Emotions and Ethics

The Intellect

THE NOTEBOOKS OF PAUL BRUNTON
(VOLUME 5)

EMOTIONS AND ETHICS

THE INTELLECT

PAUL BRUNTON
(1898–1981)

An in-depth study of
categories six and seven
from the notebooks

Published for the
PAUL BRUNTON PHILOSOPHIC FOUNDATION
by Larson Publications

International Standard Book Number (cloth) 0-943914-21-3
International Standard Book Number (paper) 0-943914-22-1
International Standard Book Number (series, cloth) 0-943914-17-5
International Standard Book Number (series, paper) 0-943914-23-X
Library of Congress Catalog Card Number: 86-82480

Manufactured in the United States of America

Published for the
Paul Brunton Philosophic Foundation
by
Larson Publications
4936 Route 414
Burdett, New York 14818

Distributed to the trade by
Kampmann and Company
9 East 40 Street
New York, New York 10016

87 89 90 88 86
2 4 6 8 10 9 7 5 3 1

CONTENTS

PART 2: THE INTELLECT

EDITORS' INTRODUCTION

This fifth volume in *The Notebooks of Paul Brunton* is an in-depth presentation of the sixth and seventh (of twenty-eight) major topics in the the personal notebooks Dr. Paul Brunton (1898–1981) reserved for posthumous publication.

Part 1, *Emotions and Ethics*, deals with two direct relationships not often adequately recognized. The first is that between character development and spiritual awakening. The second is that between personality refinement and spiritual self-expression. The evolutionary process of recognizing and developing these relationships traces a course through the animal, human, and angelic possibilities within our own individual souls.

You will know only so much of the Divine, this section seems to say, as you yourself can become. You will see its actions in your own life to the extent that you master your own baser nature and cultivate your own latent spiritual nobility. You will see its benign presence in the world around you to the extent that you first, see the working of evolutionary laws in human experience and, second, consciously place your own maturing intelligence into the service of that evolutionary development. Purification of motive and act must precede reliable revelation.

Within our hearts, this section says—under the agitations, doubts, and desires—is a reliable source of individualized ethical guidance for daily living. We *can* know what is best in a given situation and we *can* respond creatively and positively to its needs by drawing upon spiritual resources from within. But to make use of this guidance, we must first acquire enough self-discipline to discern its voice among the many that contend within us. And we must acquire enough strength of will to act as it would have us do. Only in doing this do we truly become it. And only in ourselves becoming it do we come to the calm, unshakeable certitude that it *is*.

In light of the material in *Emotions and Ethics*, Part 2, *The Intellect*, takes on deeper meaning and significance. *Emotions and Ethics* tells us that our passions, emotions, and feelings must come to be guided by reason, and that reason itself must be guided by intuition. *The Intellect* helps us to understand what reason and intuition are, and how they contribute to the individual intelligence that is born out of their creative union.

Part 2 quickly establishes three major points. First, intelligence is to be honored and developed as one of the divine qualities potential in human character. Second, speculative intellection, unguided by wisdom, is of little or no use in spiritual matters; this is as true of what this kind of blind intellection asserts about the Divine as of what it critically denies. Third, the matured and properly trained intelligence not only makes it easier for us to know when to think and when to suspend thinking; it also becomes a powerful tool for precise communication of higher intuitions and mystical perceptions. In its most developed form, this intelligence can formulate what P.B. calls a "metaphysics of truth": an inspired, fluid structure of revelatory reasoning whereby the Proficient can express, in intellectual terms, much of what has been learned through intellect-transcending inner vision and direct experience.

Editorial policy with regard to selection and placement of the material in this volume is the same as that already mentioned in the introduction to volume three. As mentioned there, (P) at the end of a para indicates that the para also appears in *Perspectives*, the survey volume to this series.

Our appreciation of the support of both Wisdom's Goldenrod Center for Philosophic Studies and the Paul Brunton Philosophic Foundation deepens with the publication of each new volume in this series. Information about this series and related activities may be obtained by writing the

Paul Brunton Philosophic Foundation
P.O. Box 89
Hector, NY 14841

Part 1:
EMOTIONS
AND ETHICS

Is there no basis of morality and taste, no standard of judgement and ethics, except that which the individual brings with himself or creates for himself? The situation is not so anarchic as it seems, for there is a progressive evolutionary character running through all these different points of view.

The human journey from mere animal existence to real spiritual essence is reflected in human ethics, where rules imposed from without are gradually supplanted by principles intuited from within.

1

UPLIFT CHARACTER

If we will bring more sincerity and more integrity into our lives, more truth and more wisdom into our minds, more goodwill and more self-discipline into our hearts, not only will we be more blessed but also all others with whom we are in touch.

2

Face yourself if you would find yourself. By this I do not only mean that you are to seek out and study the pathetic weaknesses of your lower nature, but also the noble inspirations of your higher nature.

3

Philosophy guides human conduct not so much by imposing a particular code of rules to be obeyed as by inculcating a general attitude to be developed. It does not tell us what to do so much as it helps us to get the kind of spiritual knowledge and moral perception which will tell us what to do.

4

The moral precepts which it offers for use in living and for guidance in wise action are not offered to all alike, but only to those engaged on the quest. They are not likely to appeal to anyone who is virtuous merely because he fears the punishment of sin rather than because he loves virtue itself. Nor are they likely to appeal to anyone who does not know where his true self-interest lies. There would be nothing wrong in being utterly selfish if only we fully understood the self whose interest we desire to preserve or promote. For then we would not mistake pleasure for happiness nor confuse evil with good. Then we would see that earthly self-restraint in some directions is in reality holy self-affirmation in others, and that the hidden part of self is the best part.(P)

5

These ideals have been reiterated too often to be new, but concrete application of them to the actual state of affairs would be new.

6

This grand section of the quest deals with the right conduct of life. It seeks both the moral re-education of the individual's character for his own benefit and the altruistic transformation of it for society's benefit.(P)

7

We have free will to change our character, but we must also call upon God's assistance. We are likely to fail without it and it is possible by striving too earnestly all alone to make ourselves mentally or physically ill. We should *pray* and ask for God's help even when trying to make ourselves have faith in a Higher Power as well as in ourselves.

8

We begin and end the study of philosophy by a consideration of the subject of ethics. Without a certain ethical discipline to start with, the mind will distort truth to suit its own fancies. Without a mastery of the whole course of philosophy to its very end, the problem of the significance of good and evil cannot be solved.(P)

9

The foundation of this work is a fine character. He who is without such moral development will be without personal control of the powers of the mind when they appear as a result of this training; instead those powers will be under the control of his ego. Sooner or later he will injure himself or harm others. The philosophic discipline acts as a safeguard against these dangers.

10

All those points of metaphysical doctrine and religious history like the problem of evil and the biography of avatars are doubtful, if not insoluble, whereas all the points of moral attitude and personal conduct like honesty, justice, goodness, and self-control are both indisputable and essential. Here we walk on trustworthy ground. Why not then leave others to quarrel fiercely about the first and let us abide peacefully in the second.

11

The aspirant must remember always that his immediate duty lies in self-preparation, self-discipline, and self-improvement. The building of fine character on the quest is quite as important as the efforts of aspiration and meditation, even more so, for the former will lead to the dissolving of egoism, and without this the latter are of little avail.

12

If you accept the existence of a power behind the Universe which controls its life, which is perfect, and which is bringing all things and all beings—however slowly—closer to its own perfection, you must also accept the values of hope, improvement, and evolution while you must reject those of pessimism, deterioration, and nihilism. You will never feel sorry for yourself.

13

If the moral fruits of the Spirit are absent or the evil qualities of the ego are present, all talk of having attained inward enlightenment is quite illusory.

14

To remodel his character will not interest a man if it requires great and constant effort, but to the quester it is an obligation. And this is so without his having to believe in all the windy rhetoric about the perfectibility of man.

15

The reformation and even transformation of character is as much a sector of philosophy as the practice of concentration and the study of mind. The virtue which develops from disciplining thoughts and controlling self removes obstacles and gives power to truth's pursuit.

16

The ethical ideals of philosophy are lofty but nobody is asked or expected to jump up to their realization, only to understand their direction; the rest of this inner work must develop at its own pace according to his individual possibilities.

17

Is it entirely useless to point out an ethical height to which very few can soar? No—the usefulness lies in the sense of right direction which it gives, in the inspiring love of truth and hope of self-betterment which it arouses.

18

However unrealizable the ideal may be in all its perfection, if we persist in holding it before us in aspiration we shall certainly approach it more closely in action. And the effort will give us more faith in life, make us more sensitive to its finer rhythms.

19

If the lower self disturbs you, silence it by invoking the higher self. If you are unable to do this directly, then do it indirectly by invoking it intellectually through declarations of spiritual truth and emotionally through genuflection in humble prayer. Do not accept the suggestion which drags you down, but instead seek for the pressure which lifts you up.

20

To the extent that he purifies and ennobles himself, he qualifies himself for the reception of superior insight.

21

If the aspirant will take care to fill his mind with thoughts that are always elevating, always positive, and always constructive; if he will be vigilant to keep out all thoughts that are degrading and destructive, this simple technique will keep his mind so continuously filled with the right kind of thought and feeling that he will unconsciously and little by little completely overcome the wrong kind. Thus his character will change and approach his ideals.

22

We must not, like the mystics, talk as if man were nothing else but a divine being. We are philosophical students and should not be so one-sided. We must tell men the whole and not a half-truth, which means we must tell them that they are a mixed lot, divine at the centre but slightly devilish at the circumference; altruistic in their potential nature but somewhat selfish in their actual one.

23

Everything that strengthens his better nature is useful and acceptable. Everything that weakens it is not.

24

So difficult is true self-mastery that nothing in the world's literature about it can overrate the accomplishment.

25

When the beast in man will bow in homage before the intelligence in man, when the ideal of perfected being set up for him by the serene figure of the Sphinx shall be recognized, accepted, and striven for, then indeed will he become a conscious collaborator with the universal Mind. Whoever knows how and where to look can find in himself the assurance of this ultimate victory.

26

There should be no space in his mind for negative thoughts, no time in his heart for base feelings.

27

It is not enough to repress a negative trait like jealousy or self-pity. One must also replace it by a positive trait.

28

His spiritual progress will be measured not so much by his meditational progress as by his moral awakening.

29

The truth will become truth for him not merely when he can understand it intellectually but also when he can accept it emotionally, and still more when he can incorporate it into his behaviour patterns.

30

He must look within himself for the impurities and falsities, the malice and envy, the prejudice and bitterness which belong to his lower nature. And he must work with all his willpower and thinking power to cast them out.

31

He must walk towards the highest with every part of his being, with his whole psyche matured and balanced. He must not only seek to intuit what is real, but also to will what is good.

32

It is when men come face-to-face with a real crisis, a real temptation, or a real hardship that they show their real character, not only their self-imagined or publicly reputed one.

33

It must be remembered always that mere intellectual study is not so essential as the building of worthwhile character, which is far more important in preparing for the great battle with the ego.

34

When a negative reaction impulsively shows itself before you have been able to prevent it, make as your second thought a deliberate replacement or substitution of it, by the opposed positive one. For instance, a reaction of envy at someone's good fortune should be substituted by the thought of appreciation of the good qualities or services which may have led to it.

35

When emotion is no longer able to cloud reason, when intellect is no longer able to dry up the feeling of conscience, a better judgement of affairs and a clearer perception of truth becomes possible.

36

Little by little, in tranquil moments or in deliberate meditation, there will come to him the revelation of errors in conduct and thought which, until then, he did not even know were errors.

37

Ideas influence their thinker himself; thoughts react on their generator if they are intensely held, deeply felt, and frequently born. Thus they help to form tendencies and shape character. The aspirant can take advantage of this truth.

38

His moral thought and metaphysical ideation will be so deep and earnest that they will converge upon his emotional feeling, when that has been sufficiently purified, and coalesce with it. Thus they become part of his inner being.

39

Each aspirant has to struggle with the demon inside himself if he is to realize his higher purpose in life.

40

Nature seeks to achieve its own ends, which renders it indifferent to all personal ends. It considers no man's feelings but only his level of development, that he might be raised to a higher one.

41

The only greatness he may rightfully seek is a secret one. It is not power over others that he should strive for, but power over himself.

42

He will have to grow into this higher consciousness. No other way exists for him.

43

He has not only to be brave enough to accept the aloneness that comes with every serious advance in the quest, but also strong enough to endure it.

44

How can anything be right in worldly practice if it is wrong in ethical theory?

45

The value of such study is immense. It involves a re-education of the whole mind of man. It strikes at the root of his ethical ignorance and destroys the selfishness and greed which are its malignant growths.

46

Mentally, man can do what no animal can. He can consider conduct from a purely ethical standpoint; he can struggle at heart between right and wrong, self and selflessness.

47

Every man betrays himself for what he is. He can hide his thoughts and dissemble his feelings, but he cannot hide his face. Therein are letters and words which tell plainly what sort of a man he really is. But few there be who can read in this strange language.

48

Character *can* be changed. He who habitually contemplates such exalted themes finds in time that his whole outlook is altered and expanded, as if by magic. The new outlook will gradually strongly establish itself within him. Says the Christian Bible: "As a man thinketh in his heart so is he," which may be matched with what was written in Sanskrit long before this was uttered: "As is one's thought, so one becomes; this is the eternal secret."—*Maitri Upanishad*.

49

What is to be done where a weakness becomes abnormally strong, overpowering the will and forcing him to do what his better nature rejects? The cure in the end must be based on his willingness to regard it as something not really part of himself, something alien and parasitic. If there is to be any way out toward freedom from it, he must stop identifying himself with the weakness.

50

The key to right conduct is to refuse to identify himself with the lower nature. The hypnotic illusion that it is really himself must be broken: the way to break it is to deny every suggestion that comes from it, to use the will in resisting it, to use the imagination in projecting it as something alien and outside, to use the feelings in aspiration towards the true self, and the mind in learning to understand what it is.(P)

51

The disciple who wishes to make real progress must attack, weaken, and ultimately destroy certain bad traits of character. Among them is the trait of jealousy of his fellow disciples. It is not only an unpleasant thought but may also end in disastrous consequences. It often leads to wrathful moods and raging spells. It not only harms the other disciple but always does harm to the sinner himself. It is caused by an unreasonable sense of possessiveness directed towards the teacher which does not understand that love should give freedom to him, not deny it to him.(P)

52

The pursuit of moral excellence is immeasurably better than the pursuit of mystical sensations. Its gains are more durable, more indispensable, and more valuable.(P)

53

There are five ways in which the human being progressively views his own self and consequently five graduated ethical stages on his quest. First, as an ignorant materialist he lives entirely within his personality and hence for personal benefit regardless of much hurt caused to others in order to secure this benefit. Second, as an enlightened materialist he is wrapped in his own fortunes but does not seek them at the expense of others. Third, as a religionist he perceives the impermanence of the ego and, with a sense of sacrifice, he denies his self-will. Fourth, as a mystic he acknowledges the existence of a higher power, God, but finds it only within himself. Fifth, as a philosopher he recognizes the universality and the oneness of being in others and practises altruism with joy.(P)

54

But, after all, these qualities are only the negative prerequisites of spiritual realization. They are not realization itself. Their attainment is to free oneself from defects that hinder the attainment of higher consciousness, not to possess oneself of true consciousness.(P)

55

The act must illustrate the man, the deed must picture the attitude. It is thus only that thought becomes alive.(P)

56

The more I travel and observe the more I come to believe that the only men who will make something worthwhile of philosophy are the men who have already made something worthwhile of their personal lives. The dreamers and cranks will only fool themselves, the failures and alibichasers will only become confirmed in their fantasies.(P)

57

Many people talk mysticism or play with psychism so long as either promises them wonderful powers which most other people haven't got or wonderful experiences which most other people do not have. But when they come to philosophy and find that it demands from them a renovation of their entire character, they are seized with fear and retreat. Philosophy is not for such people, for it does not conform to their wishes. It tells them what they do not like to hear. It disturbs their egoistic vanity and troubles their superficial serenity when it throws a glaring spotlight on their lower nature, their baser motives, and their ugly weaknesses.(P)

58

While the aspirant fails to take an inventory of his weaknesses and consequently fails to build into his character the attributes needed, much of his meditation will be either fruitless or a failure or even harmful.(P)

59

That it is not enough for men to think truth, that they must also feel it, is a statement with which most scientists, being intellect-bound, would disagree. But artists, mystics, true philosophers, and religious devotees would accept it.(P)

60

Buddha did not go into deeper problems before he had gone into practical ethics. He taught people to be good and do good before he taught them to venture into the marshy logic of the metaphysical maze. And even when they had emerged safely from a territory where so many lose themselves utterly, he brought them back to ethical values albeit now of a much higher kind because based on utter unselfishness. For love must marry knowledge, pity must shed its warm rays upon the cold intellect. Enlightenment of others must be the price of one's own enlightenment. These things are not easily felt by the mystic, who is often too absorbed in his own ecstasies to notice the miseries of others, or by the metaphysician, who is often too tied by his own verbosity to his hard and rigorous logic to realize that mankind is not merely an abstract noun but is made up of flesh-and-blood individuals. The philosopher however finds these benign altruistic needs to be an essential part of truth. Consequently the salvation which he seeks—from ignorance and the attendant miseries that dog its steps—is not for himself but for the whole world.(P)

61

It does not necessarily mean that he has faults to repair or weaknesses to overcome. It may mean that there is some lack in him, some quality or capacity that he needs to cultivate.

62

The real choice, decision, judgement, is made in the subconscious mind. Impulses come from it and character is formed in it.

63

Despite all the repetitive assertions that there is no ego, that the person is a fiction, that the goal is pure being unsullied by the self-illusion, here—in the various manifested signs of an individual character in a separate body—is evidence to the contrary.

64

Accept fully and without demur your self-made karma, even to the extent of refraining from asking to be forgiven your sins, for it is a just result. Ask instead to be shown how to overcome the weakness which had been the cause.

65

When negative or degrading or weakening suggestions enter his mind, from whatever source, he can deal with them in two ways, singly if that prove enough, combined if not. The first is to tense his will and by a positive commanding mental act master the suggestion and drive it away. The second is to turn away into its opposing idea and dwell firmly on that until the suggestion vanishes altogether. If, in spite of using these methods he is still defeated, then he can try remembering the Overself. Can he still carry out the evil suggestion while thinking of that serene divine presence? By aspiring to it for help and protection as fervently as he can, the negative idea may disintegrate like the ash of a cigarette.

66

A habit change or a thought change which is made under someone else's persuasion and not out of inner need brought into the open by that other person, is only a surface one and will fade and fall away.

67

If in some ways he learns to lessen egoism and practise humility, in other ways he gains a larger easier assurance. If he is now willing, to a certain extent, to be deflated, he feels he is standing nonchalantly and calmly on firmer ground than before. Perhaps this is all a play, not to be taken too seriously, for the real trial, the worst test, the last great agony, will come later—either through the terrible loneliness of the Dark Night of the Soul, or the painful crucifixion of the ego before Ascension, Liberation, and Fulfilment.

68

If each attack of adverse force, each temptation that tries a weakness, is instantly met with the Short Path attitude, he will have an infinitely better chance of overcoming it. The secret is to remember the Overself, to turn the battle over to IT. Then, what he is unable to conquer by himself, will be easily conquered *for him* by the higher power.

69

The question is whether he is to accept the baser weaknesses as human or whether he is to struggle against them as unworthy of a human being.

70

We must so centralize our consciousness as to render it strong against the onslaughts of outside suggestion, immune to the promptings of crowds and the dictation of places. Thus we learn to be our own true self not only at home, where it is easy, but also in the street and in others' homes, where it is hard. Thus we become truly individualized. Thus we are always serene among the anxious, good amongst the wicked.

71

Like a rock so firmly embedded that it cannot be moved by human force but can only be blasted by dynamite, his moral character must be embedded in the great Truths.

72

After a lifetime of world-wandering, after a varied experience among different races of people and in different classes of society, we have come to the firm and settled conviction that what is most to be looked for in a man is *character*. The best test of character is neither intellectual hair-splitting nor emotional, wordy gush, not high-flown idealistic professions, nor flowery mystical pretensions, but deeds.

73

From time to time his higher self will show him his own moral face as in a glass. But it will only show him that side of it which is the worst as well as the least-known one. He will have to look at what is thus exposed to him in all its stark fullness and hidden reality, only because he has to re-educate himself morally to a degree far beyond the ordinary. The experience may be painful, but it must be accepted. He has invoked the Overself, now its light has suddenly been thrown upon him. He is now able to see his ego, his lower nature, as it has not hitherto shown itself to him. All its uglinesses are lit up and revealed for what they really are. By thus showing up its true nature and evil consequences, this experience is the first step to making the ego's conquest possible.

74

He should begin with the belief that his own character can be markedly improved and with the attitude that his own efforts can lessen the distance between its present condition and the ideal before him.

75

It is a prime rule that quality of character and education of conscience are more important than nature of belief. And this is much more applicable to would-be philosophers than to would-be religionists.

76

In the twentieth sutta of *Majjhima-Nikaya*, Gautama recommends students who are haunted by a bad idea of undesirable character to try five methods for expelling it: (1) attend to an opposing good idea; (2) face the danger of the consequences of letting the bad idea emerge in action; (3)

become inattentive to the bad idea; (4) analyse its antecedents and so paralyze the sequent impulse; (5) coerce the mind with the aid of bodily tension.

77

But philosophy does not trust to developed reason alone to control emotion and subjugate passion. It trusts also to psychological knowledge and metaphysical truth, to developed will and creative meditation, to counter-emotions and the prayer for Grace. All these different elements are welded into one solid power working for him.

78

Just as the writer turns his experiences of society to writing use and creates art out of the best and worst of them, so the disciple turns his experiences of life to spiritual use and creates wisdom or goodness out of them. And just as it is harder for the author to learn to live what he writes than learn to write what he lives, so it is harder for the disciple to convert his studies and meditations, his reflections and intuitions, into practical deeds and positive accomplishments than to receive these thoughts themselves and make them his own.

79

It is not so much that we have to change ourselves as to give up ourselves. We are so imperfect and faulty, so selfish and weak, so sinful and ignorant, that giving up our own selves means being more than willing to part with what is not worth keeping. But to what are we to give them up and how are we to do it? We are to invoke the higher self, request it daily to take possession of our hearts, minds, and wills, and to strive actively to purify them. Much of our striving will be in the form of surrendering egoistic thoughts, impulses, and feelings by crushing them at the moment of birth. In that way we slowly give up our inner selves and submit the conduct of our outer selves to a higher will.

80

If he fails to pass a test or if he succumbs to a temptation, he should realize that there must be a defect in character or mentality which made such a failure possible. Even though the test or temptation has been provided by the adverse powers, he ought not to lay the blame upon them but upon himself. For then he will seek out and destroy the defect upon which the blame really rests.

81

After all, there must have been a corresponding inner weakness in him to have permitted him to become the victim of a temptation. Consequently it is often better not to ask for protection against the temptation. This simply hides and covers over the weakness and permits it to remain in his mental makeup. It is better to ask for the strengthening of his own willpower, to cultivate it through a creative meditation exercise specially directed to the purpose: he should picture the arousal and hardening of this willpower during the very moments of temptation by seeing himself emerge victorious by his *own* forces.

82

It has been said that ideas rule mankind. This is but a half-truth, but be it as it may, it can be unhesitatingly asserted that ideals rule the traveller on this quest. If they do not, then he is not embarked on the quest. But an ideal is only an abstract conception. Unselfishness, freedom, goodness, and justice are intangibles, and their practical application has altered from age to age according to the conditions prevailing in different times and places. An ideal must have a concrete shape or it becomes sterile.

83

Faulty characters and faulty habits can be changed by the Secret Path as the coming of the sun changes winter to spring. Greed will slowly turn to goodwill, cruelty will make its exit to allow for the incoming of kindness, and all-round self-control will gradually replace weakness. The faithful application of these teachings must inevitably influence the entire make-up of a man, and influence it most certainly for the better.

84

He must begin this preparatory work on himself by an analysis of character. This requires a sincere honest appraisal, a rigorous search for truth, not easy when vanity, for instance, may masquerade as duty among his motives.

85

As a man, it is not essential to discover and correct these faults. As a seeker, such discovery and such correction are primary duties.

86

The code of conduct which philosophy asks its votaries to practise, the set of values which it determines for them, the endeavour to transcend themselves which it inspires—these elevate the mind into nobility, grandeur, and reverence.

87

To abstain from favoured foods is a hard test; to abstain from carnal intercourse is a still harder one. To the common mind, devoid of metaphysical faculty, this may seem far enough to travel. But to the developed mind the hardest of all tests must yet be undergone—to abstain from egoistic thought, feeling, and action.

88

The more the character is purified, the easier it is to practise meditation. The more the lower nature holds a man, the shorter will be the period of time in which he will be able to hold attention on the Overself.

89

It is a great beginning of the real quest when he comes to the clear perception that the lusts, gluttonies, wraths, and passions have been lodged in him and have lived in his self yet are not him; that they are morbid creations which can be starved, exorcised, and expelled just as surely as they have been fed, nourished, and embraced.

90

What separates the lower appetites of man from his higher aspirations? The beast must obey blindly its group instinct, the human need not. He can choose between doing the same as the animal or holding himself back to think, reason, and arrive at a considered decision.

91

The lower nature does not let him keep this mood of high resolve long. Not many days pass before it seeks to discourage him. For the old cravings, the desire habits, and the emotional tendencies are still there. Soon they begin to trouble him again. "Why try?" his lower nature despondently tells him, "Why torment yourself uselessly? You can only fail in the end." Thus it creates the expectancy of failure and turns his high adventure into a dismal ordeal. Only a fixed vigilant determination and correct approach will bring forth that inner consent to the new disciplinary habits so necessary to success. Only by re-educating his tendencies and gradually making them quite willing to conform to the right way of living can the lower nature be beaten.

92

To the extent that anything lifts men up out of their animality, it serves a higher purpose. This is true of athletic training and religious aspiration, of social codes and personal self-respect. For in the end they must turn their minds away from the passions which they share with the sub-human kingdom to the fulfilment of their higher human possibilities and destiny.

93

The honourable man who lives by a decent code of ethics has to be surpassed by the seeker, since he believes in a life and goal which is still more honourable.

94

Freedom is a tremendous word whose meaning goes much beyond the average man's idea of it. He is not free who is in bondage to narrow prejudice, strong attachment, unruled desire, and spiritual ignorance.

95

The same strength which is put into negative qualities like fear, grief, revenge, and discord—to a man's own detriment—can be put into positive ones like courage, cheerfulness, fortitude, benevolence, and calmness, to his own benefit.

96

He is to work for the day when his character will be utterly transformed, when he will be incapable of meanness or animality, when he will live in constant awareness of the idea.

97

The hopeless pessimist who asserts that men cannot improve their inborn character, that they will be exactly the same faulty creatures at sixty that they were at twenty, may be right about some men but is certainly wrong about others. Every Quester who tries hard enough proves him wrong.

98

Character may be bettered by bettering conduct, which is visible, just as it may by bettering feeling, which is not. Kung-fu-tse perceived this and built his system upon it.

99

If the check to a weakness, a shortcoming, an undesirable impulse, or a negative emotion is given instantly, if retreat from it is made before it has time to swell and strengthen, victory is very largely assured. He need not be too ashamed because he has felt these things, provided he pulls himself together. They are what he has inherited from past births, plus what he has picked up in the present one, and it is inevitable or "natural" that he should experience them. Even the saints have endured them repeatedly, but those who conquered in the end knew this trick of instantly outwitting the enemy. Father John of Kronstadt, a Russian of our own century, and Saint Isaac, a Syrian of the sixth century, are self-confessed examples.

100

He will undergo periods of purification, when the animal appetites such as lust and gluttony, and the animal passions such as wrath and hate, will have to be brought under better control. The discipline involved is both a kind of penance for past sins and a preparation for future enlightenment. It may be that these baser attributes need to be pushed up out of latency nearer the surface, in order to deal with them more effectually. If so, this will come about through some sort of crisis. He need not be distressed for it will be ultimately beneficent.

101

The ability to throw negative thoughts out of his mind is so valuable that a deliberate and daily effort to cultivate it is well worthwhile. This is as true of one's self-originated thoughts as of those picked up from outside, whether unwittingly from other persons, or absorbed through susceptibility from environments.

102

Anyone can go on living but not everyone can go on living worthily.

103

We are all imperfect and the making of mistakes is to be expected. The mishandling of problems need not surprise us and the yielding to weaknesses is a common experience. Let us grant all this, but it does not excuse us from being bereft of the desire for self-improvement, of the aspiration for self-ennoblement, or of the search for self-enlightenment.

104

Man has an animal body, shares certain instinctive reactions, desires, and passions with other animals. But mentally and morally there are creative impulses, functions, ideas, and ideals which increasingly separate him from them as he develops and put him on a higher plane.

105

The ethical standards of the disciple are, or should be, as far beyond those of conventional good men, as their standards are beyond those of evil men.

106

He may have to pass successively through the three stages of intemperate idealism, disappointed idealism, and philosophic idealism. The last is as balanced and discerning as the first is not.

107

The faults of character and defects in personality which bar advancement in the quest will also bar advancement in other spheres of human life. Being in him, they will inevitably bring their results on the physical plane in the course of time. They will manifest themselves in his business or career, his home or social relations. It is not too much to say, therefore, that the self-improvement brought about by the quest's discipline will be to his advantage in other ways.

108

Where the Overself lives fully in a man, he will not need to consider whether an act is righteous or not. Righteous acts will flow spontaneously from him and no other kind will be possible. But for a beginner to practise prematurely such nonresistance to his impulses would be dangerous and foolish.

109

Woman possesses a great power in possessing the power of love. She can lift and redeem men, succour and save them, or degrade and destroy them. But with this power comes a great responsibility.

110

When we reach the Olympian heights and stand to survey the scenes of our long struggles, we shall then not regret that we were tried, tempted, and tortured by conflicting desires, for without them we should only have become mechanically good. Even our sufferings turn to sympathy.

111

All ethical paths are twofold inasmuch as they must consist of the acquirement of virtues and the expulsion of vices.

112

The less a mental conflict appears in open consciousness, the more dangerous does it become.

113

The greatness of a character is tested just as much by the temptations for ego display in success as it is by failure.

114

Many moral precepts have been preached to mankind but few practical instructions in the matter of how to carry out those precepts have been given him.

115

Is it true, as so many say, that character is stubbornly resistant to change? It is the grown man's character that is in reference here, not the phases grades and adjustments of childhood and adolescence when the acquisition of new attributes, tendencies, and traits is natural. If the idea of reincarnation is accepted, then the personality of every man must inevitably change with time.

116

Those who are willing to practise such hard self-discipline form an elite among mankind.

117

Character is as easily imperilled by the briberies of wealth and luxury as by those of poverty and lack.

118

A constructive idea is used to displace the negative one, being put immediately underneath it.

119

Habit, weakness, and desire may prevent him from following behind the philosopher as he walks his lonely road, as they may prevent him from recognizing the logic of the philosopher's teaching.

120

His human weaknesses need to be recognized, admitted, and looked at in the face realistically. To fail to see them is to walk over marsh and quagmire, bog and quicksand. They need not frighten him away from the quest for they represent opportunities to grow, material to be worked upon for his ultimate benefit.

121

The attempt to escape from such problems by first refusing to look at them, and second, by refraining from the efforts needed to deal with them, leads only to their prolongation and enlargement later on.

122

The animal instincts are valid and have their assigned place, but the cerebral ones have even more validity and a higher place, while the spiritual ones should be elevated above the other two.

123

The mind is the real root of the tree of character which, despite its thousands of branches, leaves, and fruits, possesses but this single root.

124

If man is to improve himself, he must improve his acts of will, his objects of desire, and his subjects of thought. This means an entire psychological re-education which will involve much work upon himself.

125

Those who desert the quest's moral ideals but not its mystical exercises, who seek to gain selfish victories over the rights and minds of others by the use of mental or occult power, become evil-doers and suffer an evil end. Theirs is the way of the left-hand path, of black magic, and of the sin against the Holy Ghost. Until retribution falls upon them in the end, they bring misery or misfortune to all who accept their influence.

126

Those who struggle in the work-a-day world need to learn what their higher duty is rather than what metaphysical truth is. They need a stimulant to the practice of righteousness rather than a stimulant to the analysis of intellectual subtleties.

127

From the point of view of philosophy, we ought not to be virtuous merely because of baits of peace and contentment and lessened suffering which dangle from virtue itself, but because the very purpose of life on earth cannot be achieved unless we are thoroughly virtuous.

128

It is easy to confuse respectable conventionality with authentic virtue.

129

Although philosophy wags no finger in smug portentous moralizing, it respects the validity of karmic consequences, the getting-back of what is given out, and also the need to begin curbing the ego, its desires and passions, as a preliminary to crushing it. There is solid factual ground for the excellent ethical counsel given to all humanity by Confucius and Buddha, Jesus and Socrates.

130

Many of the stupid, overworded objections to the so-called impracticability of ethical idealism will be disarmed and disproved. He will ruefully wake up to the fact that the mentality which begins by imagining rigid restrictions on what can be done to construct a better life ends by imposing them.

131

All our virtues come from that divine source. They are incomplete and imperfect copies of the abstract and original archetypes, the idea of the spirit behind each particular virtue. This is one reason why the path of being, thinking, and practising the Good, as far as he is able, becomes, for the unbelieving man, as much and as valuable a spiritual path as any offered by religion.

132

Ethical practice is the best ethical precept. Merely telling man to be kind and not cruel is utterly futile. They must be given adequate reasons to justify this precept.

133

Only as men become convinced that their further fortune and happiness or distress and trouble are closely connected with their obedience to these higher laws—and particularly the law of karma—will they discover that not only is virtue its own reward but also adds to peace of mind.

134

He will find that there is no other way, and will do better to come to it in the beginning than in the end. He *must* learn to cooperate with the World-Idea, the planetary will, or suffer from its whips. The choice is between animal-human and spiritual-human.

135

The really mature person is a positive person. He prefers goodwill to hate, peace to aggression, and self-control to unloosed passions.

136

Temperament and circumstance, happening and karma will combine to decide whether he lets go the bad tendency or habit suddenly or whether he will need a period to adjust and settle down anew.

137

We Westerners have to bring two polar opposites into harmony, for we have to adjust our temperamental inclination towards the practical, the actual, the visible, and concrete with rising other-worldly needs of the transcendental, the real, the silent, the invisible, and abstract. It is from this deeper part of our being that there arise our noblest ethics and our loftiest ideals.

138

Philosophy creates and maintains the highest standards of conduct. But they are not necessarily conventional ones.

139

It is time preachers began to realize that giving naïve admonitions to the weak and sinful is not enough. The latter must not only be told to be good but, not less important, taught *how* to be good!

140

It is not enough to repent today and forget tomorrow. Repentance should be a continuous attitude of heart until the thing repented of is expunged from it and gotten rid of.

141

We may well look with envy upon the life of Ralph Waldo Emerson, for he was a man whose course conformed perfectly to the doctrines which he taught. We may have seen high truths in our moods of vision and often written them down, but how to bring an unwilling heart and rebellious body to their subjection is ever a problem to us.

142

The forming of a high character is both a contributory cause to mystical illumination (by removing obstacles in its way) and a consequential result of it. The inner light does not shine in a vacuum. It clarifies the man's moral judgments and educates his moral conscience.

143

It is still a fact, which may be noted more in the Orient perhaps, that merely by being lofty, strong, and noble in character, a man's existence helps or comforts some of those he meets even if his circumstances prevent him doing anything outwardly useful to them.

144

There is a natural dignity which comes from inner greatness, and which is to be respected, but there is also another kind which comes from the little ego's self-infatuation, from its foolish empty pride.

145

If a man cannot make the right decision in a time of stress, if he feels bewildered in a time of crisis, this is not sufficient justification for him to expect a master to make his decisions for him. For his blindness and bewilderment measure the depth to which he is sunk in his personal self and lower nature. He would have seen his way more clearly had he kept his will free from their domination. For a master to make his decisions for him during such a critical time is not really to help him but to injure him. For it would prevent the struggle within himself continuing until it could give birth to a higher point of view, to a stronger character.

146

We must put out of our minds every weakening impulse by instant reference to the strength of the Overself, every evil thought by a call to the infinite good of the Overself. In this way character is uplifted and made noble.

147

On the degree of authority which he vests in the Overself, will depend the degree of power he draws from it to conquer the lower nature.

148

There is a perfect relation between the impression we make upon others and the mastery we have achieved over ourselves. The strength of the impression depends on the degree of the mastery. Furthermore, our power over the world outside us will be proportionate to our power over the nature within us.

149

The real tests of character are imposed through our reaction to thoughts as well as to events. Both are needed to show us to ourselves.

150

In the giant mills where steel is prepared, we may glean a great lesson. The crude material is first made to undergo the ordeal of fire, a fire so intense that the material loses its solidity and becomes a bubbling liquid. And after its temperature has been lowered sufficiently to resume a solid form again, the still red-hot material has to undergo a further ordeal. It is hammered on every side, pounded from top to bottom. Out of these processes there emerges at last a purified, strengthened, finely tempered steel which will stand up to the most trying tests during wear and work. Men who wish to make something of their lives must take the terrific pounding and suffering to which they have had to submit in the past few years as a similar process intended to turn away the dross in their character and strengthen the nobility within it.

151

The desire to serve the cause of Truth is praiseworthy, but an inner change of character is at once the basis and the beginning of such work.

152

Passion and emotion are easier to control than thought. For this and other reasons they are brought to heel—not completely, but sufficiently— as a preliminary to the practice of meditation.

153

If possible, a beginner should avoid any thing, any person, any contact, any event, or any environment which he knows will upset his emotional balance or produce negative thoughts. It is only at a later stage when he is more proficient in the art of self-control and has more strength within himself that he should not be afraid of these challenges but should accept them and try to win through.

154

Mental attitudes can be developed, thoughts can be trained in this direction, and feelings can be stimulated in harmony with it; but all this should be done naturally and not artificially.

155

Discipline without harshness, strength without coldness, balance without pedantry, these are desirable qualities.

156

If a man believes he is worth nothing and will become nothing, his seership will be confirmed. Humility can be overstretched.

157

If, as sometimes happens, an aspirant seems to have some unusual power over others, he is strongly advised to check it immediately. If allowed to continue, it could develop into black magic, which leads to self-destruction. Such a person should devote far more effort to the task of ridding himself of these dangers, to improving his thought-process, and to praying to the Overself for protective guidance.

158

There is a certain stage of development when it is more important to work on the improvement of the character than to practise meditation.

159

The fulfilment of one's Higher Purpose depends on a great deal of strenuous character building and improvement, plus the final overthrow of the ego.

160

Why purification of character should be needed in order to contact what seems to be above our lowly human characteristics is, indeed, a paradox which only the Overself can answer. Perhaps it is a test of our devotion—for it is known that the Higher Self will not surrender her revelations to anyone who does not love her completely. Purification is merely the casting out of lesser loves for the sake of this supreme Love.

161

When he begins to exercise these scruples, he will begin to question the impulse to act for its source much more than for its purpose.

162

The advantages of an excellent physique are plain enough but they are not good enough. Something more is needed to make a man. He needs excellence in character and intellect. But even this is still not enough if he is to find self-fulfilment. Intuitive feeling, which takes him into a holier presence if followed up, must be cultivated.

163

The hallucination—for usually it is nothing less—that an ideal existence can be found by emigrating to some distant spot may be turned into a reality if he who suffers from it turns himself into a different man. To the extent that he removes weaknesses from his character and expels negatives from his thinking, to that extent only will his new life be a happier one.

164

Our higher nature bids us aspire to inner growth, development, self-control, and ennoblement. It goes further and seeks freedom from enslavement by the passions, thus lifting the human nature above the animal.

165

The discontent with a spiritually unfulfilled life has a twofold origin—from personal experiences of the world outside and from vaguely felt pressures by the Soul within for the man to surpass himself. There is thus a reciprocal working of negative and positive feelings.

166

Philosophy does not believe that any man is doomed to continue to sin, but that every man is capable of rising to a life higher than that which he has previously lived. It believes, too, in the forgiveness of sins and in the truth of hopefulness. It is not pessimistic but reasonably optimistic in its long-range views.

167

Whatever within himself keeps a man from seeing the Real and knowing the True must be got rid of, or rectified. And whatever he lacks within himself and also keeps him away from them must be acquired. The struggle to attain these things may not interest most people, whose desire for self-improvement is not strong enough to move their will: but it is well worthwhile.

168

There is devilish cunning in the human ego, animalistic beastliness in the human body, angelic sublimity in the human soul. But this is only the appearance of things. All three conditions are really mental conditions. They pertain, after all, to the mind. We must root out the evil or foster the good there and there alone.

169

Occult power should not be sought until the battle for self-mastery has been largely won.

170

The nobler part of his self may exist in a man even though he has not yet come to awakening.

171

There are three activities which he needs to keep under frequent examination and constant discipline—his thoughts, his speech, and his action.

172

The quester who wants to keep his integrity in a corrupt world may not be able to live up to his ideal but at least he need not abandon it. The direction in which he is moving does still count.

173

It is not his business to reform others while he himself remains as he is. The attack on them will only provoke them to answering attack.

174

Temptation is easiest cast out at the first thought. As the number of thoughts grow, control grows harder too.

175
If you are dissatisfied with yourself, abandon your self! You can make a start by abandoning its negative ideas, its animal passions, and its sharp critiques of others. *You* are responsible for them: it is you who must get rid of them.

176
He must refuse to allow himself to become emotionally overwhelmed by an unthinking majority or intellectually subservient to an unworthy convention.

177
The man who wants the spiritual prizes of life must elevate his thoughts and ennoble his impulses.

178
He will prudently look ahead not only to the consequences of his actions but also of his thoughts.

179
He must be prepared to spend a whole lifetime in making this passage from aspiration to realization.

180
Petal-by-petal the bud of his growing virtues will open as the years pass. His character will be transformed. The old Adam will become a new man.

181
The progressing disciple who reaches an advanced state will find that his powers of mind and will develop accordingly. Where they are not accompanied by sufficient self-purification, they may become dangerous to himself and hurtful to others. His vigilance over thought and feeling must become greater accordingly. To dwell upon thoughts which belong to a lower level out of which he has climbed may open up a pitfall in his path; to hold bitter feelings against another person may throw discord into that person's life.

182
His outer conduct should be brought into agreement with the soaring aspiration of his inner life. When the one is antithetical to the other, the result will be chaos.

183
That man has attained mastery whose body yields to the commands of reason and whose tongue obeys the orders of prudence.

184
When the body's appetites and the intellect's curiosity get an excessive grip on a man, they throw an air of unreality on aspiration which soars beyond both. This makes intuitive feeling and metaphysical thinking seem irksome or trivial.

185

Those who do not have the strength of will to translate into practice the ideals which they accept in thought need not despair. It can be got by degrees. Part of the purpose of ascetic exercises is to lead to its possession. There is knowledge available, based on ancient and modern ascetic experience, which can be applied to liberate the moral nature from its weaknesses.

186

He who puts his lower nature under control puts himself in possession of forces, gifts, possibilities, and satisfactions that most other men lack.

187

If a man's inner life is repeatedly wasted by passion he will know no assured peace and attain no enduring goal. He must govern himself, rule his passions, and discipline his emotions. He must strengthen his higher will at the expense of his lower one. For the first promotes his spiritual evolution whereas the second inflames his animal nature.

188

Faith is needed to make the basic change in his thinking, the change which takes him out of the past's grip. A new life is possible if he takes up new thoughts.

189

If he lets compromise with the world, or lapses from the right moral standard, slip beyond a certain mark, he will pay commensurately for it.

190

It is not only a matter of self-betterment but also of self-respect for an honourable man.

191

The man whom he has looked upon as himself must be left behind; the New man, who he is to become, must be continually with him in thought, aspiration, will, and deed.

192

This it is to be truly human for it brings man into a more perfect state. To sneer at the philosophic ideal as being inhuman is really to sneer at it for rejecting the evils and weaknesses and deformities of the worldly ideal.

193

The moment a negative idea appears, repudiate it automatically by the use of (a) counter-affirmations and (b) imagination, which is the gate to creative subconscious mind.

194

Such negative thoughts as animosity and jealousy must be rooted out like weeds as fast as they spring up. This is both the easier and more effective way in the end.

195

The man who has not learned to control himself is still only a fractional man, certainly not the true man that Nature is trying to produce.

196

When he cannot live with his negative side any longer, illumination will come and stay.

197

Character is tested by afflictions more than by prosperity.

198

The first stage is to expunge the evil in his heart and to raise the good in it to the highest possible octave.

199

A personal character which will be beautiful, a way of life which will be the best—if he holds these as ideals, a man is more likely to come by them.

200

He needs to be as fastidious when allowing thoughts to enter his mind as when allowing strangers to enter his home.

201

If a man lives in mental and emotional negativity, the removal of his physical residence to another place will in the end benefit him much less than if he removes himself from the negativity.

202

The building-up of character naturally brings a better sense of proportion in one's dealings and outlook.

203

My good and kindly friend Swami Ramdas says: "By seeing good in all persons, you become good, but if you see evil, the evil in you will augment." We may match this with Emerson's: "People seem not to see that their opinion of the world is also a confession of character. We can only see what we are."

204

He must become thoroughly sick of his mistakes and sins before he will take the trouble to develop by self-training his discriminatory faculties and moral ideals.

205

We can combat fear by remembering that the Overself is always with us. The power of such thinking is its rightness and its constructiveness. It is right because the Overself is the real source of strength and courage so that recalling its ever-presence in us helps to tap that source. It is constructive because it uses up the energy that would otherwise have gone into the fear-thoughts.

206
He has only to resolve that he will always be faithful to his higher self and the trick is done. But alas! resolution is one thing, execution another.

207
If he finds himself attacked by a strong temptation or about to be overcome by an old obsession, he should at once think of the master, of his name and picture, and call for his help.

208
Whether you live as a labourer or a lord, it is your character that counts most in the end.

209
It is the ego that gives way to moods of sulkiness, bad temper, irritability, and impatience. Remember that on the outcome of your efforts to control yourself, your faults and emotions, your speech and your actions, much will depend for your worldly and spiritual future.

210
He who controls the mind controls the body, for the one acts upon and through the other.

211
It is not enough to overcome the jealousy which begrudges other people's having advantages denied us: we must also take the next step and overcome the envy which feels discontented at not having those advantages and continues to desire them for itself. Jealousy would go out of its way to hurt those others by depriving them of their possessions, but envy would not fall so low.

212
Once he forms this resolve to follow the bidding of intuition and reason when they oppose emotion and passion, he will find it both a safeguard and a test. If at any time he should temporarily weaken from this resolve, he may become uncertain as to the correct course to pursue when at a crossroads.

213
A willing discipline of the character by one's own self may often take the place of an unwanted and unwilling discipline by outer events.

214
He is to become an exemplar to the aspiring, a pattern-setter for those who would ennoble themselves.

215
He must establish, for and over himself, an emotional discipline and intellectual control. He cannot successfully do this all at once, of course. Emotional tendencies and mental habits engendered by years of materialism cannot be overturned and eliminated in a single night. But the goal must be there and must be kept in view.

216

The ideal man that he wants to be should be evoked, pictured, and adored daily.

217

If greater wisdom brings an immunity to other men's negative thoughts, it also brings the responsibility to stifle one's own.

218

When all malice and all envy are resolutely cast out of his nature, not only will he be the gainer by it in improved character and pleasanter karma, but also those others who would have suffered as victims of his barbed words or ugly thoughts.

219

The past is beyond recall, but the present is at our command.

220

At any place along the road of life, he may turn his back on ignorant habits and seek to create better ones.

221

If society finds him an odd creature, if it laughs at his peculiarities of belief or frowns at his departures from convention, then he must not blame society. He must accept the situation as inescapable and submit to its unpleasantness as being better than the littleness of surrender.

222

The quest is carried on always under silent and continual pressure. The earnest aspirant will strive to live well where formerly he lived ill, will keep looking for better ideals.

223

Few are ready to impose such a discipline upon themselves as if it were enforced by outside authority; but many more could do a little more if they applied what they know.

224

Some temptations come on slowly, but others suddenly and before he fully realizes what is happening to him. Whatever the way they come—and this depends partly on his personal temperament, partly on the nature of the temptation—he should prepare himself in advance by fortifying the weaker places in his character.

225

The negative quality can be rubbed away gradually by bringing counter qualities into the field against it.

226

He is expected to put forth the effort needed to dispel a negative emotion or to destroy a negative thought, since such will not go away of itself.

227
When the mind is sufficiently purified, it receives intuitions more easily and nurtures aspirations more warmly.

228
Tread firmly on negative thoughts, eject them from the mind as soon as they appear, and give them no chance to grow. Spite, envy, moroseness, despondency and denigrating criticism should all be denied entry.

229
A prompt and decisive 'No!' to the suggestion or impulse as soon as it appears, prevents it from gathering strength and becoming uncontrollable.

230
The quickness with which an impulse moves him to action may hide its beginning in him. But the moment is there: by self-training it may be perceived in time, and inhibition or control applied with more and more success.

231
His intellectual clarity must be deep and his emotional tolerance broad.

232
It is always a pity when thinkers are not equal to their own thoughts. Schopenhauer, that melancholy metaphysician, is a case in point. He extolled the Buddhistic calm of Nirvana and the supreme beatitude of living in deep thought, but he did not hesitate to beat his landlady when she committed some trivial transgression. In his attitude to events and in his relations with men, it is the business of the philosopher to display qualities flowing from the ethos of his teaching, but it is not necessarily the business of a metaphysician to do so. This is the practical and moral difference between them.

233
The gain of building an equable character and evenness of mind is not only a spiritual one, it is also a contribution to personal happiness.

234
He will not agree to act under threat. Every such attempt to intimidate him makes him only more determined to resist it and to reject the desired action.

235
The power which man spends in the passions and emotions of his lower nature will, when governed and directed upward in aspiration to his higher nature, give him the knowledge and bliss of the Overself.

236
It is not enough to follow a wholesome diet and a healthy way of life. The seeker after a better existence must match with these advances his thoughts and emotions.

237

There is all the difference between a sturdy independence and an inflated self-esteem.

238

An experience which is a blow to his ego ought to be received with humility and analysed with impartiality. But too often the man receives it with resentment and analyses it with distortion. In the result he is doubly harmed: there is the suffering itself and there is the deterioration of character.

239

We sin by wandering away from our true inner selves, by letting ourselves become wholly immersed in the thoughts and desires which surround us, by losing our innermost identity and taking up an alien one. This is the psychology of sin as philosophy sees it. But it could not have gained the knowledge for such a view of man if it had not succeeded in itself overcoming the bondage of flesh, feeling, and thought and penetrating by means of its flawless technique into the world of the divine spirit, which is the real man.

240

He is to live for the praise and blame, not of other people, but of his own higher self.

241

The distance from lip to heart is sometimes immense. Who has not known men who had God prominent in their heard speech but evil prominent in their silent desires?

242

The philosophic way of living asks for more than most men possess, more command of the passions, more discipline of the thoughts, and more submissiveness to intuition.

243

The moral injunctions which he finds in this teaching and must follow out in his life, are based on understanding the relation between his higher self and his lower self. They are not arbitrary commands but inevitable consequences of applying the adage, "Man, know thyself."

244

There is an abuse of authority when anyone takes advantage of it to bolster his own ego at the expense of those under him.

245

He will be virtuous not merely for the reasons that so many others are— it is safer, it stops the prodding of conscience, etc.—but much more for the reason that it is essential to put up no obstructions to the light flowing from the Overself.

246

All that is best in the Christian virtues, the Buddhist virtues, the Stoic virtues, among several others, you will find in the philosophic ones.

247

Few are those who are psychologically ready for philosophy's disciplines, which call, not merely for a reluctant control of the animal nature, but for an eager aspiration to rise above it altogether. Few are ready for its ethics, which call not merely for a willingness to abide by society's protective laws, but for a generous disposition constantly putting itself in someone else's place.

248

Whoever does a wrong to another man is not doing it to him alone. He does it also to himself.

249

The nature of the means used will help to predetermine the nature of the end reached. An evil means cannot lead to a good end, but only to one of its own kind, even though mixed with some good.

250

The truth comes when it is sought, but is found only when we are ready. This is why the aspirant must take himself in hand, must improve his character and discipline his emotions.

251

There is to be nothing in himself to impede the intuitive power.

252

Moral nobility is not the sole possession of either the rich or the poor, the educated or the ignorant.

253

The conflict between lower and higher values, between the false and the true interpretation of life, goes on all the time within all men. But he who brings it into the open and looks it in the face is the man who has gained more than a little wisdom from the impact of experience.

254

Unless there is honest effort to apply practically the knowledge got and the understanding gained from this teaching, unless there is real striving after personal betterment and individual discipline, the interest shown is mere dabbling, not study.

255

The first moral slip is also the worst one. For the effort to cover it up involves a further lapse. Then the road runs downhill from slip to slip.

256

Small mentalities cannot comprehend big truths. Greedy mentalities cannot comprehend generous truths. Bigotry keeps vital facts outside the door of knowledge. This is why the philosophic discipline is needed.

257

He is called upon to reconcile spiritual aspirations with life's demands.

258

Too many people are willing to make an assault upon the outward effects of evil while leaving untouched the inward causes of evil.

259

Those who want only to gratify bodily appetites and have no use for spiritual satisfactions may regard ideals as quite futile. They may find the only rational purpose in human action is to cast out all aims except selfish ones, subordinating all moral restraints to the realization of those aims in the process.

260

However stubborn and intransigent his character may seem, let him never despair of himself. Even if he keeps making mistakes let him pick himself up and try again. However slow and laborious such a procedure seems, it will still be effectual in the end.

261

He must purify the will by abandoning sin and purify the mind by abandoning error.

262

What he does in his personal relations with others or in the way he meets events is no less a part of his spiritual life than his formal exercises in meditation.

263

If the goals of life are not redefined on a higher plane, the status of life remains—hovers—between that of the animal and the human and does not become fully human.

264

He needs to be wary of his own animal self and its interfusion with his human self and its hostility to his angelic self.

265

A justly balanced picture would show every man to be good in some points, bad in other points. There is nothing exceptional in this. Therefore, there is necessity for the false pride of anyone who ignores his bad points. But in the spiritual aspirant, such pride is not only unnecessary but also deathly to his progress.

266

The tyranny of negative thoughts and negative feelings can and must be broken. For this he can look to help from the best in him and the best in others.

267

It is said that necessity shapes its own morality. This is often true. But the exceptional man listens to a higher command.

268

Standing aside from one's thoughts, as if one were no longer identified with them, observing their nature and results quite critically, becomes a means of self-betterment if repeated regularly.

269

It is tremendously important to safeguard the fruits of one's studies by purification of character. On this Quest, the aspirant's motives must necessarily be of the highest quality.

270

Each should do what he or she can to prepare himself by learning how to recognize and eliminate weaknesses. It is equally essential to keep the thoughts, emotions, and actions on as high a level as possible.

271

The discipline of self is a prerequisite to the enlightenment of self.

272

It is true that most people realize that they do not yet come anywhere near such an ideal as philosophy proposes to them regarding their personal development. At least if they are aware of the ideal and if they accept it, they will find that practice can make quite a difference. The simple practice of holding back their own negative thoughts, holding back their own negative feelings when these first appear and nipping them in the bud is the beginning of becoming their own master.

273

If a man regrets his own conduct, be it a single action or a whole course of actions, he will feel some self-contempt and get depressed. This is a valuable moment, this turning of the ego against itself. If he takes advantage of it to ferret out the cause in his own character, in his own person as it got built up through its reincarnations, he may remold it in a more satisfactory way. This inner work is accomplished by a series of creative and positive meditations.

274

He is not required to acquire a perfect character, a complete absence of all faults. In new surroundings or circumstances and under different pressures, new faults may appear. He is required to remove just sufficiently the obstructive conditions within himself.

275

The herd of men are ruled by physical instincts and changing emotions. The aspirant for true individuality must set up the higher standards of self-control, personal stability, and harmonious balance.

276

Though man assigns little importance to his thoughts, contrasted with his deeds, their total effect is to dictate his policies which in turn dictate his deeds.

277

If karmic obligations may have to be fulfilled, at least this will not be done in total ignorance. It will be with resignation rather than hatred, and with hope for higher attainment.

278

The habit of always remembering that he is committed to the Quest and to the alteration of character which this involves, should help him to refuse assent in temptation and reject despondency in tribulation.

279

The Buddhist scriptures name obstacles the aspirant may have to deal with. They are: frivolity, changeableness, unruly desires, dissatisfaction, gratification of the senses, and craving for the ego's existence.

280

Even if he finds himself in a moral solitude, as he may in the earlier years, it is still worthwhile to be loyal to ideals.

281

He must cast off the long mantle of arrogance and put on the short coat of humility.

282

A lapse in artistry may be pardoned but a lapse in sincerity may not. Be sincere! That is the message from soul to self, from God to man.

283

It is not a man's own voice which is to acclaim him as a master, but his life.

284

His willingness to acknowledge he has faults and lots of them is admirable—so few ever like to confess such a thing—but they are not so deep or so numerous as he imagines. He should not forget that he has some merits too and they are well able to balance the others and keep them where they belong. As for perfection, alas, the sage too is still striving for it.

285

Pride can take a dozen different disguises, even the disguise of its very opposite, humility. The quicker he grows and the farther he goes on this quest, the more must an aspirant examine his character for its traces and watch his actions to detect it.

286

He is indeed a prudent man who refuses to be blinded by passions or deluded by appearances.

287

He does not know in advance what he will do in every new situation that arises—who does?—but only what he will *try* to do, what principles he will try to follow.

288
He who trims his sails to the winds of expediency reveals his insincerity.

Environmental influence

289
It is true that environment contributes to the molding of character but not true that it creates or even dominates character. Thought and will are linked with our own reincarnational past. Character can be improved by effort and Grace. If we will only attend to the first and persistently carry out the inner work required on ourselves, destiny will attend to the second and not seldom remove the outer obstacles or improve the outer environment in the process.

290
Each person who enters our life for a time, or becomes involved with it at some point, is an unwitting channel bringing good or evil, wisdom or foolishness, fortune or calamity to us. This happens because it was preordained to happen—under the law of recompense. But the extent to which he affects our outer affairs is partly determined by the extent to which we let him do so, by the acceptance or rejection of suggestions made by his conduct, speech, or presence. It is we who are finally responsible.(P)

291
The victim of exterior suggestion is never quite an innocent victim, for his own quota of consent must also be present.

292
It is perfectly true that environment *does* count, and often heavily, in the sum of life. But it is also true that if one's faith is strong enough or if one's understanding is deep enough, the quest can be pursued effectively anywhere, be it a slum tenement or a stockbroker's office. It is easier to pursue it in some places, harder in others, but the law of compensation always operates to even matters out. If there is a total giving-up of oneself to this higher aim, sooner or later there will be a total result, whatever the external circumstances may be.

293
What is in a man, in his character, his mind, and his heart is, in the end, much more important than what is in his surroundings; but his surroundings have their own importance, for they either limit or they promote what he can do.

294
With most people the reaction to their environment and to events is mainly impulsive and mostly uncontrolled. So the first step for them is to become conscious of what they are doing, the second being to refuse to do

it when reflection and wisdom dictate a better course. All this implies a taking hold of the self and a disciplining of its mechanism—body, feelings, and thoughts. It leads to using the self with *awareness* and functioning in it with efficiency.

295

It is fashionable in certain circles to fix the blame for a man's erring proclivities on his faulty upbringing—or lack of it—by parents, or on his companions, temptations, and surroundings. But are they so much to blame as the man himself? And is he not the victim, the resultant, of his own prenatal past? And even this is not the ultimate cause of his sinning. He is misled by ignorance—without understanding of his deepest self and without knowledge of life's higher laws.

296

There is some kind of correspondence between the outward situations of his life as they develop and the subconscious tendencies of his mind, between the nature of his environment and the conscious characteristics of his personality, between the effects as they happen to him and the causes that he previously started. He can begin to change his life for the better when he realizes how long he has mentally been unconsciously building it up for the worse. The same energy which has been directed into negative thoughts can then be directed into positive ones. Were it not for the stubbornness of habit, it would not be harder to do this than to do its opposite.

297

The emotions felt inside the heart, the thoughts evoked inside the head, affect the environment and atmosphere outside us.

298

Without dropping into the artificial attitude which pretends to give small value to outward circumstances, he can yet try to set himself free from their mental dominion.

299

Until he has attained that inner strength which can concentrate thoughts and dominate emotions, it will be foolish to say that environment does not count and that he can mingle with society as freely as he can desert it. Without this attainment, he will be weakened by most of them or strengthened by a few of them.

300

Birth into a prosperous elegant and gracious circle is valued highly in this world: it gives a man dignity and assurance. Education, which nurtures intellect and bestows culture, is likewise well appraised. But both measure as small things in the other world of spiritual attainment.

301

The inner life is affected by physical conditions, although not to the extent to which it is affected by thoughts and feelings.

Moral relativity

302

How are we to behave toward our fellow men? Each will answer the question differently according to his evolutionary status. The young inexperienced naïve idealist will contradict the aged worldly-wise cynic for whom life, authority, celebrity, tradition, innovation, have been totally denuded of their glamour. The distance from one answer to the other will also be marked by varying views.

303

It is quite true that moral codes have historically been merely relative to time, place, and so on. But if we try to make such relativity a basis of nonmoral action, if we act on the principle that wrong is not worse than right and evil not different from good, then social life would soon show a disastrous deterioration, the ethics of the jungle would become its governing law, and catastrophe would overtake it in the end.(P)

304

The relativity of good and evil is no justification for the tolerance of wrong and evil.

305

It would be a mistake to believe that because philosophy affirms that morality, art, conscience, and religion are relative to human beings, it therefore has no moral code to offer. It most assuredly has such a code. This is so because side by side with relativity it also affirms development. It holds up a purpose, traces out a path to its realization, and hence formulates a code.

306

The virtue which he is to practise is not bounded by the standards set by law and custom, nor even by conventional morality. His standards are far higher and far nobler. For they are not measured by human weakness but by human possibility. If for so much of his lifetime they have to exist side by side with his shortcomings, the latter are not accepted but are resisted.

307

Moral relativity has led, when embraced by intellectual materialists or unphilosophical mystics, to foolish and even dangerous practical result. The fallacy is that although all points of view in morality are tenable, all are not *equally* tenable.

308

The danger of this teaching of evil's unreality and moral relativity is that in the hands of the unwise it annuls all distinction between evil and good, while in the hands of the conceited it opens dangerous doors.

309

The undisciplined or the evil-minded will always seize on such a tenet to provide support and excuse for their faults or sins. There is no reason to withhold it, however, for they will commit the same faults or sins anyway whether they have the teaching or not.

310

Because there are levels of moral growth, character, and self-control, it became necessary to lay down laws, codes, and rules for mankind in the mass. These may be of sacred origin, as with a Moses, or of secular authority, as with a ruler. Where the name of God is invoked to give them weight, this is usually a human device. But the come-back of karma is very real, and not a fancy.

311

The discovery of moral relativity gives no encouragement however to moral laxity. If we are freed from human convention, it is only because we are to submit ourselves sacrificially to the Overself's dictate. The unfold-ment of progressive states of conscious being is not possible without giving up the lower for the higher.(P)

312

Although we try to avoid fanatical beliefs and extremist views, there are certain matters where compromise would be cowardly and halfheartedness would be harmful.

313

The doctrine that ethical and artistic values are relative need not be inconsistent with the doctrine that they are also progressive. They evolve from lower to higher levels. Being ideas in some individual mind, they improve with the improvement of that mind's own quality.

314

The codes of good and bad are usually part of religion and certainly belong to the religious level. But the idea of goodness implies the idea of badness, so both are held in the mind although in different ways: one explicitly, the other implicitly. The philosopher does not depend on them but on their source, the Higher Power.

315

The ego being an illusory entity its virtues are in the ultimate sense either imaginary or also illusory. Nevertheless, moral perfection of the ego is a necessary stage on the journey to perfection of consciousness, to the Overself. To cast it aside as being merely relative, to reject ethics and virtue as being unnecessary, is a trick of the intellect to enable the ego to stay longer in its own self-sufficiency.

316

When the life and teachings of men like Muhammed and Buddha are compared, the most extraordinary differences become apparent. What in effect Buddha placed before his followers as the highest ideal was, "You may live a good life as a layman, but if you want to live a superior life you must become a monk." Muhammed, on the other hand, said literally, "No faithful follower of mine shall ever become a monk." He even told his followers that under certain conditions they could practise polygamy and have four wives. Both these men are revered as wise, and yet such divergences exist in their teaching. The divergence arose because in their wisdom they had consideration for the degree of evolution of the people to whom they spoke, of their physical, mental, and ethical needs, and of the circumstances of their lives. They gave to the people what they most needed, and the highest wisdom within their comprehension. They did not give them the hidden philosophy, the highest teaching open to man.

Even today it is useless to preach ethics to a gangster. He is not ready. Through the power of the Mind, a Sage can place himself in perfect sympathy with every man. He can see the next step ahead which can be taken without undue difficulty. It was temperamentally and climatically easy for the Indians of that period to renounce marriage, and it was therefore easy for Buddha to bring them a step further along the path by teaching complete monasticism. But the wild tribes amongst whom Muhammed lived could only grasp something much grosser, and so Muhammed in his wisdom gave them what would make them a little less savage; he gave them a practical ethical code for daily living, and at the same time stimulated their faith in after-death rewards. Instead of telling them to retire to monasteries, which they were incapable of doing, and instead of telling them to practise meditation, which they would not have understood, he said in effect "No, go on with your daily life but five times a day let go of all personal affairs for a few minutes. Kneel down, remember God, and pray." The Arab people of that time could do that, and it acted as a check on their more barbarous instincts.

Such was the wisdom of Muhammed and Buddha. But for us in the twentieth century to take the path of either would be foolishness, because it was not given to us but to a people of other times. The Sages do not give a doctrine which is once and for all delivered to all mankind. They give a teaching suited to a particular section of mankind and for a particular period.

317
If the good and evil values of this earthly existence are in the end relative, partial, and transient, there yet remains a supreme value which is absolute, total, and eternal in its goodness. It belongs to the root of our being, the Overself in us that represents the World-Mind.

318
The atheist who declares that the moral scene is entirely suggested to man by his environment has taken a partial truth, a partial untruth, and joined them together. But if he had declared that the environment was a contributory factor to the final result, he would have been quite correct.

319
The moaning of a cat has doubtless a certain musical note in it. The *Messiah* by Handel has musical notes of another kind. Metaphysical scepticism would say that both values are relative and not absolute, hence both are as worthwhile or as worthless as we believe them to be. But most of us would prefer Handel! Why? Because although as relative as the cat's sounds, it is progressively superior. We may apply this to ethics.

320
Excessive moral tolerance easily becomes moral lethargy.

321
How can you rightly give the same rules on self-control to young men, in whom the lusts are hot, and to old men, in whom they are cold?

322
Where the Hindu guru denounced anger as a blemish on character, the Greek patriot praised it as an incitement to courage.

323
To tie a code of moral values to a religious belief is safer in a simple community and riskier in a sophisticated one.

324
A virtue may be practised wrongly, when it is no longer a virtue.

325
New circumstances bring out new and different qualities, including latent and even unsuspected ones. Or a crisis in events may explode and let them appear suddenly. Thus the good may become the bad; the bad may become good. Arrogance in virtue is risky.

326
By giving his allegiance to the political system, the religious system, and the commercial system in which he lives, he has unwittingly done two things: he has made a judgement on them and he has taken a moral decision about them. But whether or not this has penetrated his consciousness, he cannot absolve himself from these responsibilities.

327

Sinfulness is relative. What is right for a man at a low stage may be wrong for him at a higher stage; and in the highest stage, he may act rightly yet sin in thought.

328

Although two different doctrines may each be relatively true, this is not the same as being on the same level of evaluation.

329

To set up relativity as an absolute truth without qualifying it, is unfair. To say that all values are alike, all codes are the same, is to say something half-false.

330

Paradox is an indispensable element of the Highest Formulations.

331

If the old moralities fall away from him it is only to be displaced by higher ones, certainly not to be bereft of any ethical code.

332

The doctrinaire who uses right ideas to support or defend wrong actions is able to do so only because those ideas are general and abstract ones. They ignore circumstances, time, and place. Convert them into specific concrete, practical, and particular cases, and their misuse becomes difficult.

333

Although he has now inwardly transcended conventional codes of good and evil, he will outwardly continue to respect them. This is not hypocrisy for he is not opposed to them. He perceives that the very relativity which deprives them of value for him, provides them with value for society.

334

Obedience to the Overself will then become the only code of ethics that he can follow.

Conscience

335

If it is not possible for the generality of mankind to practise ethical indolence permanently and to avoid the moral struggles which the situations of life lead to intermittently, it is much less possible for the minority of mankind who have begun this quest to do so. Life becomes graver for them. If they do not obey the call of conscience the first time, it may become more painful to obey it the second time. If they persist in following an ignoble and contemptible course after they have already seen that it is ignoble and contemptible, the karma becomes proportionately heavier.

It has been said that knowledge is power, but it needs equally to be said that knowledge is also responsibility.

336

As his sensitivity develops and his conscience refines, he comes to regard certain actions as sinful which he formerly regarded as innocent.

337

There is a guiding conscience in a man which develops or weakens as he responds to the forces and influences playing *on and in* him from both bygone lives and the current incarnation. It is this preoccupation with choosing good and avoiding evil, with religious feelings and moral virtues, that lift man above the animal.

338

We must interpret the word duty in a larger sense, not merely as some social task imposed on us from without, but as a spiritual decision imposed on us from within.

339

It is a faulty use of the term self-respect, when they really mean keeping up appearances before others. A true self-respect is that feeling inside a man, call it conscience if you wish, which keeps him from giving way to bestial impulses and dishonest action.

340

We shall understand the mysterious nature of conscience only if we understand its twofold character. What we commonly experience as the inward voice of conscience is simply the distilled result of accumulated past experience, and this includes the experience of many, many earth lives also. This voice is usually a negative one, inasmuch as it more often warns, admonishes, and hinders us from wrong conduct. There is a rarer experience of conscience, however, which is the voice of our own Overself, that divine consciousness which transcends our personal self. This voice is usually a positive one, inasmuch as it more often directs, guides, and explains with a wisdom which comes from beyond the fears and hopes, the suggestions and customs, that organized society and patriarchal convention have implanted in our subconscious mind. Its external development of a so-called evil course of conduct may or may not coincide with the disapproval arising from ancient experience or divine wisdom, for it is merely a matter of social convenience, cultural development, or geographical custom. It may indeed be defective, false, or even quite immoral guidance, for mob passion often masquerades as social conscience. This is the kind of conscience which has a history. It changes with changing circumstances and evolves with evolving grades of culture. The trial and death of Socrates is a classic case illustrating the conflict between genuine and pseudo-conscience.

When I was in India I learnt that to commit suicide under any circumstance was the worst of human sins whereas when I was in Japan I learnt that the failure to commit suicide under certain circumstances was itself one of the worst sins. In both countries the individual pseudo-conscience tenders its counsel to commit or not to commit suicide according to the suggestions implanted from outside in the individual mind by collective society. We may sum up by saying that the voice of outer convention is conscience in its commonest form, that the voice of personal experience is the wisdom of the human personality and the distillate of many incarnations, and that the serene monition of the Overself is conscience in its purest form, the true innermost voice of divine wisdom.

341

The ego takes his conscience over and fits it to suit himself.

342

That voice within you which whispers that one act is right and another wrong, is in the end none other than the voice of the Overself. Only it may come to you as from afar, remote and muffled, halting and intermittent, because it has to come amid other voices which are more clamant and more close to your inner ear.

343

When formalism is stretched out into hypocrisy and when compromise is accepted to the point of surrender, social conventions have drowned a man's conscience.

344

Everyone has some degree of what is called conscience. So, in relationships with others, an awareness of the promptings of this inner voice—in the light of, and supplemented by, the teachings of Masters like Jesus and the Buddha—will clarify one's course of thought and action.

345

Under the pressure of his personal ego but haunted by the commandments of respected prophets, he finds himself occasionally in moral dilemmas.

346

How shall a man meet different moral situations? What line of conduct should he follow on different occasions? How shall he resolve each conflict of duty? These are questions which he alone can best solve. It is his own conscience which is at stake. However, this does not mean that he should disdain whatever sources of guidance may be available to him. It means that what he has to do in particular circumstances at his particular stage of evolution is not necessarily what other men would have to do.

347

We can depend on making a correct ethical choice *always* only when we have consciously worked out a true philosophical basis for all our ethics; otherwise we shall be at the mercy of those many possible changes of which feeling itself is at the mercy.

348

It is not only a question of what course of action will be most effective, but of what will be most ethical. Neither of these two factors can be ignored with impunity; both must be brought into a balanced relation.

349

It is more prudent to "sense" the emanations imprinted in the auric field surrounding a person than to trust alone to the words he utters or the claims he makes.

350

Those who depend on other persons to make decisions for them or to solve problems, lose the chance of self-development which the situation offers them.

351

In trying to reach a decision about his work and how he can best serve others, the individual must turn to the Overself, and not to other sources, for direction.

352

When confronted by difficult decisions, one must be especially careful to take into consideration the future effects of his choice. A decision based on sentiment, or on other emotional reactions, unchecked by reason, cannot solve any problem—as the student has, undoubtedly, already learned. It is necessary to examine past experience—one's own, and that of others—in order to discover and profit from the lessons there presented. Failure to do so leads to painful repetition of avoidable suffering. This is particularly true of personal relationships.

353

There will come a time in the life of each student when certain critical decisions will have to be made. These, together with the quality of the ideals he pursues and his whole general attitude, will determine the circumstances of the remainder of that incarnation.

354

There are so many sides to even the simplest situation that the aspirant will at times be bewildered as to what to do or how to act. He will waver from one decision to another and be unable to take up any firm ground at all. At such a time it is best to wait as long as possible and thus let time also make its contribution.

355

If by waiting a little a man can see his way more clearly and reach a more positive decision, he should wait. But if it only befuddles his mind still further, then he should not.

356

But we are not always given the chance to choose between simple good and evil. The situations which organized human society develops for us offer not infrequently the choice only between lesser and larger evils.

357

We see among neurotics this same long-drawn inability to form decisions, or dread of their being wrong if made.

358

In every situation requiring an important decision, he will get a truer one if he can successfully analyse the personal and emotional factors involved in it.

359

Judgements made in haste, actions done rashly, without proper consideration, and decisions given out of impatience and excitement are likely to be of less value than the opposite kind.

Goodness

360

Rousseau taught that human nature was essentially good, whereas Calvin taught that it was essentially bad. Philosophy teaches that the innermost core of human nature is essentially good but the outer and visible husk is a mixture of good and bad, varying with individuals as to the proportions of this mixture.

361

The mark of true goodness is, first, that it never by thought, word, or deed injures any other living creature; second, that it has brought the lower nature under the bidding of the higher; and third, that it considers its own welfare not in isolation but always against the background of the common welfare.

362

There are three different forms of wrong action which he must carefully separate from each other in his mind if he is to adhere to the principles of philosophical living and if he is to place a correct emphasis where it should belong. First, the most important, is the sin in moral behavior; second is the error in practical judgement; third is the transgression of the social code.

363

A sharply self-accusing honesty of purpose, a blunt integrity of conscience, will have again and again to thrust its sword into his conduct of life. An ethic that far outleaps the common one will have to become his norm. Conventional ideas of goodness will not suffice him; the quest demands too much for that.

364

Few characters are completely good, totally selfless, and it leads only to dangerous illusions when this is not remembered. New evils grow in those who deceive themselves, or others, by tall talk and exaggerated ideals.

365

The goodness which philosophy inculcates is an active one, but it is not a sentimental one. It is more than ready to help others but not to help them foolishly. It refuses to let mere emotion have the last word but takes its commands from intuition and subjects its emotions to reason. It makes a clear distinction between the duty of never injuring another person and the necessity which sometimes arises of causing pain to another person. If at times it hurts the feelings of someone's ego, it does so only to help his spiritual growth.

366

This goodwill becomes instinctive but that does not mean it becomes unbalanced, wildly misapplied, and quite ineffectual. For the intelligence which is in wisdom accompanies it.

367

The goodness which one man may express in his relation to another is derived ultimately from his own divine soul and is an unconscious recognition of, as well as gesture to, the same divine presence in that other. Moreover, the degree to which anyone becomes conscious of his true self is the degree to which he becomes conscious of it in others. Consequently, the goodness of the fully illumined man is immeasurably beyond that of the conventionally moral man.(P)

368

Why did Jesus ask his followers to refrain from calling him good? By all ordinary standards he was certainly a good man, and more. It was because his goodness was not really his own; it derived from the Overself having taken over his whole person, his whole being.

369

He will awaken to the realization that the chaotic unplanned character of the ordinary man's life cramps his own possibilities for good. He will perceive that to let his thoughts drift along without direction and his feelings without purpose, is easy but bad.

370

The term "good" is used here with clear consciousness that there is no absolute standard of goodness in common use, that what is regarded as good today may be unacceptable as such tomorrow, and that what one man calls good may be called evil by another man. What then is the sense which the student is asked to give this word? He is asked to employ it in the sense of a pattern of thinking, feeling, and doing which conforms to his highest ideal.

371

What is sin? It may be defined, first, as any act which harms others; second, as any act which harms oneself; third, as any thought or emotion which has these consequences.

372

Goodness is naturally allied to the truth, is the perfume of it exhaled without self-consciousness.

373

Evil-doing is too vulgar. The spiritually fastidious man does not find himself set with a choice between it and the opposite. He cannot help but choose the good spontaneously, directly, and unhesitatingly.

374

In the end the question of goodness involves the question of truth: one may be correctly known only when the other is also known.

375

Whatever else he may be, he is no aspirant for sainthood. That admirable goal is quite proper for those whose innate vocation lies that way. But it is not the specific goal for would-be philosophers.

376

The same truth, ideal, or master that shows him the glorious possibilities of goodness within himself, will also show him the ugly actualities of evil within himself. No sun, no shadow.

377

Morally, emotionally, and intellectually, no man is all weaknesses or all strengths. All are a mixture of the two, only their proportion and quality varies.

378

The good in man will live long after his faults have been forgotten.

379

He who has achieved goodness in thought and feeling cannot fail to achieve it in action.

380

Sin is simply that which is done, through ignorance, against the higher laws. Virtue is the obedience to, and cooperation with, those laws.

381

Human sin derives from human ignorance of the Presence which is always within man. Who that is aware of It could possibly transgress, could oppose Its benignity or forget Its teaching of karmic come-back?

382

It is true that a face may proclaim the possessor's character, but it is also true that often only a part of this character is revealed and that the hidden part is, schizophrenically, of an opposite kind.

383

The fact must be admitted, as every saint has admitted it, that there are two poles in human nature, a lower and a higher, an animal and an angelic, an outward-turned and an inward-turned one.

384

It is more just to say that each man's nature is compounded of both good and bad qualities. This must be so because the animal, the human, and the angel are all there in him.

Altruism

385

The need today is not for compromise or patchwork. It is for one, outright, generous gesture.

386

The selfish person thinks only of satisfying his own wants first of all, not caring if he harms others. The next higher type thinks also of his immediate circle of family and friends. But the highest type of all gives equal regard to himself, to his family, to whoever crosses his path, and to all others. He feels for everyone, never satisfying his desires by wrongfully taking away from, or harming, another.

387

One fruit of the change will be that just as the old idea was to watch out selfishly for his own interests, so the new idea will be not to separate them from the interests of others. If it be asked, "How can anyone who is attuned to such impersonality be also benevolent?" the answer is that because he is also attuned to the real Giver of all things, he need not struggle against anyone nor possess anything. Hence he can afford to be generous as the selfish cannot. And because the Overself's very nature is harmony and love, he seeks the welfare of others alongside of his own.

388

He is entitled to seek his own profit and advantage, but only in equity with and considerateness for those of the other person concerned.

389

Those who regard altruism as the sacrifice of all egoistic interests are wrong. It means doing well by all, including ourselves. For we too are part of the all. We do not honour altruistic duty by dishonouring personal responsibility.

390

Up to a certain point in development, man does right in seeking self-gain. But beyond that point, he must stop the process and seek self-loss.

391

The attitude of non-interference in other people's lives is a benign and justifiable one at certain times but an egotistic one at other times.

392

The best charity in the end is to show a man the higher life that is possible for him.

393

By selfishness is meant seeking advantage to self in all transactions with complete indifference to others' welfare.

394

It is useless to prate and prattle of altruistic motives when the essential motive imposed on us by Nature is self-interest. Every man has a complete right to be selfish. Trouble arises only when he hurts others in order to fulfil this aim. Then the same Nature which prompted him to concentrate on his own existence will punish him. For the law of compensation cannot be evaded: that which we have given to others, of woe or good, will some day be reflected back to us.

395

Be careful not to limit the third element in the quest—action—to altruism or service. It is rather the re-education of character through deeds. Thus this includes moral discipline, altruistic service, overcoming animal tendencies, temporary physical asceticism, self-training and im-provement, and so forth. It is the path of remaking the personality in the external life both through thought-control and acts so as to become sensitive towards and obedient to the Overself. Altruism will then become a mere part of, a subordinate section in, this character training.

396

Whoever labours worthily at a worthy task which does not afflict his conscience is rendering service to humanity. It does not matter whether he is a peasant or a businessman, a bricklayer's apprentice or a spiritual teacher.

397

The isolationist individual who stands unmoved by a crime being committed on his doorstep, is tempted by selfishness not to burden himself with another person's troubles.

398
Ambition can be transformed into service.

399
No right action, done through unswerving faithfulness to the philosophic ideal, is ever wasted even if its results are not to be seen. It will surely bear its good fruit at some time in the individual's existence, however long deferred and however far off that may be.

400
We must learn not only to develop right qualities of character, but also not to direct them wrongly. Misplaced charity, for instance, is not a virtue.

401
In ethics we are to seek a sublime common sense which means that we are not to help ourselves to the ignoring of others, not to help others to the ignoring of ourselves.

402
To treat others too softly may not be the wise way when life itself may treat them more harshly because of their mistakes, sins, or weaknesses.

403
He needs to protect himself by the truth which, applied here, means he must strengthen himself against their negative, slushy emotion. A misconceived and muddled pity brought in where toughness and reason are needed, would only harm them and him, both.

404
The continued study of this philosophy will inevitably lead the student to accept its practical consequences and thus make the universal welfare of mankind his dominant ethical motive.

405
I have more respect for the man who builds a career of usefulness and service to his community than for the man who turns his back on cares or responsibilities so as to sink into the smug peace of retreat. At the best the latter will address useless appeals to mankind to be better, whereas the former will do something more positive and more effective.

406
Excerpt from John Steinbeck's *The Log from the Sea of Cortez*: "Perhaps the most overrated virtue in our list of shoddy virtues is that of giving. Giving builds up the ego of the giver, makes him superior and higher and larger than the receiver. Nearly always, giving is a selfish pleasure, and in many cases it is a downright destructive and evil thing. One has only to remember some of our wolfish financiers who spend two-thirds of their lives clawing fortunes out of the guts of society and the latter third pushing it back. It is not enough to suppose that their philanthropy is a kind of frightened restitution, or that their natures change when they have enough. Such a nature never has enough and natures do not change that

readily. I think that the impulse is the same in both cases. For giving can bring the same sense of superiority as getting does, and philanthropy may be another kind of spiritual avarice."

407

Pure altruism is a rare and difficult quality, remote from the actuality of human conditions. The cautious person is also entitled to ask whether it is justifiable, whether a man is not entitled to do justice to himself as well as to others. The obvious reply is that there is no reason why his own good should not be included in that of the whole community. It is an arguable question whether the Buddhist story of a man who gave his own body to feed a starving tigress acted very wisely, although we must admit that he acted most generously.

408

He may love mankind without being in love with mankind. He may act with unwearying altruism and compassion towards them and yet with clear sight of their moral uglinesses and mental deformities.

409

An intellectual enlightenment not accompanied by a moral purification, can lead only to a meagre result when turned to the service of humanity. The altruist must educate his own character before he can influence effectually the character of others. Only then are false steps and dangerous missteps less likely to be taken.

410

A generous act not only helps the beneficiary but, if the motive is pure, ennobles the doer. The wisdom of the act is, however, a different matter and requires separate analysis.

Patience, perseverance

411

If he has cultivated the quality of calmness, then he will automatically derive from it the quality of patience. If he has not done so, he will yet get something of its atmosphere quite involuntarily and unconsciously from the stretching-out of his intellectual outlook by his metaphysical vast studies, with their unveiling of the cosmic plan, the eternal cyclic laws, and the ego's own long-drawn evolution. How valuable a trait of character patience can be is best revealed in the domain of action. It will stop premature deeds, it will guide him to the knowledge of when to act, and it will teach him that wise activity is a well-timed, ripened activity.

412

The student will now see how necessary it is to develop the quality of equipoise. Without it he is at the mercy of every desire and passion, every emotion and impulse, every negative thought which rises from within himself or is picked up from contacts or neighbours outside himself. But with it there will be at least a conflict before surrender or a conflict leading to victory.

413

When a mystic's words are spoken or written from too high a level for the aspirant, so that he can see no trail leading up to that level itself, the aspirant is likely to become depressed and discouraged at the magnitude of the climb before him. Let him not lose heart too quickly at this point of his upward course, for the path does indeed involve the work of many reincarnations. Here is his chance to learn two useful qualities: resignation and patience. Yes, there is hope for him, but it is a realistic and not a dramatic one. He must learn to be patient because his labours are not in vain. He must learn to be resigned because the hour when he will gather their fruit is in God's hands.

414

He must discipline himself in patience, where patience is needful. He must learn to wait and let a situation ripen until it is really ready for him to use advantageously. On the other hand, it would be foolish for him to delay and over-prepare, for an opportunity which occurs once may never occur again.

415

It is the work of a lifetime to venture on such a great improvement of character as will place the lower self under our control, instead of our being controlled by it. We are likely to get disheartened at times by the seeming slowness of progress. This is partly because we are too apt to think in terms of this single incarnation only, whereas those who understand life's actual range think of it in terms of dozens and scores. Hence we have to learn a certain tolerant patience with ourselves, while at the same time maintaining an ardent aspiration for self-improvement and a critical attitude towards our weaknesses. This sounds contradictory but it is not really so. It is rather a matter of getting a proper balance between the two attitudes.

416

We find by rueful experience that years are needed to begin to correct a weakness, let alone to complete the correction. The moral adjustment to truth is a long-drawn affair. This is disheartening if we seek quick results. The formidable nature of our task of self-changing thus discloses itself. Tendencies built up through many a lifetime cannot be altered, without Grace, in a single year. Patience is called for in dealing with them.

417

However disheartening the slowness of his growth may be to his emotions, the remembrance that he is a sage in embryo should always be encouraging to his reason.

418

Patience is needed, and confidence in the path chosen. Resignation rather than rebellion brings results.

419

The practice of calmness amid all occasions and the exercise of an unruffled patience in all situations are indeed two valuable elements of the philosophic discipline which contribute definitely towards the student's growth. It is easy to be patient sometimes and with some men but the philosophic discipline calls for unruffled patience at all times and with all men.

420

Each man has to fight his lonely battle which nobody else can share with him, has to work out personal problems in the solitude of his own mind, has to gain command of his passions in the secrecy of his own heart.

421

Where the good and the evil are so closely blended together, as in human character, unless he makes his self-portrait harsh, uncompromising, and unbeautiful, he will waste many years in illusions, only to find at the end that everything still remains to be done.

422

If he will be strong enough to rise above the cowardice of conformity and above the embarrassment of setting himself apart from others, he will receive a proportionate though intangible reward. He will know the delight and strength of being himself to that extent.

423

A man will do the best he can in his personal situation, not the best that someone else could do in the same situation. His action is relevant to his strength and understanding. All this is true. But it is equally true that he has untapped inner resources. Why not try to better his best?

424

Self-reliance is not a quality which can be given to others. Only by providing them with your own example can you contribute to this end.

425

Each virtue is the fruit of a long self-discipline, a constant self-denial. It is not picked up easily, but has to be cut from the solid rock.

426

He must not let himself be swayed by emotions into unreasonable actions nor lured by intellect into unintuitive ones.

427

He cannot help being what he is but he can help remaining what he is.

428

When we enlarge our love of the Divine by making it a matter of the will as well as feeling, we ennoble it.

429

Where self-confidence is based on the possession of adequate knowledge and innate ability, and not on arrogant conceit, where furthermore it arises from a conscious and logical carrying out of predetermined courses, it is a useful attribute.

430

All aspirants on this spiritual quest have to go through periods of discouragement from time to time and I myself was no exception. Physical nature does not easily permit us to escape from her grasp and her resistance to the individual spiritual effort is inevitable. Perseverance is therefore an indispensable quality.

431

An ordinary fortitude of the will is enough to enable one to bear the trifling disappointments of life, but a deep philosophic courage is needed to bear the crushing blows of life.

432

Such power is not easily gained. A man must overcome much within himself, must hold his spine unbending and his effort undeviating. All those negative qualities which act as encumbrances to true understanding of situations, occasions, events, and persons must be guarded against in attitude and action.

433

Amid his gross brutalizations and maniacal exaggerations, Nietschze's evil mysticism expressed some truth. He affirmed rightly that life must be hard if it is not to be trivial.

434

His quest of the Overself must be an untiring one. It is to be his way of looking at the world, his attitude toward life.

435

It is far more important to develop the strength within himself needful to break the spell than to beg for preventative protection against it. In the first case he progresses enormously and rapidly; in the second, he is static.

436

Each difficulty surmounted, each weakness resisted will fortify his will and increase his perseverance. It will evoke the better part of his nature and discipline the baser, and thus fit him more adequately to cope with the next ones.

437

He must be equally steadfast in adhering to this attitude whether other people utter complaints against him or make compliments to him.

438

We must retain our determination and our loyalty to the quest in all circumstances. Physical pains, climatic extremes must not deter us. We must console ourselves with the thought that these things are certain to pass away. They are mental figments, ideas which will be negated, whereas the truth and reality we seek belong to the immutable, and can never be negated.

439

Few of us can withdraw from the world and most of us must engage in its activity. But that is no reason for accepting the evils which are mixed in with this activity.

440

Tenacity of purpose is a characteristic of all who accomplish great things. Drawbacks cannot disgust him, labour cannot weary him, hardships cannot discourage him in whom the quality of persistence is always present. But to the man without persistence every defeat is a Waterloo.

441

Indecision of purpose and infirmity of will must yield to the resolute mind and the determined act. The person who sways uncertainly between one side and the other misses opportunity.

442

The student's inner reactions to outer events provide him with the opportunity to use his free will in the right direction. His attitude towards his own lower nature, that is, how far he encourages or discourages it, is another. And his recognition of what are good opportunities and what should be avoided, together with his acceptance or rejection of them, is still another.

443

Mental indolence and moral lethargy are hardly likely to waft us into the high haven of spiritual peace. We must learn to think fearlessly and courageously about every problem that faces us; we must try to elevate our hearts above the level of the moral lepers and spiritual cripples of our time.

444

He will learn to endure the blows of misfortune with a bravery heretofore unknown and a serenity heretofore unexperienced.

445

The strength of will which can lead a man to command of his sexual desires, cannot stop there if he is to achieve a full self-mastery. It must also go on to his diet and feelings, his speech and habits.

Value of confession, repentance

446

The man who seeks to release himself from moral responsibility for his actions or his fortunes can in no way make any real progress on the spiritual path. He may improve his capacity to meditate, he may become more sensitive psychically, but his real battle—against the ego—remains unfought and therefore unwon.

447

It would be a grave error to believe that philosophy is merely the practice of reflection over lofty or lovely thoughts. It is also the shedding of tears over low or unlovely ones, the remorseful weeping over past and present frailty, the poignant remembrance of errors and incapacities. We who practise it must examine ourselves periodically. This means that we should not, at any time, be satisfied with ourselves but should always recognize the need of improvement. Hence we should constantly strive to detect and remedy the moral, temperamental, and mental defects which disclose themselves. We will need to look into our hearts more deeply than ever before, and search their darker labyrinths for the motives and desires hiding away from our conscious aspiration. We are called upon to make the most searching criticism of ourselves, and to make it with emotional urgency and even profound remorse.

This advice to look within would be idiotic if it meant only looking at our human frailty and mortal foolishness. A morbid self-obsession, a continuously gloomy introspection and unending analysis of personal thoughts and experiences is to be avoided as unhealthy. Such ugly ego-centricity does not make us more "spiritual." But the advice really means looking further and deeper. It means an introspective examining operation much longer in time, much more exigent in patience, much more sus-tained in character, than a mere first glance. It means intensity of the first order, concentration of the strongest kind, spiritual longing of the most fervent sort.

Although philosophy bids us avoid morbid thoughts of depression, doubt, fear, worry, and anxiety because they are weakening and because they represent only one side—the dark side—of a two-sided situation, this counsel must not be misunderstood. It does not bid us ignore the causes which give rise to such thoughts. On the contrary, it bids us take full note of them, face up to them frankly, examine them carefully, and understand the defects in our own character which led to them. Finally we are to adopt the practical measures needed to deal with them. But this once done, and thoroughly done, we are to turn our back upon them and let them go altogether in order to keep our serenity and contain our spiritual detachment. In every painful problem which is ultimately traceable to our own wrong-doing, the best way to rid ourself of the worry and anxiety it brings is first, to do what is humanly possible to mend matters in a practical way; second, if others are concerned, to make such reparation to them as we can; third, to unmask our sin pitilessly and resolutely for what it is; fourth, to bring clearly into the foreground of consciousness what are the weaknesses and defects in our own character which have led us into this sin; fifth, to picture constantly in imagination during meditation or pre-sleep, our liberation from these faults through acquiring the opposite virtues; sixth, and last, when all this has been done and not until then, to stop brooding about the miserable past or depressing future and to hand the whole problem with its attendant worries into the keeping of the Overself and thus attain peace concerning it.

If this is successfully done, every memory of sin will dissolve and every error of judgement will cease to torment us. Here, in its mysterious presence and grace, whatever mistakes we have made in practical life and whatever sins we have committed in moral life, we need not let these shadows of the past haunt us perpetually like wraiths. We may analyse them thoroughly and criticize ourselves mercilessly but only to lay the foundation in better self-knowledge for sound reform. We must not forget them too soon, but we ought not hug them too long. After the work of self-analysis is well done, we can turn for relief and solace to the Overself.

448

Human nature is universally frail; his is no exception. Nevertheless, if he is appalled at his mistakes, if this anguish is doubled because what he has done wrongly is irreparable, is there nothing else left to do than to give himself up to helpless despair? The true answer is more hopeful than that. "I know that if I keep patient while cultivating humility and silencing the ego's pride, I shall grow away from old weaknesses and overcome former mistakes"—this should be the first stage of his new attitude. For the next one, he can at least go over the events of the past and amend them in thought. He can put right mentally those wrong decisions and correct those rash impulsive actions. He can collect the profits of lessons expensively learnt.

449

The first value of self-confession of sin is not so much getting rid of an uncomfortable sense of guilt over a particular episode or series of episodes as getting at the weakness in character responsible for it or them, and then seeking to correct it. Merely to remove the sense of discomfort and to leave its moral source untouched is not enough. Any priestly rite of forgiveness is ineffective until this is done. It must produce repentance if it is to be real and that in its turn must produce penance if it is to be successful in purifying his character. The second value of the confession is to induce the sinner to make amends or restitution to those he has hurt and thus balance his karmic account with them.

450

Men commit many sins and fall into many errors before the failure of their own conduct finally dawns upon them.

451

By raising his point of view regarding any grievous situation, whether it involve himself alone or other persons, he attracts the entry of a higher power into it which will work for his benefit and in his favour. He will learn to endure the blows of misfortune with a bravery heretofore unknown and a serenity heretofore unexperienced.

452

What then is all this repentant religio-mystic activity in prayer and reflection since his novitiate began but a form of confession of his sin? Confession is a rite as necessary to those outside the church as it is to those inside. The object is a kind of psychoanalytic procedure, to bring the sin to the surface by reliving the past if forgotten in the past, and to correct it mentally and imaginatively as well as in the character by resolves for future change. The result is purificatory.

453

It is better for his real progress that his eyes should fill with the tears of repentance than with the tears of ecstasy.

454

When a man lets go of his ego, *all* the virtues come submissively to his feet. If he can let it go only for a little while, they too will stay only a little while; but if he can make the parting permanent, then the virtues are his forever. But this is a high and uncommon state, for it is a kind of death few will accept.

455

Everything that belongs to the ego and its desires or fears has to go. For some men it is hard to put aside pride, for others it is harder to put aside shame, but both feelings have to go.

456

His thoughts, his feelings, and his actions must work in combination to effect this great self-purification which must precede the dawn of illumination. And this means that they must work upon themselves and divert their attention from other persons whom they may have criticized or interfered with in the past. The aspirant must reserve his condemnation for himself and leave others alone to their karma.

457

You are right to shut the door on the past if you have analysed its meanings and profited by its lessons, but not otherwise.

458

It is a useful practice, both for general moral self-improvement and for combatting our ego, every time we become aware that we are preoccupying ourselves with other people's faults, to turn that preoccupation upon ourselves and let it deal with our own faults, which we usually overlook. For we earn the right to judge others only after we have judged ourselves.

459

But although the aspirant will be greatly helped by a calm analysis of the transiency, suffering, and frustration inherent in life, he will be greatly hindered if he uses it as an excuse for a defeatist mentality and depressive temperament. The gallant inspiration to go forward and upward is indispensable.

460

The self-righteousness which prompts him to criticize others, and especially his fellow-questers, is a bad quality which ought to be excised as quickly as possible.

461

He may come to self-approving attitudes, but only after he has plumbed the depths of self-distrusting ones.

462

Every time he takes the harder way of acknowledging a fault, repenting a wrong, and then earnestly seeking to make reparation to whoever has suffered by it, he will be repaid by the sudden descent of gratifying peace, of a happy serenity absent from ordinary hours.

463

His attitude towards those situations in life which are difficult or trying will show how far he has really gone in the Quest. If he has not undergone the philosophic discipline, he will either analyse these situations in a wrong egoistic way or else avoid analysing them altogether.

464

Tolerate weakness in others but not in yourself.

465

If this process of self-examination is to bear fruit, the disciple must pick out those virtues which he lacks or in which he is partially deficient and he must set to work, as a practical exercise, to cultivate them. If his practice is to be complete it will take him into the emotional, intellectual, and volitional parts of his being. He should constantly strive to think, to feel, and to do what he should be and do.

466

So long as a man carries a flattering picture of himself, deterioration of character waits in ambush for him.

467

To acknowledge past perceptual error, to confess intellectual mistake, and to retrace one's steps accordingly may be bad policy for politicians, but it is sound policy for truth-seekers. The superficial or the conceited may feel that they lose in character thereby, but the earnest and the humble will, on the contrary, know that they gain.

468

No one else is to be regarded as responsible for his troubles, irritations, or handicaps. If he will analyse them aright, that is, with utter impersonality, he would see that the responsibility is not really in the other person, who apparently is the agent for these calamities, but in his own undisciplined character, his own egoistic outlook.

469

No man can follow this Quest faithfully without finding that the very weaknesses which he conceals from other men will eventually be brought to the forefront of his attention by the play of circumstances, so that he will be unable to postpone work on them any longer.

470

The very fact that he has become aware of these faults arises because the light has come into existence and begun to play upon the dark places in his character, thus generating a conscious desire for self-improvement. This awareness is not a matter for depression, therefore.

471

To wish one's past history to have been different from what it was, to pile up blame for one's bad deeds, choices, and decisions, is to cling to one's imaginary ego although seeking to improve it. Only by rooting up and throwing out this false imagination which identifies one with the ego alone can the mind become freed from such unnecessary burdens.

472

You are to be penitent not only because your wrong acts may bring you to suffering but also, and much more, because they may bring you farther away from the discovery of the Overself.

473

To repine for past errors or to wish that what has been should not have been has only a limited usefulness. Analyse the situations, note effects, study causes, draw lessons—then dismiss the past completely.

474

If the ego is discarded, all regrets over past acts are discarded with it.

475

He may be ashamed of what he did in the past but then he was that sort of man in the past. If he persists in identifying himself with the "I," in time such feelings will come to him and cause this kind of suffering. But if he changes over to identifying himself with the timeless being behind the "I" there can be no such suffering.

476

Repentance must be thorough and whole-hearted if it is to effect this purpose. He must turn his back upon the former way of life.

477

If Nature is hard, truth is cruel. It is unsparing to our egoistic desires, merciless in ferreting out our personal weaknesses.

478

If it is right to forgive others their sins against us, it must also be right to forgive ourselves and not constantly condemn ourselves to self-reproach. But we ought not do so prematurely.

479

When a man becomes aware of his wrong-doing and realizes its meaning for himself and its effect upon others, he has taken the first step towards avoiding its inevitable consequences. When he becomes deeply repentant he has taken the second step. When he tries to eliminate the fault in his character which produced the evil conduct and to make amends to others, where possible, he has taken the final step.

480

The quest will uncover the weakest places in his character, one by one. It will do so either by prompting him from within or by exposing him from without. If he fails to respond to the first way, with its gentle intuitive working, he must expect to endure the second way, with its harsh pressure through events. The only protection against his weaknesses is first, to confess them, and then, to get rid of them.

481

The constant nagging of those with whom he is compelled to live, work, or associate, so far as there is any truth in their exaggerations or misunderstandings, can be made to serve a most useful purpose by arousing in him the necessity of change and self-improvement. However much his self-love is wounded and however long it may take to achieve this and to correct his faults, he will only profit by it. With his success a separation may occur, and they may be set free to go their own way. It may be brought about by their own voluntary decisions or by the compulsion of destiny. When a relationship is no longer useful to evolution or karmically justified, an end will come to it. This acceptance of other people's criticisms, humbly and without resentment, may be compared to swimming against the current of a stream. Here the stream will be that of his own nature. In this matter he should look upon the others as his teachers—taking care however to separate the emotional misunderstandings and egoistic exaggerations from the actual truth. He is to regard the others as sent by the Overself to provoke him into drawing upon or deliberately developing the better qualities needed to deal with such provocations, and not only to show him his own bad qualities.

482

Out of the shadows of the past, there will come memories that will torment as they teach him, pictures that will hurt as they illustrate error, sin, and weakness. He must accept the experience unresistingly and transmute it into moral resolve and ethical guidance for the future.

483

The seeker should try to regard his weaknesses and faults from a more balanced and impersonal point of view. While it is correct for him to be ashamed of them, he need not go to the other extreme and fall into a prolonged fit of gloom or despair about them. Sincere repentance, coupled with an unswayable determination to prevent further recurrences, is the philosophic way to deal with them.

484

To have discovered a sin in oneself, and to have gone on committing it, is to sin doubly.

485

He is not interested in defending his past record or denying his errors. He understands that there are no excuses for excuses and that to make them habitually is to confess failure to overcome the ego.

486

In this blend of analysing the results of past actions, reasoning about the probable results of present tendencies, measuring up to the standards of spiritual ideals, and obeying the quiet whispers of intuition, he will find a safe guide for shaping his future course of conduct.

487

One should be eager and quick to judge, condemn, and correct himself, reluctant and slow to judge, condemn, and correct others.

488

When he can bring himself to look upon his own actions from the outside just as he does those of other men, he will have satisfied the philosophic ideal.

489

His errors and shortcomings can be excused by his sincerities and intentions, but that is not enough. He may accept such excuses but life itself will not.

490

Each is so accustomed to obeying the lower ego that he finds his greatest comfort in continuing to do so, his greatest discomfort in disobeying it. Insofar as the quest seeks to bring about such a reversal of acts and attitudes, it becomes the most difficult enterprise of his whole life. Much new thinking and much new willing are required here.

491

To accept our moral weaknesses, to overlook our failure to practise control of thoughts, and smugly to condone this unsatisfactory condition by calling it "natural," is to show how powerful is the ego's hold upon us.

492

When a man comes to understand that he has no greater problem than the problem within, he comes to wisdom.

493

The fact that he is becoming aware of his weaknesses more acutely and that he now sees egoism in himself where he formerly saw virtue, is a revelation made by his progress towards truth.

494

Even temptation can nourish a man, make his will stronger, and his goal clearer, if he considers it aright and understands it as it really is.

495

To make amends and fast, acts as a purification after a sin.

496

The memory of past wrong-doing whether to others or to self may make a person shrink with shame. Such feeling is valuable only if it creates a counter feeling. It should originate a positive attitude: the remembrance or belief or recall of Plato's archetypal ideal of The Good. This should be followed by new determinations. Not out of someone else's bidding but out of his own inner being he may lay this duty upon himself.

497

The willingness to say, at least to himself, "I was wrong. What I did was done under the influence of my lesser self, not my better one. I am sorry. I repent" may be humiliating but will be purifying, when completed by attention to self-improvement.

498

Until a man freely admits his need of true repentance, he will go on doing the same wrongs which he has done before.

499

Some over-anxious aspirants fall into the error which the sixteenth-century Roman saint, Philip, warned against when he said that prolonged expression of remorse for a venial sin was often worse than the sin itself. I think he meant that this was a kind of unconsciously disguised and inverted spiritual pride.

500

Since he is called upon to forgive others, he must likewise forgive himself. He need not torment himself without an end by the remembrance of past errors and condemn himself incessantly for their commitment. If their lesson has been well learnt and well taken to heart, why nurse their temporary existence into a lasting one by a melancholy and remorse which overdo their purpose?

501

No decision, no action is really unimportant and none should be underrated. By the light of this view, no event is a minor one, no situation is an insignificant one. A man may display negative traits in the littlest occurrence as in the greatest; the need for care and discipline always remains the same.

502

An excuse for one's action is not the same as a reason for them. The first is an emotional defense mechanism, the second is a valid, logical justification.

503

If the aspirant has any grievance against another person or if he be conscious of feelings of anger, resentment, or hatred against another person, he should follow Jesus' advice and let not the sun go down on his wrath. This means that he must see him as expressing the result of all his own long experience and personal thinking about life and therefore the victim of his own past, not acting better only because he does not know any better. The aspirant should then comprehend that whatever wrongs have been done will automatically be brought under the penalty of karmic retribution. Consequently, it is not his affair to condemn or to punish the other person, but to stand aloof and let the law of karma take care of him. It is his affair to understand and not to blame. He must learn to accept a person just as he is, uncondemned. He certainly should try not to feel any emotional resentment or express any personal ill-will against that person. He must keep his own consciousness above the evil, the wrong-doing, the weaknesses, or the faults of the other man and not let them enter his own consciousness—which is what happens if he allows them to provoke negative reactions in his lower self. He should make immediate and constant effort to root such weeds out of his emotional life. But the way to do this is not by blinding himself to the faults, the defects, and the wrongdoings of the other. Nor is it to be done by going out of his way to associate with undesirables.

504

Since a mistake will not rectify itself, he must go on, write to the person he has wronged and humbly make amendment and apology.

505

He should not be satisfied with being contrite alone. He should also do something: first, to prevent his sins or errors happening again and, second, to repair the wrongs he has already done. The first aim is fulfilled by learning why they *are* sinful or erroneous, perceiving their origin in his own weaknesses of character or capacity, and then unremittingly working at changing them through self-improvement. The second aim involves a practical and sacrificial effort.

506

Whatever mistakes he has made, whatever sins he has committed, let him learn their lessons, correct his thinking, improve his character, and then forgive himself. Let him joyously receive Jesus' pardon, "Go thou and sin no more!" and accept the healing grace which follows self-amendment.

507

If he engages in honest and adequate self-appraisal and blames himself for the inner fault which really accounts for some outer trouble, and if he sets out to correct that fault, he will in time gain power over that trouble.

508

You will learn the truth about your character in easy stages. No one can take it all at once: one might have a nervous breakdown or even a physical sickness. The truth has to be given gradually for safety's sake.

509

A point is reached when remorse has served its purpose, when carried further it becomes not only a torment but useless. This is the time to abandon it, to lose it in the remembrance of one's inner divinity.

510

His character improves whether or not he tries to impose disciplines upon it. The process is spontaneous and proportionate to the improvement in his point of view, in the disengagement from the ego's tyranny.

Truthfulness

511

Among the moral self-restraints which an aspirant is required to practise is that of truthfulness. It is the second of Patanjali's five ethical injunctions for the would-be yogi. There are several reasons for this prescription. But the one which affects his quest directly is the effect of untruthfulness upon his inner being. It not only spoils his character and destiny but also deforms his mind. In the liar's mouth the very function of language becomes a perverted one. He renders defective the very instrument with which he is seeking to make his way to the Overself; it becomes spoiled. If he meets with any mystical experience, it will become mixed with falsity or hallucination. If he finds spiritual truth, it will not be the pure or whole truth but the distortion of it.

Where situations are likely to arise which make truth-telling highly undesirable, the earnest aspirant should try to avoid them as much as possible by forethought. The pattern of indifference to truth-speaking must be broken up. The pattern of scrupulous respect for truth must be built up. The discipline of his ego must include the discipline of its speech. His words must be brought into correspondence with his ideals. Every word written or uttered must be steel-die true. If the truth is awkward or dangerous to say, then it may be advisable to keep silent. May he tell a small white lie to liberate himself from an awkward situation? The answer is still the same: "Thou shalt not bear false witness." Not only will he refrain from telling a conscious lie of any kind but he will not, through bragging vanity, exaggerate the truth into a half-lie. Any tendency in these directions will be crushed as soon as he becomes aware of it. He will take the trouble to express himself accurately, even to the point of making a fad of the careful choice of his words. Let him not maim his heart nor deform his mind by formulating thoughts which are false. If philosophy be the quest of ultimate truth, then it is certain that such a quest cannot be carried to a successful conclusion if this rule be broken. He who seeks truth must speak it.

512

We have begun to question Nature and we must abide the consequences. But we need not fear the advancing tide of knowledge. Its effects on morals will be only to discipline human character all the more. For it is not knowledge that makes men immoral, it is the *lack* of it. False foundations make uncertain supports for morality.(P)

513

Men ask, "What is truth?" But in reply truth itself questions them, "Who are you to ask that? Have you the competence, the faculty, the character, the judgement, the education, and the preparation to recognize truth? If not, first go and acquire them, not forgetting the uplift of character."(P)

514

The time may come when he may have to choose between his ethical life and his material livelihood. In this agonizing experience he may choose wrongly unless his hope and belief in the benevolence of whatever Powers there be is firm and strong. But a wrong choice will not dispose of the problem. Sooner or later it will present itself again with more compelling insistence. For a glimpse of truth once given is like a double-edged sword: a privilege on one side, a duty on the other. A man's allegiance to Truth must be incorruptible.

515

If every momentary passion is to cloud a man's judgement and confuse his reason, if he is to become angry with every doctrine which he dislikes, if he is swept away by the emotional claims of mere prejudice when examining a theory or a viewpoint, if his heart is agitated with bitterness over personal injustices incurred to the extent that he declines to see both sides of a matter, he can never come to a right conclusion but will be tossed about like a rudderless ship—his emotions of hate, fear, or love forever interposing themselves between him and the truth. He who exhibits anger at views which he dislikes, for instance, is exhibiting his unfitness to study philosophy. For psychoanalysis of his state of mind yields the fact that he gets angry not because the views are untrue, but because they are repugnant to him, the individual named "X." We must learn to seek after truth not by our heartfelt emotions, nor by our vivid imagination, but by our keen reason.

516

The kind of truth you will find will depend on the kind of person you are, the kind of thinking of which you are capable, the kind of experience you have had, and the kind of instruction you have received. The man with a distorted mind, for instance, will discover only distortions of truth; that is, there will be a basis of truth beneath his ideas, but their structure will be perverted or distorted.

517

Canting moralists busy themselves with drawing up the catalogue of virtues. They could better employ their time by first coming to an understanding of the one who is to possess these admirable virtues, the Self. For then they would find, if they find the Self, the very fountainhead of all virtues.

518

Clarity of vision goes much better with purity of heart.

519

We must not crucify truth to assist a political cause.

520

Nevertheless, however ready to come to terms with an imperfect society, however intimidated by the political power of an institutional religion, the philosopher will not feign his assent to false doctrines. He must be true to the best that is in him when such assent is demanded of him.

521

The use of falsehood to propagate truth has always ended, historically, in the persecution and suppression of truth.

522

When a man begins to excuse in his own mind an evil course for the sake of an excellent objective, he begins unconsciously to change his objective.

2

RE-EDUCATE FEELINGS

The proper cultivation and refinement of feeling is necessary for the philosophic path, but this must not be confused with mere emotionalism. The former lifts him to higher and higher levels while the latter keeps him pinned down to egoism. The former gives him the right kind of inner experience, but the latter often deceives him.

2

It is right to rule the passions and lower emotions by reasoned thinking, but reason itself must be companioned by the higher and nobler emotions or it will be unbalanced.

3

As man's impulses to action come mainly from his feelings, hence it is necessary to re-educate his feelings if we would get him to act aright.

4

There are three kinds of feeling. The lowest is passional. The highest is intuitional. Between them lies the emotional.

5

It is not emotion in itself that philosophy asks us to triumph over but the lower emotions. On the contrary, it asks us to cherish and cultivate the higher ones. It is not feeling in itself that is to be ruled sternly by reason but the blind animal instincts and ignorant human self-seeking. When feeling is purified and disciplined, exalted and ennobled, depersonalized and instructed, it becomes the genuine expression of philosophical living.

6

The heart must also acknowledge the truth of these sacred tenets, for then only can the will apply it in common everyday living.

7

Those are much mistaken who think the philosophic life is one of dark negation and dull privation, of sour life-denial and emotional refrigeration. Rather is it the happy cultivation of Life's finest feelings.

8

The hardest thing in the emotional life of the aspirant is to tear himself away from his own past. Yet in his capacity to do this lies his capacity to gain newer and fresher ideals, motives, habits, and powers. Through this

effort he may find new patterns for living and re-educate himself psychologically.

9

But it is not all his ideas which govern man's life. Only those are decisive
which are breathed and animated by his feelings, only they prompt him to
action. Hence a merely intellectualist acceptance of these teachings, although good, does not suffice alone.

10

The aspirant needs to rise above his emotional self, without rising above
the capacity to feel, and to govern it by reason, will, and intuition.

11

Sentimentality is a disease. The sooner the aspirant is cured of it, the
quicker will he progress.

12

The idea that perfectly harmonious human relations can be established
between human beings still dominated by egoism is a delusional one. Even
where it seems to have been established, the true situation has been
covered by romantic myth.(P)

13

It is possible to attain a stoic impassivity where the man dies to disturbing or disquieting emotions and lives only in his finer ones, where the
approbation of others will no longer excite him or the criticism by others
hurt him, where the cravings and fears, the passions and griefs of ordinary
and everyday human reactions are lacking. But in their place he will be
sensible to the noblest, the most refined feelings.

14

By "heart" I mean the central abode of human feeling, the symbolic
reminder that the "head" or cold dry intellect is not enough to touch the
reality of Spirit.

15

There is one relationship which takes precedence over all others. It is the
relationship with the Overself.

16

A wrong relationship with the Overself must inevitably lead to a wrong
relationship with men.

17

We are not called upon to renounce our human affections, our earthly
ties, as the ascetics demand, but we are called upon to liberate our love
from its egoism.

18

He is indeed free who is no longer liable to be tossed about by
emotional storms, whose mind has become so steadied in the impersonal
Truth that his personal feelings shape themselves in accord with it.

19

If and when we can reconcile our feelings with the hard, sharp truths of philosophy, we shall then find the secret of peace.

20

The disciple must have no room for false sentimentality if he seeks truth. Consequently, he will not apply the phrase "a broken heart" to himself at any time, for he knows that what it really means is a broken ego, a severed attachment to some external thing which has to be given up if the way is to be cleared for the coming of Grace. It is only when he is unwilling or unable to do this for himself that destiny steps in, taking him at his word in his search for truth and reality, and breaks the attachments for him. If he accepts the emotional suffering which follows and does not reject it, he is able to pass into a region of greater freedom, and of progress to a higher level. His heart is not broken arbitrarily or capriciously, but only there where it most needs to be broken—where passion, desire, and attachment bind him the most strongly to illusion and to error.

21

Only after long experience and severe reflection will a man awaken to the truth that the beauty which attracts him and the ecstasy which he seeks can be found free of defects and transiency only in the Soul within.

22

Philosophy will create within him a disgust for evil, a disdain for what is ignoble, a taste for what is refined and beautiful, a yearning for what is true and real.

23

It is not that in the process of dying to self he is to become a man without feelings, but that he is to die to the lower phases of feeling. Indeed, such a victory can only be achieved by drawing the needed forces from the higher phases of feeling.

24

In the world of values, the truth is the synthesis of opposites, as for instance the synthesis of optimism and pessimism.

25

The quest remains unfinished and unsuccessful so long as it lacks this element of rich feeling, so long as it has not become a warm devotion.

26

The Quest is not all a matter of psychological readjustment, of severe self-improvement. Man is not just a character to be remolded. Deep reverential feelings have also to be cultivated.

27

His life will be extraordinarily enriched, and not bleakly impoverished, by discovering the higher relationship that is possible between men and women than that which begins and ends with the flesh.

28

Intense concentrated feeling may fill a man with self-destructive or murderous antagonism but lead another into self realization—depending upon the thoughts and acts which flow from him at its bidding.

29

First comes the capacity to recognize these higher feelings; then to understand them for what they are; next to appreciate their intrinsic worth; and finally, to give oneself up to them entirely.

30

The real philosopher *feels* what he knows: it is not a dry intellectual experience alone but a living one.

31

Why become resentful and bitter at the loss? Why not be grateful at having had the good fortune at all, and for possessing memory of it that cannot be lost? Why not regard it as enough to have experienced such happiness, even for a little time, when in the chances of life it could have passed you by altogether? Why not receive the gifts of destiny humbly without trying to own them with a tight vampire-like grip?

32

The higher human feelings such as kindness and sympathy, patience and tolerance have to be nurtured.

33

This species called Man has shown its finer possibilities in the kindness of Christ, the compassion of Buddha, the love of Saint Francis, and the skill of Michelangelo.

34

He will not lose the capacity to feel; in this he will still be like other men: but it will be free from false sentimentality and debased animality.

35

He who enters upon this quest will have to revise his scale of values. Experiences which he formerly thought bad, because they were unpleasant, may now be thought good, because they are educative or because they reveal hitherto obscured weaknesses.

36

Aesthetic appreciation, the feeling of delight in art, is not enough by itself to bring humanity into the perception of reality, that is, into truth. Artistic feeling, even poetic emotion, is not less exempt from the need of being equilibrated by reason than the other functions of man's nature.

37

No one can be devoid of feeling, and the philosopher will not be exempt from this rule. But whereas the ordinary man's feelings are transient emotions, passions, stresses, or moods, the philosopher's feelings nourish a sustained, elevated state.

38

The mistake of taking personal feelings as fit judges of truth or reality is a grave barrier which often lies across the portal of philosophy. People put a grossly exaggerated value on them and are thus led astray from the true knowledge of a fact or a situation.

39

Without changing a person's feelings, no change for the better in his own life, in himself, and in his relationship with other persons can be stable.

40

When his feelings are really a conscious or subconscious cover for other feelings, nothing will help, save the uncovering of what the ego has hidden.

41

Generous feeling must be directed by sound judgement, fervent devotion must be led by wise discrimination.

42

The longing for inward security and invulnerable peace is one which a man can certainly satisfy. But he cannot satisfy it on his own terms. Life has always and inseparably dictated the price which must be paid for it.

43

It is easy to talk vaguely of lofty ideals, hard to put them where they belong—in our personal relationships.

44

The line of conduct which impulse suggests is often different from that which deliberate reflection or deeper intuition suggests. Only when a man so develops himself that the two lines harmoniously coincide will he know the peace of never being torn in two—either mentally or emotionally. Then only, when desire and duty agree perfectly with one another, will he be happy. For, when reason approves what feeling chooses, and the inner balance is perfect, the resulting decision is more likely to be a right one than not.

45

Cheerfulness is an excellent mental attribute and worth cultivating; but where it results from mental blindness it is not worth having, for then it may become a real danger.

46

Feelings, emotions, and passions should not be allowed to submerge reason, unless the feeling is genuinely intuitive, the emotion truly impersonal, and the passion a passion for the highest Truth.

47

Feeling can be *trained* to become finer, more delicate, responsive to higher urges and ideals.

48

The baser feelings go away of their own accord as the higher ones are let in and encouraged.

49

The man who is seeking regeneration of his character will not often have repose of his feelings, for he is called by himself to struggle with himself.

50

It is in the very nature of emotion to vary like the wind. Consequently, he who would attain inner peace cannot base his attainment upon emotion alone. He has to find something much more stable than that, much more constant than that. This is not to say that the life of the spirit is without feeling, but it is a calm, unbroken feeling.

51

He may legitimately take pride in the fact that he is called to the philosophic life, that he has accepted the philosophic ideal. For it is not the kind of pride which can vaunt itself over other men; its aims are to be fulfilled rather by humbling the ego and reducing its sway.

52

The Roman Stoics, who sought to control their emotions and master their passions, placed character above knowledge. We pursue a similar albeit less rigorous discipline in controlling feelings by reason because we place knowledge above character. The latter is made a preliminary to attainment of the former.

53

Goethe says: "I prefer the harmful truth to the helpful falsehood. Truth will heal the wound which she may have given." And again he says: "A harmful truth is helpful, because it can be harmful only for the moment, and will lead us to other truths which must become ever more and more helpful. On the other hand, a helpful lie is more harmful, because it can help only for the moment and then lead to other lies which must become more and more harmful."

54

When he can bring himself to see clearly that no woman has anything to offer him which the Overself cannot offer more satisfyingly—be it ecstasy or beauty, intimacy or love, comfort or companionship—the glamour of sex will pall.

55

No possessive relationship between two human beings can last forever. To ask for such a thing is to ask for the impersonal universe to change its laws of growth for the sake of pleasing its ungrown progeny. God is entirely self-sufficient and if God's children are to grow increasingly into his likeness, they can do so only by becoming less dependent on others, more sufficient unto themselves.

56

A false, showy, and pretentious cheerfulness which ignores facts, re-presses truths, and hides evils is not really cheerful at all.

57

It is well to remember not to let oneself become the victim of negative feelings or harsh thoughts. They do not mend matters but only make you suffer more, and also suffer needlessly.

58

It is one of the side effects of philosophy that it purifies human affection, takes the littleness out of it, and lifts it to a higher and wider plane. This may bring some pain or it may bring a shared pleasure, depending on those involved in the experience.

59

It is excellent but not enough to be well-meaning, to have a pure intent, to be guided by feeling alone, if ignorance, credulity, naïveté, or imbalance are the accompaniment. For there are traps and quicksands, illusions and deceits in life as on the quest.

60

No human being has the right to claim another as his own. Each stands ultimately alone and essentially isolate. Each is born out of and must find his way back to spiritual solitude. For each must learn to be divinely self-reliant and self-sufficient. This is so because the soul is of the nature of God. How much misery has come into contemporary life through non-recognition of this fact! How much bitterness has come to the unwilling possessed ones or to the defeated would-be possessors!

61

The way to get rid of an obstinate negative feeling is to supersede it by a new positive one of greater intensity. Right thoughts about the wrong feeling will help to correct it, right imaginations about the new one will help to bring it in, but feeling itself must be invoked and fostered if success is to be attained.

62

In most human relations, egoism in one person is replied by egoism in the other.

63

He has feelings but they are so poised that they never disturb, so balanced with reason that they never agitate, and so harmonized with intuition that they never excite him.

64

If anyone is to carry out Christ's bidding of reconciliation with enemies and forgiveness of those who have harmed him, he can do so only by giving up the ego.

65

In the New Testament Apocrypha we find a curious sentence: "For the Lord himself, having been asked by someone when his kingdom should come, said, 'When the two shall be one, and the outside as the inside and the male with the female.'"

66

The loss of property and the break-up of possessions may be a terrible happening, but it may also have the effect of driving the sufferer into himself. He may disintegrate with his things, or he may steel his mind and school his emotions to endure the event while he tries to start life anew. So in the end he will become stronger than he was when the world's pleasures and riches were available to him.

67

We may wallow in the lowest kind of emotions and passions, or we may raise the whole feeling-nature to a level where love and beauty, refinement and sensitivity reign serenely.

68

When the good in him overbalances the bad, his selfishness will be purged by pity.

69

He can transcend sex by turning inward and finding the inner bliss. He should cultivate therefore joy, love, and happiness as attributes of the inner self.

70

The man who reposes his emotional strength or mental peace on any single person is taking a chance whose outcome may disappoint him.

71

The feelings of the transformed man no longer come out of the ego but out of the Overself's life deep within the ego.

72

A fuzzy sentimentality which passes for mystical feeling is only its counterfeit.

73

If a man has trained himself to reject self-pity as an emotional egoism that is harmful, he is not likely to encourage its display in other men merely because they conventionally expect him to be sympathetic. Yet it must always be remembered that when pity, which begins in the emotions, is filtered through the reason, it is not destroyed but balanced.

74

A man may have to free himself from being unduly dependent on or overly attached to another person if he is to attain the freedom and assume the responsibility of true adulthood.

75
Values are imposed upon things by human feelings, human desires, and human purposes. The common criterion of value is whether a thing or an occurrence brings an agreeable feeling or satisfies a personal want. But as wants and feelings are subject to change, so likewise first valuations are subject to revision with time. Indeed, it may happen, as indeed in the case of marriage it often does happen, that what was formerly valued as good is later branded as bad.

76
That he should seek the delight of shared understanding and confirmed attitude with friend, family, or co-disciple is to be expected.

77
Muhammed knew the power of tears. He bade his followers to weep whenever they recited the *Koran*.

78
In these changing times, we all have to reorient our external lives occasionally, so it is useless to try sentimentally to fix forever relationships that once were.

79
It is essential that the student keep his romantic inclinations under constant surveillance of reason, caution, and reflection upon consequences. He is well advised to avoid emotional entanglements; for in this region there is often, for those who have a special spiritual destiny, a thorn concealed beneath every rose.

80
When two people, emotionally involved with each other, have a misunderstanding or difference of opinion regarding the Quest itself, it is best that they deliberately discontinue their relationship for a while. In this way they avoid a revival of the discussion which can only lead to exacerbation and further confusion. Time will solve the problem. Probably there are faults on both sides, since we are all human, but we have to carry on with the Quest despite these faults.

81
Being on the Quest need not prevent the continuance and even the development of a friendship with one of the opposite sex, provided that it be kept on a high plane above the physical. Karmic ties may be involved and these have to be carefully negotiated. The relationships can be beautiful, platonic, and mutually helpful but a strong discipline of the ego is called for.

82
Great men can liberate great feelings in others or lift them toward acceptance of true ideas.

Love, compassion

83

Few people know what love really means because with nearly all it is filtered through the screens of bodily and selfish considerations. In its pure native state it is the first attribute of the divine soul and consequently it is one of the most important qualities which the seeker has to cultivate.

84

The love for which man is searching exists; it is as perfect, as beautiful, as perpetual, and as healing as he can imagine it to be. But it does not exist where he wants to find it. Only the inner kingdom holds and gives it at the end of his search. No other human being can do so unless he or she has previously entered the kingdom, and then only through all the limitations and colourings of the earthly consciousness.

85

Although we have stated in *The Wisdom of the Overself* that a love restricted to the limited circle of wife, family, or friends is unphilosophic and should be extended in universal compassion to all mankind, this should not be mistaken to mean that such a restricted love ought to be abandoned. On the contrary, it should have its fullest place within the larger one. We have also written in the same book that "love" is one of the most misused words in English. We may now add that it is also one of the most debased words. Why? Because, very often, it is based on sheer self-interest and not on the beloved's interest and gives only so long as it gets; because, not seldom, the greater the ardour with which it begins, the greater the antipathy with which it ends; and because it frequently mistakes the goading of animal glands for the awakening of human affection. True love does not change or falter because the beloved has changed and faltered or because the physical circumstances wherein it was born have become different. It cannot be blown hither and thither by the accidents of destiny. It is not merely an emotional attraction, although it will include this. "Love is not love which alters when it alteration finds, . . . O no! it is an ever-fixed mark. . . ." wrote Shakespeare.

86

It expresses itself outwardly in an exceptionally kindly behaviour. He will not hurt others unnecessarily. He feels that one of the best pieces of advice he can give others is: "Be kind." In this way you abrase your own egoism and show forth something—just an echo—of this love which emanates from the indwelling spiritual self. The cost in thus weakly and briefly identifying yourself with others is little: the gain in moral growth is large. When your duties, activities, or responsibilities in life call for critical judgement of any person, that is allowable. But when you fall into it for the sake of idle gossip or, what is worse, when you are nastily censorious, slanderously back-biting, for the sake of malice, that is unkind and unpardonable. Above his own deliberate willing or wishing, quite spontaneously and impulsively, a feeling of pure love begins to well up within him. It is unconnected with physical or egoistic causes, for all those who touch his orbit benefit by it. It does not stop flowing if they are foolish or ugly, sinful or deformed, unclean or disagreeable.

87

No one has ever unraveled the mystery of love as it exists between a man and a woman. Since it is usually beyond our power to accept or reject, we should regard it as a Divine Message and seek out its meaning to our spiritual life.

88

At its peak moments, which can arise only in its first or last stages and which belong only to its affectional rather than passional side, human love catches and reflects feebly the nature of divine love.

89

The romantic aureole which young persons put around love, the demands made on it for that which it cannot give, point to the need of maturer instruction. Yet there is a relationship where two can grow in virtues side by side, learning wisdom from one another, harmonizing more and more with each other. But this calls for self-control, eliminating negatives, cultivating positives.

90

No one has the right to bind, hinder, or restrict the free spiritual movement of another person—no matter how close his blood, contractual, or emotional relationship may be—who enters into the pursuit of higher well-being. If it is done in the name of love, then that word has its meaning sorely misrepresented, for it is really being done in selfishness.

91

This quality of "love" is not to be measured by the exhibitions of effusiveness on the part of its possessor; it is to be measured by the presence or absence in him of egolessness.

92

Whoever talks of his love for mankind will reveal it better by positive deeds than by sentimental displays. The fact is, however, that such love is hard to feel when brought down to individuals. Only the sage really possesses it.

93

By loving the Overself within you in worship you are loving it in all other men, because it is present in them, too. Hence, you don't have to go out of your way to love any individual specially, separately, although you will naturally feel affection for some.

94

The capacity to give and receive love is not to be destroyed, nor can it be. Nature has planted its roots too deeply for that destruction to be attempted with success or desired with wisdom. But the man or woman who aspires to the highest cannot let it stay ungrown and benefit from its finest fruits. He should nurture it, purify it, exalt it, and spiritualize it. He should direct it toward his best self, his Overself, aspiring and yearning. And when it comes back to him in the blessed form of Grace, he should be ready and fit to receive it.

95

Love mixed with the sense of bodily touch, or with the emotion of personal companionship, is what most people take to be love itself. They have not experienced it as it is, unmixed with anything else. Yet if its adulterated forms give them so much satisfying feeling, how much more could they get from seeking it at its source, pure and intense!

96

Passion, with its savage insistencies and appeasements, its animalist intrusion, has no place in this serene, tender affection which unites their minds—the hushed peace, the mesmeric strangeness, and the golden felicity of this mood.

97

It is by trial and error, reflection and experience, that the paradoxical art of loving without becoming possessive, of being affectionate without becoming attached, of accepting outward attachments with inward detachment, is learnt, and this applies to family.

98

Miguel Unamuno's declaration that "love is the child of illusion" is one of those statements which are themselves the product of illusion. For the pure state of love is the Cosmic Energy which holds together and continuously activates the entire universe. It is those shadows of shadows of love which appear in the beasts as lust, in the humans as affection, which represent states that are transient and in that sense unreal. This transiency is obvious enough in the beast's case but less so in the human's.

99

We may divide these different kinds of love conveniently into animal-physical love, emotional-mental love, and impersonal-spiritual love.

100

When Saint John of the Cross was prior of the Monastery of Segovia, he was unjustly dismissed from his high position by his own superiors in the Order and banished to an unhealthy hermitage in semi-wild country. But he bore no ill-will against his persecutors, and even wrote in a letter: "Where there is no love, put love and you will get back love." This is so, but he did not state that the returning love might take a long time to appear, so long that a whole lifetime in some cases, or several incarnations in other cases might be needed. The lesson is that it must be accompanied by patience. If we look for quick results, we may look in vain. Indeed, we ought not to look for any positive results at all. In all such relationships with hostile persons, we ought to do what is right, forgiving, extending goodwill, if we wish, but leaving the outcome to take whatever course it did. "Act, but do not be attached to the consequences of your action," was the counsel which Krishna gave the young prince Arjuna. Be patient if you want to practise goodwill.

101

We have been told by well-meaning ministers of religion and counsellors in psychology to practise Jesus's words, "Love thy neighbour." Now there are two different ways in which we can do so, because there are two different interpretations of these words—the religious and the philosophic. According to the first, we have at least to be amiable toward our next-door neighbour, or at most to throw our arms around him and express our warm feeling for him in a gushy, sentimental, hyper-emotional manner. According to the second and philosophic interpretation, we have to understand that every person who crosses our path is our neighbour, everyone with whom we are thrown into momentary or continuous contact is our neighbour, whether at home or at work. It is in these immediate contacts that irritations are bred, differences are noted, and dislikes appear. It is much easier to love humanity as a whole or in the abstract than it is to love humanity in the individual and in the concrete. In spite of the instinctive urge to manifest irritability, dislike, anger, resentment, or even hatred against those with whom you are thrown in contact, you can steel your will and resist the negative feeling. If you can take all these negative feelings and sublimate them into understanding, tolerance, and goodwill based on the teachings of philosophy, you are actually loving your neighbour in the sense that Jesus meant it. You will then see that such philosophic love is far removed from and far superior to the hyper-emotionalism which blows hot and cold.

102

How can I love my enemy, it is asked, or anyone who is outwardly or inwardly repugnant to me? The answer is that we are not called on to love what is evil in our enemy nor what is ugly in anyone. We are called on, however, to remember that alongside of the evil there is the divine soul in him, alongside of the ugliness there is the divine beauty in him. His non-awareness of it does not alter the fact of its existence. And because he is a bearer of something grander than himself, unconscious of it though he be, we are to meet his hostility with our goodwill, his baseness with our nobility, and thus help him by our thought or our example to move onward—even if no more than one millimeter—towards the discovery and realization of his own divine soul. When we are enjoined to love others we are really enjoined to sympathize with them as fellow living creatures and to have compassion for their sufferings or ignorance. If the thought of our enemy arouses hatred, dislike, or fear, he will continue to haunt. The only way to be free of him is to arouse our compassion for him, to extend goodwill towards him. In the moment that we feel like this we exorcise his wrath and are liberated.

103

"Love thy neighbour as thyself," the dictum preached by Jesus and practised by the sages, seems to offer a remote and unapproachable ideal. But it will not seem so if we come to understand what Jesus meant and how the sage is able to realize it. Every man does indeed love himself, but he does not love the whole of himself. There are defects and weaknesses in himself which he hates. He cannot therefore be expected to love them in his neighbour. But he can be expected, if he perceives that these faults eventually bring painful karmic results, to feel compassion for those who suffer from them. In the case of the sage, not only is such a consideration operative but also the perception of his neighbour's existence within the one universal Mind in which he feels himself to be rooted. It is easy and natural for him, therefore, to practise loving kindness towards his neighbour. Here, at this final stage of knowledge which is sagehood, the "I" in a man becomes inseparable from the "you." Both exist simultaneously *within* him, whereas in the ordinary man they stand fundamentally opposed to each other. No longer is the personality the sole content of the mind: it is now but a partial content. In his inmost attitude he is conscious of unity with others and consequently emanates a perfect sympathy towards them. This is not the sentimental attitude which often goes with the superficial emotion called love. It is profoundly deeper. It can never change, whereas emotional love may turn to dislike or even hate. This inner sense of unity can in no wise alter. It is always there. Nor can it even be impeded by physical or selfish considerations. There is nothing in another man's face or body, fortune or misfortune, mind or heart, which can obstruct the ceaseless flow of the blesser. "We two are rooted in the same Overself" is the remembrance which he cherishes in himself. He has understood the inner-penetration of the many in the One and of the One with the many. What he *feels* for himself is not different from what he feels for others; but what he *does* for himself will be necessarily different, because wisdom demands recognition of the superior and hence more responsible role which has been allotted to him in his game of life.

104

Plotinus' belief that in all his lesser loves, man is seeking the divine, that it is the object he really permanently wants much more than these temporary ones, is the truth to which he must come one day. And he will come by a double movement: the first, away from them by successive disenchantments, the second by progressive glimpses of the divine beauty.

105

A life without love is a life emotionally starved and therefore stunted in growth. But do not limit the meaning of the word *love* either to a selfish or an animalistic definition.

106

How many unreflective and selfish persons have uttered the words "I love you" to someone else—wife, friend or teacher—when what they actually if unconsciously meant was, "I love myself and use you to serve *my* interests or to satisfy my feelings."

107

A merely physical or purely emotional love will fade and die when events test if it really seeks the happiness of the beloved rather than the pleasure of the lover.

108

The idea that ordinary people can love one another, including those they have never met as well as those they meet day after day, is a pleasant piece of sentimentalism. It sounds well when solemnly uttered by ministers of religion before their respectful congregations or when published as advice by professional psychologists. But where are the individuals who succeed in following it? If we look at history or at the cities and villages we already know, we find that the only form where something like it is discovered is that of organized philanthropy. This is excellent, this is commendable, but still it is not strictly love. Most ordinary people cannot get closer than this to the full sympathetic identification with another person which love really is. Only saints can achieve complete empathy; only they are capable of washing the leper's sores. For all others the idea is vague and unreal, although convenient to use in talk at Christmas time.

Karamazov, a character in one of Dostoevski's Russian novels, drily said, "One can love one's neighbour in an abstract way occasionally perhaps, even from afar, but in close contact, almost never. . . . It is precisely the neighbour, the one who is physically close to us, whom one cannot possibly love. At best one can love those who are far away."

Now this may be a little exaggerated but it does speak openly of the difficulty many people experience in their attitude towards those with whom they are in daily contact. It is still more difficult if they are forced to live with unscrupulous or unliked people. Then it will be all they can do to numb their revulsions.

But ordinary people have to come to terms with their associates or have at least to take care not to show their dislike. They must particularly learn to endure others who are different from themselves in habits, leaving aside the case of those who are thoroughly repulsive to them. Unless they do achieve this capacity, there is no hope for the human race, which must otherwise go on fighting and warring until, with the frightful weapons now coming into its hands, it destroys itself.

Such tolerance is still only the first station on the route to that active goodwill which the more idealistic persons who take the Quest seriously must try to achieve eventually. Many of them find it hard to reach even this first halt. They are sensitive, they are often heterodox, and they cannot warm up to those whose ideas, habits, mannerisms, or orthodoxies irritate them. The Quester who does not eat meat, for instance, may not enjoy sitting down at table with those who delight in it. If he has the fortunate circumstances to do as he likes, he need not do so. But most are not so free. He may put up with the meat-laden table and its diners with bad grace or good grace, but put up with them he must. Or take another case, that of having perforce to associate with someone who indulges in frequent sniffles when such a personal habit is felt to be most repulsive. Again if he is a Quester and if he is free to do as he likes and to avoid the other person, he is entitled to do so. But suppose he is not free? Instead of straining himself in the futile task of trying to love unlovable people, it is better to learn how to give them enough goodwill to tolerate them. This is within his capacity. If he has to live with them, or associate with them, he must try to put up with them, which means trying to put himself in their place. And that is a most desirable spiritual exercise, an advanced stepping-stone toward love itself. The practice of goodwill helps the practiser by creating good karma and shaping a good character. The thought of it, habitual and sustained, helps those who touch, or move within, his orbit. The profound meditation upon it repays him with blissful feelings and mystical harmony. If a man can be nothing else, let him be kind to others. Each time he does this he goes out of his own little ego. He comes a little closer to expressing the spiritual self dwelling hidden in his heart.

109

Gandhi (and spiritual pacifists like him) believed that love shown to a man like Hitler would call forth its like from him. This is a typical belief among mystics down through the centuries. When tested by experience, we find that it is successful in some cases but a failure in many more. And where it fails it harms the criminal because he believes the more strongly that his crimes can go unpunished, and it harms society because it is a misapplication of a good ideal. Everything, even love, must be applied at the right time and at the right place, for when misapplied even a virtue becomes a vice. We must not forget that wise old Latin proverb which warns us that when the best is corrupted it becomes the worst of all.

110

The love for all humanity which many a religionist professes to feel would not need much testing to find out the shallowness of its reality. The saint possessed by his higher self may, perhaps out of excessive kindness, be able to give it to the undesirable and the disgusting types. But the more impersonal philosopher has a wide goodwill, which is not the same as love.

111

When one's love for another is of the highest type and leads to an expansion of understanding, compassion, and tolerance of others, he has glimpsed the greater purpose of personal love: how the surrender of his "heart" may lead to its opening to, and becoming united with, Universal Love.

112

Being aware of the weaknesses or faults of another does not necessarily mean we love him less. It is an essential part of the message of love that we learn how to forgive surface characteristics by contemplating the essence of the beloved, to see what "is," while also seeing deeper to what truly IS—the Divine evidenced in a particular form.

113

Only when love ceases to be personal and becomes impersonal, when it passes out of the local into the universal, does it fulfil itself and attain its own unmixed and unadulterated integrity.

114

Real love is not something to be withdrawn abruptly when the person who is its object annoys or offends you.

115

If the human race has not yet learnt to love its neighbour, it is not likely to take the farther step of loving its enemy.

116

It is not only unnatural to put one's neighbour before oneself, but also unwise. Both Buddha and Ramana Maharshi pointedly said that the duty to oneself is primary. Only—one had to find out what was behind the self before that duty could be properly accomplished.

117

Those who cannot make the leap and rise above human love to their higher self—with its impersonality and immateriality—may continue to draw a happiness from it. But the limitations will be there, inexorable, unconquerable, of time and body, relativity and change.

118

Fear weakens a man, hate destroys him in the end, but love brings him his best.

119

More than four hundred years before Jesus' time, Mo Tzu was teaching the Chinese that "if everyone in the world would practise universal love, then the whole world would enjoy peace and order." But he also took care to teach them to rise above the emotions, and to understand by this kind of love a state of mind, not a state of emotion.

120

Those who glorify romantic love avert their eyes from the truth that there is a negative side to it. However ignored, it will one day come into focus.

121

There is a common notion that love, to be worth its name, must be highly emotional and dramatically intense. That, of course, is one kind but it is not the best kind which is calm, unchanging, and unexcited.

122

The sentimental gush which is talked so often and so freely in religio-mystic circles about loving one's fellow humans is usually quite shallow and will not stand deep analysis. Nor is it the most important of all the virtues as such circles seem to believe.

123

When a woman comes to a man for spiritual help or even spiritual companionship, he should not ask her for more than the chance to serve. This remains true even if she is not conscious of having been sent to him for this purpose, or even if she mistakes the spiritual attraction for a merely human one. It would be a spiritual failure on his part to ask for more than the opportunity to serve her. The service he gives must be given with a pure motive. Therefore, her appearance in his life is a test for him.

Should he fall in love with her the test still holds good, but its character may change. He is to keep the relationship at a high level. He is not to attempt to possess her but to be content with knowing and loving her. He must accept the situation with calm resignation and complete nonattachment.

124

Does the unified man have to like everyone he meets? Some students believe that because Jesus commanded us to "love thy neighbour as thyself" and because the *Bhagavad Gita* bids us hold no aversions and no attractions, this question ought to be answered with a resounding Yes! But in actual life we find that some unified men succeed in doing this whereas others frankly do not feel that way nor make any such effort.

125

To make the love of everybody else a compulsory ethic ought not to be demanded even from a quester, much less from the masses! To make the cultivation of goodwill desirable as a general attitude would be more reasonable. Even so it should grow naturally out of the cultivation, not be forced.

126

When a man discovers that the same Overself dwells in his enemy as in his own heart, how can he ever again bring himself to hate or injure another?

127

It is easy to believe mere softness to be compassion. It is easy to deceive oneself in this way. But a vigorous analysis of one's thoughts and observation of their results in action will expose the very real difference between them.

128

What did Jesus mean when he enjoined his disciples to love their neighbours as themselves? Did he mean the sentimental, emotional, and hail-fellow-well-met attitude which the churches teach? How could he when in order to become what he was, he had once to hate and turn aside from that part of himself, the lower part—that is, the ego and the animal nature—which is mostly what neighbours show forth? If his disciples were taught to hate, and not to love, their egos, how then could they love the ego-dominated humanity amidst which they found themselves? The injunction "Love thy neighbour" has often led to confusion in the minds of those who hear or read it, a confusion which forces many to refuse to accept it. And they are the ones who do not understand its meaning, but misinterpret it to mean "Like thy neighbour!" The correct meaning of this age-old ethical injunction is "Practise compassion in your physical behaviour and exercise goodwill in your mental attitude towards your neighbour." Everyone can do this even when he cannot bring himself to like his neighbour. Therefore, this injunction is not a wholly impracticable one as some believe, but quite the contrary.

Whoever imagines that it means the development of a highly sentimental, highly emotional condition is mistaken; for emotions of that kind can just as easily swing into their opposites of hate as remain what they are. This is not love, but the masquerade of it. Sentimentality is the mere pretense of compassion. It breaks down when it is put under strains, whereas genuine compassion will always continue and never be cancelled by them. True love towards one's neighbour must come from a level higher than the emotional and such a level is the intuitive one. What Jesus meant was, "Come into such an intuitive realization of the one Infinite Power from which you and your neighbour draw your lives that you realize the harmony of interests, the interdependence of existence which result from this fact." What Jesus meant, and what alone he could have meant, was indicated by the last few words of his injunction, "as thyself." The self which they recognized to be the true one was the spiritual self, which they were to seek and love with all their might—and it was this, not the frail ego, which they were also to love in others. The quality of compassion may easily be misunderstood as being mere sentimentality or mere emotionality. It is not these things at all. They can be foolish and weak when they hide the truth about themselves from people, whereas a truly spiritual compassion is not afraid to speak the truth, not afraid to criticize as rigorously as necessary, to have the courage to point out faults even at the cost of offending those who prefer to live in self-deception. Compassion will show the shortcoming within themselves which is in turn reflected outside themselves as maleficent destiny.

When the adept views those who are suffering from the effects of their own ungoverned emotion or their own uncontrolled passion and desire, he does not sink with the victims into those emotions, passions, and desires, even though he feels self-identity with them. He cannot permit such feelings to enter his consciousness. If he does not shrink from his own suffering, it is hardly likely that the adept will shrink from the sufferings of others. Consequently it is hardly likely that the emotional sympathy which arises in the ordinary man's heart at the sight of suffering will arise in precisely the same way in the adept's heart. He does not really regard himself as apart from them. In some curious way, both they and he are part of one and the same life. If he does not pity himself for his own sufferings in the usual egoistic and emotional way, how can he bring himself to pity the sufferings of others in the same kind of way? This does not mean that he will become coldly indifferent towards them. On the contrary, the feeling of identification with their inmost being would alone prevent that utterly; but it means that the pity which arises within him takes a different form, a form which is far nobler and truer because emotional agitation and egotistic reaction are absent from it. He feels with and for the sufferings of others, but he never allows himself to be lost in them; and just as he is never lost in fear or anxiety about his own sufferings, so he cannot become lost in those emotions or the sufferings of others. The calmness with which he approaches his own sufferings cannot be given up because he is approaching other people's sufferings. He has bought that calmness at a heavy price—it is too precious to be thrown away for anything. And because the pity which he feels in his heart is not mixed up with emotional excitement or personal fear, his mind is not obscured by these excrescences, and is able to see what needs to be done to relieve the suffering ones far better than an obscured mind could see. He does not make a show of his pity, but his help is far more effectual than the help of those who do.

The altruistic ideal is set up for aspirants as a practical means of using the will to curb egoism and crush its pettiness. But these things are to be done to train the aspirant in surrendering his personal self to his higher self, not in making him subservient to other human wills. The primacy of purpose is to be given to spiritual self-realization, not to social service. This above all others is the goal to be kept close to his heart, not meddling in the affairs of others. Only after he has attended adequately—and to some extent successfully—to the problem of himself can he have the right to look out for or intrude into other people's problems.

This does not mean, however, that he is to become narrowly self-centered or entirely selfish. On the contrary, the wish to confer happiness and the willingness to seek the welfare of mankind should be made the subject of solemn dedication at every crucial stage, every inspired hour, of his quest. But prudence and wisdom bid him wait for a more active altruistic effort until he has lifted himself to a higher level, found his own inner strength, knowledge, and peace, and has learnt to stand unshaken by the storms, passions, desires, and greeds of ordinary life.

Hence it is better for the beginner to keep to himself any pretensions to altruism, remaining silent and inactive about them. The dedication may be made, but it should be made in the secrecy of the inmost heart. Better than talk about it or premature activity for it, is the turning of attention to the work of purifying himself, his feelings, motives, mind, and deeds.

Just as the word compassion is so often mistaken for a foolish and weak sentimentality, so the words egolessness, unselfishness, and unself-centeredness are equally mistaken for what they are not. They are so often thought to mean nonseparateness from other individuals or the surrender of personal rights to other individuals or the setting aside of duty to ourself for the sake of serving other individuals. This is often wrong. The philosophical meaning of egoism is that attitude of separateness not from another individual on the same imperfect level as ourself but from the one universal life-power which is behind all individuals on a deeper level than them all. We are separated from that infinite mind when we allow the personal ego to rule us, when we allow the personal self to prevent the one universal self from entering our field of awareness. The sin lies in separating ourselves in consciousness from this deeper power and deeper being which is at the very root of all selves.(P)

129

Jesus' preachment of love of one's neighbour as oneself is impossible to follow in all fullness until one has attained the height whereon his own true self dwells. Obedience to it would mean identifying oneself with the neighbour's physical pain and emotional suffering so that they were felt not less keenly than one's own. One could not bear that when brought into contact with all kinds of human sorrow that shadow life. It could be borne only when one had crushed its power to affect one's own feelings and disturb one's own equilibrium. Therefore, such love would bring unbearable suffering. By actively identifying oneself with those who are sorrowing, by pushing one's sympathy with them to its extreme point, one gets disturbed and weakened. This does not improve one's capacity to help the sufferer, but only lessens it. To love others is praiseworthy, but it must be coupled with balance and with reason or it will lose itself ineffectually in the air. Not to let his interest in other matters or his sympathy with other persons carry him away from his equilibrium, his inner peace, but to stop either when it threatens to agitate his mind or disturb his feelings, is wisdom.(P)

130

Love of the divine is our primary duty. Love of our neighbour is only a secondary one.(P)

131

Compassion is the highest moral value, the noblest human feeling, the purest creature-love. It is the final social expression of man's divine soul. For he is able to feel with and for another man only because both are in reality related in harmony by the presence of that soul in each one.(P)

132

There must be an end, a limit to his sacrifices on behalf of others. They must not play upon his kindness to the extent of ruining his own life. He may help them, certainly, but there are various other ways to do so than by surrendering what is essential to his own life to satisfy their emotional demands or material desires.

133

In the ninth chapter of *The Wisdom of the Overself* I wrote:

> For this notion of love is a sadly limited one. To bestow it only on a
> wife or a child, a sweetheart or a sister, is to bestow it in anticipation

of its being returned. Man finds in time that such giving which hopes for a getting is not enough. Love cannot stop there. It seeks to grow beyond the restricted circle of a few friends and relations. Life itself leads him on to transcend it. And this he does firstly, by transcending the lure of the pitiful transient flesh and secondly, by transforming love into something nobler and rarer—compassion. In the divine self-giving of this wonderful quality and in its expansion until all mankind is touched, love finally fulfils itself.

This last sentence may lead to misunderstanding. The paragraph in which it appears is, I now see, incomplete. For compassion is an emotion felt by one ego when considering the suffering condition of another ego. But spiritual development eventually lifts itself above all emotions, by which I do not of course mean above all feeling. The wish to help another person should not spring out of compassion alone, nor out of the aspiration to do what is right alone, nor out of the satisfaction derived from practising virtue for its own sake alone. It should certainly come out of all these, but it should also come even more out of the breaking down of the ego itself. With that gone, there will be a feeling of oneness with all living creatures. This practice of self-identification with them is the highest form of love.

134

False compassion, like false sentimentality, does harm under the delusion that it is doing good. The abolition of flogging in England and the eruption of youthful merciless brutal criminal violence are not unconnected. The legal punishment of birching was not cruel: but the use of it on the wrong persons—starving men, for instance—was cruel. For hooligans and bullies it is a fit deterrent.

135

Some students have expressed disagreement with my use of the term "compassion" when describing the enlightened man's loftiest social quality. They believe the common term "love" would be more correct. Now one of the fundamental terms of the New Testament is, in the original Greek, "agape"—which is always translated as "love." But this is unsatisfactory because man's love may be selfishly motivated whereas "agape" has the definite implication of unselfish, or better, selfless love. And the only English word which I can find to express this idea is the one which I have used, that is, "compassion." If we cast out its selfish, sentimental, or sensual associations, the word "love" would be enough to express this attitude, but because these associations thickly encrust its meaning, the word "compassion" is better used. The kind of compassion here meant is not condescending toward others. Rather does it stretch out its hands through innate fellow-feeling for them. It puts itself in the shoes of others and intellectually experiences life from their standpoint.

136

"Hatred ceaseth not by hatred," declared the Buddha, "It ceaseth only by compassionate love." This counsel is much the same as Jesus' injunction to love our enemies. Many people, who wish to do what is ethically right and feel that their best course is to follow the ethics prescribed by such great souls as Jesus or Buddha, get confused here and wallow in sentimentality under the mistaken impression that they are following these counsels.

But the sentimentalists misunderstand Jesus if they believe that he taught us to practise outwardly and practically unconditional and universal forgiveness. On the contrary, he made repentance the prerequisite of such visible forgiveness. Those who refuse to repent and persist in wrongdoing must be *inwardly* and *silently* forgiven, but otherwise left to suffer the karma of their actions. What is really meant is that we should be big-hearted enough not to exclude our enemies from our goodwill to all mankind and that we should be big-minded enough to comprehend that they are only acting according to their own experience and knowledge of life. This is to "forgive them for they know not what they do." When we hold them in thought and when we image them with feeling we must do so without anger, without hatred, without bitterness.

All doctrines which are based on hatred emanate from the blackest of evil forces. Hatred is always their indicator just as compassion is always an indicator of the good forces. By practising great-hearted compassion, we help to counteract whatever ill-feelings have been generated. Therefore let us not at any time or under any provocation lose ourselves in emotions of resentment, bitterness, and hatred. We must not hate the most misguided of our enemies. We may oppose their false ideas resolutely, we may hate their sins, but not the sinners. We must pity even the most violent of them and not spoil our own characters by accepting their example. We must not sink to the low level of seeking revenge. The desire for revenge is a primitive one. It is apposite to the tiger and reptile kingdom, but in the human kingdom it should be replaced by the desire for justice.

These two attributes—hatred and pity—stand at opposite poles to each other: the one as being the worst of all human vices and the other as being the best of all human virtues. This, then, is a further reason why we must take care not to fall into the all-too-easy habit of hating enemies. For they are still members of this great human family of ours, still creatures planted like us on this woeful planet both to learn its immediate lessons and to share its ultimate redemption.

137

A gushy sentimentality which refrains from saying what needs to be said or doing what needs to be done because it will hurt people's feelings, is mere weakness and cowardice, not true compassion. It will not help them by giving them the truth when this is called for.

138

He must give out that love of which Jesus spoke. But it is not to be an unbalanced sentimentality; rather it is a serene self-identification with others without being thrown off one's own centre. That is why reason is a helpful check here. Above all, he must love the Real, the Overself.

139

The ideal relation to our neighbour, and indeed the ultimate one, is a loving one, as Jesus said. If it is to be perfect, it means a self-identification with him. But who can create this attitude of his own free will, by his own mere wish? It cannot be done. Only growth and time, or grace, can bring it about.

140

We can harm others and ourselves by practising a sloppy sentimentality in the name of love, a misguided humanitarianism in the name of service.

141

To practise love towards our fellow men is to hold goodwill toward them, to accept them as they are and even to identify ourselves intellectually, if temporarily, with them in the attempt to understand their viewpoint.

142

"Love thy neighbour," preached Jesus. Perhaps! but that does not mean I must also love his ill-mannered vulgarity, his insensitive crude commonness, his unfair class, race, and national hates, his malice towards all and charity toward none.

143

A silent compassion which does things is preferable to a voluble sentimentality which does nothing.

144

He whose goodwill and pity extend to all men will understand all men.

145

T.M.P. Mahadevan says that the higher meaning of "Love thy neighbour" as revealed in meditation is to (1) confer a blessing, and (2) identify with his higher self.

146

Total goodwill is, after all, only an ideal because it must be practised towards our enemies and those we dislike not less than toward our friends and those we like. We can only *try* to come close to it in difficult cases. The attempt may elicit grace, which will carry us further in the same direction.

Detachment

147
The philosopher achieves what is rare—a cool mental detachment from things or persons, united with a tender feeling for them.

148
No man can become philosophical and yet derive complete satisfaction from or attach complete importance to whatever is favourable in his external life. He sees too clearly how transient, how imperfect, and how compensated by disadvantages it all is. Indeed he outgrows the excessive common interest in and the excessive common preoccupation with the ebb and flow of external life. He finds more and more trivial what he once found—and the generality of men still find—worthy of serious attention.

149
Is it possible to be inwardly aloof from the pleasurable things of the world and yet be outwardly able to enjoy them? Is it possible to love another in a human way but yet retain the inner detachment requisite for resting in philosophic peace? Can we make the best of these two worlds? The answer is that just as we can learn by practice to remain inwardly peaceful in the midst of outward turmoil, so we can learn to remain peaceful in the midst of outward pleasure. But this practice is hard to learn and most beginners fail at it. For a man to train himself in emotional control over the mad loves and insane passions, the recurrent longings and tormenting desires, is like training himself to die. Let no one underestimate this tremendous task.

150
The philosophic attitude is a curious and paradoxical one precisely because it is a complete one. It approaches the human situation with a mentality as practical and as cold-blooded as an engineer's, but steers its movement by a sensitivity to ideals as delicate as an artist's. It always considers the immediate, attainable objectives, but is not the less interested in distant, unrealizable ones.(P)

151
Disinterested action does not mean renouncing all work that brings financial reward. How then could one earn a livelihood? It does not mean ascetic renunciation and monastic flight from personal responsibilities. The philosophic attitude is that a man shall perform his full duty to the world, but this will be done in such a way that it brings injury to none. Truth, honesty, and honour will not be sacrificed for money. Time, energy, capacity, and money will be used wisely in the best interests of mankind, and above all the philosopher will pray constantly that the

Overself will accept him as a dedicated instrument of service. And it surely will.(P)

152

He will rise above personal emotion into perfect serenity rather than fall below it into dull apathy.(P)

153

To be pure in heart means not only to be separated from animal tendencies, not only from egoistic impulses, but also to be detached from everything and everyone. Thus we see that the word "pure" is not as simple in connotation as it is short in length, and purity is harder to achieve than the newly converted religious enthusiast believes.

154

The act of renunciation is always first, and only sometimes last, an inward one. It is done by thoroughly understanding that the object renounced is, after all, only like a picture in a dream and that, again like a dream, it is ephemeral. Its illusoriness and transitoriness must be not only mentally perceived but also emotionally taken to heart. If we give up our wrong belief about it, we may not have to give up the object itself. Now this admonition cannot be made to stop with visible things only. To be honestly applied, it must be applied to visible persons also. No matter how fondly we love somebody, we must not flinch from seeing the meta-physical truth about him nor from accepting the consequences of such perception.

155

How can we renounce the attachments to everything and everyone and yet enjoy life, fulfil obligations, or remain in the world? How do this without flight to a monastery? How remain an affectionate husband, a devoted father? In the case of things, the answer has been given earlier. In the case of persons, the answer ought now to be given. We renounce the "materiality" of the loved one and with it the clinging to her material image, her physical possession, her personal ego. We hold on to the concept of her "spirituality," her essence, her real being. We then know that this true self of hers cannot be separated from our own; the illusory relationship is replaced by a real one, the perishable pseudo-love by an undying essential one.

156

He may try to keep up the illusion that he is a well-fitting part of these surroundings called civilization, a member of the society into which he was born, but in the deepest layer of his heart the reality will deny it. He no longer belongs to a race caught up in appearances, ensnared and hypnotized by them to the point of self-destruction.

157

It may take some time to get familiar with this impersonality of attitude, this detachment of heart, before he can realize how fine it is, how precious its worth and rewarding in result. The first impression may be cold and frightening. The last will be calm and soothing.

158

If indifference and detachment mean that the man has ceased to care, then he has ceased to understand philosophy.

159

Deep within his heart he will strive to depersonalize his relations with his wife, his children, his family, and even his friends. But in the domain of action we should find him the best of husbands, the most loving of fathers, and most faithful of friends.

160

The demand which the quest makes upon his feelings is often a harsh and exacting one. He has to see each troubling situation which concerns him without allowing personal emotions to interfere with the truth of vision. He has to displace hot resentment, for instance, by calm detachment. It is a battle of self against self and consequently invisible to and unnoticed by other men. No one will help him here.

161

To be detached simply means not letting yourself get into the power of anything or anyone who can hurt, damage, or destroy you inwardly.

162

The *Gita* recommends those who live in the world but are not of it to work with complete detachment from the fruits and results of their activity. But how could any aspiring student achieve this? Only the master, the man who has uncovered his identity as Overself could succeed in labouring without caring what rewards he got or what effects he brought into being.

163

It is not a petrifying ascetic coldness but a benevolent inherent calm.

164

The practice of detachment helps in the practice of meditation, while the reverse is also true.

165

It is pure but calm feeling unmixed with the desires, passions, perturbations, and inflammations of the ordinary unawakened and unevolved man.

166

Does this detachment mean that nothing is to make any difference in him? No, it means rather that he may let the different effects produce themselves but only under the check and control of a deeper abiding serenity.

167

He who can detach himself from emotion even while he continues to feel it, becomes its true master.(P)

168

It would be a mistake to confuse detachment with callousness or to think that the conquest of emotion means the lack of all feeling. He who is possessed by the one and has achieved the other, may still have his sympathies unimpaired, and even brought to a greater self-identification with other men than before. But they will not be uncontrolled. Wisdom and knowledge, ideality and practicality will balance them.

169

The degree of attachment is measurable by the degree of emotional involvement. Therefore to become detached is to become emotionally detached.

170

The disillusionments which come from personal contact with the defects or deficiencies of human nature will not make him cynical, will not even make him sad.

171

A cold, heavy and death-like apathy is not the indifference, or the detachment, taught here.

172

In the world of artists—using the word broadly to include all who practise any of the arts—one too often notices an easy, careless way of living, a lack of any worthwhile purpose, and consequently a lack of any worthwhile self-discipline. This merely egoistic casualness drifting through the years, is a counterfeit of the true detachment taught by philosophy.

173

It is not so easy to assume an air of detachment in the deeper levels of one's being as it is on the surface.

174

To be unattached gives one a lighter touch in dealing with the affairs and events of life, takes out some of the unnecessary solemnity and nerve-racking hurry.

175

The emotional results of undergoing a misfortune or an affliction can be made a part of oneself or can be separated out by refusing identification with them. One may seek the real *I* which never changes and so become detached from them. It is this self whose presence in one makes it possible to be conscious of those results.

176

The wise man had better cast the plaudits of the multitude out of his ears; it is all noise, for the mob does not understand him. He has pleased them for today; but tomorrow, when he displeases them, they will be as ready to destroy him. He should be prepared to receive abuse with the same equanimity with which he is ready to receive praise.

177

It is comparatively easy to be detached from past circumstances, for the feelings they aroused are now quiet or dead; but can he be so detached about present ones? Yet no less an achievement than this is required of him.

178

When detachment is used as an excuse for escape, it is being misused.

179

It is not that he is above having admirations and aversions, preferences and distastes, but that he tries to stand aside mentally even while they register on his feelings.

180

Detachment does not mean that he regards his outer performance in the world and his inner thoughts about the world with the utmost solemnity. No! the day will not pass without a little lightheartedness about it all. Why? Because he knows very well that it is just like a dream into which he is peeping—a passing show, as Shakespeare also knew.

181

We may express our disenchantment with life in exactly opposite ways—either with a grim scowl or with a quiet smile. It is not only a matter of temperament but also of our world-view. The two combine to make the result which we express. In the last and supreme disenchantment—which is death itself—a third factor enters to effect this result.

182

Out of the understanding which ripens and deepens with the philosophical work, he becomes grateful for one result. This is the transmutation of those resentments and bitternesses which follow some experiences into needed instruction and growing detachment.

183

His aim being the contrary of most people's aims, he tries to depersonalize his attitudes and reactions. What relief he feels with even partial freedom from the burden of self-consciousness! How heavy a load is borne by those who see or react with ego-centered nervousness.

184

The eventual aim of human evolutionary experience is to make us learn to love the Overself more than anything else. Therefore, any personal attachments which we continue to hold within the heart must be purified in quality, while at the same time kept subordinate to our larger attachment to the Quest.

185

He must fully understand his situation, both with regard to business responsibilities and the duties towards his family—perhaps a wife and mother. It is part of this belief that such responsibilities have to be honourably and effectively discharged and truth should be able to help him to do so rather than relieve him from them.

186

The detachment which is taught by philosophy is not to be confused with the detachment which is preached by religio-mysticism. The first is a personal lifestyle for coping with the world; the second is an indifference to the world.

187

It comes to this: that we have to view our own life's events in a bifocal manner, both impersonally and personally.

188

The right way to regard possessions and property is to replace the sense of ownership by the sense of trusteeship.

189

When earthly things or human entities hold our heart to the exclusion of all else, they obscure the Overself's light and shut out its peace.

190

Such nonchalant detachment is not easy to attain. It is easy to renounce the things which we value lightly but very hard to become inwardly aloof to those which we hold precious.

191

Human preferences do exist; it is possible to pretend that they may not be there when they actually are—but this has to be paid for by self-deception.

192

It is natural and pardonable for a married man with responsibilities to worry if he has lost his employment or to be anxious if serious illness descends on his family; but if he is also philosophically inclined, he will check his worry and anxiety by calm reasoned analysis followed by prayer, meditation, and finally a handing of the problems over to the higher power.

193

It is not that he is to be without pity for the misfortunes and miseries of others—such a thing would be impossible—but that he insists on taking a larger and longer view of them.

194

It is better that we pass by unnoticed rather than be praised or blamed. For then there will be no strain on our peace of mind. If praised, we may swell with pride. If blamed, indignation may disturb our feelings.

195

He may not give more than a part of himself to these lesser loves. His deepest feeling must remain remote from them.

196

Conquest of the emotional nature and knowledge of the true character of death will be evidenced when, at the actual passing of a near one, he seems insensible to grief.

197

To be detached from anything means that he can take it or leave it alone.

198

Ambition wears thin with time or even wears out altogether. The hour may come when it means nothing and when a man feels nothing of it. Only the young are so eager to risk the perils of upward flight to fame. The reflective man is indifferent to worldly ambitions as the aged man is tired of them. Philosophy leads its votaries to a somewhat similar detachment, but, by supplying new incentives, does not lead to negative results.

199

The process of inner disentangling in the quest of total freedom may have to be wide-sweeping. Not only desires but also duties may have to go, not only long-hoarded possessions but also relatives and friends.

200

There are those who regard such detachment as too cool, perhaps even too inhuman. They are displeased with this rule. They will let nothing disturb their tenderest affections, yet the ego lurks here too.

Family

201

His family life—if there is one—provides the first scene for his application of philosophy. There his opportunity is plainly visible, the area for the self-judgements of his philosophic conscience plainly marked out.

202

When the family circle prepares the younger members for mature life, it does its duty. But when it sets itself up as the supreme value of human existence and its loyalties or attachments as the supreme forms of human ethics, it overdoes duty and breeds evils. It stifles individual growth and crushes independent thought. It is nothing more than enlarged self-centeredness. It turns a means into an end. Thus the influence of a useful institution, if over-emphasized, becomes unhealthy and vicious. Parents who refuse to release their children, even when the latter are fully adult, who constantly fuss around them with over-solicitousness and hover around with over-protectiveness, belong to the patriarchal age. They stifle the children's development, breed the daughter-in-law's or the son-in-law's resentment, and fill their own minds with unnecessary anxieties.

203

The desire for motherhood is Nature's urge in the individual; it is entirely on a par with the illusions of sex. See it for what it is worth, no more or less, and leave the rest to fate; you may then enjoy it if it comes or remain undisturbed if it does not.

204

The parent, the husband, or the wife who demands continuous attention and undivided devotion, who assumes as a natural right the duty of making decisions for one, turns a home into a gaol.

205

The only relatives he recognizes are not blood ones but love ones, inner not outer, lasting spiritual affinities not temporary physical accidents, mental and not geographical ones.

206

Family life gives great joys on the one hand and grave anxieties on the other. It was always like that and we cannot alter but must accept it. With all its ups and downs the householder life is the best after all. Most of the qualities needed for spiritual development can be got from it.

207

Parents should respect the child's individuality and not let it get too dependent and too attached, thus robbing it of the capacity to grow mature and self-reliant.

208

The over-protectiveness of fear-ridden mothers toward their children and the over-possessiveness of dominating mothers show a lack of faith in the one case, and a lack of understanding in the other.

209

It is a part of family relationship for the children to identify themselves, *by extension*, with their parents. Thus, it is what the French call "egoisme a deux."

210

Relationship is a matter of soul, not a measure of blood.

211

Once across the threshold of puberty the girl or boy begins the unfolding of the emotional nature. Each will then develop her or his own individual feelings and passions as a process of growth towards womanhood or manhood. How can this be done unless the young begin at the same time to develop away from utter dependence upon the mother? They must begin in however small a degree to claim their freedom and move away emotionally from their physical source. All this is to be accomplished by stages and not all at once until maturity is reached. Then, just as the fledgling bird has to emerge from the nest and learn to fly even at the risk of falling, so the young must learn to stand on their own feet in order to reach maturity.

212
It is questionable whether family love is a break out of the ego's shell or merely an extension of self. More often perhaps it is a mixture of both.

213
The family link becomes unhealthy when it becomes exaggerated. No personal relation is enduring. All end with the efflux of time. Even the most enduring of all—the disciple-master one—must end too with the disciple's own graduation.

214
It was Jesus' closest relative, his own mother, who sought to sidetrack him from his mission, compelling him to exclaim, "Woman! What have I to do with thee?" It was Ramana Maharshi's own mother who sought to drag him back from his meditation-cave to a worldly life, compelling him to tell her, in effect, not to alter a course already preordained for him. The duties towards one's family are limited ones, whereas the duty towards one's soul is an unlimited one.

215
A family problem may have to be considered again and in a fresh light, judged and considered not merely by his personal feelings but from the point of view of duty, as perhaps to his children. It is necessary to make sacrifices at times if one wishes to follow the spiritual Quest, even if those sacrifices involve crushing the ego.

216
When children are grown up and past thirty, their lives are largely their own affair: they are then entitled to a measure of freedom from possessive parents.

Friendship

217
Once he has found out his true relationship to the higher power, the problem of settling his relationship to other human beings becomes easy.

218
"Friends are friends if nothing can separate them," observed the Buddha. He spoke not of the superficial relation which subsists between persons belonging to the same class, rank, profession, or locality. True friendship is not formed as are most of these by self-interest, vanity,

custom, or habit. It is a profound tie formed not seldom between those who have lived together and died together under remote skies and remoter centuries no less than in familiar lands and more recent times. We are bound to each other by links that have lost themselves in the archaic past, links of affectionate studentship and hallowed trust, and—not seldom—the mutual suffering of sharp persecution, when the prison cell and the torturer's stake were the punishment for expressing or believing truth.

219

We often imagine we have made a new friend when we have merely made a new acquaintance. He only to whom we can speak our private thoughts is our friend, and none else. He who flies to our aid when all others flee away is our friend, and none else. Above all, he whose sympathy is so perfect that he understands and forgives our failings is indeed worthy to be our honoured friend.

220

Where minds are great and hearts are large, two persons can remain cordial friends even though their outlooks differ.

221

There is a silence between two persons which is full of nervous tension, but there is another which is full of healing peace. This is rare, uncommon, but it is found through real harmony, full trust, surrendered ego.

222

It is not necessary to give up personal friendships in order to follow the Quest. They are quite permissible in their place and have their instructive value.

223

Those who pursue such an ideal as ours have always to live inwardly, and sometimes outwardly, apart from the mob—that is, to live in a loneliness which makes true friendship double its worth.

224

Sometimes a quick friendship means that he is reviving an old spiritual relationship out of the hidden past, out of the numerous incarnations which have been lost in time. Therefore understanding and recognition come quickly, explanations and introductions are not waited for and are not necessary in the real soul-realm.

225

There is the common friendship in which the emotional attitude may one day pass from affection to animosity, and there is this rare friendship which, because it is based on something deeper, diviner, and more enduring than mere emotion, witnesses only the ripening of affection into real love.

226

We each possess our own heavenly latitude and must seek out our true compatriots on that line.

227

"As iron sharpeneth iron, so a man sharpeneth the understanding of his friend," says Solomon.

228

The course of life's friendships is sometimes like a turning wheel. We think we grasp the hand of a friend but one day the wheel turns and he is gone. In the end we cannot escape from our solitariness.

229

Only those who hold the same spiritual conception of life can be true affinities in friendship.

230

There are times in personal relationships when eagerness for friendship, on one side, would mean cruelty on the other side, if an individual wished to break away from any continued acquaintance completely. In such an instance one should try to continue seeing the other but make the association on a different level if possible. The other person may have awakened to the Quest of truth, and any unfortunate experience between them would be no reason for deserting her but only for learning how to handle persons of the opposite sex who are led across his orbit for spiritual help.

Marriage

231

Each of us being individually complete in his inmost godlike self, no other person is needed for self-fulfilment, no mate or affinity is required to bring him to the realization of life's goal. But each of us being incomplete in his outer self, the longing for such a mate or affinity is human, natural, and pardonable. There is nothing wrong nor contrary to the Quest in seeking to satisfy this longing, although unless this is done with wisdom and after prudent consideration, rather than with ignorance and in impulse, the result may bring more unhappiness rather than more happiness. Nor must such a longing ever be allowed to obscure the great truth of individual completeness on the spiritual level.

232

Those ascetics who vehemently denounce marriage because, they say, it caters to the passions are themselves showing the baneful effects of passion repressed but not sublimated.

233

Personally I do not accept the Christian and Hindu conceptions that marriages are made in heaven and that we are allied as husband-wife for all eternity; but I do accept the strict duty of acting with the utmost consideration for the other party, of being ready to renounce one's own happiness entirely rather than destroy the happiness of the other person.

234

The aspirant who seeks to live spiritually in the world should marry for something more than physical enjoyment and comfort, more even than intellectual and social companionship. He must find a woman whose inner being is polarized to the same ideals as his own, who will walk by his side through every vicissitude as a fellow-pilgrim and a wholehearted seeker.

235

One general guiding principle as to whether or not a young aspirant on the quest should enter into marriage is that it is necessary that there should be spiritual harmony. Both must pursue the same ideal, for if disharmony enters this would lead to disaster. Both must stand within measurable distance of each other on the spiritual path. In addition to that, it is advisable that there should be physical, magnetic, and temperamental suitability to each other. In any case this decision is a matter which should not be rushed and it will be well to take enough time for consideration. It would be well also to ponder the opinions of wise friends who have met the other person. A decision about marriage should not be made on the basis of emotion alone, but the checks of critical reason and outside judgement should also be introduced.

Committing oneself to a life-partnership in marriage is not only of vital importance to worldly life but also to spiritual life. It may either help inner progress or else lead to spiritual disaster. It is necessary, therefore, that a man, for example, should explain his views to the lady that he is interested in, and if she is unable to accept them sincerely within a reasonable period then he may face the fact that he would be headed for a stoppage on his spiritual journey if he married her. To make a mistake in marriage will bring both pain and trouble to his wife as well as to himself. He should resolve to choose correctly or else to wait patiently until the right girl appears.

236

The marriage partner should fulfil both the human characteristics needed for satisfaction and the spiritual qualities needed for affinity. Where fate denies this, wisdom counsels abstention from marriage altogether. Otherwise, unnecessary unhappiness is invited.

237

Philosophy says that the marriage state is necessary for most people, the less advanced. It also says that even for the others, the more advanced, the smaller love of two persons mating can coincide with, and remain within, the larger love of the individual for the Higher Self. Of course, this is only possible if the relationship is a successful and harmonious blending of the two personalities.

238

For some people marriage does take away from the higher life, but not for others. It all depends upon the two individuals concerned in it as to which of these results will come about.

239

Marriage hinders some aspirants because of the distractions and burdens it imposes, but it helps others because of the release from sex-tormenting thoughts which it may give. When sensibly fitted into the framework of a spiritual understanding of life, marriage need not be a bar and success may be achieved.

240

It is true that men who are lonely or young or romantic are likely to marry a young woman with whom propinquity has brought them in touch. In such cases he puts an illusion around the woman to the pressure of desire. When the illusion goes and the facts show themselves he is left alone with the hard lesson of discrimination. The situation can repeat itself with the victim being the woman.

241

Many marriages are based on calculation, not on love. They are business transactions bearing social or financial rewards, not emotional ones. Yet if animated by goodwill they may be successful.

242

One man who seemed to make no spiritual progress generally, and little progress in meditation particularly, found the situation completely altered when he adjusted himself to a new attitude towards his wife. She was a shrew and a scold, hostile to his higher aspirations and quite earthy. He was several times on the brink of leaving her but the thought of responsibility toward their growing children restrained him. He did leave her mentally and bitterly resented her presence in his life. When he was taught how to bring a new viewpoint to bear upon his marriage, he began to regard it as a perfect opportunity for the better development of his character and his wife as an unwitting instrument for the better control of his mind. He learned to accept her in his life without complaint. He came to regard the marriage as a piece of Self-Created destiny to be worked out, in its own unpredictable time, by his fostering the needful qualities. He set to work upon himself and gradually unfolded patience, calmness, strength of will, and unselfishness. Within a few years he not only became expert at meditation but also gained higher awareness. Nor was this all. In his work as an executive in a large commercial office involved in accounts, calculations, and business decisions, formerly he would easily become excited, irritated, or angry with subordinates over their mistakes, their inefficiency or stupidity. Now he taught himself how to hold on to the inner peace found in periods of meditation until the time arrived when he could pass through the whole day's activity without losing or disturbing it.

243

If a woman has done all that was humanly possible to hold her husband and has failed, she must realize that acceptance of the inevitable—even the temporarily inevitable—is the only way to bear this painful result. The husband's weaknesses may have found their expression in outer action. But through the painful results of that expression he may eventually discover a truer set of values. If she has tried to appeal to his better nature and failed, she must now let him do what he wishes and try the path of personal experience in the satisfaction of his desires, which is the common path for most people.

244

It is not necessary that he remain married in order to pay a karmic debt, nor on the other hand is he free to follow personal desires in the matter. It is a mistake to think that such a debt must continue to be paid until the end of one's life. Yet, it must be paid off if one's inner life and path are not to be obstructed. Only the voice of his own deeper conscience may decide this point.

245

An individual may keep the ideal of a true mate but understand that one can't be absolutely certain to meet him or her on this earth. The spiritual path is a call to renunciation of personal attachments, inwardly at least, and to a renunciation of the animal nature also. Both have to be overcome if inner peace is to be obtained. But once overcome, the world can be enjoyed without danger because his happiness no longer depends on it. If he lets the natural desire for a mate be included in but transcended by the higher desire for spiritual realization, he stands a chance to get both. But if he feels that the first is wholly indispensable, he may miss the chance to get either. The truth is that the Soul will not give itself to you unless you love It more than anything or anyone else. He may have great capacity for love in his nature which, properly directed by wisdom, may lead him to great spiritual heights and human satisfactions. But directed by impulse, unchecked by reason, it can bring him into situations productive of much misery to himself and others. He must therefore make it a part of his spiritual discipline to secure this balance. Until he has secured it, he should not commit himself to any decision without consulting with a spiritually mature person. Much harm has been done by the pseudo-romantic non-sense and false suggestions put out by cinema, magazines, and novels.

246

Marriage is a risky affair when one of the two belongs in every way—spiritual, intellectual, and social—to a class higher than the other. If they cannot meet on these levels, where can they? The bad in both is brought out and made worse; the good is diminished. This was one of the original reasons why the caste system got established in some form or other among the Orientals as if it were an essential part of religion.

247

Marriage multiplies burdens, entanglements, anxieties, difficulties, and worldly preoccupations. The single man has a better chance to wed his life to a single undistracted aim. Nevertheless, philosophy does not condemn marriage but leaves it to individual choice. Indeed, when two persons are temperamentally harmonious and spiritually suitable, it definitely approves of marriage.

248

If he could find a companion who had the character and capacity to help, and not to hinder, his own inner pilgrimage, then it might be useful for him to marry; but if she were to fall short of this ideal then greater inner misery would descend upon him. There is a certain fate about such matters and if she has to come, she will come into his life of her own accord. In any case it will be advisable to wait to make sure that the inner harmony does really exist.

249

Some questions asked about marriage problems ought not to be answered by anyone other than the individual's own higher self. Let him hear the voice of the Overself, which concerns itself neither with conventional contemporary attitudes, out-dated Oriental teachings, nor merely personal reactions. Let him listen mentally in profoundest meditation to hear this voice.

Happiness

250

It would be a profound error to believe that because the philosophic life is so deeply concerned with self-improvement and the philosophic mind so attached to serious studies, therefore the philosophic student must be a gloomy, dreary, and miserable individual. But the contrary is the fact. His faith uplifts and upholds him, his knowledge brings joy and peace to him.

Nor should the renunciatory preachments of Buddha, the bitter complaints of Job, the harsh pessimism of Schopenhauer, and the appraisal of the World's life as vain foolishness in Ecclesiastes make us forget the cheerful optimism of Emerson and the bright rapture of many a mystic.

251

The quest for an ideal place or person can never be satisfied; consequently, it can never really end. What we may hope to find are better places, better persons. The dream of the Best will always remain only a dream.

252

Where is the earthly thing, attraction, creature, which can compete successfully with THAT in the deepest heart of men? Without knowing what he is really doing, he is seeking THAT amid all other activities, loving THAT behind all other loves.

253

It is possible, given certain conditions, to attain happiness thinking only of oneself and without care for the welfare of other men, but it is not possible to keep it. For if destiny or nature do not interrupt or destroy it, some among those others will become envious and may turn into a potential danger to one's happiness.

254

We shall secure personal happiness only to the extent that we unfold ourselves to the light of the impersonal Overself.

255

The happiness which everyone wants can be found only in the eternal, not in the temporal. But everyone continues to try this or that, with the same endlessly repeated result. Nobody listens to the prophets who tell this, or listens with more than his ears, until time teaches him its truth. Then only do his heart and will begin to apply it.

256

The danger of seeking for personal happiness over and above self-improvement is one of nurturing egoism and thus hindering that improvement. And how could anyone find happiness so long as the causes of his suffering lie so largely in his own frailties?

257

With a single exception, no living man is ever really content either with his lot or, what in the end is the same thing, with himself. That exception is the illuminate. The reason is that all living men are unconsciously striving to become, in the timed state, what they already are in the eternal one. That is, they are unwittingly in search of themselves. This is the hidden cause of all their discontent, all their restless desires, endeavours, and ambitions.

258

Happiness cannot be found by those who seek it as a goal in itself. It can be found only by those who know it is a result and not a goal.

259

It is true that the student of philosophy, understanding the impermanent and imperfect nature of this world, has in one sense renounced the quest of personal happiness, but he has renounced it only as an end in itself. He comprehends, on the one hand, that it is futile to demand perfection and permanence when the ever-changing world cannot by its very nature give them. To seek to establish personal happiness under such conditions is to travel farther away from it. He comprehends, on the other hand, that so long as he feels for and with other living creatures he cannot be fully happy whilst so many among them are immersed in suffering. But all this is not to say that he need forgo the quest of the higher transworldly happiness which is entirely independent of persons, places, and things and which is to be found within the Overself alone. Moreover, he realizes that it is his duty to attain it precisely because he must attain the power to lift those suffering creatures above their misery and gloom, to infuse in them the life-giving qualities of hope, courage, and serenity which will help them triumph over difficulties. Thus there is no adequate reason why he should be less happy than other men. The depth of his thinking and discipline of his senses do not prevent his sharing in the beauty-bringing arts, the laughter-raising fun, and the lighter diversions of human living. Indeed, by his efforts to reshape his thought and conduct, he is eliminating a number of causes which would otherwise bring him future worry and misery, just as he is fortifying himself to bear present trouble with calmness and wisdom. Moreover, he is on the path to realizing for himself—if he has not already partially realized it—that inexpressible inner beauty and satisfying bliss which accompany the consciousness of the Overself. Even from afar its reflected light shines down upon his path, to cheer the mind and warm the heart. No—he cannot be a miserable man. He is in the process of finding an exalted and enduring happiness which is not bought at the expense of others, but rather shared with others.

260

Some worthwhile lessons may be got by analysis and reflection from experiences of human love, if it is approached with reason, impersonality, and the determination to learn wisdom. We may see the risks in permitting happiness to depend upon another person, whoever that other person may be. The first love must be given to the divine soul within one's own heart, because it alone will never desert, betray, or disappoint. Then and then only may an individual turn to human love for comfort.

261

Is not excessive melancholy just as undesirable, and as much of a stumbling block in the path of spiritual progress as, for instance, excessive drinking—or any other fault? What is being gained by these self-demeaning tactics? Is anyone benefiting from them? The time has come to ask himself these questions. Certainly he is not alone in having made mistakes—everybody makes them! Consider what would happen, however, if everybody continued to punish themselves over and over again, needlessly remaining on the level of their own errors? What then is to be done? His gloomy situation can improve only when he is willing to change his attitude towards it. He must make a deliberate attempt to *cultivate happiness!* Just as he raises the windowshade in the morning to allow sunshine to pour into the room, so must he open himself to the higher power and let hope pour into his heart! As long as he continues to cling to despondency and to misunderstand, he is shutting out the Overself and preventing its message from reaching him. Every day *is* a new day, with new possibilities of a fresh, determined, and more courageous approach to all daily difficulties. Let him *forget* the past, and start planning for a happier tomorrow! No one else can do this for him, but he can draw faith from the knowledge that his efforts will count towards his joyful resurrection.

262

It is an heroic and stoic goal to set before a man, that he shall not be dependent upon others for his happiness and that he shall be emotionally self-sufficient. But it is a goal reachable by and, in the present kind of faulty human society, useful to, only the few.

263

If a man reaches finality of decision and recognizes that enlightened self-discipline is to be achieved and not resisted, he takes the first step to true happiness.

264

So long as we believe that some other person is essential to our happiness, so long shall we fail to attain that happiness.

265

Happiness is not the monopoly of the successful. One of the happiest men I ever knew was an aged tramp who wandered from poorhouse to poorhouse across the country. His eyes were blazing with a strange light.

266

Happiness? Is it so important and so necessary? Are not strength, understanding, and peace of mind more indispensable to a human life?

267

When inner conflict goes out, inner harmony comes in. There can be no happiness without such harmony.

268

Only they who have brought all the different sides of their being into equilibrium, as well as they who have lived fully between the opposite poles of human experience, can appreciate the quest for serenity over the quest for happiness. Goethe in Europe was one man who appreciated this superiority as Buddha in Asia was another.

269

It is as erroneous to expect perfect happiness through another person as it is to expect perfect salvation. Each must find the one or the other for himself in himself. No one else can bear such a great and grave responsibility, or ought to bear it. No human relationship can adequately or properly be substituted for what everyone must in the end do for himself.

270

He who asks for happiness asks for something he cannot and shall not get while his body breathes. The wise man does not ask more from life than it can yield. If it cannot give happiness, it can give peace.

271

"Are you happy?" is a question people often ask him. But he has not sought happiness. He has sought to find out why he is here and to fulfil that purpose.

272

The aim of getting as much personal happiness as he can out of every situation is no longer the dominant one. Other and loftier aims now coexist with it in some cases or even displace it in others.

273

During no one's lifetime are all desires fully realized. To look for a happiness that is complete is to look in vain. It is more philosophic to look for peace of mind.

274

Happiness may leave a man in a single moment or come to him in the same way. But this can only happen if he identifies it solely with the ego and nothing more.

275

If a man has inner peace he does not have emotional disturbances or mental agitations. Who then, really enjoys living—the disciplined philosopher who has the peace, or the undisciplined sufferer from the agitations?

3

DISCIPLINE EMOTIONS

Higher and lower emotions

The emotions are uppermost in primitive man. With time and evolution, reason begins to mix with them and eventually to rule the lower ones. With further time and further evolution, intuition appears as the fruit of the finer ones. This is the place of emotional life in man.

2

Few persons can separate—in their consciousness—emotions from thoughts. The capability of doing so is essential both to self-knowledge and to self-conquest. Therefore it is important to every Quester.

3

We must keep the emotional issues separate from the intellectual ones. But this is not to say that the intellect is to live an emotion-proof existence. Such separation always needs to be kept up only so long as the lack of it is likely to impair the quest of truth. This danger arises only during the earlier stages of man's seeking. When he has attained a balanced personality, cultivated a serene disposition, and mastered the egotistic urges within himself, then emotion and reason join forces with intuition in producing the quality of intelligence. Henceforth he feels what he thinks and thinks what he feels, his emotions are rightly directed and his thoughts are truthfully formed. They work together harmoniously, satisfactorily, and unitedly.

4

He who seeks to arrive at the truth about a matter must banish his personal inclinations and egoistic desires about it during the time that he contemplates it. He must make his emotions submit to the facts which displease them and he must compel his reasonings to accept the conclusions which surprise them. Otherwise, his emotions may betray him and his reasonings delude him, so that white will appear black and illusion will appear as reality.

5

There is a special quality which we will do well to develop during this particular period in which we live, and that is calmness. For wherever we turn our gaze, we perceive great upheavals of thought and emotion, great stirring of violent passion and bitter hatred, mass excitement and mob restlessness. In such a disturbed atmosphere we are liable to be swept off our feet against our better judgement and may thus injure the true interests of ourselves or of our country. We should remember that to keep a cool head is the way to act wisely and successfully, whereas to yield to hot impulsiveness is to act rashly and often wrongly. We should also remember how the unfortunate younger folk of Germany were cunningly swept into the Nazi current of blind impulses and became the bomb-fodder for the insatiable ambitions of a hysterical maniac like Hitler. Let this be a lesson on the need and value of calm judgement and levelheaded-ness.

We may also draw a further lesson from Germany, that is, the impor-tance of practising goodwill to all. The continent of Europe could never have arrived at the present unhappy condition of its people had it realized this virtue. The more we try to be kindly and helpful to others, no matter what class or creed they belong to, the more others are kindly and helpful to us. Therefore, even from the purely selfish point of view it pays good dividends to practise goodwill. Moreover, it will help us as much as anything else to get on in life, for it will bring friends, gratitude, and even opportunities.

6

Once engaged on this Quest it becomes necessary to attend closely to the emotional and mental movements within himself, rejecting the lower ones and consenting to the higher. He must study carefully the differences between them, so that he may be able to recognize them.

7

He must come to the discipline of passion and emotion not through fearing their bad effects but through willing consent to the truth that his real being is above them and that it is better to live in reality than in illusion.

8

We hear much from the new moralists about the need of encouraging young men and young women to express themselves and of not letting society impose its will upon them, as we hear much from the psycho-analysts about the need of liberating them from secret inhibitions and of satisfying their repressed emotions. Both these movements are excellent. They are antidotes to the tyrannic soul-crushing, hypocrisy-breeding, and self-deceiving conventions of the old society. But a good overdone may become an evil, a virtue stretched too far may become a vice, and a method which ignores all the facets of the diamond of psychological truth except a single one may become unbalanced. The new morality may free people to the point where liberty is merely license and expression a dangerous disregard for the knowledge yielded by experience and age. The new psychoanalysis may free them to the point where mental liberation is mere lack of self control and emotional satisfaction is dangerously anti-social. This is not to say that we would belittle the value of either. Both standpoints may be philosophically used, which means they may be used in a balanced manner as a part of a wider one.

9

The whole man is the natural man. Whoever sets up a cleavage between the intellectual and emotional functions, and would ignore the latter in order to enthrone the former, is unnatural and cannot attain that truth which is the voice of nature. This is not to say that emotion or reason should run riot; it is proper and necessary to give reason the reins, but this done, any sharper division will lead to unbalance, distortion, and error.

10

Yes, the emotions of a person who is called hard and dry may need to be released, but this applies only to the positive ones. The negative ones are not worth releasing and should be got rid of.

11

Anger and hatred are dangerous emotions to carry about with you. Whether or not they lead to actions harmful to the person they are directed against, they are certainly harmful to you. Conquer them quickly, get these psychological poisons out of your system.

12

There is another kind of negative trait which, although unaggressive, is only less unpleasant by a matter of degrees than the aggressive ones. It is the black and bitter mood of sullen coldness, of the self-centered, self-tormenting, self-pitying sense of being wronged by the other person, the introverted, withdrawn, sulky, resentment at being hurt, a resentment so deep as to find no fitter expression than gloomy, frozen, and tense silence. He places all the blame for the situation on the other and consequently adopts a grieved unconciliatory attitude towards the other. He wounds by saying nothing, doing nothing, and being boorish. The atmosphere around him is full of sustained and hostile emotional tension. It is, of course, an adolescent trait and cannot endure when spiritual maturity is really attained.

13

What the unawakened man feels as fear, the awakened one transmutes into needful caution and careful forethought.

14

It is a feat of emotional surgery to relinquish attachments and to renounce possessivenesses.

15

Emotions unchecked by reason may become our betrayers. Beware of them when exceptionally strong and unduly excessive.

16

The fears which are natural or necessary should not be confused with the fears which are neurotic or excessive.

17

If the aspirant is to remake himself effectively, he must begin by attacking the lower emotions. They must be killed and eliminated from his life-scene. So long as they dominate it, so long will experience yield poisonous fruits instead of health-giving ones. Every fresh situation will only give fresh life to his ego because those emotions will involve themselves in that situation and cause him to misread it. The first enemies, the hidden sources of his own difficulties, are within himself.

18

To take the attitude in a depressing situation that the only action is to sit down and be depressed by it is unphilosophical.

19

He should never give himself up to despair, although he may give himself up in hard situations to gravest reflection and deepest resignation.

20

He may become so sensitive as a consequence of meditation that other people's thoughts, feelings, or passions may reflect themselves into his own nature temporarily when he is physically near them or mentally dealing with them. In such cases he will probably mistake the result for his own, thus expressing what is really alien to his mind or acting outside of his individual pattern of life. This is particularly true when a strong emotion like anger is directed against him. He may then feel instinctively angry with the other person. Unwittingly, he may become disloyal to the Ideal merely through being ignorant of what is happening psychically, and unguarded against it.

21

The longer he lives the more he discovers that real peace depends on the strength with which he rules his own heart, and real security depends on the truth with which he rules his own mind. When he leaves his emotions in disorder they bring agony—as the accompaniment or the follower of the happiness they claimed at first to be able to give. When he lets his thoughts serve the blindnesses of his ego, they deceive, mislead, or trouble him.(P)

22

The aspirant must not act, live, or think under the sway of merely sentimental, emotional, and self-centered feeling alone but should strive for mature truthful feeling. This is intuition. When dealing with a complex personal situation, he should detach himself and follow such intuition instead of emotion. Then it will be solved rightly. He will not be karmically free of an unpleasant relationship until he has mentally freed himself from all negative thoughts and negative acts concerning it. Then the outer karmic forces will free him, or else he may be shown inwardly how to free himself outwardly.

23

Of what use, in such serious matters as survival, to live in so many illusions? Sentimentalists and emotionalists who desert reason at the bidding of well-intentioned, high ideals or religion to preach unrealistic attitudes do not know the difference between religio-mystic ethics and philosophic ethics. Only the latter is practical in the highest sense as well as the worldly one. Foolish teachers, professors, and those whose lives are spent in academic circles are suborned by these emotions more easily than are other people, just because their distance from the world of practical decisions and realistic affairs have made them one-sided.

24

All this emotional energy which neurotics waste in self-pity, hysterics in crises, and unwary ordinary persons in trivialities and negatives, is to be conserved, controlled, and constructively redirected.

25

If it be observed that young people and women at times display emotional instability, let it also be stated that to them is given by Nature tasks which can be fulfilled only in great love, and which call up in them commensurate emotional capacity. Where much is given, much is required, and they in particular need to learn control and wise use of the emotional drive so generously placed in their keeping.

26

An excessive humility or a morbid self-depreciation may prevent a man from seeking outside help. This too is a manifestation of the ego, which cunningly uses such emotion to keep him away from a contact which threatens its rule.

27

This quality of a continuous calmness—so highly prized by the Brahmins of India—is hard to come by but exceedingly precious when gained. He who possesses it, who is unfailingly one and the same not only toward others but also toward himself, becomes a rock of upholding strength in their crises, an oasis of hidden comfort in his own. This beautiful serenity makes many other qualities possible in his own development while leaving a benedictory afterglow of encouragement with all those who are still struggling with their own refractory emotions and passions.

28

Emotion is an unreliable adviser but refined, purified, and liberated from egotism, it becomes transformed into intuition.

29

As all worries and fears are aroused in the ego, they are lulled when, by meditation, the ego-thought is lulled and the meditator feels peace. But when the ego is rooted out by the entire philosophic effort, they are then rooted out too.

30

There are two kinds of inner peace. The first is somewhat like that which the ancient Stoics cultivated: the result of controlling emotions and disciplining thoughts, the result of will and effort applied to the mastery of self. It brings with it, at best, a contentment with what one has, at least, a resignation to one's lot. The second is much deeper, for it comes out of the Overself. It is the blessed result of Divine Grace liberating one from the craving for existence.

31

To attain this inner equilibrium, the emotions need to be brought under control. It is not enough to repress them by will alone: they need also to be understood psychologically in a far deeper sense than the academic one. It is not enough to analyse their obvious surface causes and workings: their relationship to the real self at the centre of being must become quite clear. The 'I' who experiences them must be sought.

32

To sustain this inner calm will not be easy. Many a time, in test situations, he will fail. But even when the negative, explosive, or depressive emotion asserts itself strongly, he is not to show it in behaviour nor express it in speech. For this is a step towards that control of self, that impersonality, which is what the quest means. If mind influences body, body also influences mind. From the physical control he may proceed to the mental.

33

When calmness has been well practised for a sufficient period, it will occasionally of itself lead the practiser into sudden brief and ecstatic experiences of a mystical character.

34

He should calmly recognize that suffering has its allotted function to perform in the divine plan, that other people have their lessons to learn through it when they will learn in no other way, and that the spectacle of its operation should, in such cases, be met with intelligent understanding rather than with neurotic sentimentality. He should face the fact that many people will not learn from reason, intuition, or teaching and that no one can really liberate them from their sufferings except themselves. Every other kind of liberation is a false one. Others may effect it today only to see the same condition return tomorrow. He should not, in certain situations calling for hard decision, for instance, show unjustifiable weakness under the belief that he is showing forbearance, nor submit to antisocial egotism under the thought that he is practising love, nor abandon his highest duties for the sake of making a false and superficial peace with interfering ignorance, nor passively accept a flagrant wrong because God's will must always be borne.

35

The lower emotions and the moods they produce are his first enemies. Every antagonism and envy, every wrathful temper and animal lust, every self-injuring desire and socially harmful greed bars his way. And it will not move out of the way without a long fight.

36

This spiritual quest takes the aspirant through many moods. He will alternate at times between blank despair and exalted joy. Though naturally affected by these moods, he ought nevertheless to try to keep a certain balance even in their very midst, to cultivate a kind of higher indifference towards them, and patience towards their results. This can be achieved more easily by obtaining a firm conviction of the transient character of such moods.

37

Both emotion and reason have their proper place in practical life, but in the philosophic life where the Quest is for truth alone and not for satisfaction, there is no place for emotion other than a secondary one. Its power over man is so great however that it will continually come into conflict with this ruling, it will struggle desperately to resist reason and to silence its voice, it will contradict the dictate of calm considered judgement and seek by sheer force to dominate the mind. Again and again the uprush of emotion will disturb the would-be philosopher and destroy his equanimity, thus rendering impossible a correct appreciation of the truth he seeks.

38

The melancholy feeling that he is missing something joyous in life, that a happiness which so many others have captured is running away from him with the years, is one of the emotional snares likely to beset the aspirant's path. If he yields to its self-pitying suggestiveness, it will weaken his resolve and disturb his peace. From that it is only a step or two to descend into a painted and delusive animality.

39

Those who waste themselves in emotional excesses weaken themselves spiritually, for the power of feeling is an essential part of the higher nature.

40

With the pressures brought down upon them by his total philosophic effort, the grosser desires will gradually be flattened out anyway. But it will not be to his detriment if he deliberately and directly assists them to enter that condition.

41

We must command our thoughts if we are to command our deeds, but much more, we must command the emotional impulses behind those thoughts and those deeds.

42

When he is tempted to be angry with some irritating person, he is faced with two choices: either to identify himself with this lower emotion or with his higher aspirations. If, following bad habit, he succumbs to the first, he weakens himself still further. If, following good resolve, he overcomes the temptation, he strengthens himself for the future.

43

Strong emotional attachments to another person may only tighten the ego's hold, may narrow, limit, warp, or prevent the seeing of truth. This happens all-too-often in family relationships and in the affections of the young. It can even happen in guru-disciple relationships.

44

Until that joyful time comes when negative moods or thoughts have ceased to cross the threshold of his consciousness, he must struggle with them by a combination of different methods. First, his will must follow them at once after their entry and remove them forcibly. Second, his imagination and reason must attack them in the meditation period set aside each day for that purpose.

45

Whether or not it is possible to attain a perfection of calmness that is secure against all assaults, it is surely possible to attain sufficient calmness to keep off many or most of the emotional disturbances and mental turmoils which derive from the petty incidents of everyday life.

46

Some have to learn that rashness is not courage, and only the painful results of their actions may succeed in teaching them this lesson.

47

The personal emotions entangle us in the events of life, whereas the impersonal intuitions enable us to see them from above.

48

Even if the intuitive leading or reasoned reflection opposes his wishes, the imperativeness of following truth and preserving integrity will force him to desert his wishes.

49

Emotion is valuable as a driving power, but doubtful as a means for discovering truth. If unbridled by reason and ungoverned by will, it may even drive a man to foolishness and disaster.

50

The neurotic introduces emotional factors into purely business matters, creates hysterical scenes, and cannot take a single word of constructive criticism or admonitory counsel.

51

Look through the miserable emotions of the ego and go beyond them to the smiling serenity of the Overself.

52

It is not the emotions which are to be kept out but the disturbances to which they may give rise.

53

Do not respond to negative or base emotion with the like. The greater the animosity shown you, for instance, the greater is the inward calm with which it should be met.

54

There is a vital difference between being merely callous in the presence of other people's suffering and being philosophically calm.

55

A settled composed disposition will be one of the fruits of perseverance in rejecting negative moods and undesirable thoughts as soon as they arise.

56

Self-control is your greatest friend through all the incidents and accidents of life.

57

Shanti means not only peace but also tranquillity, calmness, equanimity.

58

Whoever prolongs resentments belonging to past years and chapters long left behind, himself adds to the injury he suffered. Such brooding brings on negative moods.

59

Personal feelings must be studied and analysed, not to become more neurotically self-wrapped but to correct, discipline, and lift them to a higher level.

60

The more emotional a person is the more easily is she (or he) hurt. The way to lessen such hurts is to bring up reason to the same strength and to deepen calm.

61

The more he practises keeping calm in the confrontations of worldly stress, the less difficult will it be to practise meditation. The practice not only makes it easier for intelligence to operate but also for thoughts to come under control.

62

A panicky feeling disorganizes the whole of a man, throws him into confusion. This is avoided if one cultivates inner calm constantly.

63

He cannot afford to imitate those who show a calm exterior while raging furiously within themselves. Not necessarily—nor only—for the sake of appearances or personal advantage does he remain calm, but also because the ideal of self-control is very close to his heart.

64

But although philosophy refuses to accept a wild emotionalism or an unbalanced one or an egotistic one, it would be a grave mistake to think that it refuses to accept emotion altogether in its own sphere. On the contrary, it asserts that without the intensest possible feeling, a genuine devotion to the Overself cannot be given. And without such devotion, the Overself in turn is unlikely to give its Grace. What philosophy does ask, however, is that emotion should be balanced, purified, and deepened.

65

Pessimism will corrode our better nature, optimism may disillusion itself in the end. The middle way is the better way—and also the truer way—for it gives both sides of the case.

66

It is not only in practical life that emotional control will be needed but also in mystical life. The very intensity of his emotions—however noble and aspiring they be—will confuse the reception of the truth during meditation and mingle it with the meditator's own preconceptions.

67

We believe first and think out our belief afterward. This is because emotion rather than reason is our driving force. Reason actuates us from a deeper level and is therefore slower to arouse and harder to keep going than feeling.

68

The Stoics in old Europe tried to put the emotions under the absolute control of reason. The Buddhist yogis in old India tried to do exactly the same. But whereas the Stoics did this in order to meet the everyday alternations of fate, health, and fortune with great courage, the yogis did it in order to escape from those alternations. The Stoics were practical men who accepted the world but sought to conquer it through the power gained by conquering themselves. The yogis rejected the world and, like the desert monks of early Christianity, wanted to be done with its struggles and afflictions.

69

If he sulkily takes constructive, well-intentioned criticism as if it were a personal insult, if his emotional self falls discouraged into a slough of despond at the smallest discovery of his own faults and weaknesses, then he is likely not ready for this quest. Some self-preparation is first needed.

70

Merely to recollect that he is on the quest should soften his angers, if not quickly subdue them.

71

They should deliberately face whatever it is they fear. When they become frightened, they should not seek escape, but, in times of meditation and prayer, should turn full attention on its cause. Then, they should call upon latent resources and if the call is made in the right way, the response will appear in their conscious will. Thus equipped, they will be capable of compelling fears to subside and, in time, of overcoming them.

72

This inner quiescence, this emotional calm, this being at peace with oneself, this refusal to be upset or feel hurt, is one of those conditions which make possible the discovery of the true being.

73

The truth crushes all the falseness and all the deceptiveness in sentimentality and emotionality, but leaves intact what is sound in them. The ego eagerly wants to nourish itself with these pitiful illusions, therefore.

74

It is even helpful in certain cases to put the physical body under the strain of hard manual labour, or hard physical exercise for some weeks. This counterbalances the mental tension.

75

To eradicate anger he should cultivate its opposite—forgiveness.

76

According to ethics of the hidden teaching, hatred and anger are twin branches on the same tree.

77

How far is the moral distance from Buddha's purity to the modern pseudo-Zen plausibly concealed laxness! How immense the distance from self-mastered Founder to self-indulgent follower! The often used word "freedom" is conveniently misunderstood, its true meaning twisted to suit their sensual appetites.

78

Conduct is a deliberate, consciously purposeful, and willed activity whereas behaviour is general, casual, and not specifically directed.

79

Security of earthly possessions is hard to find and harder to keep in the quick-changing world of today. So anxieties and worries get multiplied. Because of this, inner security, the close friend of inner peace, becomes proportionately more valuable. If it is to be attained, the first practical requirement is to train oneself in the art of keeping emotionally and mentally calm.

80

This deliberate practice of calmness is a preparation for the deeper state of Mental Quiet, which comes by itself when meditation is sufficiently advanced. It is effort consciously and quickly made to keep a hold on passions and emotions so that the work of getting nearer the realization of ideals is not hindered.

81

Whether, or how much, philosophy removes fear must depend on either his capacity to withdraw part of awareness from the body or on a higher level to remain unmoved in the non-dual identity. Most people are captive, in different degrees, to some kind of fear. It may be caused by their surroundings, by their religious upbringing, by those in authority over them, by their bodily condition, by suggestion received from others or self-made.

82

It is prudent to keep away from temptation—at least until enough positive strength has been developed to risk the test. But if development is not sought and obtained, then untempted and unproven virtue may be merely negative.

83

Many aspirants pass through fluctuating moods, because they have yet to face the battle of Reason against Emotion, and to make their emotions the servants of their thought-out principles of living.

84

If he has strong emotions naturally, his problem is to check, guide, and rule them where they are of the lower human kind. But of course, the highest and noblest emotions need not be checked, and he may safely give himself up to them. He must get a better balance of temperament by disciplining his feelings, cultivating the moments of calmness which come to him, and by developing the reasoning faculty. He should also practise the exercise of constantly thinking over his past. But his thoughts should be tranquil, impersonal, self-critical, and he should be eager to learn the lessons to be gained from this practice. Especially should he look for the mistakes made, the faults displayed, and—by studying the results to which they led—try to get rid of these weaknesses of character.

85

There is nothing wrong with the human desire for affection, companionship, and marriage. But he who has embarked on the spiritual path should remember that more is expected from him than from ordinary people. He is expected to have a definite measure of control over his emotions and impulses and must not be carried off his feet into extremes where he loses balance. It is not possible to make good progress on the spiritual path unless some triumph over the impulsive nature is secured.

86

Evenness of temper is a valuable possession where it comes from self-mastery and not from a low vitality physically.

87

When you feel these fits of depression and despondency coming on, you must learn to stand aside from them and refuse to identify yourself with the emotions which express them. They are simply other forms of ego manifestation. With time and practice, you *will* be able to do this. The Short Path affirmations and meditations are essential at such a time, for they help you to acquire the detachment necessary to recognize the moods for what they are.

One student asked: "But how can one identify oneself with something one doesn't know?" Another one replied: "That is where faith in something beyond the intellect comes in!" P.B. said: "Yes, if that faith is intense enough it will be sufficient to lead to the desired result. If not, if one cannot have faith in the Overself, then a Teacher is necessary. It is through faith in the Teacher that the student is helped to knowledge of the Overself which he finds so difficult to reach by himself."

In this matter of sadness and depression, one should also be careful not to take on the moods of others. Sometimes, people who are sensitive do this. If extra-sensitive, they can even take on for a short time the symptoms of their ailments.

88

When critical moments arrive in a man's life his best recourse is first to calm not to panic, second to remember and turn towards the Overself. In that way he does not depend on his own small resources alone, but opens himself to the larger ones hidden in his subconscious.

89

So long as anyone lives in a state of uncontrolled emotion, and especially of ungoverned desire, so long does he remain unready for entry into the higher consciousness. For he is unable to bring his mind into that unruffled balanced state which is necessary to reflect like a mirror the truth and peace of that consciousness.

90

When anyone is carried away by an emotion, in most cases it happens before he knows it. This is why some sort of training in self-awareness, self-observation, and self-control becomes a requisite. All of these can be practised during the day at odd times more easily and effectively if the day itself is reviewed at night.

91

The emotional agitations will certainly come to an end when he finds his real inner peace, for he cannot have the two together. To have the peace he has to give up the agitations.

92

There will be no relief from this continual oscillation between opposite moods until he reaches the sixth degree.

93

His capacity to recover quickly from, and react positively to, the unexpected shocks of life will be one of the benefits of this cultivation of calmness.

94

When uncontrolled, emotion may be very destructive to oneself and to others, but controlled it becomes constructive and beneficial to all.

95

If they uselessly seek to achieve moral perfection, they may hopefully seek to achieve inner peace.

96

The man who holds to this discipline of the emotions will not be easily embarrassed when friends desert him or enemies attack him. Where the hands of another man may tremble, his heart bleed, and his eyes fill with tears, the philosopher will know peace.

97

The impressions which other persons make on him are to be separated from the emotional and personal feelings they arouse in him. How else is he to know the truth about them?

98

The practice of calmness frees a man from the fretful, nervous tension so many carry around with them; he brings a pleasant air of repose with him.

99

This coolness where other men might see them with passion or emotion, this detachment from events and persons, things and places, is exacerbating to those who misunderstand it.

100

Why was it required of candidates for entry into the Pythagorean School of Wisdom that they be of a "contented disposition"? Why does the ancient Hindu Scripture *Svetasvatara Upanishad* forbid the teaching of the deepest knowledge to one "who is not tranquil in the mind"?

101

The practice of calmness means that no emotions are squandered, no negative thoughts entertained.

102

Walter Hilton, the medieval English religious mystic, remarked on the fact that the advanced Christian is no longer bubbling with religious devotion or weeping with religious fear, since emotional feelings are subject to changes, hence unstable, for he "is now wholly at peace, and there is little outward indication of fervour."

103

The pathological resentment in their hearts contributes toward the ideological resistance in their heads to truth.

104

He who values inner peace will resist being swept away by strong negative emotions, will try to keep in command when the pressure of fear, anxiety, wrath, or hate threatens this peace.

105

As we win control of our feelings they become less a source of negative thoughts and more of upholding ones.

106

We use the term "emotionalist" in the same derogatory sense that we use "intellectualist."

107

Only an unflinching devotion to truth and an unyielding exercise of reason can see through these insincerities of sentimentality.

108

Intelligent generosity is philosophical. Sentimental generosity is not.

109

So long as he mistakes his own longings for actualities, so long will disappointment wait for him in the end.

110

If we let it stay in the mind long enough and feed it often enough, a worry can easily become an obsession.

111

Baruch Spinoza wrote in his *Ethics*: "Human power in controlling the emotions consists solely in the Understanding, it follows that no one rejoices in blessedness because he has controlled his lusts, but contrariwise his power of controlling his lusts arises from this blessedness itself."

112

The passage from jealousy to hatred is not a long one.

113

The negative, discordant, and disruptive emotions require treatment by psychological means just as much as the physical body may require treatment by medical, surgical, herbal, naturopathic, magnetic, or manipulative means.

114

The first step is to deny every form of outward expression to those emotions which are definitely harmful to his spiritual progress: to resentments, wraths, envies, and hates.

115

How can he discover the truth that some of his strongest desires arise out of imagined needs if he lets them envelop him in a haze of excitement or of emotion?

116

If the value of a calm stability in our emotional life could be sufficiently known and appreciated, we would have less unhappiness, less tragedy, and less inefficiency.

117

In moments of unusual calm, he may recognize the truth of these statements, but never in moments of personal agitation, whether it be painful or pleasurable agitation.

118

He must learn to master his baser emotions and to free himself from emotional frailties which, while not objectionable in common everyday life, may weaken his capacity to comprehend the truth.

119

The free indulgence of undesirable personal emotions leads to neuroticism. Those who most need the excellent discipline of checking such emotions by the power of will and eventually extinguishing them by the activity of reason, are unfortunately those who are least ready to submit to it.

120

He may put each irritating situation of his life in a truer perspective if he asks himself whether when dying he would like to remember that he had reacted to it in a negative way when he could have reacted positively.

121

Since a kind of order reigned in Nature, argued Confucius, it should be made by men to reign among themselves. They ought to live in an orderly manner and thus they could live in civilized harmony. This requires them to control emotions and not allow themselves to be swept hither and thither.

122

The individual who is touchy and irritable should beware lest his traits flare up into open anger, still more lest anger grow by degrees into intense hate and aggressive spite.

123

These neurotics seeking comfort, who invade mysticism to its detriment, display their self-willed, petty egotisms by resenting the discipline of their emotions, and thus contribute to their own further suffering.

124

The man who is constantly petulant and consistently pessimistic obstructs the inflow of higher forces.

125

Sentimentality may enfeeble a person and mislead his impulses.

126

To keep emotion under control is one thing; to keep it altogether out is another. It is well to be cautious about how we feel, but not to be so overcautious that the day comes when we can no longer feel at all.

127

The emotional moods between which so many undisciplined men and women oscillate, with black despair at one end of the scale and golden joy at the other, belong to the ego.

128

It is not enough to create these new ways of thinking. They must be supported by emotional steadiness if they are to be maintained and not lost again. Emotional enthusiasm is not enough.

129

Diderot took this view, too, and asserted in *The Paradox of the Actor* that a good actor is inwardly calm and self-possessed even in the most passionate moments of his roles.

130

He finds that this serenity can be kept only if he drops many previously held superstitions, such as that it is necessary to be liked by everyone he meets everywhere.

131

If he starts with wildly unbalanced over-appreciation, glorifying and magnifying only its good points, he will probably end embittered in inevitable disillusion. But if this is pointed out to him, he is affronted.

132

Two men may be blood-brothers and yet greedily fight each other where property inheritance is at stake; two other men may be close friends and yet treacherously betray each other where a woman's love is at stake. Where personal desires or ambitions are at stake in the conventional world, such insincerities are always possible.

133

When the response to these teachings is merely emotionalist then it is also mostly untrustworthy.

134

He who follows such a regime finds he is more and more the master of himself, better and better able to subdue passions.

135

Don Quixote found his frightening giants were only windmills after all. So exaggerated are many of our fears.

136

To look only for pleasant effects upon the ego's feelings, whether it be our own or other people's, is a mistake.

137

Emotion is expert at inventing reasons for its aversions and dislikes.

138

One of the very important tasks of the Quest is to bring the emotional nature and the passional nature under control. If this is not done, it is certain that the man will be so affected by the various persons, so changed by the various environments he meets with as the days move forward, that he will not be able to achieve that serene poise which is the Quest's goal, nor depend on what he will be like tomorrow. That is, he will not be able to depend upon himself.

139

There are feelings which should be distrusted. There are reasonings which should be discarded. Only when the philosophic discipline has purified the heart and tranquillized the head can we safely rely on ourselves for judgement.

140

Most people are, in fact, very far from the stage where they can sagely trust their emotions or indiscriminately yield to their instincts.

141

Is it not better to take counsel of reason than to yield to the ardour of impulse, the throb of emotion, or the stir of passion? For if these are leading in a right direction, they lose nothing but, on the contrary, get confirmed by being reasoned out.

142

If one has to meet other persons who tend to put one into a condition of unease, then the most practical wisdom is to have as little personal contact with them as possible.

143

Emotions must be held within bounds. Intuition and intelligence must set those bounds. Otherwise imbalance, fanaticism, narrow-mindedness will thrive like weeds in the human heart.

144

Young James Dean, brilliant cinema-acting genius, was not protected by the golden Saint Christopher medal, given him by Pier Angeli, which was found close to his battered and broken body at the scene of the auto accident which ended his short life. This tragic result was directly caused by his own reckless temperament; it was the bitter fruit of a defect in his own character. No religious medal could avert the result itself; only a modification of temperament, a correction of weaknesses, could have done so. To believe otherwise is to believe in superstition.

145

Incompatibility is inevitable, but not unconquerable.

146

Our private emotions need not less control than our public behaviour.

147

The aim of the self-denial and self-discipline is to bring the aspirant through the period of emotional adolescence into the healthy state of emotional maturity.

Self-restraint

148

No aspirant is asked to remain emotionally neutral regarding his personal hopes and fears. He is asked to strive for impartiality in his decisions, to recognize that it is wrong action which secures his own enjoyment at the cost of other people's suffering or his own gain at the cost of their rights.

149

He is to try at all times to see directly into his own personal situation without being misled by emotions, blinded by passions, or confused by suggestions; that is, he is to see it just as it really is. This practice is intended to help disentangle him from his ego.

150

The same human characteristic of emotion which enslaves and even harms him when it is attached to earthly things alone, exalts and liberates him when it is disciplined and purified by philosophy.(P)

151

Just as inordinate fear evoked by sudden catastrophe could drive someone quite insane, so calm resignation evoked by sudden bereavement could bring a glimpse of full spiritual sanity.

152

He who keeps a silent tongue in his head when the air is filled with anger is on the way to holding down his own wrath. But he who keeps a silent mind will conquer it more quickly and easily.

153

There is the caution which comes from timidity and the caution which comes from experience. They are not the same.

154

He must keep a part of himself in such reserve that no event and no person can ever touch it.

155

In the case of an ordinary man, the emotional reaction to a situation is all he is conscious of during the situation itself. The intellectual or intuitional judgement of it comes some time afterwards, if it comes at all. But in the disciple's case, his self-training should be directed toward a side-by-side working of the two at one and the same time.

156

The silent, taciturn, reserved man makes fewer friends but guards his present and future better. To be cautious in speech and writing today—whether private or public—is to save trouble tomorrow. A single indiscretion may mar a lifetime's honourable reputation.

157

The same act which is wrong when done in anger and on impulse may become right when done in calmness, after due reflection. Such an act might be, for instance, the protection of other persons against an unjust invasion of their rights or a violent aggression against their bodies.

158

At a certain stage of one's evolutionary development, personal emotions form the greatest obstacle of all. It is extremely difficult and painful to stand aside from one's emotional nature at a time when it wants most to be insistent—but that is the very time the quickest progress can be made, if he does.

159

One should try, so far as possible, to avoid anxiety about his problems, whether they are of a worldly or spiritual nature. It is necessary to develop a calm, hopeful attitude toward the future.

160

Anything that may be written or thought at a time when one is plunged in pain or grief must be evaluated again after enough time has elapsed to allow the upheaval of emotions to subside, lessening the hurt. Only then can a calm, philosophical appraisal of the entire situation be satisfactorily achieved.

161

Inner strength of a remarkable nature can be shown in the manner in which one responds to disappointment. One could so easily become wildly hysterical at the breakdown of his hopes. We are forced into admiration for the way in which another may take the breakdown of his dreams.

162

Nothing should ever be done in a great hurry or in a sudden outburst of enthusiasm. He should sleep on his decisions and discuss them with older people who have themselves demonstrated by their own success that their judgements are worthwhile.

163

In one's relationship with others, the emotions involved in carrying out a duty tend to confuse the duty itself with unnecessary matters.

164

The emotional hurts which meant so much and felt so deep when he was spiritually juvenile, will come to signify less and less as he becomes spiritually adult. For he sees increasingly that they made him unhappy only because he himself allowed them to do so, only because, from two possible attitudes, he himself chose the little ego's with its negative and petty emotionalism as against the higher mind's positive and universal rationality.

165

There will be times when he, who built on philosophic coolness through the years, who thought himself proof against tears, will yield to them all too readily and all too helplessly.

166

He should keep a cool, philosophical perspective even when everyone else seethes with violent emotion and bitter prejudice. He should preserve his independence even when everyone else submerges his own in a fashionable party or a popular group.

167

Whilst utterly and apologetically patient with other people's pitiful or romantic illusions, he should firmly and austerely have none of his own. His needs are too high, too distant from those of fools and weak beings, to be satisfied with anything less hard than reality itself.

168

Small minds are the victims of every trying situation because they are the victims of every immediate reaction to it. The student of philosophy, with his metaphysical powers and personal self-discipline, is not. He looks many years ahead of it and much more deeply into it. He does not blindly accept the first feelings about it that arise within himself or are suggested to him by others.

169

The need is to live according to principles, not according to impulses.

170

Men who seek a higher kind of life must practise self-restraint whatever faith they hold or to whatever religious society they belong.

171

Those who demand the freedom to live as they wish, who seek to be undisciplined and unregulated by any authority, ask too much.

172

No one can avoid sometimes reacting badly to outer experiences or circumstances, but the aspirant should not react without trying to practise self-control.

Matured emotion

173

With regard to the emotions, the path is a crucifixion of the personal ego. The aspirant's heart must be searched and searched until it is free from all reservations and utterly surrendered to the higher self. It is impossible to pass through such a process without undergoing the terrible ordeal of crushing some feelings and surrendering others. The adept is indeed the man who has triumphed over his emotions, but it would be an indefensible and inexcusable error to think he lives in a complete emotional vacuum, that he is a man without feeling or sensibilities of any kind. Bulwer Lytton has pictured for us in his brilliant novel *Zanoni* a character of this type, the Rosicrucian adept Mejnour. This picture is close to reality in certain respects but it is far from reality in other respects. Let us not make the mistake of believing that the adept does not know the meaning of the words affection, sympathy, compassion, joy, enthusiasm, and even ecstasy. He does, but he knows them all within the higher self, which rules them. The only emotions he does not know are those lower ones, such as anger, resentment, hatred, prejudice, bitterness, lust, pride, and intolerance. Yes!—the philosophical life does not lack emotional content but it is not the kind of narrow, selfish, vacillating emotion so many human beings are accustomed to.

174

If a man is to attain a durable peace, he must commit emotional suicide. But does this mean he is to become utterly devoid of all feeling? Not at all. It is only the lower emotions that have to be liquidated. Yet it is these which play so large a role in human life today, whether in their grossest form of hatred or their most refined form of romantic nonsense miscalled love.

175

The frenzies of passion let loose, the manias of the lower emotions run wild are never again to be known to him. This high standard is the goal. It may seem unattainable to a human entity, yet history and biography prove that it is not.

176

It might be thought that the philosophic discipline seeks to eliminate emotion. The truth is that it seeks to maturate emotion. The disciple's feelings—no less than his thoughts—must grow up and assume their philosophic responsibilities.

177

It will be easy for critics to misunderstand the statement that he is to become intellectually feverless and emotionally passionless. We do not mean that he is to be deprived of all feeling, bereft of all enthusiasm, incapable of all affection. We mean that he is to seek an inward serenity which no feeling, no enthusiasm, and no affection can distract.

178

The adept who attains perfect inner serenity can do so only by paying the price of forgoing the emotional agitations, attractions, and repulsions which constitute much of the inner life of most people. Having attained it himself, he can lead others to it only by pointing towards it as a reachable goal for them, too. He may not yield to personal favouritism or egotistic caprice based on likes and dislikes in selecting those whom he is to help. Indeed, because of this it is said that he is more interested in mankind collectively rather than as individuals. Now if he had to commit emotional suicide to reach his present height, it is unreasonable to expect that he should flatter or encourage those who, although seeking the same height, seek also to preserve or nourish their egoistic emotions. The latter are nearly always closely linked to egoistic desires. An inward detachment from all eagerness for earthly life is the grim price that must be paid before entry into the kingdom of heaven can be got. Such detachment requires soft sentimentality to yield to hard recognition of the impersonal realities of the human situation. And this recognition must assuredly lead the seeker far away from conventional points of view concerning his personal duties, his family relations, and his social behavior.

179

It is not that he will not feel desires and aversions, attractions and repulsions, but that he will not be moved by them. They will be under control, not only of the ego but of a power higher than the ego. Thus the tensions which agitate the uncontrolled man and stresses which animate him, will not be present.

180

It is an error to regard him as inhuman, as lacking in feeling. What he rejects is negative feeling: what he seeks to overcome is animal wrath, lust, hatred; what he affirms is positive feeling of the best kind—delicate, sensitive, aesthetic, compassionate, and refined. Thus his stoic imperturbability is not *rigor mortis*.

181

To talk of his condition as simply being one of controlled emotion is not quite correct; much rather is it one of balanced emotion—which is markedly different.

182

The idea of a philosopher being an utterly aloof person, coldly indifferent and quite unapproachable, a man who restricts his human feelings to the degree that hardly any are left, is applicable only to those who follow narrow, rigid, and incomplete systems.

183

The notion that a philosopher is melancholy is arguable: there is no reason why he should not show joy and appreciate humour. But since he is a balanced person, he will put the governor of deep seriousness to control these qualities.

184

If a human price has to be paid for such emotionless behaviour let us remember that it must also be paid for too emotional behaviour.

185

A portentous gravity is not at all a hallmark of the sage.

186

Is mental tranquillity indistinguishable from emotional death? Is it not better to guide feelings, educate desires, and uplift emotions into the proper channels than to kill them? Such questions show a confused comprehension of the philosophic discipline. The latter's aim is not to produce an insensible human stone but a true human being.

4

PURIFY PASSIONS

The same power which, when misgoverned, drags men down into materialism, also lifts them into spiritual awareness when directed upward.

2

Where all a man's acts are merely the reflex behaviour dictated by his sense-impressions, he has hardly any life higher than an animal one. It is the business of this quest to insert the influence of consciousness of the causes and results of his actions, reason, and will into such behaviour.

3

There are certain indestructible truths which reveal themselves through the ages to every man who, for a time at least, sufficiently masters his animal self and sufficiently quietens his human self. Those which we most need to learn today are simple and ancient, yet completely relevant to the modern scene and completely adequate to the modern need.

4

It is everywhere the state today that most people are automatons, merely reacting to the outward world of the five senses in a mechanical manner. They do not really control what is happening to them but merely drift with the forces playing through the sense-stimuli. The consequence is that they do not actually possess or use the power of free will. They are puppets on Nature's stage.

5

When any emotion takes full possession and reaches an extreme stage, it becomes a passion.

6

One does not easily discard the various passions. The decision to do so does not lead, or even contribute much, to their conquest. It merely announces the beginning of a long war. They return, in spite of one's wishes, again and again for they belong to the animal body which, itself, cannot be discarded. But in the end a man must claim his birthright to a higher kind of life, must fulfil his nobler possibilities, must set up reason and intuition as his most reliable guides.

7

If your thoughts are energized by a noble passion and your deeds inspired by a lofty enthusiasm, they are the better for it. But if your thoughts are distorted by a foolish passion and your deeds wasted by a misdirected enthusiasm, they are the worse for it.

8

The same ambition which stretched his mind and capacity for money-making or power-hunting can, when transformed into aspiration, stretch them for truth-seeking and character building.

9

It is not even that he has to give up all desires but that he has to purify them and put them all under the dominance of his one supreme desire for attainment—which may or may not mean their extinction.

10

Man's true intelligence is feeble while it remains imprisoned in egoism and narcotized by sensuality. He must liberate it by the philosophic discipline before it can become strong.

11

So many of our feelings and so many of our thoughts have until now been dictated by the body. Is it not time to think and feel also as the true self would have us do?

12

The animal heritage has given him instincts, appetites, impulses, and desires; the human holds out higher possibilities to be worked for and realized.

13

One message of the Sphinx is to *balance* the human mind with the brutish animal in us. This is not the same as the ascetics' message, which is to exterminate the animal altogether.

14

He who has not overcome his passions finds himself compelled to act against the clearest warnings of his reason.

15

What really moves a man to act is his feeling; this is why the passions, which are strong feelings, need more deliberate effort of the will to bring them under restraint.

16

An action which is spontaneous and not a calculated one—that can be safe only for the enlightened man. For others it may be mere impulse or mere passion.

17

The point is not that natural impulses of the body are wrong—how could that be?—but that men have made them wrong. Originally the satisfaction of the pleasure-instinct was in harmony with higher will as a lesser part of a greater function. But now human will has reversed its role and exaggerated it to first place. The result is disharmony and disease.

18

On one thing all men in all lands are agreed, that it is immeasurably more preferable to be released from anxieties than to suffer them. Yet, these same men throw themselves into situations or bring about events which will rivet the chains of anxiety upon them. How is it that such a contradiction exists everywhere? What causes them to do this? It is the strength of their desires, the power of their ambitions, the tendencies inherited from past births. This being the cause of the trouble, the remedy for it becomes plain. The more a man frees himself from desires, that is, the more he masters himself, the more is he freed from numerous anxieties. And even if he too is subject to the painful tests and unpleasant ordeals which inescapably affect human existences, he does not consider them to be misfortunes but as devices to draw out his latent qualities.

19

The way out from tyrannical desires may have to be staged. First become a witness—indifferent and dispassionate—every time there is a surrender. This way is taking a new direction, starting to disidentify from the desire.

20

On the one hand he must tear himself away from his earthly passions. On the other hand he must give himself up to his sacred aspirations.

21

The eagerness of desire betrays him into romantic self-deceptions and leads him into wounding frustrations. The ego lures his hopes constantly onward only to lacerate them in the end.

22

Whilst we are still limited by the body and its inescapable needs, it is an impossible task to extirpate desire and negative self-interest. Philosophy adds that it is also an undesirable one. Only, put desire and self-interest down in their proper place, it says, do not permit them to obstruct higher and spiritual needs.

23

It is not that they have to abandon joy but to purify it. If the joy which comes from debased pleasures is thereby lost, the joy which comes from ennobled thoughts and refined feelings is gained.

24

When earthly desires are extinguished, calm befalls a man.

25

He must needs declare open war on his own passions, for he now sees that he cannot have them and peace too. Like all war this one will witness both victories and defeats, hardships and sufferings. But out of these battles with himself he may progress, learning discrimination and gaining willpower.

26

He realizes that he has to break his passions or, if uncontrolled, they will break him.

27

In this work of purification the need of moral intellectual and emotional honesty will have to be stressed. It is satisfied by discriminating examination of thoughts, feelings, and motives, with constant self-distrust as a guide in the work.

28

The more he trains himself to recognize and reject the impulses that come from his lower nature, the more will clarity of comprehension become his.

29

The animal that he is must be kept at bay; his freedom as a man must be gained by degrees.

30

It is true that thought precedes action, that actions express thoughts, and that to rule mind is to rule the entire life. But it is also true that man's battles with himself proceed by progressive stages, that he exerts will more easily than he changes feeling. Therefore, the discipline of inward thinking should follow after—and not before—it. To counsel him to take care of his inner life and that then the outer life will take care of itself, as so many mystics do, is to be plausible but also to show a lack of practicality. Man's heart will feel no peace as his mind will know no poise until he abandons the lower instincts and gives himself up to this unearthly call. First, he must abandon them outwardly in deeds; later he must do it inwardly even in thoughts. This will inevitably bring him into inner struggle, into oscillation between victories and defeats, elations and despairs. The way up is long, hard, rugged, and slow to tread. It is always a stage for complaints and outcries, battles and falls. Only time—the master power—can bring him to its lofty end. Only when the lessons of birth after birth etch themselves deeply and unmistakably into his conscious mind through dreadful repetition can he accept them co-operatively, resignedly, and thus put a stop to the needless sufferings of desire, passion, and attachment.(P)

31

When a man's desires and yearnings, thirsts and longings are so strong as to upset his reasoning power and block his intuitive capacity, he is stopped from finding truth. In this condition he shuts his eyes to those facts which are displeasing or which are contrary to his desires and opens them only to those which are pleasing or agreeable to his wishes. Thinking bends easily to desires, so that the satisfaction of personal interest rather than the quest of universal truth becomes its real object.(P)

32

Reforms that begin with the lowest in man lead the way to the highest in him. The mastery of animal passion opens the door to the birth of spiritual intuition.

33

Whether the cage be made of gold or the net fabricated from silk, the reality of their inner captivity still remains.

34

A discipline which is not stern but gentle and easy is best suited to modern man.

35

The faculty of will is immeasurably more important to the progress of the inner life than that of intellect. For the passions and appetites of the body are controlled by will; the strength of the lower nature is at the service of the ego's will rather than of its intellect.

36

He is called on, in his higher life, to transmute the animal calls of his nature to what—however dimly he sees it—is really the god within him.

37

It is unpleasant to break away from long-lived habits, and this is true both in our mental and our physical life. Yet in times of crisis such as severe illness and breakdown, people do do that because they have to. How much better to do it not violently and abruptly—under outward compulsions—but to do it little by little, gently and easily, taking our time by doing it through application of wisdom.

38

When control is so perfect that he can never again raise his voice in anger, he need turn attention to only one other passion—the sexual.

39

Such a chaste aloofness from the lower desires may be reached only in part by their firm repression. If it is to be reached in full, there must be even more an ardent pursuit of the highest desire—for the Soul.

40

The Taoist masters did not make, as the Buddhist and Hindu masters made, complete freedom from desire an essential prerequisite. They were satisfied to ask for "fewness of desires" only.

41

When desires die without regrets, he begins to taste real peace. When cravings slough off naturally, like a serpent's skin, he finds tranquil happiness.

42

The man who can win his way to freedom from anger and finally liberate the mind from passion may need much of his lifetime, if not all of it, for the work; but what he gains is of inestimable value. For this brings him closer to awareness of the Overself.

43

As aspiration for the Overself grows stronger, other desires grow weaker.

44

You must possess an insatiable longing for light if you are ever to emerge from the darkness.

45

He arrives at purity by a cultivated discipline of the mind rather than by a forcible atrophy of the senses.

46

The thread-like intuition which will lead him out of animality into serenity will be his best guide if he can find it and heed it.

47

It is not possible for these finer elements to become, little by little, paramount in his outlook, consciousness, and conduct without a corresponding decline in the coarser ones. He will gradually become the ruler of his physical appetites and then master of his bodily desires. Indeed, as all his longings for the Overself slowly gather themselves together into a great dedicated life, there is an equally great shift-over from the animal part of his being to the truly human, allied with an opening-up of the angelic or divine part.

48

The fruits of sexual extravagances, the harvest of sexual promiscuity, the gleanings of sexual irresponsibility, and the gratifications of sexual license must be subjected to the hard discipline of reason. Those who will not do so must sooner or later pay the price in fears, anxieties, irritations, regrets, disillusionments, shames, and despairs.

49

So long as a man identifies himself with the physical body, so long will he perforce have to identify himself with its desires and passions. Only when he transfers this self-identification to the infinite mental being can he completely detach himself from them.

50

Of what use is it for men to talk of freeing themselves from subjection to egoism when they are still in subjection to passion?

51

The student of philosophy will try to comprehend the sensations got from sensual pleasures impartially and impersonally. Man knows instinctively what will give him momentary emotional satisfaction; he must wrestle with reason to know what will give him deep enduring happiness. Reason must arbitrate when different pleasures compete for suffrage or when duty competes with desire. Desire carried to an undue extent becomes a passion disturbing to the equilibrium of life and character. When a man finds that despite all his efforts to improve himself and reform his character, he still remains the same, it is an indication that new methods must be tried.

52

The scourging of the flesh may be needed by, and may help, those who find their overheated passions and lusts get out of hand. But it will not end these troubles of man, even though it may tame them for a time. Something more must be added, or must replace them—first, knowledge; second, work on the process of attention.

53

The instinctual animal urge plus the ambitious drive for power and the personal desire for property keep men from spiritual aspiration.

54

If he is filled with selfish interests alone, seeking the fulfilment of personal ambitions irrespective of any higher considerations; if animal passions drive him and greed dominates him, he blocks his own way. Purification from such attachments must be the first endeavour.

55

Pleasures which corrupt character are undesirable; but those which uplift character (like the finest works of Beethoven and Handel) are desirable.

56

The reputed Oriental teachers advise—nay insist—that seekers must eliminate all desires. But is not the search itself not only an aspiration but also a desire? Can there be peace of mind while this one remains? So it is needful to put all the others in a worldly category. This is what the more semantic minded teachers do. But since the last act in this spiritual drama is played by the Higher Power, why not let it decide what to do concerning the matter?

57

There is the blindly instinctive and passioned animal will in man, which violently drives him to seek and be satisfied with bodily satisfactions. There is also a higher will which gently draws him to transcend the body altogether.

58

If the only enjoyment a man knows is that of physical sensations, he is only a dressed-up, walking, and thinking animal.

59

It is an essential part of the Quest's work to separate the man from his passions, to subjugate the animal in him so as better to cultivate the godlike in him.

60

Both desires and fears bind a man to his ego and thus bar the way to spiritual fulfilment. They could not exist except in relation to a second thing. But when he turns his mind away from all things and directs it toward its own still centre, it is the beginning of the end for all desires and all fears.

61

The end of all this long self-training to cast out personal grief and animal passion is blessedness.

62

The heart must become empty of all desires. This brings about the emotional void, which corresponds, in its own place, to the mental void experienced in the depth of *mystical* meditation. To this emptiness he must give himself, with it he must satisfy himself. In this way he obeys Jesus and becomes "poor in Spirit."

63

What is it worth to a man to be free from the passions, and free from the inner divisive conflicts which their activity must necessarily produce in him? Are they not the chief obstacles which prevent him from attaining that inner calm wherein alone the ego can be faced, caught, and conquered? And this done, what is there to keep the Overself from taking possession of him?

64

Few men are moved by a single motive. For most men the contrary is the fact. This is because first, the ego itself is a complex and second, the higher and lower natures are in conflict.

65

Discrimination is needed to penetrate the thin surface of so many pleasures, while the strength is needed to say "No" when this is wiser than accepting them.

66

It is not only needful to understand the characteristics of one's desires but also their source. This knowledge will help him to improve character and attain true self-reliance.

67

It is a strange paradox that on whatever desire a man wields the axe of non-attachment, he will thereafter become possessed of the power to attain it.

68

There is this great paradox on the Quest: that the more the disciple obtains the power to bring about the fruition of his desires, the more he loses those desires!

69

If we lack the willpower to overcome bad habits that have become popular and conventional, at least let us try not to justify our indulgence by specious reasons.

70

The blind impulses must be checked by willpower, the lower nature must be disciplined and the lower energies directed into higher channels. It is perfectly possible, where fate ordains, to live continently and chastely, however strongly sexed a man may be. But to achieve this he must utilize the analytic reason, the creative imagination, and the active will in understanding and disciplining his energies and then he must redirect them towards aspirational, intellectual, or moral ideas or transmute them into practical work.

71

He who begins by refusing to be a slave to the palate's perverted appetite will find it easier to go on to refusing to be a slave to lust. A triumph over the one prepares the way for, and helps in the achievement of, a triumph over the other.

72

It is true that we all share an animal body with the lower creatures. But that does not force us to stay on their level emotionally.

73

Every desire conquered feeds his strength and fortifies his will.

74

The man who has made his way to the top of his profession but failed to make the conquest of his passions, is still an unbalanced creature, an unsatisfied human being.

75

The extremes of abstention which follow repugnance, indifference, or self-struggle and the satiety which follows helpless yielding are both undesirable.

76

The necessities of Nature hold us in their thrall but there is first, a difference between them and the desires of the ego and second, a difference between the true necessities which are inescapable from physical existence and the false ones which have been imposed on us by age-old habits, traditions, environments, and outer suggestions.

77

That desire is a true one whose source lies in a genuine need, not in mere greed.

78

Tantra redeems man, lifts him above the lustful dog to the loving human being, distinguishes him from the mere animal.

79

The danger of tantrik yoga exists when it mistakes its own lust for spiritual direction or special privilege—which happens all too easily and all too often.

80

We are cast out of heaven by our own passions and kept out by our own attachments. If today we are miserable exiles, the way to remedy such a situation is clear. We must free ourselves from the one and disentangle ourselves from the other.

81

He should desire that which will itself cut off all desires.

82

Whoever puts a moral purpose into life automatically lifts himself above the physical level of mere animality. For him begins a struggle between the slavery of sense and the freedom of enlightenment, between blind emotion and deliberate will, between inward weakness and inward strength. Henceforth, he seeks happiness rather than pleasure, the calm of a satisfied mind rather than the excitement of satisfied senses. If this is a stoic ideal, it is a necessary one, for he must conquer himself. He hates himself, and no man can live in peace with what he hates.

83

Make sure what you really want before you go after it. The bitter experience in life is to find after years of effort that the thing you have gained is not the thing you want.

84

It is admittedly painful to tear one's will away from one's desires but it is still more painful to have it torn away by life's experiences. Hence, the philosophical method to conquer desire is a twofold one. We must let it wear itself out by submitting to it through experience and letting it come up against inevitable disappointment, disillusionment, or suffering whilst alongside this we must become reflectively and analytically aware of its causes, self-deceptions, and consequences. It is a matter of gradually letting the desires lose their intensity until we become free of them not through their forcible renunciation nor through the long-drawn process of waiting for old age to come but through the process of learning to live more and more within the satisfactory beatitude of the Overself. We give up our desires not by negating them but partly by comprehending their mechanistic cause and mentalistic nature and partly by superseding them with the exalted peace of the Overself.

85

The undeveloped mind lives only for the day. It can see the immediate events in a series but cannot conjure up the ultimate ones. The disciple dare not risk such a blind condition. He must deliberately set out to bring the two together, by the use of creative imagination or by analytic reflection or by both. If passion rises in him, at least its counterbalance, the mental picture of the evil consequences of passion, rises a second later with it.

86

If a man is not free from lust, fear, and anger, be sure he is not united with the Overself, whatever other qualities, powers, or virtues he shows.

87

Long continued reflection turned sharply and analytically upon desires and cravings helps to counter them, but does not basically weaken them. For that, contrary emotions must be aroused. This is most effectually done by happenings and experiences. But because these are mostly beyond our choice, the third way left to us is to seek Grace. One way to invite this Grace is by sitting in meditation upon the non-self.

88

He may complain of his weakness and immediately submit to a temptation. Or he may recognize that the Higher Self is also him; he may try to use will and grow in strength by this resistance.

89

He finds that he is perceptibly pulled away from fleshly lust to a deeper level where the calmness and the judgement enable him to realize that the lust belongs to his animal physical inheritance and not to his inmost character and that, therefore, it may be brought under control and discipline. If he acquires the power to achieve this, it will come imperceptibly for it will come mostly by grace.

90

The satisfaction of passion has a claim on the animal body, but it must always be subject to the higher claims of reason and intuition and the need for the sense of human responsibility.

91

The amoral is always the first step to the immoral.

92

The idea that he has to attain mastery over the desires of the flesh is a correct one. But that this mastery will lead to reunion with a "soul-mate" is not the teaching of the best mystics or philosophers. What really happens is a reunion with the true "Beloved," who is none other than the

Soul of the individual, his higher Self. This is a real living entity, whose presence is felt, whose words are heard, and whose beauty arouses all one's love.

93

Where man is open only to worldly forces and not to inner ones; where he submits to the world's demands and ignores the soul's; and where he submits to his own animal forces without thought of regulating, controlling, and disciplining them, we may expect to find that he is quite insensitive to any teaching of this kind. He is like a person who has been caught in a mire and with every movement gets deeper into it.

94

He will learn the pleasures of self-control. It is not always easy but all effort for the rewards bears fruit. The man who can develop emotional placidity and rise above passions begins to know what peace of mind means. That is only a beginning for in its fullness it can come only with the knowledge and the enlightenment of Truth. Until then this placidity will free him from the constant alternation, the rise and fall of feeling, the elation and depression to which the average person is subject.

95

Whether it be to acquire fame or accumulate wealth or any of the other major desires, what he wants from life will in the end rest on his stage of spiritual evolution.

96

The animal in man is there, but it must be brought under control or it will claim too much and diminish his aspirations. Then they become fitful, coming less and less, departing more and more. At an interview he gave a man, the Buddha warned against the passions—their futility, danger, and defilements.

97

Self-conquest must be his secret wish; deliverance must become his impassioned yearning.

98

When wholetime meditations and his sparetime thoughts are unremittingly given to uprooting passions that hinder spiritual progress and cultivating ideas that promote it, the neophyte will not be left without reward.

99

Restricted by no monastery's vows and obeying no order's rules, he may yet be purer in thought and conduct than most of the monks.

100

The animality of our inheritance will then be kept in its proper place, subjugated, its strength absorbed into his higher will.

101

Passion conquers the young man in the end and forces him into an affair, a relationship, or a marriage. But he who withstands its drive, and conquers passion itself, is a hero.

102

A blind obedience to the urges of physical sense-satisfaction, indifferent to the restraints of ideals, reason, knowledge, or intuitive feeling, weakens concentration and meditation, but strengthens the lower nature.

103

The unruled passions are responsible for a substantial part of the difficulty in summoning up enough aspiration to make men do what they ought, and enough penetration to clear the mind of its illusions.

104

Those with some mental development wisely add tomorrow to today, consequences to causes, and thus finish the picture. Others are ruled by the moment's impulse or the day's trend or by passion rather than reason.

105

It is supposed to go so far that even such a lofty desire as one for desirelessness itself can no longer remain acceptable.

106

He may feel the temptation but he need not submit to it.

107

It is the emotion, still more the passion, which anyone pours into an attachment which may make it an obstacle on his quest.

108

Men who are driven by strong ambitions will have little energy left for strong aspirations.

109

In the Sphinx sits the symbol of that enterprise which offers the candidate for initiation his greatest reward but which paradoxically brings his greatest suffering. This is the conquest of passion by reason and will and the overcoming of personal emotion by impersonal intuition.

110

The Sphinx is a perfect image of the adept in whom the man controls the animal. The attainment is a rare one—too many are satisfied to remain hardly more than animal, with a few human traits.

111

If he cannot put the objects of his desires completely outside his heart, then he must do the next best thing and put them on its borders.

112

The *Bhagavad Gita* teaches that thought creates attachment, and this in turn leads to desire.

113

When a man, with his impulses and passions, meets life with its paradoxes and illusions, he soon falls victim to the deceit of appearances.

114

If the passions dry up, is there any real loss? Are anger, hate, and lust worthy expressions of a being whose spiritual possibilities are so wonderful as man's?

115

The man who has learnt in some way—whether by personal experience or by a wise old man's instruction or through an inspired book—that excessive ambition may be folly, excessive luxury has no end to the labour of collecting it, knows that the monks who are content to live barely and simply may not be fools after all. But it is also possible for another man who has cultivated an inner detachment to have the same feelings and nevertheless seek to enjoy life.

116

To feel free at last of nagging desires and frustrating attachments brings a large measure of contentment.

117

What is the use of studying philosophy unless we are to become wiser in the future and unless we use its lessons to discipline the impulses and dominate the senses?

118

The white lotus lives in the black mud. It is both an example and an inspiration to man.

119

There is danger in a view of life which makes men unable to be satisfied with a simpler life and which stimulates their desires endlessly.

120

Even if it is beyond his power to kill these passions without Grace, it is within his power to curb them.

121

We get muddled and worried by problems which have been manufactured for us by our own desires, instincts, and passions. The need of disciplining them is evident.

122

If the energy used in the pursuit of ambitions or pleasures could be diverted to the following of aspirations, if he had the strength to remove everything else from his life except the quest, how could he fail?

123

He may discover that the battle is not really over, that atavisms of the old animalistic life, rooted either in the present or in former births may come pouring over the threshold of the conscious ego.

124

When the intellect is enslaved by desires, by greeds, by ignorance, it readily finds several defenses against the call of the Quest. When it has become a little freer and listened to the call, it just as readily finds defenses against making any practical application of what it has learnt.

125

If your passion is transferred from a passing object or human body to the more durable and beautiful soul, you will be progressing from a lower to a higher plane.

126

Many complain about being troubled by sensual desires. They ask a prescription to cure this trouble. One was given by the Buddha in *Dhammapada*. Here it is: "As when a house roof is not properly secured, then the rain finds a way through it and drops within, so when the thoughts are not carefully controlled the desires [sex] will soon bore through all our good resolutions. But as when a roof is well stopped when the water cannot leak through, so by controlling one's thoughts and acting with reflection, no such desires can arise or disturb us."

127

How few of the images which fill his mind come from his higher self, how many from his animal self!

128

It is not enough to refrain from sensual acts. It is no less needful to refrain from sensual thoughts.

129

As this diviner self displaces the earthly one in his will, heart, and mind, it is natural that what he hitherto felt as temptation will be felt as such less and less. On the philosophic path he will attain to this without immuring himself in any cloister, but rather in the very midst of worldly activity.

130

These acts of self-denial, these austerities, are to be valued not for their own sakes but for the sake of the purification of the soul.

131

They can take to a simpler life. It does not demand a bare and spartan existence. It means only that they can eliminate useless luxuries and excessive pleasures, stop buying what they need not buy and keep money they cannot afford to spend. By living a simpler life, by becoming more frugal and less spendthrift, they can cut down their wants, diminish their desires, lessen discontent, and perhaps even become happier. It will be easier to call their soul their own.

132

We live on different layers of desire from the beastly to the angelic.

133

When lust is merely submerged and not supplanted, it will sooner or later reassert itself.

134

Lust is an extreme intoxication of the bodily senses, a fire of carnal passion which submerges reason, and an enslavement of desire which tyrannizes over countless victims.

135

A wiser course than total suppression is to limit desires and govern passions.

136

"We are conscious of an animal in us," exclaimed Thoreau, and then cried out, "If I knew so wise a man as could teach me purity, I would go to seek him forthwith."

137

When the pursuit of pleasure, and especially physical pleasure, becomes excessive, it becomes a vice.

138

Where is his mind's peace when he is racked by desires, irritated by frustrations, and denied even the compensation of knowing *why* he is suffering?

139

Instinct fights with intellect but purified, elevated, and instructed, it can harmonize with the other, both working together for the benefit of man.

140

The irony of this picture of men rejecting their freedom and preferring their chains would be unbelievable, did we not know how gilded those chains are.

141

The animal in man may be recognized by the ferocity, the gluttony, the hate, and the violence in man.

142

It is certain that the heart which is agitated again and again by the yearning for sensual joys will not know the calm happiness of spiritual joys.

143

To what better use can a man put his will than the eradication of hatreds and the subduing of passions? For out of these two sources alone come so many wrong deeds and so much consequent suffering.

144

A man may be so infatuated with his lower nature that he prefers to be agitated and disturbed by its passions rather than to attain the unruffled calmness of his higher nature.

145

Desire is satisfied by possession but not ended by possession.

146

Only when the gathering of earthly gains seems futile, and the gains themselves mere dross, will he stop bartering his precious years for them.

147

When a desire lurks hidden in the heart, it may sway actions or influence thoughts without resistance. But when it rises to the surface and is seen for what it is, then it can be fought and conquered.

148

As his desires quieten, he finds to his surprise that many things hitherto thought indispensable to existence, he can do well without.

149

He who submits his emotions and passions to reason, and his reason to intuition, will save himself many regrets.

150

So long as he is buffeted between his passionate desires and his self-hating guilt, so long will a distressing tension be sustained.

151

So far as they distract the mind and disturb its peace, the struggle against the passions must go on.

152

When passion, uncontrollable and blind, irrational and violent, is behind action, the consequences may be harmful to its owner but they may also be instructive—if he is willing to be instructed. For life is an educational process, which everyone has to undergo whether the pupils like it or not.

153

We are not always the same person. At one period of life a desire may almost enslave us which has no power over us at a later period.

154

The world can be overcome only to the extent that we overcome ourselves, our endless desires and snaring ambitions, our passions and habits.

155

He has not only to deal with his tendencies but also with his compulsions.

156

But passion is an insurgent, a rebel against reason whose counterbalance it fears and avoids.

157

Even such normal factors as curiosity and ambition become disturbing when they become excessive, unbalanced, and drive the enslaved mind.

158

As the heart opens to this call of the inner self, the demand comes to the will for a more austere habit of living.

159

It is the difference between gentle austerity and harsh asceticism.

160

The passions of men are so resistant to control that in no single method is there sure hope of overcoming them. Only in a combination of methods does this lie.

161

The high moments of heavenly inspiration are laid low in the dust of obscenity or lust.

162

The effect of passional indulgences spreads out on physical and mental levels.

163

If we learn by bitter experience to drop the burden of one particular desire, we do so only to pick up another soon after. We are not content to be at peace.

164

The desires of human beings are never satiated, nor can they ever be since human beings must go on searching for final satisfaction. It is in their nature to do so. But what cannot be satiated by outer things can turn in on itself and find rest at last within.

165

How morally helpless many persons allow themselves to become is shown by the compulsive nature of their deeds and the obsessive nature of their thoughts.

166

It is the strength or feebleness of his attachments and desires which largely govern his first and earlier paces in the relinquishment of ego.

167

When insight arises, the passions become subdued and the problems which beset man become solved of their own accord. We may quarrel and kill whilst we remain in ignorance, but we must needs feel for and with each other when we comprehend at long last that in the Overself we are one.

168

All too easily do luxurious habits become insatiable habits, ever demanding more and more and meanwhile creating tension or discontent.

169

Whereas the conventional good man seeks to leave behind only the gross and flagrant forms of sin, the philosophic disciple is much more scrupulous. Whereas the one is content to moderate the strength of his lower nature, the other tries to subjugate it altogether.

170

We are to discipline, and when necessary abstain from satisfying, the lower impulses of our nature because we are to cultivate its higher intuitions. The clamant voice of the one drowns the soft whisper of the other.

171

We must try to turn the flow of our passions into a sublimer channel than the senses alone.

172

Men and women who have reached or passed the age of the late forties are more ready for, and better suited to, disciplining the animal nature and human passions than younger folk.

173

It is more difficult to conquer lust than to walk on the edge of a sword. But it can be conquered. And the way is essentially wise: slowly supplant lust of the flesh by a lust (love) of the divine. "No matter how much you feed your desires," says the *Vishnu Purana*, "they will never be satisfied." Therefore direct them gradually towards the Infinite, in which they may ultimately merge, and from which there is no return.

174

A resolute effort to banish from his heart the desire that caused his failure, an effort prompted by the miseries of that failure, will thus be the next step, after its recognition, in converting a weakness into a power.

175

Where passion rules, truth trembles!

176

Continued feeling of freedom from obsessing desires, inordinate urges, and undue cravings is generally a suitable indication that the character is sufficiently purified to enter a further stage.

177

It is men who condemn themselves to this abject, undisciplined servitude of the passions and senses; so it is men themselves who must seek and win freedom from it. It is hard to do so, but it is also hard to suffer the consequences of not doing so.

178

If you recognize that the feeling, the desire or body-sensation is pulling you away from the ideals set up for the Quest, hoist yourself out of it *at once*.

179

Let others look for the second-rate and third-rate: let him be more discriminating, more fastidious, and seek the best alone.

180

The senses will stupefy a man into foolish desires if he allows them, if he lets them go beyond his control. Wisdom and security alone dictate that he shall become self-mastered. For this it is necessary to call up the will and to practise using it until it is developed into something strong.

181

If before performing an impulsive, undisciplined, and irresponsible deed he would remember what the consequences are and that he will have to bear them, then he will have taken the first step towards self-mastery.

182

The rising generations have legitimate complaints against their ancestors. But in the matter of winning full freedom to follow their desires and upset the old Christian moral codes, the Mosaic decalogues, Confucian precepts, and the Indian taboos, they need to pause. Puritanic ideals are denounced but are not entirely inhuman: they have to be sifted and the good in them taken out. Stoic, simple living and self-discipline can be softened, its harshness also taken out, and the residue will be what the moderns need if they are to travel up higher and not sink lower.

183

In what manner are men free who, in some way, to some extent, are enslaved by sex, society, ambition, swelling desires, possessions, neighbours, associates, and family?

184

Only by releasing ourselves from our desires can we hope to find lasting peace. If this seems like a heavy price to pay, we have only ourselves to blame.

185

When animal desires rage in a man, each satisfaction of them seems to be an asset, something gained; but when he is more awakened and freer from them he begins to see how much of a liability these desires are, how wise and prudent it is to check them and finally transmute them.

186

If he is no longer a victim of passions or at the mercy of emotions, it will not be because his blood temperature is too low, but because his control of himself is high.

187

The animal gives way to its desires and feelings more quickly than the human because it acts by instinct. The human, so far as he is an animal, also acts by instinct. But to the extent that he has developed reason and will he has developed a counter to that instinct which moderates or controls his desires and his feelings. Those humans who are nearer on the scale of evolution to the animal kingdom give way to passion and anger more readily because they have less self-control.

188

A silent but self-declaring presence comes into knowledge whenever he puts a brake on that downward and earthward movement of daily life which is the common lot—not to stop it altogether but to halt it for short periods or to slow it down so that he is not wholly carried away.

189

The control of the lower nature which society may demand and religion may encourage, which makes a good man by conventional standards, is not enough for philosophy. It is only a stage of the mountain's ascent: the summit has yet to be conquered. The transformation of this nature, making it utterly responsive to the Overself, is the philosophic goal. Self-effort can lead to its control but only Grace can lead to this transformation.

190

All this does not imply that he is to become perfect and faultless before he can see the Overself, but that he has to become much more developed before he can stay in the awareness of it.

5

SPIRITUAL REFINEMENT

Courtesy, tolerance, considerateness

The philosopher's easy self-assurance and dignified serenity, as notice-able in calamity as in prosperity, mark him as being in some mysterious manner superior to circumstances. He will always be a gentleman, but not in the narrow, formal sense of clinging to a code of etiquette which may become faulty the moment he crosses the border into another country, or which will certainly become falsified a thousand years hence. He will be a gentleman in the broader sense of behaving always with human dignity and kindly consideration towards all others who cross his path.

2

That alone is true culture which refines taste, improves character, lifts standards, corrects behaviour, and teaches self-control.

3

A refined taste, delicate and subtle, delighted by the harmonies, melo-dies, or beauties in Nature and art, offended by the grossness in man, can express itself socially and instinctively only through refined manners. If others lack this taste but for class reasons keep up the appearance of such manners, the outer social value is still present even when the inside is empty.

4

His general attitude in discussion or study should be unbiased and unprejudiced, his observation of men and their situations impersonal and serene. He must realize that small men cannot entertain large views, that he is called upon to be big enough to put aside his personal sympathies and antipathies at certain times. He must realize too that whilst a man's mind moves at the low level of harsh prejudice or hot passion, it cannot possibly arrive at just conclusions. Before he can arrive at the truth of a highly controversial matter, he must detach himself from partisan feeling about it. Only in such inner silence can he think clearly and correctly about it. Where his criticism is directed against others, it should be the result of calm, impersonal reflection, not of emotional chagrin. This poised spirit will help him to avoid foolish extremes and dangerous rashness. He should not adopt a violent partisan spirit towards a problem or a principle for he knows that such a spirit always obscures the truth. Instead, he should always calmly view all sides in a balanced way. It is because he himself holds no rigidly partisan view that the earnest philosophic student can see better than other people what is true and what is false in every partisan view. It is not often that all the truth lies on one side and all the falsehood on the other. His ethical attitude should be more tolerant and less unfriendly than the average, as his intellectual attitude should be more inclusive and less dogmatic. He should refuse to imitate the irresponsible multitudes, with their surface judgement and facile condemnation. He should seek to understand and to respect the views of others; he should take the trouble to put himself in their place, to give an imaginative sympathy to their standpoint. He need not fall into the error of necessarily sharing them and may still stand on the intellectual foothold which he has secured.

Although this attitude will more and more show itself in personal and social situations and in practical and general affairs as a matter of course according to his growth, it will also show itself in his spiritual life. The unprejudiced study and unbiased comparison of various systems of religions, metaphysics, mysticism, and ethics will be for him valuable parts of philosophic culture. He should be both willing and desirous to understand all of the chief points of view, all the leading variants of doctrine in these systems, but at the same time he will know his own mind and views. Even while he is seeking to know the minds and views of others, he should estimate how limited, how distorted, how falsified, or how large an aspect of truth each represents. He can do this with the help of the philosophic conception of truth, which lights up all these others, because it stands at the peak toward which they have climbed only a part of the way.

5

Tolerance and mutual accommodation is the way of true spirituality. There is room in life for the other man's opinion also. Let him keep it if he wishes, so long as he refrains from forcing it upon us and so long as he himself does not preach or practise intolerance. His own experience of the ups and downs of life have combined to bring him to that belief; why should he not have it then? We may dislike it intensely but we must admit that from his standpoint he is right enough. When his experience broadens out and he sees life in larger perspective, be sure that he will change his opinion too. When his circumstances alter or his environment changes, he may learn how limited was his former view. When the long-drawn lesson of suffering or a thought-provoking book or powerful personality swings the balance of his mind in a new direction, he will desert his opinion or modify it. Meanwhile, let us set the world an example—and be tolerant.

6

Those who give enough thought to behaving politely do so from different motives, some of which may be merely hypocritical, others the slavish following of blind custom, still others simple obedience to selfish interest; but there still remains the remnant who do so sincerely, honestly, because generous enough to consider the feelings of those persons they meet.

7

The good manners prescribed for civilized living may have varied from century to century, or from continent to continent, but whatever their form, they represent that man in society must have some consideration for society, and not be utterly and selfishly indifferent to the effect of his conduct upon others. There is also the further point that if he lacks self-respect he needs to be taught it, to keep civilization from falling back to barbarism; so personal dignity and appearance, cleanliness and inoffensive speech are involved.

8

At some point and place, whether in the home or at school or in society itself, the young have to learn, and to be trained, in acceptable manners. And this, not chiefly to improve their quality, which it does, nor decorate their behaviour, which it will, or even refine their speech, which it must, but because it lifts them up from being animal to being human and thus contributes toward their spiritualization.

9

Is it really pretentious to give importance to politeness in behaviour in an age when the decay of manners is plainly visible? To those old enough to have seen better, the difference points up moral value of consideration for others in human society.

10

It is no man's fault that he lacks breeding, but it is *his* own fault if he lacks the courtesy which comes from breeding or else is self-acquired.

11

To become a fuller human being a man must acquire education and culture. Both he and his life will be enriched. But unless he keeps humility, his egoism may grow too.

12

We may affirm the factuality of caste *in nature* without turning ourselves into snobs who adopt condescending airs and utter patronizing remarks to those they consider socially below them.

13

We have to recognize the fact of caste in the development of the human species through successions of repeated earthly embodiments. That which comes through inherited or acquired wealth is not necessarily the same, may be a mere shallow copy, an empty vessel. When caste comes with arrogance, and especially with cruel arrogance, be sure it is not a carry-over from past births. The same situation holds with refinement of nature, conduct, taste, manner, and speech. When it is real, inward, the quality shines through; but when it is artificial, contrived, outward, it comes with snobbishness, especially a proud snobbishness.

14

All creatures are rooted in the same primal Being, but all remain at different levels of awareness or distance from this Being. Because of the oneness we must practise goodwill to all, but because of the distances we must see them for what they outwardly are.

15

Those who object—as so many young people do today—against formal social behaviour or conventional courtesy such as Confucius propagated and such as well-brought-up persons were taught to accept in our own modern West until recently, do not see how much it smooths everybody's way including their own and how much it oils the wheels of social existence for all of us.

16

Behind time and ego, behind all the conditions in which we find others to be, there is that which is divine within them. For the sake of that we may honour them even when their outer self is unworthy of it and dishonourable.

17

It is not a question of defective social manners or wrong accents but of two traits of good character—consideration for others and respect for oneself.

18

The conventional and not seldom hypocritical smile, the pretense of goodwill where there is none, constitute false manners, not good manners.

19

Courtesy is the oil which lubricates the wheel of life.

20

At a time when goodwill and courtesy seem to be fading out, we need all the more to support them staunchly.

21

What is called correct social behaviour can vary from period to period, century to century. It is not the same as, and not to be confused with, courtesy.

22

There are those who dismiss the subject as unconnected with philosophy, unessential to spiritual self-cultivation. But a sage like Confucius thought otherwise and constantly exhorted his disciples to cultivate courteous manners and gentlemanly behaviour.

23

Is it not better that men should learn to discipline their unpleasant traits, instead of inflicting them on other people? It is not only better for society but also for the men themselves, for it is a part of their spiritual evolution.

24

If it becomes an empty arid formality, devoid of the corresponding feeling, it is not courtesy, but hypocrisy.

25

If we are asked to resist our innate natural selfishness and include other people's welfare along with our own, it is only because in this way they too are being asked to include ours. This at least helps us and them. This is the practical benefit of politeness.

26

Refinement is not so much a matter of birth as of quality, which may be born in a man or fashioned for himself.

27

The young child should be taught how to grow up into a civilized well-behaved person, who naturally and not hypocritically behaves with consideration for the feelings of others.

28

Culture is not only the enrichment of personal experience: it is the enrichment of the person himself.

29

Suppose you knew that this was to be your last day on earth. How would you behave towards others? Would you not sink all short-range attitudes and rise above the petty selfishness, the pitiful enmities, and the harsh discords which may have marred your past? Would you not try at least to feel goodwill toward all men? This is how philosophy bids you behave at all times and not merely on your deathbed.

30

We must see men not only as they are today, but also as they shall be in an evolutionary tomorrow. If we listen to the voice of experience, we tend to become cynics, if to the voice of the Overself, optimists. A shrewd appraisal of humanity should combine the two, recognizing and not denying ugly faults and dark frailties, but at the same time being graciously tolerant and forgiving.

31

He is open-eyed enough to see men as they are, but also generous enough to see them as they must one day become.

32

As the full meaning of reincarnation and of karma sinks deeper and deeper into his mind, a generous tolerance will rise higher and higher in his feelings. He will begin to see that every wrong-doer is what he is because of his past experience and present mentality and has to act in the way he does and cannot act in any other way. The life of such a man develops inevitably and naturally out of his character, out of his mode of thought, and out of his experience on this earth in the present and in former lives.

33

If a man's attitude towards spiritual truth is determined by the fact that he was born in a particular place and not by wide search and deep thought, he does not deserve and will not find the highest truth.

34

If he practises goodwill to others, it is more likely that the higher power will bestow grace upon him through others.

35

There is never any justification for being unmannerly, or worse, rude.

36

The man of such immeasurable goodwill will express it in all ways all the time.

37

The more he refuses to let negative emotions capture him, the more will an inner harmony permeate him.

38

He will keep a secret untroubled poise amongst those who are utterly bereft of any reverence for life's higher meaning as amongst those who possess it.

39

Beware of projecting your own negative reactions, ideas, colourings, or feelings on displeasing situations and abrasive persons.

40

If he is to keep his inward peace unruffled he must live above the level of those who have it not. This can be done only if he obeys the practical injunctions of Jesus and Buddha, only if he keeps out of his emotional system all the negatives like resentment, bitterness, quarrelsomeness, jealousy, spite, and revenge. These lower emotions must definitely be outgrown if philosophic calm is to be the supreme fact and philosophic wisdom the guiding factor in his life. When other men show their enmity and meanness toward him, he is to retaliate by showing his indifference and generosity. When they falsely assail his character or enviously calumniate his work, he is to forbear from harsh feelings and not let them forfeit his goodwill. He is not to succumb to the human temptation to retaliate in kind. For he is engaged on a holy ascent, and to succumb would be to slip grievously back. Indeed, out of the base actions of others, he may kindle noble reactions which assist his upward climb.(P)

41

Whoever expands his consciousness in advance of the contemporary level must not expect more than a few to understand him. Yet it is his business to understand them as it is their misfortune to misunderstand him.

42

The man who is no longer disturbed by the presence or working or characteristic of his own ego will not be disturbed by that of others. No negative feeling will enter his attitude toward them.

43

Although the repulsions to uncongenial persons may be acknowledged frankly, he can and should rise high above them. On the practical level it is necessary to rectify the outer and visible causes of the disharmony between him and the other person, as far as that is possible. On the mental level it is necessary to deal with the inner and invisible causes. The easiest way to begin such work is to begin it in creative meditation. There he should take up the picture of that person and mentally rectify the relation with him, adjust the thought of it to what it should be from the highest standpoint. He should finish by prayerfully sending good thoughts for his inner improvement, and by forgiving any sins against himself. Thus instead of criticizing or attacking the person against whom he has a grievance, with results that may provoke still more trouble, he should remain emotionally undisturbed whilst using constructive endeavours in right meditation and unselfish prayer for that person. This may bring about a remarkable change in him, or else in the relationship with him, or at least in the aspirant's own attitude towards that person. For whatever is given out to others, in the end comes back to oneself.

44

When superior patrician ancestry, or higher education, or greater wealth, or influential social position, lead in speech or behaviour to arrogant hauteur and scornful contempt for the less fortunate, it leads to the snob. In him, outward and formal good manners do not come from the heart; in him, the spirit contradicts the letter. Consequently they are not really good manners at all.

45

The question has been asked: what is one to do in the face of another person's rudeness pushed to a point which is almost insulting? This could be ignored in many instances if on the belief in reincarnation it is viewed as a sign of the other person's ill-formed character and low caste. But when it is not of such a kind and where one is constantly thrown into contact through work or relationship or residence so that one is exposed constantly to the same kind of contact, how should a spiritual aspirant deal with it?

The answer is to regard it as a test and a challenge. It is a test of certain qualities which must be sought within oneself and drawn upon, such as patience, calmness, and learning. It is a challenge, and if one lacks those qualities it is necessary to seek deeper and try to draw from the inner resources of the Higher Self. This means working previously both in meditation and in thought to picture the needed emotional and mental response, plus the resulting physical conduct, as a daily exercise, until this reaction has become somewhat regular.

Or we can supplement this with moving to the metaphysical field and remembering at the end that it is all part of the dream-like experience which, in appropriate conditions, or on sufficient degree of mental perception being attained, one sees life to be.

46

When one has had a large experience of the world, with widely different groups of people, races, tribes, nations, classes, and castes, one is unwilling to offer admiration without some sort of qualification to any human institution or any human being. And when one has studied the human entity metaphysically and psychologically, discovering the place and power of the ego, one finds philosophical support of this mental reservation. But this need not imply cynicism: the presence of goodwill and the faith in ultimate salvation of all would preclude it.

47

Since he needs to rule emotions and not let them rule him, to overcome passions and not become their victim, he must cultivate a diamond-like hardness. But this is not directed toward others, only to himself, unless evil or foolish influences are seeking to sway him.

48

No person who is really refined, that is to say by character and taste and not by birth or wealth, can bear the crudity, the ugliness, and the decadence of those literary, artistic, psychoanalytic, or "progressive" circles which take a delight in uttering filthy four-letter words. Spirituality shrinks into silence in such garrulous company, takes curtained-off refuge in its own natural fastidiousness and refinement; but again I say these develop from within and are not imposed by the family or the "finishing school." Whatever superficial interest these circles may take in so-called mystic experience, materialism and egotism are their real religious creeds, just as courtesy is not a genuine characteristic of their behaviour, whatever outward show of it they may hypocritically have to make at times. The noisy cheap mannerless and brassy cafés of Montmartre and Montparnasse are their familiar spiritual homes.

49

One quality of his everyday conduct which will be noticeable to others will be his self-effacement. He is immediately ready to enter into their standpoint, sympathetically and helpfully, to listen patiently whilst they talk only about themselves and their own affairs.

50

The student of philosophy must free himself from all narrow racialist views, national prejudices, class feelings, and personal selfishness. Philosophy in practice demands no less than this because it brings the realization that in actual fact all men are inseparably linked with each other. "He who regards impartially friends and foes, foreigners and relatives, the righteous and unrighteous, he excelleth." —*Bhagavad Gita*

Racial animosity is really a pathological state which clouds vision and falsifies judgement. It raises prejudice to the dignity of a principle. Hate is a mental poison. It is the worst possible sin of our thought life. It damages those we hate, infects our own environment, and in the end it severely damages ourselves. The ability to treat all kinds and classes of people equally, and with universal goodwill, does not imply the inability to observe the comparative differences and even defects among them.

51

It is not enough to possess a wide tolerance in these matters; it should also be a *wise* tolerance. Otherwise one may merely condone and increase self-destruction.

52

Not to tell another person "No!" when all prudence, intelligence, foresight, and experience bid us do so is simply moral and verbal cowardice.

53

He can be polite without being fulsome and effusive. His sincerity will dictate the proper measure.

54

The need for finer manners where coarse vulgarity, aggressive obscenity, and raucous noisiness prevail, speaks for itself to those who seek escape from materialism. In an atmosphere of disorderly or non-existent manners, materialistic thought flourishes all the more.

55

He has much contempt for human folly but much tolerance for human weakness.

56

He will keep serene, even-tempered, detached amid the recurring irritations of life and the petty provocations from persons who cross his path. They may affront him but they cannot hurt, much less infuriate, him. But all this aloofness of spirit would not be possible if he identified himself with the ego alone.

57

But it is not only inner calmness that he needs to acquire; inner clearness is also requisite. Both the intellect with its ideas and the character with its qualities should share this effort to secure greater clarification.

58

His tolerance is so vast that he will not intrude upon others' freedom, not even to the extent of seeking the betterment of their character or the improvement of their mind.

59

As a man advances in inward development, gaining ever richer experience in fresh embodiments, he comes to see that he will gain more by practising co-operation than by selfishly seeking his own isolated benefit alone.

60

It is at such moments of remembrance that he is here also to ennoble his character that it becomes easier to extend goodwill to those he dislikes, or who dislike him, those who have brought him trouble and others who radiate materialism or destructiveness.

61

It would be a mistake to believe that because he makes no sharp exclusions and practises such all-embracing sympathy toward every possible way of looking at life he ends in confusion and considers right and wrong to be indistinguishable from each other. Instead of falling into mental vacillation, he attains and keeps a mental integrity, a genuine individuality which no narrow sect can overcome. Instead of suffering from moral dissolution, he expands into the moral largeness which sees that no ideal is universal and exclusively right.

62

Although generally he will be infinitely considerate of other persons, there will be certain situations wherein he will be infinitely hard upon them and utterly indifferent to their emotional feelings.

63

All are benefited by remembering at all times the practice of harmlessness towards all creatures in thought, word, and action. He should not consider himself alone, but ought also consider his duty to those other beings who cross his path, including animal beings.

64

Elegance is often found as an accompaniment of refinement. This is not only true of physical things, behaviour, and conduct, but also of character and mind.

65

The true gentleman does not cast aside fine manners however much one may become intimate, familiar, or friendly with him.

66

The man of exemplary manners will always have an advantage over those who have none. The charm of dealing, or conversing, with him gives him the preference, all else being equal.

67

Assert the ego aggressively against others and you provoke their egos to assert themselves. Hostility breeds hostility, violence encourages the others to be violent.

68

He keeps this composure. If he has moods, ups-and-downs of feeling, others will not know it. By presenting them with an imperturbable front, they are helped without his particularly seeking to do so.

69

A well-mannered child is a testimony to a well-mannered home.

70

It does not mean that he is to force himself to like everyone under the sun equally well, or that he is to negate every personal preference and deny every personal repulsion. It does not mean that he is no longer to discriminate his perceptions of human status and quality.

71

He is never the enemy of any human being, but only of the sin in that being. All his social-relational thinking is governed by goodwill, but his conduct is ruled by reason added to the goodwill. In that way, he does not fall into unbalanced sentimentality nor harm others under the delusion that he is benefiting them.

72

He shows an uncommon patience because that is Nature's way. He expresses an impartial understanding because that is Truth's way. He accepts people just where they are and is not angry with them because they are not farther along the road of life.

73

He is not only different in that he seeks *both* to commend and to criticize, whereas the ordinary man seeks only to do the one or the other, but also in that he seeks to understand the world view and life-experience which have given rise to such a viewpoint.

74

He must be ready to bestow an intellectual sympathy towards the attitudes of other men, no matter how foolish or how wicked these attitudes may be. Such a sympathy enables him to understand them, as well as the experiences and the thoughts which have led to them. But it does not necessitate acceptance of the emotional complexes and spiritual ignorance which accompany them.

75

It is not necessary to be sullen in order to be serious. The man who walks rudely through the crowded streets of life, who flings his contempt from mien and speech, is but a melancholy misanthrope, not a philosopher. He thinks he has surrounded himself with an atmosphere of detachment, when he has merely succeeded in surrounding himself with an atmosphere of surliness.

76

It is time to stop when such a flexible all-things-to-all-men attitude begins to destroy strict honesty of purpose and truth of speech. No sage can stoop so low, but pseudo-sages may.

77

With each coming of this experience, there is a going of bitterness out of his heart. More and more he sees that people cannot help being what they are, the products of their own past experience and present characteristics, the living milestones of a cosmic evolutionary process. How can he blame, resent, or condemn them? More and more, therefore, does tolerance suffuse his attitude and acceptance mellow his contacts with the world.

78

The blood and violence, the fear and suffering associated with the production of meat, should be enough to make kindhearted, sensitive people shun it.

79

In the sphere of human relations, he will hold himself to certain attitudes which eradicate the negative tendencies in him and stimulate the positive. When thrown among those who do wrong and practise evil, he will not fall into anger, hatred, resentment, or bitterness, but will use the occasion to rise into patience, detachment, or indifference, knowing that such persons will sometime and somewhere infallibly receive the painful return of what they have given out. When, on the contrary, he is brought into the company of those who do right and practise virtue, he will rejoice in their goodness and be glad to witness their conduct. When he finds himself among those suffering misfortune he will pity, and when among those enjoying good fortune he will feel no envy.

80

It is not possible for every man to establish harmony with every environment in which he finds himself, but it is possible for him to understand all environments so thoroughly as to react rightly to them.

81

"You must neither defraud your neighbour nor allow him to defraud you," said the Persian prophet, the Bab, to a disciple who had paid an exorbitant price for some bazaar article.

82

If he has to resist the influence and pressure of society in many directions to keep his spiritual integrity, he need not do so in an aggressive, uncouth, or tactless manner. Some have unfortunately behaved in this way, not because philosophy bade them do so, but because their individuality was strong and their ego pronounced.

83

Unless some quirk of destiny puts him in a public situation where duty and responsibility compel attention to negatives and criticisms, he may prefer to draw attention to the good and the beautiful, to spread harmony.

84

So long as we let other people's faults or blunders evoke our own in angry response, so long do we foolishly add an inner hurt to whatever outer hurt their fault or blunder may have caused us.

85

Where harshness, coarseness, brutality, and vulgarity reign, where no touch of kindness, beauty, gentleness, or love enters the atmosphere, there the soul stifles.

86

He is neither a sentimentalist nor a simpleton, but expects from humanity that dual nature, that thorn with the rose, which corresponds to the positive-negative nature of the universe itself.

87

One may note these defects in a man's character not to judge, certainly not to condemn him, but solely to understand any person with whom one has to deal in some way.

88

The good have existed in all countries, at all times, among bad people and at bad times. We ought to welcome them as persons whatever low opinion we hold of their kindred.

89

The idealist who expects too much from people is as mistaken as the cynic who expects too little.

90

His tolerance is such that he accords to others the right to be, to act, and to live the way they want to be, to act, and to live. He trusts the evolutionary laws to take care of their corrective education.

91

It is of the highest importance for older people to look after the manners of younger ones. But the bad behaviour of many parents towards one another as well as in society is reflected in that of their children.

92

Aggressive, naughty, ill-tempered, or disobedient traits in children need a measure of discipline from parents, or life will provide it in later years much more harshly. But there is a special need for parents to provide it *lovingly* as education, not scolding and punishing.

93

If we can give nothing else, we can always give others our kindly thoughts and not our personal troubles.

94

The word *ahimsa* in Sanskrit signifies harmlessness, non-injury to others. It was a quality at the heart of Gandhi's gospel and Saint Francis' preaching. The saint of Assisi knew no Sanskrit but his instruction "to cause no offense whatsoever to anyone" could also be used as a definition of *ahimsa*.

95

It is not always fair to scorn someone as a hypocrite for past frailties and lapses of the bygone past who behaves properly in the living present. There may have been a genuine awakening accompanied by moral reform inwardly and outwardly, so that instead of condemnation, the attitude should be congratulation.

96

His duty to himself calls on him to protect the personal interests. But his duty to the All calls on him to respect others' interests too.

97

There are rude and wild young people who assert that civilities and politenesses intensify class divisions and status differences. They claim that in being wild and rude they are simply being natural and sincere whereas the others whom they denounce as holding bourgeois values are hypocritical and insincere. If the background of these misguided young persons is scrutinized, it will usually be found that at least three-quarters of them belong to working class origins while the others who are themselves probably of comfortable middle-class origin are pathological, mentally disturbed, emotionally upset persons. No, the courtesies of decent social intercourse are part of the proper evolution of the human race, and its refinement from the grossly animal to the truly human. This is an evolutionary advance.

98

Good breeding is a quality which must be acquired through the incarnations, for it is a quality of good Quality itself.

99

The practical realistic desire to live well whilst he is living on earth can still leave plenty of room for idealism and spirituality. Free from the mental fatigue of ghost-haunted traditions and emotional poisons which weigh so heavily on others, he is able to search vigourously for great art, vital religion, inspired mysticism, and the highest philosophy—and appreciate them adequately when found.

100

Toleration does not mean acceptance of anything, however evil it be. It means the avoidance of fanaticism, the practice of goodwill, and the recognition that by reason of their past re-incarnatory history, many wide differences of opinion, belief, practice, and character do and must exist in human beings.

101

It would be of no avail to mention the further stages until he is ready for them. But the teacher can say that the ultimate discovery is of the oneness and infinitude of Mind, hence of all mankind as arising out of That. This provides the basis of his ethics, and makes him seek the common welfare alongside of his own.

102

The person who cultivates tidy arrangements and orderly habits in the little things of everyday living unconsciously imitates the tidiness and orderliness of the Mind behind the whole universe.

103

He may still believe as the Brahmins believe that caste is a fact in Nature, but he will be without that pride in social rank which has too often ended with the Brahmins in some sort of arrogance or even cruelty to those of lower status.

104

The refinement, manners, and culture which Confucius wished to see in a properly developed human being may be different in outer form from those which a modern sage would wish to see, but they are not different in spirit. Those who now denounce them angrily as class-marks must therefore praise grossness, crudeness, coarseness, and ignorance as ideal. And others who can see no spiritual usefulness being served by fine quality simply do not look far enough. The practice of true philosophy should reduce, or remove, coarseness of character, behaviour, and speech.

105

He will find less and less pleasure in the chatter of society, clubs, and drawing rooms, which when it is about self, is quite inane, and when about other people, is often cruel.

106

In this world he has to deal with people. To deal efficiently with them he needs to understand their characters. But to turn a blind eye towards their weaknesses will only mar this understanding and spoil this efficiency. Even where he seeks to help them, such results will only hinder his compassionate aim.

107

The range of his goodwill excludes none, includes all. He recognizes no enemies, only unevolved men.

108

By "good manners" is not meant "formal etiquette" although the two may often coincide.

109

Teach elementary manners, that is, a warm smile.

110

In a truly civilized society courteous manners and refined tastes would be the rule.

111

One man can hate another man, but if the first has renounced his ego— the source of hatred—how can he continue to do so?

112

A smile will say to others what words may fail to do, will express your basic attitude of, in Jesus' phrase "good will unto all men."

113

He will in the end unfailingly draw to himself what he gives out. If hate, hate returns; if love, love returns.

114

We may dislike a man and disapprove of his opinions but this ought not prevent us from giving him our goodwill.

115

It is not enough to show an outward good temper—excellent discipline though that be—if thought irritates and feeling boils.

116

There is a tolerance which springs from mere indifference, but there is also a tolerance which springs from inner largeness of spirit.

117

Differences between men—whether in external things or internal thinking—there must be. But they need not become the occasion of hate between men.

118

With enough goodwill on both sides, a compromise can usually be reached in most disputes.

119

By refinement I mean a quality of good breeding, either natural or acquired.

120

The easiest way to express this feeling, described by Jesus as "goodwill unto all," is to be courteous to all.

121

Always good-natured and good-willed because always up-lifted by the Overself, he is a true gentleman, strictly courteous from within, not put on for appearance's sake.

122

We may practise goodwill untainted by selfishness towards all mankind without becoming mushily sentimental about "universal brotherhood."

123

The hermit who behaves rudely may be showing his individualism, as he believes, but he is also showing his lack of spirituality. Polite manners imply thought for others.

124

Nor is his tolerance grown out of laziness. It is grown out of understanding mated to kindliness.

125

In his upward climb he should slowly learn to drop the emotional view of life and to replace it by the intelligent view. Thus he will show his passage from a lower to a higher level. But it is to be an intelligence that is serene in activity, impersonal in judgement, warm in benevolence, and intuitive in quality. There should be no room in it to hold bias or bigotry, on the one hand, or dead logic-chopping on the other.

126

He will not only take care not to exceed his own just rights, not only be scrupulous not to invade other people's rights, but he will even take care not to interfere with their free will.

127

Be strong without being stubborn.

128

Much good behaviour is thinly veneered, being the consequence of social prudence rather than personal virtue.

129

There is the danger, however, that those who begin by being spiritually insensitive may end by becoming spiritually offensive.

130

He should bestow an intellectual sympathy on all, even though he cannot bestow an emotional sympathy.

131

If you can go to a man you greatly dislike and remember that he, too, will one day discover his spiritual identity and express a finer, more lovable self, it will be easier to be calm, patient, just, and at ease with him.

132

The relationships which develop between him and other people become a further channel for expressing what he has of this understanding, this peace, this self-control.

133

He cannot meet hatred with hatred, but only with resignation. His answer to enmity is to condone it. His attitude to opposition is to be tolerant.

134

Those who are not deceived by the fictitious good-fellowship of saloons and taverns may find his calm cool presence more truly cordial than those who seek emotional displays.

135

It is not a virtue but a weakness to be unable to stand up for your own rights or to be unable to rightly say "No!" or to submit to being bored by someone you want to get away from.

136

His actions will affect those with him, his dislike or hatred may provoke theirs, his kindness may create kindly reactions from them. A man needs to be careful in such matters.

137

It is not easy for any man who has the ideal of living by truth. He will find himself forced to talk little, to cultivate a reticent manner and follow his own way of life.

138

Bad-mannered children become so partly because of their parents' failure to correct them, which may be through having had similar parents themselves. And where this is shown by the child pointing out and ridiculing a stranger, neighbour, schoolchild, or foreigner because of his different or unusual appearance, clothes, and so on, it is also cruel.

139

Do not expect nobler action or higher motives from any man than experience suggests you should expect.

140

Whoever cultivates goodwill to others will inevitably throw out whatever ill will he encounters in himself towards particular persons. For as goodwill grows in a broad generous way so ill will dies in a personal way.

141

Let him accept others as he accepts himself, with all their and his defects, but with the addition that he will constantly aim at improving himself.

142

He persists in showing a proper courtesy to those who themselves behave badly.

143

He may argue if others wish to do so but he will never argue acrimoniously.

144

When the actions or words of others provoke us, it is easy to become irritable, resentful, or indignant; it is hard to practise a bland patience and exercise a philosophic tolerance. But that is just what the aspirant must do.

145

A child whose parents fail to discipline it at the proper occasion in the proper loving way will be encouraged by the omission to continue its mistaken attitude.

146

If they cared enough, they would show it in being affable, pleasant, kind—that is, they would suppress their egoism sufficiently to make such decent manners possible. But they don't: they care too much for their own ego to let it happen.

147

Knowing the nature of human nature; knowing, too, the universality of Yin and Yang's existence and applicability: there is no need to be surprised at anything which anyone does.

148

If he must assess men's motives and examine their characters, he will do so only to understand them, not to judge them. He will not use it to gossip about their personal frailties.

149

Ingratitude fails to embitter him—does not even make him feel hurt.

150

To a person of refined feeling, the crudeness of animal passion is repellent.

151

It was an act of reverence among pious Chinese, or of courtesy among polite ones, to hold the hands with the right palm inside the left one.

152

Those who make a virtue of bad manners, who know nothing or want to know nothing of the laws of decent social intercourse, should be avoided.

153

If his family failed to bring him up to practise self-discipline, to control behaviour and refine his speech, to avoid violence and roughness, then he must himself supply these things and acquire these habits.

154

He not only learns that it is impossible to please everyone but that it is impossible even to avoid giving offense at some time to some human beings.

155

It is true that fine manners may be put on, to make a more favourable impression on his victim, by the exploiter, the swindler, or the seducer. But this is the misuse of manners and offers no valid criticism of them.

156

He naturally feels a warmer emotion about his own kith and kin, his own friends, than about other people. He not only knows them better but they affect him more deeply.

157

All reaching out towards the transcendental is to be encouraged, however elementary it be.

158

The philosopher does not exhibit the common fault of rejecting and condemning every other standpoint in order to support his own.

159

Neither the mockery of insensitive sceptics nor the malice of sectarian fanatics should be allowed to sway him from a fixed resolve to accord goodwill unto all, including them also.

160

He should try to keep discussions of opposing views within the codes of amicable courtesy and good manners.

161

Why must we be always grabbing at others, staking out claims and making demands upon them? Why not leave them free?

162

He has not only to separate himself from his own lower principles, but just as much from other people's when he is in contact with them.

163

If disunion reigns in the psyche within, then disharmony must reign in the life without.

164

A quarrelsome man carries his enemies with him for he creates them wherever he goes. There is no peace in his outer life because there is none in his inner life.

165

When it is not possible for his relatives or friends to share with him the acceptance of spiritual ideas, he should be tolerant, understanding, and patient toward such disagreement.

166

The logic of a higher life compels him to recognize the divine element in the hearts of those who hate or malign him, and he honours them for it; but it does not compel him to waste precious years in unnecessary struggles against them. The years which are left to him and to them on this poor earth are too few to be lost in unworthy squabbles.

167

He will express his faith positively but not aggressively.

168

Even simple human ethics, let alone divinely given commandments, tell us to treat others as we wish them to treat ourselves.

169

Whoever looks for the negative aspects of others should also remember that there are usually some positive ones also and that in fairness he ought to recognize them too.

170

If anyone or anything, a man or a book, can contribute to free us from the resentments towards others or the bitternesses towards life which poison feelings, thoughts, and health, he has rendered us a great service or the book has proved its worth.

171

His virtue is not cold and selfish and self-admiring, although it may seem so to those who have insufficient knowledge of these matters.

172

Conformity has its uses, its merits, its place and time. Given these, it is quite acceptable.

173

Ill-mannered people mistake invective for argument.

174

The insatiable curiosity whose satisfaction fills so many columns of personal gossip in newspapers, is reflected in those who intrusively ask private questions where they have no right and no encouragement to do so. It is a breach of good manners, a blow at personal rights. It is a lack of respect for human dignity and independence.

175

Being different from the crowd may mean being lonely but it also means being inspired, protected, blessed. Jesus was not holier *in essence* than he is, only that man had manifested all this holiness, whereas he has hardly begun to do so. The task is to reflect the attributes of divinity in the conduct of humanity, involving the bringing-in of his metaphysics and his mysticism to actuate his conduct.

Spiritual value of manners

176

I cannot recall any statement by mystics—ancient, medieval, or modern—that one aspect of spiritual union is an exquisite refinement. Everyone writes of its moral fruits, its religious insights—even its creativity, artistic or intellectual—but who seems to note this aesthetic effect on manners, feelings, speech, and living?

177

That breeding and culture can contribute to spirituality may not be evident to the ascetically mystic mind or the simpler religious mind. That fastidious refinement (but not arrogant snobbish refinement) can come with inner growth may be likewise obscure. But the long association of holiness with asceticism or with bareness of living has confused the understanding of truth. A lifestyle touched with beauty in manners, surroundings, character, or taste, can better express what philosophy means than an ugly and unclean one. That the lack of opportunity is responsible for a part of crudeness and inferiority and immaturity is, however, obvious enough. But it is a fact which ought not be used to cover up the correct view of these things.

178

Good manners are not only an end in themselves, emblems of a finer personality, tokens of willingness to be of service, but also part of a means to higher spiritual attainment—the ultimate courtesy and supreme generosity of human behaviour.

179

Ill-mannered conduct is ordinarily incompatible with spiritual realization: the cases of those Tibetan and Japanese masters who historically behaved badly towards would-be disciples are special cases, and ought not to be taken as guides.

180

Refinement is as valuable a quality, and as spiritual, as truth-seeking.

181

Good manners and finer feelings, courtesy and graciousness—these inhere in one who possesses a true spirituality. It is true that many aspirants consider this to be mere surface polish, unimportant, a cloak quite often for hypocrisy and falseness. That may be so in a number of cases. But even it if were correct of all cases the fact remains that the manners which aspirants adopt, the code of behaviour which they practise, possess a definite place on this quest. Those Chinese and Javanese mystical cults which regarded and used etiquette as part of their way toward inner unfoldment, as part of their yoga path, were not wrong. For it creates forms of conduct which not only refine and uplift the practiser's character, but also can be used to defend his inner life—where he is developed enough to possess one—against society's onslaughts. There is a moral element in it, too. For where etiquette trains a man sympathetically to consider the emotional reactions of other persons to his own behaviour, it transfers his point of view from an habitual selfish one to a more impersonal one. Again by smoothing the relations between both of them, it puts the others not only more at peace with themselves but also with him. Lastly it requires and fosters some measure of self-control. For we are not only victims of aggression from our enemies. We are just as much, or even more, victims of ourselves, attacked by our own weaknesses and faults.

182

We should learn and teach children to learn to respect the need for respect—whether it be shown to elders or to authorities, as Confucius taught, or whether it be shown to other people's religious beliefs. Respect is something which can later grow into a higher quality and that is reverence. Through reverence we can begin to sense higher atmospheres which produce a feeling of awe whether the atmosphere be found in the beauties of nature, of music, of art, or of saints and sages. People of the lower classes are apt to loose their temper more quickly than those of the upper classes because they have not been brought up to respect self-control or to value it and thus to respect themselves. Thus self-respect becomes a moral quality and when traced to its ultimate meaning it becomes respect for one's own higher self.

183

The connection between the good life and good manners is not usually brought out by those who would uplift humanity spiritually, except of course by such shining exceptions as Confucius in the East and Emerson in the West. In a period like the present—when the young generation ridicules all mention of manners, courtesy, etiquette, and so on as hollow, hypocritical, and insincere—the values so criticized must be clarified again and their connection with the higher life made plainer.

184

Everyone knows the social value of culture and breeding and refinement but everyone does not know that they should, and could, have a spiritual one too. For they share this in common with the value of art that they can uplift a man or, misused, degrade him. The point lies in their effect.

185

The refinement of tastes, the improvement of understanding, the betterment of manners—this is the cultural preparation for the path.

186

Philosophy accords a place and value to culture and refinement, to quality of character and enrichment of mind. It rejects the narrowness of view and negativity of attitude which allows salvation *only* to those who exhibit their detachment in bare squalid homes, devoid of beauty, or their indifference in minds unresponsive to intellectual power and poetic feeling.

187

Where good manners are sincerely felt and sincerely practised, they represent consideration for other people, abandonment of the self-centered habit we are born with. And what does this in turn represent but a surrender of the ego? This helps to explain why Hilaire Belloc could write:

> Of Courtesy it is much less
> Than courage of heart or holiness,
> Yet in my walks it seems to me
> That the Grace of God is in Courtesy.

188

The difference between those who behave rudely and those who behave politely is not only a social one: it is also a spiritual one. For it is goodwill which inspires good manners, where they are genuinely felt, that same "good will unto all men" which Jesus enjoined us to practise. The lack of courtesy has a deeper negative meaning than most people comprehend.

189

Confucius was not merely a teacher of ethics or of etiquette, as is so often believed here. He set up an ideal, called "The Superior Man." He defined the latter's general education, social behaviour, and moral character. He prescribed forms of polite civilized conduct, but these were not at all his sole mission. He made it quite clear that even the finest manners were hollow and vain if not supported by inner integrity and personal sincerity. He tried to show kings, dukes, and government officials their proper functions, responsibilities, and obligations. He taught common men the need of self-control, especially over passions. He sought the reform of education and of scholarship. But although he did not venture outside his proper sphere into religious discussion this does not mean he was without religion itself.

190

Confucius set up the ideal of what he called the superior person, roughly equivalent to what we Westerners call the "perfect gentleman."

191

Underbred and overbearing persons imagine that they are showing the world their importance when all the while they are merely showing their littleness. Good manners, when sincere and spontaneous, are spiritual virtue. In all human contacts the good man expresses himself naturally in good manners. In the management of both transient and lifelong relationships the master shows by grace of manner the grace of God.

192

By upbringing and temperament, by education and environment, a man may grow into refinement from childhood, easily and naturally. But he who comes into it from harsh, low surroundings by his own determination and effort, advances spiritually.

193

The accepted canons of good manners may vary from one part of the world to another, but deeper than these conventions is a courtesy which relates to the spiritual side of one's nature.

194

Politeness if sincere is a spiritual quality. Those who lift their eyebrows at such an assertion do not look deeply enough into it. In those cases where it is empty formalism they are right, of course; but in those where it expresses genuine consideration for others, they are wrong.

195

The thin courtesy which is hollow and insincere, the good manners which are acted and artificial, the pleasant words which are false and untrustworthy, do not of course hold spiritual value.

196

There are deeper reasons than merely social ones why Confucius preached politeness: their roots go down into moral training.

197

If people practise good manners merely and only as a part of their paid job—as, for instance, head waiters in restaurants—that is their affair. But the motivation can also be on a far deeper level even in ordinary social intercourse. Under the finest manners there can be—not hypocrisy, as a Colonial once informed me—but utter sincerity and true feeling. They can express goodwill to all, poor and rich, black and white, servant and superior. If the world all too easily puts them on like a mask, to disguise antipathy or even hate, the quester who has had, or hopes to have, a glimpse of his Higher Self, does not need to wear such a mask at all. Without a hollow, ridiculous obsession with formality and decorum, such as Confucian China eventually fell into and then had to rebel against, he can simply *be* what he now knows a human being ought to be in his relationship with others.

198

Courtesy should be recognized as one of the desirable spiritual virtues. Social manners and outer etiquette are only the local forms taken by courtesy. They may change or drop out, what matters is the inner attitude.

199

To be well-bred is not solely an innate blood-born attribute as so many narrowly believe; it can also be shaped by philosophy, which is no less a matter of refinement of manners than it is of consciousness. It is not concerned with snobbish social elegance, as others also narrowly think, but with goodness and with aesthetics. It avoids vulgarity because that is so ugly. All these qualities may not usually be associated with philosophers, but that is because in such cases there is not enough depth in them.

200

Whether it be in the forms of art, music, poetry, literature, or those of living, dress, behaviour, manners, or speech, the quality of a person reveals himself in his coarseness or refinement. By that I mean whether he is or is not on the quest which is after all an attempt to refine ourselves from materialism to spirituality and therefore from low quality thoughts and feelings to higher and nobler ones.

201

It is not only manners which must be refined, if higher development is sought, but also consciousness.

202

Whatever helps to refine character, feeling, mind, and taste is to be welcomed and cultivated as part of the philosophic work.

203

I think it was Emerson's view, if memory is correct, that a person's manners show outwardly the degree to which the Spirit is working within him. It was certainly the view of some Far Eastern sages, but explanation may be necessary for those to whom it is new.

204

Without referring to polish and elegance—which are a different thing—decent manners in the sense of being considerate to others come closer to a spiritual man's conduct than rude manners.

205

The graceless discourtesies and little brutalities of those who are either too ill-bred or too selfish to be considerate of others, advertise spiritual emptiness. They defend themselves by ascribing mannerliness and charm to snobs, because they dare not face what they are and see their own poverty of soul.

206

Confucius saw the moral worth of proper manners, the ennobling value of dignified living, the formative power of right custom.

207

If society did to Confucius' canons of propriety and conduct what it did to all religions, if it made the externals and forms more important than the realities and spirit, that was not Confucius' fault.

208

Mencius makes even the movements of the body one of the features which exhibit outwardly the Superior Man's virtue.

209

Considerate behaviour is spiritual behaviour.

210

A formal elaborate politeness, such as the better class Chinese and neighbouring peoples practised for over a thousand years, perhaps under the impetus of Confucius, is not meant here, but rather one coming from the heart.

211

The awakening of higher quality of consciousness should bring with it a higher quality of manners.

212

Refinement is a beautiful quality for anyone to possess, but for someone with a soul above materialism it is charged with a higher meaning. It not only involves consideration for others and respect for oneself, but also an attitude of aspiration.

213

The quality of consciousness is affected by the way we live. Food, hygiene, surroundings, personal habits, speech, manners, and auric atmospheres should be in harmony with the spiritual ideal—that is, *sattvik*.

214

Put these qualities in opposition and the truth about them becomes plain enough. Vulgarity contributes nothing to spirituality, but refinement gives much.

215

If high birth or much wealth makes a man arrogant or snobbish he would not come under the philosophic classification of "gentleman" whatever his society declares.

Discipline of speech

216

Whoever loves the Ideal must expunge coarse language and obscene words from his personal speech, still more from prose writing offered to the public, and most of all from finely felt and shaped poetry.

217

Not to stray from the truth is a prescription which is more important than it seems, whether in speech or writing. But in the activities of those seriously set on the higher life, it is even more important. The divorce from outer expression affects the man's inner invisible psyche and harms it. As a sequel it distorts what he believes to be true. The consequences are deplorable.

218

Discipline of speech. It requires great tact and great wisdom to talk frankly and give someone constructive criticism or make needed correction without hurting him. But even if both are absent, great love will achieve the same result.

219

The fact that people feel they must speak constantly, talking to each other whenever they are together, is simply an outer sign of their inner restlessness, of their inability to control the activity of thought. That is to say, it is a sign of their weakness.

220

Discipline of speech. When a man has this feeling of inner harmony it leads to a harmonious attitude toward all others. He suffers no nervous tension with them. He can sit, unspeaking, unplagued by tacit suggestions from society to break into his mind's stillness with trivial talk, useless chatter, or malicious gossip.

221

In many men silence in conversation may betray their nervousness which is a form of inner weakness. But in the sage such silence is on the contrary a form of inner strength.

222

Discipline of speech. The man who, in his speech, has no reverence for fact, is unlikely to find truth.

223

He is friendly without becoming familiar, brief in speech without becoming discourteous.

224

It is better for him to have a reputation for taciturnity than to be so intimidated by the crowd as to conduct himself and conform his speech to common, shallow, obvious, and vulgar ways.

225

There is an interchange of trivialities which too often passes for conversation which is both a waste of time and a degradation of speech.

226

He should act on the principle that if he cannot say what he means, he should say nothing.

227

Those who *must* speak of their emotional distresses or irritating problems, their misfortunes or disagreeable illnesses, should learn something from the Japanese attitude and at least do so with a smile.

228

The Discipline of Speech (Essay)

Too many people use their voices to hinder what is good in their own character, or even to despoil it, instead of using them as instruments of service. How pitiful to see so many employ their tongues in empty chatter and idle gossip for most of their lifetimes! When anyone becomes a quester, this matter may no longer be ignored. Buddha did not ask laymen to undergo the rigours which he asked monks to undergo, but he did state a few rules of self-discipline which were essential for all alike. Among them he included, "Abstain from foolish talk and harsh speech."

Since no utterance can be recalled into the silence whence it came, the quester will be more than ordinarily scrupulous about all his utterances. This does not mean that he is to abjure all trivial talk, certainly not all humorous talk, but it does mean that he is to bring some degree of discipline to bear upon his vocal activity.

He will not, for instance, waste time in uncharitably analysing the character of others when no business in which he and they are involved really calls for any analysis at all, let alone the backbiting uncharitable kind. This practice of criticism and slander is a common one and is often the result of the habit of gossiping. It helps no one but hurts everyone—the speaker, the persons spoken about and those who readily listen to condemnatory gossip.

He must attend to his own life, even to the extent of often refraining from talking about other persons. If this calls for a quality of generosity it is he who will be the gainer in the end. If he cannot say anything good about a person, he will prefer to say nothing at all. If he cannot praise, he will practise silence. And if the situation is one where doing that would ultimately lead to a worse result, then he will criticize helpfully and entirely constructively, not condemn hatefully. If he finds it necessary to be outspoken, he avoids making personal attacks. Sometimes it may be needful to speak sharply, to utter words which may be odious to the other man's ego but necessary to his welfare. In those cases, however, he should first put himself in the calmest, quietest mood and second, speak in the kindest possible way. Is it not better to disagree gently with the other man without being disagreeable to him? When he hears someone filling speech with negative statements and there is no duty laid on him to correct them, he puts his mental attention elsewhere. Better still, he starts affirming and holding the positive ideas which counteract the other person's remarks.

It will help a quester overcome the fault of habitually speaking harsh words or occasionally speaking angry ones, if he practises the following exercise. Let him sit for meditation and think in turn of some of the persons whom he has offended in this way. Then, seeing the other person's face and form before him, he is in imagination to speak with the utmost kindness in the one case or with the utmost calmness in the other. He may take any situation or incident which usually provokes his fault into expression. Let him do so with closed eyes and as vividly as he can bring them before his mind's eye.

Further, the discipline of speech requires him to pause momentarily but long enough to consider the effect his words will have on those who hear them. Too many people—and of course especially impulsive people—are too eager to speak before they are ready, or before their words are chosen. The quester tries to avoid using words without awareness of their meaning or responsibility for their effect.

Since experience properly assimilated tinges the character with caution and the speech with reticence, even the right thing if said at an unpropitious time may too easily become the wrong thing. If energy is often squandered in needless talking and trivial babble, the capacity to concentrate the mind on its deeper levels becomes weakened. This is why the *Mahabharata* praises the practice of silence for the would-be yogi. The *Mahabharata* even asserts that the practice of silence is conducive toward gaining the capacity to discriminate between good and evil.

He will not allow a single word to fall from his lips which does not fall in harmony with the ideal in his mind. Even the slightest deviation from this ideal may be followed by uneasiness.

Speech brings down to the physical level, and so puts into swifter activity, what thought has initiated. To a slight or large extent—depending on the individual power—it may be creative. Hence a person whose daily talk is mostly negative, filled with reports of dislikes and aversions, wrongs, evils, mishaps, and sicknesses is a person who is better avoided by those whose own inner weakness makes them susceptible to the influences carried by others.

If evil things are falsely said about him, he is neither to be surprised nor be annoyed. People see themselves in him, as in a mirror, and he must learn to accept what must needs be. Instead of feeling insulted or hurt, he should thank those who criticize him, for letting him see what may be true about himself and therefore need correcting.

Under this discipline he should recognize that searching for truth must begin with speaking it. To be a liar and a hypocrite is as obstructive to the pursuit of truth as it is distorting to the reception of truth. Every lie—and even, to a lesser extent, every "white" lie—obstructs the light on his path and to that extent prevents him from finding his way to that region where the false simply does not and cannot exist. He will be as truthful in his most trivial utterance as in his most solemn one. He will take care to avoid exaggerations and to shun mis-statements.

The pursuit of truthfulness must be inflexible, even in situations when it becomes uncomfortable. All questions ought to be answered correctly but awkward questions may be answered with part of the truth, if that will be less harmful than the whole of the truth. The changing circumstances of life will present him with temptations from time to time when it will be much easier to speak falsely than truthfully, or with opportunities to exaggerate for the sake of personal vanity or selfish gain.

If he has trained himself to love truth and abhor falsehood, to fortify the respect for factuality and avoid even the slightest tendency to desert it, there may grow up inside his consciousness a remarkable power. He may be able to detect instinctively when other persons are lying to him. But whatever unusual psychic power unfolds in him, he must protect it well. In this matter prudence puts a bridle on his tongue, which he uses to conceal rather than to reveal, if that should prove necessary. He may not talk to others about the higher teaching or the inner experiences if the act of talking about them makes him feel self-important, if it is stained with conceit and egotism. He must discipline himself to keep silent about them and, when this power has been attained, to give truths and revelations to others under the restriction of their real need and degree of receptivity. It is a foolish aspirant who rushes to tell of each new inner experience, each fresh glimpse that he gets, each little psychic happening or occult revelation that comes to him. The price of babbling verbosely and egoistically about his experiences and beliefs may be a definite inner loss or stagnation. As his ability to practise meditation enters its deeper phases, he will naturally become less talkative and more silent. The quietness which he finds there begins to reflect itself in his speech. But if he speaks fewer words, they carry greater significance behind them and greater responsibility for them.

Some Indian gurus go so far as to throw out of their uttered speech and written communication all use of the personal pronoun "I," referring to themselves by name in the third person, that is, as if they were referring to someone else. Certain Catholic orders of nuns discard the possessives "my" and "mine" from their speech. Is it an affectation, a pose, or a sign of tremendous advancement, to speak of oneself always in the third person? The answer is that it could be any one of these things: only each particular case could provide its own material for a correct judgement.

229

Within his own mind he will live his inner life fearlessly, but his public acts or utterances will be with careful regard for their effect on others.

230

Personal colouring of the truth is inevitable the moment it is given a shape in thoughts or words.

231

If he speaks at all—for in the divine presence he hangs his head—let it be with the high voice of true authority. Let it come out of the great stillness to shame lesser voices of the mean, the petty, and the ignoble.

232

What is permissible about such topics in a private talk may not be in a printed or public statement.

233

Abrasive, provocative, violent, or hostile speech is objectionable and unsuited to a philosopher.

234

"You keep silent and It speaks; you speak and It is silent." —Japanese Master.

235

He must always remember that what he feels is not necessarily felt by everyone else, that caution and restraint in speaking of it to others need to be exercised.

236

The more speech and thought are kept free from negative statements about other faiths, other teachings, other persons, and other organizations, and the more we practise courtesy and silence in matters where we do not agree with them, the better will it be for our true development.

237

The mind has to be cleansed. Speech and thought must be undefiled by treacherous backbiting, slanderous gossip, and all unkind words. The law of recompense declares: "As you speak of others so shall you be spoken of."

Accepting criticism

238

Be grateful to the one who criticizes you, whether he be a friend or a foe. For if his criticism be true, he renders you real service. He may point out a flaw in your character that you have long neglected, with unfortunate results to yourself and others. His words may prompt you to remedy it.

239

Where a relationship is unfriendly or irritating, there is often some fault on both sides, although more heavily on one particular side. If the student either wishes or is compelled to continue the relationship, or if his conscience troubles him, he must consider those faults which lie on his side alone, and try to correct them. Neither his personal feelings, nor even those of the other man, are so important—for they are both egotistic—as the need of self-improvement and self-purification.

240

When dealing with the impulsive, independent, irritable, but large-hearted type, do not offer criticism, however constructive, and do not preach. Offer instead a silent example of superior conduct, as this may be followed. Do not answer angry words with the same kind but change the subject or remain silent. Show warm appreciation of the other's good work or deeds or qualities; such favourable notice may create harmony. Be unfailingly kind.

241

When great men are criticized by other great men, they should be all ears. When they are criticized by small men, they should be quite deaf.

242

The only gentlemanly thing to do when the raucous clamour of falsehood grates on the air and the frightful spectre of animosity gibbers at him is to oppose them with silent fact of what he is and leave it at that. It is better therefore that he let personal abuse find like-minded ears and pay it back only with dignified silence. He who understands what he is about and who is conscious of the purity of his motivation can afford to smile at his "critics" and remember the Turkish admonition: "Let the dogs bark: the caravan marches on." His sense of dwelling in the Overself would be of little avail if he reacted to these unpleasant events and unfortunate experiences in the way which personal emotion would persuade other men to react. It is natural for the egoistic part of him to feel resentment, indignation, bitterness, disillusionment, and even sadness over base calumnies, the personal hatred, and prejudice he has endured. But it is equally natural for the diviner part of him to feel undisturbed, unsurprised, and compassionate over the same treatment. For here there is a perfect understanding that these opponents can only act according to their knowledge and experience, can only view him, because of the limited facts at their disposal and the limited evolutionary character they possess, through the spectacles of ignorance. Karma will assuredly take care of their deeds; his business is to take care that he send them his kindliest thoughts, keeping the devils of separateness out of their relation, holding firmly to the feeling that they are all members of the same grand life.

243

He should take care that opponents are not permitted to disturb the equanimity of his mind. Conscious of the loftiness of his motives where they suspect sordid ones, aware of the true facts of a situation which they construe falsely, he must discover his own strength by trusting the higher laws to take care of them, while he takes care to protect his thoughts from being affected negatively.

244

If an enemy, a critic, or an opponent accuses him of committing a sin or having a fault, he need not get disquieted over the event nor lose his inner calm nor feel angry and resentful nor retaliate with counter-accusations. Instead he should give it his attention, coolly, to ascertain if there is any foundation for it. In this way he disidentifies himself from the ego.

245

The man who requites me with ingratitude or betrayal does not deserve my resentment anger or hatred but my pity. Someone, somewhere, will requite him in the same way. If he needs punishment for thus wounding me, that will be a part of it. The other part will be what he does to himself by strengthening the faults which led him to act in this way. And these in turn, although inside himself, must lead to the eventual appearance of troubles corresponding to them outside himself.

246

If he cannot afford to take offense at the criticisms of others, but should use them as food for self-examination, neither can he afford to become elated at their praise. For if he does, then that also will be a triumph for his ego, a worship at its altar which would become in time a source of fresh weakness.

247

If misunderstanding comes to him from other people, he will meet it with a calm smile rather than a resentful thought. If misfortune comes to him from a source seemingly outside his own causation or control, he will meet it prudently, endure it bravely, and emerge from it profitably. If he can get nothing more, he will get the lesson of nonattachment.

248

If he trains himself in thought control as a means to ego control, then neither flatterers nor critics can reach him with their praise or blame.

249

He comes to a point where he is not only willing to identify his own faults without having to wait for some self-made misfortune to wring the admission from him, but where he does so calmly, without emotional distress, as if he were identifying them in someone else. Even more, he will seek criticism from others in order to profit by it.

250

The disciple should be as relentless in his periodic, critical observation of himself as he should be merciful in his observation of other people. He must never shrink from exposing his own faults to himself and he should not trouble himself with the faults of other people, except that his dealings with them render it essential to allow for such faults.

251

Although he should heed criticisms of himself to sift them for their truth or falsity, he need not be too concerned about them. His real judge is his own Overself, not any human being.

252

If his actions are right in the Overself's sight, he is under no compulsion to justify, explain, or defend them to meaner or lesser minds.

253

He will never take personal umbrage about the criticisms other people make of him. On the contrary, he will take an impartial and objective view of them. Whoever thinks more of himself than he ought to, or lets the praise of others cause him to forget the weaknesses which he alone knows, needs to drink from the cup of humility.

254

When he feels that unjust criticism is levelled against him, let him remember that it is wiser to keep silent than to stir up a hornet's nest. At such times it is his duty to extend the utmost goodwill and compassionate forgiveness to the parties concerned and to their dupes. For they act as they do through ignorance or misunderstanding. When they begin to love truly they will begin to understand aright. To the sage, these are pinpricks, for he is not interested in his personal fortunes but in the Quest for truth.

255

He has quite enough to do to attend to his own faults and to criticize himself without going about criticizing others. To turn the critical faculty on himself exclusively is the best way to improve personal character.

256

But because few persons can detach themselves from their own egos sufficiently, few persons are fit to be the sole judges of their own actions. It is therefore useful to ask for criticisms from other people.

257

He trains himself to talk without rancour of those who criticize him, and without bias of those whose ideas or ideals are antithetic to his own. In the face of provocation he seeks to keep his equanimity.

258

He learns like a second habit to compose himself into detachment before snubs, to respond with gay half-whispered laughter to attacks.

259

It is admitted that someone else may well have been the principal cause of personal hurt or ill from which we suffer, but it is also needful that we honestly examine whether we ought not to take a share of the blame ourselves. For there is in us an instinctive wish to escape from our own responsibility in every painful situation.

260

He should be vigilant against his own violations of ethical standards but indifferent towards other people's sins where duty does not call upon him to deal with them.

261

Whether belittled by some men or flattered by others, he remains unmoved. Denigration must be examined, to his spiritual profit, to see how much truth there is in it, and adulation to see how much falsity is in it; but in both cases it is more important to keep his equilibrium up and to keep his ego down.

262

A sincere aspirant will not only expect criticism, he will demand it.

263

What is the proper way to receive criticism? Accept what is true, reject what is false, but do so unemotionally, without egoism.

264

We shall make the curious discovery that the more men worship their own fallacies of thought and belief, the firmer the conceit that they know the truth.

265

In many circles, the man who exhibits moral superiority irritates and provokes others into accusations of hypocrisy and pretension.

266

By considering his opponents as his friends, his enemies as his helpers, he turns their opposition and enmity into practical service to himself.

267

He should humbly accept and gratefully profit by the constructive criticisms of his more advanced, more experienced fellow disciples.

268

The unblurred clarity of his conscience gives him a secret joy and strength, a silent triumph over detractors.

269

The man who criticizes us does us a favour: we ought to feel obliged to thank him. For if the criticism is unjust, we have to laugh at its absurdity. If true we ought to be spurred to self-correction. The first provokes a smile, the second confers a benefit.

270

To take a merited rebuke humbly, perhaps even gratefully, is a sign of superior character.

271

Enmity from others stirs him, not to infuriated anger but to calm perception of its cause.

272

He must try to understand the inner meaning of such happenings. The more he meets with criticism and enmity, the more he must ask himself what truth they contain. And he himself must provide the answer with perfect impartiality. If they contain no truth at all, so much the better. But such self-examination cannot be properly done if he allows emotion to get the upper hand, especially the emotions of resentment against his critics and bitterness against his opponents.

273

Neither the bitterness of resentment nor the thirst for revenge enter his heart when he is defamed by others. He keeps his serenity unbroken, his goodness intact, his gentleness ever constant.

274

If it is right to forgive others their sins toward him, it is equally right to forgive his own toward them. But it's not right to absolve himself and forget before he has fully learned the lessons and resolutely made a start to apply them.

275

Whoever accepts praise must be prepared to endure blame, unless his acceptance is quite impersonal and disengaged.

276

They and their words will perish into the dust with time, but that source whence he draws his peace "passeth their understanding," and will endure when time is not.

277

If others persist in uttering negatives to him during conversation, he is entitled to have recourse to a polite inattention.

278

If he is not concerned about his ego, he will not be concerned about critics and what they say about him. Such attacks will arouse no ill-feeling in him.

279

One shouldn't brood over fancied wrongs which he believes have been done to him nor dwell on another's faults. The law of recompense will deal with the situation. Emotional bitterness is harmful to both persons. On this path, the student must learn to overcome such feelings; they act as obstacles which hinder his advancement.

280

It is not the enmity of others towards him but the apathy inside him which is the more dangerous in the end.

281

Although he should study and observe the errors and weaknesses of other men, he should not do so unduly. Such study must not include gossip about them or disparagement of them. His business is to learn from them, not to censure them, so that he can better know how to deal with himself.

Refraining from criticism

282

When talking or even merely thinking of other persons who show some fault, weakness or sin, people are too apt automatically to judge them. This is an unnecessary and uncharitable habit. Unnecessary, because it is neither a duty nor a benefit to any one; uncharitable because the judgement is based on incomplete evidence. It is better to mind one's own business, to become detached from others, to practise tolerance and to displace such judgements at once by criticizing oneself instead.

283

Some well-meaning moralists who say that the disciple should no longer look for the evil in others swing to the other extreme and say that he should look only for the good. Philosophy, however, does not endorse either point of view, except to remark that we have no business to judge those who are weaker than ourselves and less business to condemn them. It further says that to look only for the good in others would be to give a false picture of them, for a proper picture must combine the bright and the dark sides. Therefore it prefers mentally to leave them alone and not to set any valuation upon them, to mind its own affairs and to leave them to the unerring judgement of their own Karma. The only exception to this rule is when a disciple is forced to have dealings with another man which make it necessary for him to understand the character of the person with whom he is dealing; but even this understanding must be fair, just, calmly made, impartial, and unprejudiced. Above all, it must not arouse personal emotions or egoistic reactions: in short, he will have to be absolutely impersonal. But it is seldom that a disciple will have to make such an exception. He should refrain from giving attention to the imperfections and shortcomings of others, and he should certainly never blame them for these. He should turn his critical gaze towards himself alone—unless he is specifically asked by others to examine them—and exercise it to correct himself and improve himself and reform himself.

284

Why blame a person for what he does if his higher faculties have not yet awakened and possessed him? He is only doing what he can. Moreover it is prudent never to condemn others. For others will then by karmic law condemn you.

285

We need not be blind to the faults and lapses of inspired men, but we ought to forgive them. A balancing of accounts justifies this attitude. Those who bring this rare gift with them deserve a wider indulgence than others.

286

We should always remember that everyone, on all the different and varying levels of spiritual advancement, has his own difficulties and problems. To accept these without giving way to negative emotions is the first step in the right direction. Coming to terms with life and oneself is a never-ending procedure from which no one is exempt. The very nature of existence is synonymous with the individual struggle for self-development.

287

Do not belittle any human being who is awake to his higher nature.

288

Do not condemn another soul for his misdeeds, even though he be the wickedest of all men. Firstly, because he cannot be other than he is, for time, experience, tendencies, and destiny have brought him to this particular point and way of self-expression. Secondly, because the worse his misdeeds the greater will be the redemptive suffering to which he unconsciously condemns himself.

289

What historian has complete and true information on any past event or obscure personage when he does not even have it on any present event or celebrated personage? Unless business or duty brings the responsibility into our hands, it is fairer to refrain from sitting in judgement.

290

So many are so quick to think ill of others, to spread calumny and give out malicious gossip, that the man who reverses this debased trend and minds his own business is coming closer to spirituality than he perhaps knows himself.

291

The man who respects himself will not degrade others.

292

He will have eyes open enough to see the sordid evil in men yet a world-view large enough not to become cynical about them.

293

What is the use of reproaching a fly for not being a bird or for its inability to travel as far or look as beautiful? Yet this is what they do who deplore others' bad behaviour and spiritual ignorance.

294

By blaming other persons, one's own ego is served by its implied superiority.

295

Ignorance and immaturity in others should call forth, not his irritability, but his patience.

296

The largest activity in the world is criticism, the smallest creation.

297

We aspirants ought not to waste our time or sully our minds to criticize the weaknesses of others. There are countless people in this world who expend their energies in this useless task. It brings them no gain. It keeps them tied to the lower nature. It attracts worldly troubles to them. We are to be as constructive and positive as they are destructive and negative. This will lessen the disharmony in our surroundings and increase the harmony in our hearts.

298

There are times, occasions, situations, and responsibilities which may make fair criticism a moral duty. But no aspirant can fall into the all-too-common habit of criticizing for its own sake, much less for malice's sake, without thwarting his spiritual progress. Condemning others for their real or supposed sins is even worse.

299

From the time that he perceives that he does not and can not know all the circumstances, he ceases to condemn others.

300

It is not for him to judge others, for this would imply finding fault with the divine World-Idea, of which they are a part. He knows well that, in their own proper time, they will unfold their better characteristics.

301

Since every man is guided in his mind by, or is the end-result of, his own experience of life, it is conceit to act as a judge and criticize his actions. If he were perfect he would not be born at all. Of what use, then, is blaming him? Since every man is—by the mere fact of his reincarnation here on earth—admittedly imperfect, no other man has the right to upbraid him for this and yet become indignant when his own imperfections are pointed out and condemned.

302

There is a certain quality missing from their psychological makeup which Saint Paul called "charity" and which is the outcome of broad views and generous feelings, of spiritual insight and mental serenity. It is this lack which accounts for the harsh, unfair, prejudiced, and even spiteful treatment which they afforded me. Nevertheless it is not my duty as a student of philosophy to blame them for not possessing a quality which, after all, is not a part of their goal, but to display it towards them myself. And in the last reckoning it does not matter how people—even reputedly spiritual people—behave to me, but it does matter how I behave to them.

303

He may register what others are by the measure of his own sensitivity, but he must not set up to judge, criticize, and condemn them.

304

"If you are to love men you must expect little of them." —*Helvetius*

305

Let those who wish complain of evils or criticize: that is their affair. But to take such adverse attitudes is not a laudable way of life. They, men or women, could find enough material to occupy whole days at a time. We are all vulnerable. Denouncing negatives is unhealthier than announcing positives.

306

He is too psychologically perceptive not to understand the character of others but too generous to judge and condemn them.

307

The student should not go about criticizing or abusing others. He should not do so because it is mentally unhealthy and hinders his own progress, because it will one day bring down criticism or abuse upon his own head, because he has to foster a compassionate outlook, and because he ought to understand that everybody on earth is indeed here owing to his own imperfection so that the labor of showing up faults would be an endless one.

308

The wise student should emulate the masters when encountering a man who insists on controversial argument but who has no desire to learn the truth, no humility to accept it from those who, from broader experience, know more about the matter or who, from superior intelligence, judge it better than himself. The student should lapse into silence, smile, and take the earliest opportunity to get away! He should not waste time and breath or fall into friction and disharmony by letting himself be drawn into further talk. For the truculent and bull-headed man who argues against every standpoint he takes, who disputes each explanation he gives, will be impervious to whatever truth is given him. It is better meekly to acknowledge what he asserts, without criticizing it or correcting its errors. It is better to let the man remain in the smugness of his mistaken views and let the situation be accepted, since its change is not possible.

309
Such people do not come to hear the truth about themselves or to learn the truth about life. They come for confirmation of their own ideas, flattery about their own character, and endorsement of their own conduct. This is why they will vehemently reject all criticism or correction.

310
It is stupid to bring into conversation with others beliefs which they are certain to scoff at but which one cherishes as holy.

311
The philosopher would not waste his time in hair-splitting arguments or bickerings about trivial, unimportant details when discussing a metaphysical or mystical theme with the unconvinced.

312
It is useless trying to explain his loyalty to the philosophic ideal to those who can see no use and no truth in philosophy itself.

313
Those who are unready for the higher truth will also be ungrateful to anyone who foolishly brings it to them.

Forgiveness

314
The necessity of forgiving others what they have done to us is paramount. Nay, it is a duty to be constantly and unbrokenly practised, no matter what provocation to disobey it we may receive. Our contact with others, or our relation to them, must bring them only good! never bad.

315
To the degree you keep ego out of your reaction to an enemy, to that degree you will be protected from him. His antagonism must be met not only with calmness, indifference, but also with a positive forgiveness and active love. These alone are fitting to a high present stage of understanding. Be sure that if you do so, good will ultimately emerge from it. Even if this good were only the unfoldment of latent power to master negative emotion which you show by such an attitude, it would be enough reward. But it will be more.(P)

316
Noble indignation and just resentment are on an immensely higher level than grossly selfish indignation and greedy resentment. But in the case of

the disciple, for whom the scale of moral values extends farther than for the "good" man, even they must be abandoned for unruffled serenity and universal goodwill. To the definitely wicked and the evilly obsessed he need not give his love. But he must give them and all others who wrong him his forgiveness, for his own sake as well as theirs. Every thought of resentment at another's action against him, every mood of bitterness at the other's refusal to do something he wishes him to do, is a crude manifestation of egoism in which, as disciple, he cannot indulge without harming his own self and hindering a favourable change in the other person's attitude towards him. The man who burns with hate against an enemy is, by the fuel of his own thoughts, keeping the fire of the other man's mutual hate alive. Let him remember instead those glorious moments when the higher self touched his heart. In these moments all that was noble in him overflowed. Enemies were forgiven, grievances let go and the human scene viewed through the spectacle of tenderness and generosity. Only by such a psychological about-turn towards goodwill and forgiveness will he open the first door to abatement of his enemy's feeling.

317

Ordinarily it is not easy, not natural, to forgive anyone who has wronged us. The capacity to do so will come to us as understanding grows large enough or as meditation penetrates deep enough or as grace blesses us.

318

If an enemy who is guilty of doing wrong toward him comes to him, whether out of personal need or by the accident of social life, there will be no hard feeling, no bitter thought, no angry word. For the other man, he sees, acted out of what was truth for him, what was valid by his own understanding. Even if his enemy had sought to gain something through injury to himself, then it must have seemed right to the greed in his enemy's ego, which could not then have acted otherwise. In this attitude there is an immense tolerance, and an immeasurable forgiveness.

319

The moral purification involved in casting out all hatred and granting complete forgiveness opens a door to the Overself's light.

320

If it is proper to forgive a man's crime, it is not proper, through emotionalism and sentimentality pushing forgiveness to the extreme, to condone his crime.

321

The true mystic harbours only goodwill towards one who chooses to be his enemy, together with good wishes for the other's well-being and for his coming closer to the higher self, hence closer to the truth.

322

To serve humanity is in the end to serve yourself. This follows from the working of karma. To forgive those who, in ignorance, sin against you is, for the same reason, to forgive yourself.

323

In the end the heartlessly cruel punish themselves, though whether here in this life, in purgatory after death, or in some future re-embodiment is another matter.

Criticizing constructively

324

Where other persons are good but mistaken, the uttered criticism of them should be gentle; where they are well-meaning but weak, it should be cautious. For in such cases the character has what is admirable and what is blameworthy mixed up in it.

325

The first step in dealing with one who is difficult to live with, who is irritable, impulsive, quick to take offense, explosively bad-tempered, condemnatory, and sulky is to control in yourself what you wish him to control in himself—to set an example through self-discipline, to stimulate his higher will, and to give out love.

When correcting his mistakes or shortcomings, remember it is not so much *what* you say as *how* that matters. If done calmly, gently, kindly, and unemotionally, it will be effective. If not, it will arouse his ego into antagonism or resentment and fail of effect.

Every time he speaks to you, do not answer at once. Instead, pause, collect yourself to the dangers of the situation and answer slowly, taking special pains to be more polite than circumstances call for. If you do not do this, his fault may be aroused in him immediately and you may pick it up sensitively, too; then both will display it.

Remember that negative fault-finding acts as an irritant to him and as a poison to your inner relationship. Correct him by positive, affirmative suggestions of what to do rather than harass him with criticisms of what not to do.

In short, be polite outwardly and surrender the ego inwardly. Only by first conquering the weakness inside yourself can you rightly hope that he will ever even begin to struggle against the same weakness inside himself. If he is the unfortunate victim of temperament, that is, of his ego, remember that he is a younger soul, that you are older, and check yourself. Iamblichus tells us that the Pythagoreans did not punish a servant nor admonish a man during anger, but waited until they had recovered their serenity. They used a special word to signify such "self-controlled rebukes," effecting this calmness by silence and quiet.

Pythagoras himself advised that the scars and ulcers which advice sometimes causes should be minimized as much as possible: "The corrections and admonitions of the elder towards the younger should be made with much suavity of manners and great caution; also with much solicitude and tact, which makes the reproof all the more graceful and useful."

326

It took me a long time to learn that if you want to improve a man, do not reprove him. Leave that to life itself. But then it will do so in harsher, more inconsiderate terms than those you are likely to use.

327

Criticisms should always be *balanced* ones, should avoid the tendency to go to extremes or to be one-sided when revealing defects.

328

He should not waste thought or harm others by destructively criticizing them. Instead, if his life-path forces him to deal with them and therefore to understand them exactly as they are, he will calmly and constructively, gently and impersonally, analyse them. He will see their weakness without involving himself in egotistically emotional reactions to it—unless they are compassionate recognitions of the sorrowful results it must inevitably bring.

329

It is sometimes necessary when a man is acting stupidly, unwisely, or unethically, to speak out straightforwardly if he is to be helped, rather than remain silent. If he has aspiration, if he is seeking self-improvement, his faults can be corrected. But if they are concealed from him and no one tells him about their existence, they will live longer and he will suffer more from them.

330

The fear of hurting his feelings is, in such a case, a foolish consideration. For it condones present error instead of correcting it. Yielding to this fear keeps the man imprisoned in a wrong view, where rejecting the fear might be the first step towards his liberation from it.

331

If sometimes a criticism is called for if harsher experience is to be avoided, then let it be given by a constructive suggestion of the opposite positive quality only, not mentioning the actual negative one. But if that is unlikely to be accepted and a plain warning seems the only way, then it should be uttered humbly and tactfully.

332

To offer someone constructive criticism and to avoid its being taken as a reproof, one should phrase the sentences carefully as if making a helpful suggestion and not as if making an attack.

333

Criticism based on passion, anger, prejudiced bias, hatred, or ignorance is of little worth. If it is to be constructive and healthy, it must be based on fact ascertained in the way in which the scientist ascertains facts.

334

If men are to be judged at all, then they should be judged not by the understanding which others possess but by their own.

335

The aspirant who resents being told that there is room to improve himself in a particular way, is unfit to be a disciple. If he takes a constructive helpfully meant criticism in such a way, what is the use of saying that he wants to lift himself to a higher plane?

336

A fair appraisal of any thing or person should leaven appreciation with criticism.

337

"He who spares the bad hurts the good," warns the old Roman proverb. Yet the critic, who is at the same time philosophically minded, will always seek to be constructive and will only show up the bad where he can also show us the good.

338

It is his business as a student of philosophy to be constructive.

339

He will make it easier to make a needful criticism if he prepares the way for it with an offering of praise.

340

Criticism is rarely acceptable when it comes from outside, for it is then supposed to have a hostile motivation. Neither the spirit of genuine truth-seeking nor that of friendly constructive helpfulness will be correctly understood; they will only be misunderstood.

341

Help in growth comes also from friends—if they are superiors or at least equals and if they have the courage to criticize shortcomings.

342

Being blamed in a hostile spirit is not the same as being criticized in a friendly constructive one. Yet over-sensitive egocentric persons usually react as if it were!

343

A close friend or kindly spiritual guide will render him a better service by making him more aware of his frailties than by remaining silent. For it is these latter that are the seeds of his future sufferings, as well as the bars to his future progress.

344

Every man whose orbit touches your own is unwittingly your teacher. He has something of value for you, however small it be. Let him perform his mission, then. Do not dim the lesson by covering it with clouds of negative emotion.

345

Most neurotics cannot take any criticism—no matter how helpful, constructive or well-meant it be—but only exaggerated praise.

346

Moral advice is not usually wanted, liked, or obeyed. The more it is pressed upon a person, the more it is likely to be resisted. He is content to stay as he is.

347

Criticism of others should be benevolent, constructive, and suggestive, firm yet sympathetic.

348

He needs to learn that it is not necessary to be rude in order to be outspoken.

349

It is a brutish sign to be unable to put vigour, emphasis, and feeling into a criticism without using obscene four-letter words.

350

Keep an even balance and affirm what is positive in life even while you are criticizing and protesting against what is negative.

Sympathetic understanding

351

He can give others full understanding, but only by intellectually identifying himself with them. This is an inner process which must be temporary, even momentary, if it is not to be dangerous, too.

352

To give others who hold different beliefs a mental sympathy—enough to understand what it is they hold and why—calls for a capacity to detach oneself temporarily from one's own beliefs. This is not to be done, of course, by rejecting them in any way but by just letting them stand as they are while moving over and into the other person to get an understanding of his point of view. Such a capacity cannot be acquired without enough humility and selflessness to make it possible to entertain a distasteful viewpoint even for a single second.

353

Even if he finds the opinions, beliefs, and actions of others repulsive and not to his taste he should experiment at times in the development of tolerance and in the knowledge of human nature. This can be done by entering imaginatively into their history and into their experience until he understands why they think and act as they do. That need not result in the acceptance of their attitudes, but in the comprehension of them.

354

He should be able to give an *imaginative* sympathy to those whose outlook is far from his own, lower than his own. He should be able to probe understandingly into the mind and heart of men with whose views he profoundly disagrees and whose actions he instinctively abhors. He should be able even to put himself without wincing into the shoes of a hardened criminal. But he should do all this only momentarily, only just enough to glimpse what is this mystery that is his fellow man, and then return to being himself, broadened but untainted by the experience.

355

His handling of an uncongenial person with whom he has to live or work will fail or succeed according to his practice of identifying himself with him when he deals with or speaks to him. If he fails to do this, it means that he persists in identifying himself solely with his own little ego and its personal interests, activities, or desires—hence the irritability, bad temper, and negative reaction to the other's deficiencies. But if, on the contrary, he instantly tries to feel with him, to identify himself with him, to give him temporary intellectual sympathy—that is, to practise love—there will be forgiveness of the other's failings and mistakes, good humoured acceptance of his deficiencies, and laughing patience with his shortcomings. Both persons will then make more progress more rapidly.

356

If his tolerance, sympathy, and understanding are wide enough to enter every point of view, this does not mean that his judgement, balance, and discrimination are inactive.

357

He is to see men and women not only as they are with their meanness and frailty, their wrong-doing and cruelty, but also as they are unwittingly struggling to become—perfectly expressive of the divine in them. And if the uglier one is to be the first impression, the lovelier one must follow quickly as the final impression. In doing this he makes truth out of life, instead of bringing falsity into it, as some rainbow-dreaming cults would have him do. More, he gives the best possible help to others in their struggle because he brings the kingdom of heaven to their earth in the only way it can be brought.

358

Try to understand other persons not in order to blame them but in order to understand better the operations of mind itself, the human mind.

359

If he catches himself criticizing his critics, being indignant with those who oppose him or despondent because others have denounced him, he ought to pull himself up sharply. Instead, let him enter into their shoes for a few moments to understand why they dislike or attack him as they do, and then to give their attitude his *mental* sympathy for these few moments. Their statements about him may be totally false or quite true, somewhat exaggerated or wilfully distorted. Nevertheless, let him continue to step imaginatively into their shoes. This attempt will not be easy and an inner struggle will probably be unavoidable before he can bring himself to make it. He is not asked to endorse their attitude or approve the emotions which give rise to it, but only to practise this useful exercise for developing tolerance and diminishing egoism. Even if the others have tried to bolster up their own egos by deriding his, the activity may seem pleasant but will prove unprofitable. For not only does it break any harmonious relation with him, but it poisons their own psyches. Thus they punish themselves. Why should he let resentment drag him into the same error? On the contrary, they offer a chance to deny his ego, to exalt his ethical outlook, and to shift his emotional centre of gravity from the negative pole to the positive one. Let him regard them as his tutors, possibly his benefactors. Let him take these episodes as chances both to do needed work on himself and to refuse to identify himself with negative emotions. They are to be used for present instruction and future guidance. Thus he lifts himself out of his personal ego, actually *denying himself* as Jesus bids him do.

Until it becomes perfectly natural and quite instinctive for him to react in this philosophic manner to every provocation, temptation, or irritation, he needs to continue the inner work upon himself. He needs to drill himself every day in those particular qualities in which he is deficient. Each new problem in his relations with others must be accepted also as a problem in his own development, if the foregoing is to be practised. But after that has been done and not before, since it is an indispensable prerequisite, he may dismiss the problem altogether and rise to the ultimate view, where infinite goodness and calm alone reign and where there are no problems at all.

360

His sympathetic understanding will include both those to whom religion is vital and those to whom it is suspect.

361

Where sympathy is prolonged excessively, when this shift of personality from oneself to another is not limited to gaining understanding of that other's need, and is not guarded by wisdom, there will be a denial of one's own individual being. This can lead to harm on both planes—spiritual and physical.

362

Mental sympathy with others must go only as far as a certain point: if it begins to affect us negatively, we must refrain from proceeding farther.

363

He need not stray either from the line which his thinking has been following nor the direction along which his conduct has been moving, even though he tries to give mental sympathy to different characters.

6

AVOID FANATICISM

Let us feel that we are trying to become good men of warm hearts, not good statues of cold marble.

2

It would appear that ideals that seem too remote for realization and goals that seem too high for achievement are not worth the trouble of setting up. Yet to abandon them altogether would be to lose the sense of right direction. That would be a mistake. It is wiser to keep them as ultimate ideals and goals, drawing from them inspirational and directional value. It is here and for such a purpose that the dreaming idealists themselves have their place, not in the all-or-nothing revolutionary way that they themselves think they do. It is needful to make a compromise between the facts about human nature in its present state and the ideals which it can hope to realize only in some future state. It is not necessary to go all the way with the extremists, whether in art, mysticism, politics, or economics in order to realize that we can learn something from each of them. Let us take what is adaptable in their views, but let us reject what is decidedly extreme.

3

There are not only sins against moral virtue; there are also sins against balance and proportion.

4

All extremists, whether in politics or theology, are fond of propounding either false or artificial dilemmas. Either you are an X-ist or a Y-ist, they assert. That you need limit yourself to neither of these things alone does not enter their brains, any more than that you may often treat the competitives and alternatives of those false dilemmas as complementaries. It is not only wrong to take up such an extremist attitude, it is also dangerous to the quest of truth. Manifestly, both attitudes cannot be right at the same time. If we want the truth we must accept neither and search with less fanaticism for it. And we shall then discover that it is not so black or not so white as the extremists and partisans would have us believe. The choice before us is never really limited to two extremes. Philosophy refuses to confine itself so rigidly to them and points out that there is always a third alternative. But unphilosophic minds are too partisan to perceive this. They operate mechanically on the dialectic pattern. It is as natural for the ordinary enquirer to be a partisan, to suppress what is good and proclaim what is bad in an opponent's case, as it is natural for the philosophic student to bring both forward because he is genuinely a truth-seeker. Consequently, most public discussions of any case present a picture of it which varies entirely with the mentality and outlook of the discusser. Even if the philosopher finds it necessary to take one side in any controversy, this never prevents his perceiving, admitting, and accepting what is true in the opposite side. With this understanding of the relativity of all human knowledge and experience, he will understand that a multiplicity of possible standpoints is inevitable. Consequently, he will become more tolerant and less inclined to accept the hard, dogmatic "either this ultimate or that one" attitude. Nevertheless, if philosophy affirms that different views of the same subject may each be right from their respective standpoints, it does not affirm that they are equally right. It recognizes ascending levels of standpoint and consequently the progressive character of the resultant views.

5

The illumined man will not condemn the unillumined one for not being better than he is, for not having developed a higher standard of thought, of feeling, and of conduct. He does not make the mistake of confusing the two levels of reference, of setting up his own criterion as being suitable for others. This must not be understood to mean, however, that because he gives them his intellectual sympathy, he also excuses them morally, for he does not. A misdeed is still a misdeed even though its relativity may be recognized.

6

We are not in full agreement with those who attack all success as unspiritual or better living as materialistic. Whoever has realized his early purpose, if he has done so honourably and if the purpose itself is worthy or conducive to society's well-being, is a success. If he receives rewards for his accomplishment, there is nothing unspiritual in accepting them. And whoever appreciates attractive clothes, good quality food, modern aids to efficient comfortable living is—if he develops his self-control alongside this appreciation—taking better care of his physical instrument and making more of his physical environment. He is not necessarily materialistic. The meaning of the word "spiritual" should not be unjustly circumscribed.

7

We believe that the battlefield of the quest is more within the mind than the flesh. Ascetics who gaze with disdain upon a useful life in the world have hitched their wagon to a cloud, not to a star.

8

The unsuccessful, the sick, the disappointed, the unfortunate, the pleasure-satiated, the defeated, the neurotic, the bored, and the sad have not found happiness. In their discouragement they turn either to worldly escapes like drink or begin with what seems the next best thing—inner peace. They perceive that peace can be got but only at the price of partially or wholly renouncing bodily passions, earthly desires, human prides, personal possessions, and social power. This sense of frustration drives many of them to religion, some of them to yoga, and a few of them to philosophy. All entrants into these portals are not similarly motivated, for others come through higher urges. It is a good start all the same because it marks an awakening to the need of higher satisfactions. But it is only a start. For the ultimate goal of life cannot be merely the negative denial of life. It must be something more than that, grander than that. The ascetic ideal of liberation from desire is good but not enough. The philosophic ideal of illumination by truth both includes and completes it, bringing the positive qualities of joy, happiness, and contentment in its train.

9

Even the sincere aspirant can become too anxious about the quest because he is too self-centered. He must learn to let go also. Let him remember the sage. He is satisfied to be anonymous.

10

If a man becomes cold, pitiless, impenetrable, if he sets himself altogether apart from the life and feelings of other men, if he is dead to the claims of music and the beauties of art, be sure he is an intellectualist or a fanatical ascetic—not a philosopher.(P)

11

We need not become less human because we seek to make ourselves better men. The Good, the True, and the Beautiful will refine, and not destroy, our human qualities.(P)

12

We ought never to wish that any harm should come to anyone. If a man is behaving in a dastardly way, even then it would not be right to do so. In that case we should wish that he should awaken to his wrong-doing.

13

The simple uncluttered life is a sensible idea. But if pushed by fanaticism, exaggeration, and extravagances to its ultimate, logical, and inevitable consequence, it would not only lead to the complete abandonment of all gadgets, appliances, and tools but—by steps—to life in a cave and clothes made of skin.

14

The desire to achieve unity in various sections of human life, belief, and activity—and in humanity itself—is only a dream. The differences are there, and will, in some altered form, still be there even under the surface of any cheerful pseudo-Utopia of a unified world, or section of the world. There is no profit in denying them, only self-deception. The only real unity can come out of inner expansion, out of a great heart which excludes nothing and no one; but this will still not be uniformity.

15

What we have to allow is that those who live only to satisfy the ego and its earthly desires are not lost or sidetracked. They need and must gather in such experiences. It is a part of their necessary involvement.

16

He should guard against those foolish tendencies of so many mystically minded people to hero-worship some man into a god, to over-idealize this man's personal statements as infallible oracles, or to exaggerate some helpful idea he propounds into a universal panacea.

17

With fanaticism there comes unbending rigidity and, in fact, unwillingness even to look at the evidence—which it finds of no interest.

18

It is not enough to be eager for the truth; he must also be open to the truth. No bias, prejudice, fear, or dislike should stand in the way.

19

If excessive pride in his attainments, virtue, knowledge, or devotion is an obstacle which hinders a man's growth, excessive humility is also another. This may surprise those who have read again and again in spiritual manuals of the need to be humble.

20

Goethe's journey to the Harz Mountains prompted a poem by him which is very inspired. Brahms wrote the music for it. It was written after visiting a man who saw only the negative side of life and became a hermit. Goethe specially went to see him to point out the positive side of life.

21

Why demand perfection from others when you find it impossible to attain yourself? Why impose ideal standards on them when they mock your own strivings and aspirations?

22

When virtue is too self-conscious, it becomes Vanity.

23

The path from arrogance to madness is a short one. It is safer to keep humble if we want to keep sane.

24

When mysticism leads to stolid apathy toward world-suffering, when it paralyses all sympathy for fellow creatures, it is time to call a halt.

25

The holier-than-thou attitude which condemns the sins of other men implies its own sinlessness. This is not only to commit the sin of spiritual pride but also to fall into the pit of self-deception.

26

Do not maintain a position which conscience, common sense, or intuition show you later to be wrong. Have the willingness to withdraw from it.

27

He should shun the unphilosophic attitude which sees one side as all black and the other as all white, for he should understand that both have a contribution to make. Nothing is to be hated but everything is to be understood. Nobody is his enemy for everybody is his tutor, albeit usually an unconscious one and often only teaching us by his own ugly example what to avoid.

28

It is in the nature of unbalanced and unphilosophic mentalities to see everything in extremes only and to confront others with the unnecessary dilemmas which they pose for themselves.

29

A book that has not taken a laugh at life somewhere in its ramble, becomes a bore. A man who has not found the fun in life at some time, has somehow failed. But at the same time everyone cannot give years and years of intense thought and concentration to trying to solve the most difficult problems of life without becoming stamped with gravity, not only in mind but also in body. If he is well-balanced, however, he will appreciate the lighter side of life and enjoy it without losing his earnestness.

30

No single factor is usually responsible for a particular evil and no single remedy can cure it. Reformers are usually one-eyed and take our attention away from important contributory causes in order that we may fasten it upon the one which they happen to have picked out. They are doubtlessly well-meaning, but are apt to be dangerously fanatical.

31

When fears and wishes wholly control a man's thinking, instead of reason and truth, we must guard ourselves against his statements, commands, doctrines, and ideas.

32

The average American wants economic security because he wants to satisfy a higher standard of material living than exists anywhere else in the world. And the average American is right. Let him not degrade himself materially at the behest of monks and ascetics who wish to impose an ideal on others which was never intended for the world at large.

33

Philosophical mysticism cannot appreciate, much less accept, the kind of nonattachment which runs to fanatic extremes or which makes too great outward fuss of itself. It cannot find any enthusiasm for Ramakrishna's refusal to handle money because he regarded it with such horror that the auto-suggestion brought a painful burning sensation to the palm of his hand when, accidentally, he did touch it. It cannot admire Chertkov, who was Tolstoy's closest friend and disciple, in his refusal to handle money to the point of necessitating his wife to sign his cheques and his secretary to pay for his purchases. It admits the moral purity and sincerity of both these men but deplores their mental unbalance.

34

His cheerful enjoyment of life did not pull down the blind between Whitman and his mystical experience of life. Asceticism is certainly a way, but it is not the only way to the goal.

35

The cynic who despises and distrusts human nature is seeing only a fragment of it, and not the full circle.

36

It is good in a world where there is so much evil, so many wrong-doers, to be cautious. But carry this quality to excess and you breed timidity or fear, which are evils in themselves.

37

He should beware lest in his recoil against trying to satisfy the demands of an unworthy sensuality, he falls into the opposite extreme of trying to satisfy the demands of an impossible renunciation.

38

It is possible to show a faithful devotion to principles without becoming either fierce or fanatical about them.

39

These extremists tell us that such a reconciliation of the spiritual with the human is impossible, that the two aims are mutually discordant and utterly irreconcilable, that they contradict each other and if attained would destroy each other, and that either the first or the second will eventually and inevitably have to be abandoned. Sometimes it is better to be suspicious of such an oversimplification. It may lead us more quickly to truth, but it may also mislead us. And this is one of the times when such caution is called for.

40

It is a common phrase in the literature, instructions, and rules of totalitarian movements—especially political movements—to say that not the slightest deviation may be made from the line laid down by the authority.

41

The ascetic demand that we renounce art, turn our backs on aesthetic feelings, and reject beauty may seem a necessary one. But we have to beware here of falling into the danger which Angelique de Arnauld, Abbess de Port Royal, fell into. She said: "Love of poverty makes one choose what is ugliest, coarsest, and dirtiest." She was the same Mother Superior who refused to allow any form of recreation to her nuns, so that some of them had nervous breakdowns and others went mad.

42

Those lovers of excessive asceticism who shiver at the sight of beauty, shrink from the thought of refinement, and brush off all suggestions of cleanliness as time-wasting, thereby proclaim the opposites by implication. That is to say, they proclaim dirt, squalor, and ugliness as being spiritual.

43

This insistence on interfering with other people's lives on behalf of some fanatical belief, this minding every business but one's own is a great troublemaker. It is the cause of the world's division into two fighting camps today.

44

One of the signs of fanaticism is its conceited assurance; another its lunatic extremist attitude which denounces a moderate position as heretical.

45

If he overdoes his remorse and stretches out his repentance too far; if his self-examination and self-criticism become unreasonably prolonged and unbearably overconcentrated, the actuating motive will then be not true humility but neurotic pity for himself.

46

Take the spiritual life seriously, but not too seriously to the extent of becoming a fool or a fanatic when active in the world.

47

The fanatic mutilates himself, deprives his mind of all the great accumulation of wide experience, original thought, and intuitive feeling which exists in the rest of the human race or in its records.

48

He who has caught the spirit of philosophy cannot become a narrow-minded fanatic or a conversational bore. He does not shut out the activities of human intelligence and human creativity from his interests, but lets them in.

49

With fanatic hatred as his spirit and verbal violence as his expression, a man can never make a bad state of affairs better. By thinking such false thoughts, he can only make it worse. When views are so wide of the truth and so violent in expression, he cannot become a leader of people but only their misleader. He is an unfortunate sufferer in a psychopathic state and needs remedial treatment to restore his lost mental balance.

50

Violently emotional exaggerated statements, reckless hysterical extremist screams should warn us that they come out of some sort of imbalance, that it is time for caution, prudence, reserve.

51

He can be quietly enthusiastic about his cherished beliefs without indulging in propagandist shrieks.

52

The discipline of passion, the checking of emotion, and the ruling of the flesh do not demand that we are to turn into inert wooden creatures. We may still keep the zest for life, the enthusiasm for worthwhile things, and the appreciation of art and beauty, but we shall keep these things in their proper place.

53

It is one thing to set up such a goal in life; it is another to find the way to reach it. For the attempt to live in celibacy—unless wisely managed and informed with knowledge—provokes the animal in us to revolt.

54

When his involvement in the Quest has become a desperate affair to the point of morbid self-analysis endlessly repeated, it is time to restore his balance.

55

How many misguided persons have condoned bringing harm to a fellow human or animal creature by quoting a text or a doctrine!

56

Without discipline the passions and emotions may run wild. With excess of discipline the heart may freeze, the man become fanatic and intolerant.

57

He must constantly make allowances for the possibility that his own attitudes are not the higher self's.

58

He will be neither a slavish sycophant of modern sophistication nor an over-enthusiastic votary of ancient folly.

59

To feel detachment from earthly pleasures is one thing, but to feel distaste for them is another.

60

He must not so clamp himself in the rigidity of any system as to turn it into a superstition.

61

When criticism becomes so harsh that it becomes hysteria, the man has lost his balance.

62

A mind surcharged with hysteria or neuroticism will not be able to appreciate, let alone find, the highest truth.

63

A man must know his limitations, must know that there are certain desires he can never attain and certain people with whom he can never be at ease. Moreover, he must know other men's limitations too, must realize that he can never make some understand, let alone sympathize with, his mystical outlook and that he can never bring the unevolved herd to give up their materialistic, racial, or personal prejudices.

64

The simple life need not be a squalid one. The austere life need not be an ascetic one. There is room for aesthetic appreciation in the first and for reasonable comfort in the second. Both must respect the finer instincts and not decry them.

65

The "renunciate" who gloats over the miseries of life and points continually to its horrors is not necessarily wiser than the hedonist who sings over its joys and points continually to its beauties. Each has exaggerated his facts; each is too preoccupied with a single facet of existence. Wisdom lies in the impartial appraisal and the balanced view.

66

We need all these virtues, yes, but we also need to practise them on the proper occasions—or they lose their value and do more harm than good.

67

It is not the ordinary use and ingenious or aesthetic development of material things which corrupts man, but it is the excessive use of, and infatuated attachment to them which does so.

68

The life of some unbalanced persons seems to be a periodic swing from one side of the pendulum to the other—that is, from extremes of emotional and physical sensuality to extremes of fanatic and wild asceticism. Their existence is filled with contradictions and discrepancies.

69

The unseen source which suggests or encourages fanatical austerities, extreme self-ordeals, or dramatically exaggerated sacrifices is suspect.

70

When detachment is overdone it becomes a coldbloodedness. The man then moves and acts like a marionette.

71

There is a constant preaching of renunciation: abandon possessions, embrace poverty, chill off desires, and turn aside from luxuries. The high evaluation of poverty by holy men—in their preachments—is not seldom contradicted in their practice.

72

Why should he go out of his way to destroy religious ideas which others put their faith in, if such ideas are not used to support harmful actions?

73

We must recognize that men are at different stages of response to the commands of Moses, the counsels of Jesus, the admonitions of Gautama, and the teachings of Krishna. Consequently it is vain to hope that they will accept or obey a universal rule of behaviour.

74

Enthusiasm may degenerate into exaggeration.

75

Every beginner must remember that his own way to truth is not the only way. However perfectly it suits his need and temperament, it may not suit another man's. Each gains his understanding of it according to the level of his evolution.

76

Failing to establish himself in the truth, he hides the weakness of his position under the abusiveness of his phraseology, and conceals his lack of rational arguments beneath the plenitude of his personal innuendoes.

77

If we simply compare the two attitudes, instead of arbitrarily opposing them, we shall find that they usefully counterbalance each other.

78

Why should we deny our human needs and human nature because we claim our divine needs and seek our divine nature?

79

All external austerities are helpful in training the will but only some of them have any other value in themselves. And when they become fanatical and extreme and merely external, they become perilous and illusory.

80

He is not so foolish as to seek to impose the austere ethical standards of the higher philosophy upon those who are still unable to get beyond the level of the lower religion.

81

The sages were never so unpractical as to offer a rule of life whose logical application could only be that all men should enter monasteries and all women enter convents.

82

How often in history do we find men and movements whose purpose is admirable but whose execution of it is execrable! A bad means used to attain a good end, turns the end itself into a bad thing.

83

The man who sits encased in his own virtue, may unwittingly become encased in spiritual pride.

84

Both conservative followers of tradition and progressive rebels against it may have something to offer which is worth welcoming. Why not admit the truth and scrutinize each offering justly? Why immediately react against or in favour of it, only by looking at the name of its source? It is better for everyone if there is willingness to accommodate the other, to get the entire picture and then only make decisions.

85

We must fly the kite of idealism, but we must also be able to jerk it back to earth on a minute's notice.

86

The single-idea enthusiast, the fanatic persecutor, and the disproportioned extremist—these are all out of focus, out of harmony, and out of balance.

87

The danger of adopting extremist attitudes is that, each being insufficient, its results are imperfect.

88

The unbalanced fanatic merely makes a new attachment out of his attempted detachment.

89

The type to which a man belongs, the temperament which he possesses, will direct him to go along a certain way as being easiest for him. This limits his outlook, and leads to intolerance of other ways and imbalance of his own development.

90

He should not fall into extremes and, in his care for self-protection, fall into an excessive prudence that risks nothing and consequently gains nothing.

91

Your creed is immaterial in mysticism. You may be a philosophic Buddhist or a doctrinaire Baptist.

92

Do not in enthusiastically winning new qualities and virtues ignore and neglect the one which must regulate them all—balance.

93

The beginner who develops a self-conscious measured spirituality is dangerously near to the vice of spiritual pride.

94

In trying to mold himself on a higher pattern, a new fault may insert itself—the tendency to become self-righteous.

95

He is in a hard state who is unable to make compromises and untempted to make concessions.

96

Like the rudder on a boat, or the governor on a spring, the very quality which he lacks is needed by a man to keep him from going astray into extremes, follies, quicksands, and disasters.

97

When behaviour or ideas are pushed to an incredible extreme, they are held up to ridicule either by mild humorous irony or by strong sarcasm. This brings a needed corrective to their exaggeration.

98

Any good quality may be pushed to fanatical extremes, whereupon it may become a bad quality.

99

It is hard to walk with the pessimists and deny the will to live because birth is evil and deny the natural needs because desire is evil. A juster evaluation would find evil forms of living and evil desires, but the great current of Life itself is surely beyond such relativities as good and evil.

100

A temperate self-discipline is certainly inculcated by philosophy but it does not call for the extreme of rigorous asceticism. A reasoned austerity at certain times and a wise self-denial at other times fortify and purify a man.

101

Ascetic disciplines take four channels: physical, mental, emotional, and vocal. This last one, the restraint of speech is threefold: first, some of the mantra yoga practices; second, the observance of strict silence for specified periods; and third, the carefulness never to depart from truthfulness.

102

The purpose of all balanced asceticism, whether physical or metaphysical, emotional or mental, is to pull the consciousness up from a lower outlook to a higher one. But this is only to make it possible for the aspirant to get the loftier outlook. This cannot be done if he confuses asceticism with fanaticism. It is properly a training of the body and thoughts to obey and work with his higher will.

103

To practise the necessary trainings and disciplines which any improvement of self calls for is to embrace the correct kind of asceticism, not to fall into the unnecessary and unbalanced ways which turn it into fanaticism.

104

"We practise asceticism," said a Mount Athos monk, "not because we hate the body but because it calms the passions."

105

Life makes no sense if we have to deny its most powerful manifestations, if we are taught to deny the body and ignore the senses, if we are to reject the natural satisfactions and renounce the aesthetic ones.

106

To deny Nature in the name of some narrow ascetic doctrine, to judge men and art by its standards, is to introduce ugliness into life, prejudice into affairs, and imbalance into character.

107

Not in ascetic despisal of the flesh nor in fascinated enslavement to it will peace be found.

108

Two representative examples of those forms of asceticism which may be listed as unreasonable, extreme, or fanatical, and which are therefore taboo in philosophic practice are wearing hair shirts to cause irritation or itching of the skin, and deliberately inflicting pain by scourging or mutilating the body.

109

An asceticism which makes a moral distinction between the body and the Spirit is exaggerated or false.

110

Asceticism is useful as a training of the self but harmful as a shrivelling of it.

111

Asceticism serves a useful purpose, but the balanced man will not cling to it when the purpose has been achieved. He will let it go in order to reach the next step higher, where there is no room for one-sided things.

112

Among the dangers of asceticism are its aptness to breed an intolerant mind, its proneness to harsh judgement on nonascetic human beings.

113

An asceticism which rises from within, which is wholly spontaneous, natural, and unforced, which at the same time avoids fanaticism and imbalance, is not objectionable and may even be admirable.

114

The ascetic who is ashamed to possess a body is as foolish as the one who hates it for the weaknesses he thinks it produces in his feelings.

115

The ascetic seeks for the impoverishment of life and the worldling seeks for its enrichment. Both are right in their place. But whereas the ascetic would impose his rule of life upon all others as constituting the highest one, the philosopher knows that it is but the mark of the beginner who has to disentangle himself from the dominion of desire and worldliness.

116

I accept the Chinese Confucian view which asserts that taste or flavour is essential to enjoy food but reject the Chinese Buddhist view which requires spiritual aspirants to deny themselves such enjoyment.

7

MISCELLANEOUS ETHICAL ISSUES

The moral precepts which philosophy imparts to its votaries are based not only on the familiar laws of goodness being coincident with happiness and of suffering being a reaction of evil, but also on the lesser-known facts of psychic sensibility.

2

If you have renounced the world outwardly and wear the monk's cowl or the nun's robe, you would be right in regarding ambition as a sin. But if you still live in the world and have renounced it inwardly, it would not be wrong to work like those who are ambitious and so fill a more useful and more powerful role in society.

3

Capital punishment is unethical because it commits a second murder to punish the first one.

4

Ideals are good and needed, but impracticable ones are not. Their failure tests and shows them up for the mere theories that they are. The balanced, practical idealist does more for humanity than the hazy, muddling theorist.

5

So far as advertising uses its powers of suggestion and repetition to increase the desires for food, clothes, and things which are basically harmful, it becomes a means of debasing or perverting people.

6

Today they are legalizing abortion in several countries and making it easier for the act to be committed than it ever was before. Nevertheless it remains what it is. On its own level it is an act of murder, even though that level is an early one in the life of the human being in the foetus. There is, there must be, a bad karma connected with such an act.

7

To abort a foetus is to destroy a child, to take its life. This is an act which must carry its own karmic penalty. And for a woman, whose very function in Nature is to bring a child into the world, such an act is doubly strange.

How sad that, through ignorance of higher laws, such mistakes made in judgement and conduct have to be paid for—sometimes with many years of unhappiness or suffering, sometimes with recurring regrets over opportunity missed and gone.

8

It is not enough to try to secure peace between the nations. We must also try to secure it between men and animals by ceasing to slaughter them.

9

To take advantage of the helplessness of so many animals when confronted by man's deadly weapons, cruel snares, or powerful contrivances is a sin. The karmic scales of life will read off an appropriate penalty for it. Ordinary human brutality to these creatures is bad enough but scientific brutality by vivisection is worse.

10

I would not go out of my way to destroy a mosquito but if it insists on attacking me, disturbing my daily activity or nightly sleep, then my killing of it in self-defense is ethically justified, if harmless precautions like screening windows and netcurtaining the bed have been taken but fail to keep it away.

11

In this matter we must distinguish between creatures that live on the distress of others, that represent the principle of evil in the universe, from those that do not. The ethics of nonkilling need not be applied to parasites, vermin, vampires, and maggots. In destroying them to take a higher nonverminous form, we do no wrong.

12

Sassoon story. The poor monkey-chieftain gave out a loud cry of distress, a last scream of despair before it fell dead to the earth. But in that moment his eyes met the hunter's; there was an immense heart-broken reproach in the monkey's, and in the man's heart a feeling like that which would follow had he slaughtered a human being.

13

Whether shooting animals is cruel is arguable when they are instantly slain but it is unquestionably cruel when they are impaled on spikes or hooked in a trap.

14

To take a beast from the hot tropics to the cold north, to confine it in a cage or cell for the remainder of its life is not compensated by guaranteeing all its meals.

15

I lament the cutting of flowers and the caging of animals: the one because it condemns living things to swift decay and early death, the other because it condemns living creatures to the utter hopelessness of lifelong imprisonment.

16

Why should the last dying days of cut flowers bring joy, happiness, uplift, and inspiration to anyone?

17

If we are not to slaughter mosquitoes, because they are living creatures, then logically we ought not to slaughter the germs of syphilis with Salvarsan or penicillin. We ought to let them destroy a man's flesh and poison his descendants, for these germs too are living creatures. Let us not anthropomorphize the mosquitoes' sufferings. When we kill them they do not feel anything like that pain that creatures with more developed nervous systems feel.

18

He takes care not to hurt the body of any living creature, however tiny it be, nor to harm its well-being. The only exceptions to this benevolent vigilance will be those cases where still greater evil will result by failure to defend himself against wild animals or verminous parasites.

19

Those who can only find their fun by the wanton killing of harmless animals, show no mercy and, at the appropriate time, will receive none.

20

Dr. J.C. Lillie in *Man and Dolphin*: "Animal training is effected by isolation and contact with humans, withholding food until the starving animal has to approach a human being or die. This is the usual training maneuver in circuses." E. Westacott in *Spotlights on Performing Animals* shows every kind of cruelty is forced on the unfortunate creatures.

Nonviolence, nonresistance, pacificism

21

The doctrine of nonresistance, as taught by Tolstoy and practised by Gandhi, seems noble and lofty but is actually founded on misunderstanding and misinterpretation of the true doctrine. What its modern exponents have done is to make it mean nonresistance to human evil; what its ancient advocates meant was nonresistance of the human ego to the divine Self. Its most philosophical advocates always taught that we should put aside our personal will and our personal desires and sacrifice them to the higher being, the higher Self, unresistingly. They taught a wise passivity, not a foolish one, a self-surrender to the divine power not to the diabolic power.

22

"Ahimsa," described as the highest ethical duty by the *Mahabharata*, and so often translated as "nonviolence" would be more correctly translated for the Western mind by "non-harmfulness." It does not necessarily mean that its practiser must abjure the use of physical violence when defending himself against aggression.

23

Philosophy is as opposed to violence and bloodshed as a method of ending conflicts as is pacifism but it stops where the latter walks obstinately on. It makes a clear distinction between aggression and self-defense, and justifies the use of force in the second instance.

24

He will defend himself and others against evil aggression, but he will not retaliate against it.

25

Justice often demands that force be used in order to implement its decisions. Philosophy sets up justice as one of the guiding principles of personal and national conduct. Therefore philosophy has no use for pacifism or nonviolence.(P)

26

The resistance of evil is a social duty. Its strongest expression heretofore has been defensive war against a criminally aggressive offending nation. If resistance is itself an evil, war is the most evil form of that evil. The appearance of the atomic bomb is a sign that a new approach must be found today, that the old way of defensive war will not meet the new problems which have arisen. If man is to end war once and for all and find peace, he must do so both internally and externally. He can do the one by ending the rule of the animal aggressive emotions within himself such as greed, anger, revenge, and hatred, and he can do the other by abandoning the slaying of his fellow creatures, whether human or animal. He may take whatever defensive preparations he pleases, but he must stop short at the point of killing other men. The refusal to slaughter would then evoke powerful spiritual forces, and if enough persons evoke them the end of war would be assured. However it is unlikely that such an idealistic course would appeal to more than a small minority of mankind, so that if the end of war is to be brought about in another way it can only be by the political method of an international policing army operated by a world federation of peoples. Since such a federation does not exist today, its only possibility of coming into existence is through the hard lessons learnt out of the appalling destructiveness of an atomic war. There is no other alternative to such a war than the renunciation of the right to kill.(P)

27

Philosophy is essentially realizable hence practical. It uses the idea of nonviolence only under the governance of wisdom. If violent punishment or causing pain will be better in the end than refraining, it will not hesitate. They have their place. But because philosophy combines and balances its wisdom with compassion, with mercy and, if advisable, forgiveness, its violence operates side by side with nonviolence.

28

To meet the assaults of vicious human beasts with sympathetic nonviolence in the optimistic belief that this attitude is not only morally correct but may also change the attacker's character, is to deceive oneself.

29

Such passivity invites the continuance of attack and promotes further crime. It persuades the criminal individual to turn potential victims into actual ones. It actually contributes to the other man's delinquency by encouraging him to adventure farther into wrong-doing.

30

The materialist resists evil from a selfish standpoint and with angry or hateful feeling, the mystic practises nonresistance to the point of martyrdom, the philosopher resists evil but from the standpoint of common welfare and in a spirit of calm, impersonal duty.

31

Sir Arthur Bryant: "Christ's injunction to *the angry and revengeful* to turn the other cheek was addressed to *the individual*, seeking by forbearance to render unto God, for his soul's sake, the things that are God's, and not to the rulers of society. Christ never . . . bade his followers to turn someone else's cheek to the lawless and aggressor."

32

He who would trust to the goodness of human nature at its present stage of evolution may meet with justification in some instances but with disappointment in many more.

33

The primary and justifiable use of destructive weapons should be for self-defense. When however, through greed or fondness for fighting, they are turned to offensive and aggressive uses, he who thus violates ethical laws, will, sooner or later, have to pay the karmic penalty. This is equally true of individual gangsters as of imperialistic militarists.

34

When the bloodshed and horrors of fighting have to be experienced by one on the Quest, let him steel his nerves and toughen his feelings by sheer effort of willpower. Let him console himself in the knowledge that it is only a temporary affair and will have to come to an end, at which time he can then live the kind of life he wants to live. Such a state of affairs, although a terrible business, underlines Buddha's teaching about the ever-presence of suffering and the consequent necessity of finding an inner refuge from it. Whatever happens, he must try to keep his moral outlook undegraded by outside pressures. Good character is the foundation of a worthwhile life, spiritually and materially.

35

It is the duty of pioneer thinkers to help mankind move up towards a higher life. This duty will be made clearer when the implications of the destructive period through which the world is passing are made plain. The ideals of pacifism are for those who have renounced the world. For all others the full discharge of responsibilities is necessary. The truth is that the present crisis has no parallel in history except that which preceded the destruction of Atlantis. For present-day circumstances are the material objectifications of the struggle between unseen powers representing good and evil, light and darkness. In the last war, the Nazis and the Japanese were the focal points for an attack upon the highest ideals of mankind, were the human instruments for a vile eruption of evil and lying spirits. It is the duty of those who care for these ideals to protect them. This can only be done by fighting and defeating the instruments of the forces of darkness. This battle must be waged in an impersonal spirit without hatred and with deep recognition that mankind without exception forms one great spiritual family and with the consciousness that this must constitute the ultimate ethical ideal for every nation. Thus mankind must first be purged by suffering and later healed by love.

36

Pacifism and conscientious objection to war are unworthy of a student of philosophy. They are ideals which are correct only for monks, hermits, and those who have renounced the worldly life, but quite incorrect for those who remain in the world to serve mankind. During the last war, when we were fighting such devils as the Nazi gangsters, who would destroy all spirituality, all truth, and all religion, pacifism was sheer idiocy. The *Bhagavad Gita* explains that selfless action is much higher than self-centered renunciation. So philosophy supported the war as a sacred duty but it was done without hatred and simply to teach the Germans and the Japanese that crime does not pay. If they have learned this lesson, we have helped them spiritually.

37

We take from those we associate with some of their characteristics. We may take only a little, and that unconsciously, but the result is unavoidable even if the association is only one of hate and war. This truth would provide the advocates of nonresistance and nonviolence with a good argument for their cause but other factors need to be taken into consideration. What is the benefit of slightly uplifting the character of some men at the terrible price of degrading the character of an entire culture for generations? For when a nation is handed over to an invader, its culture is handed over at the same time. All expressions of the arts, the intellect, religion, mysticism, and philosophy are then at the mercy of, and will be reshaped by, inferior minds and brutal characters.

38

Nonviolence is, and always has been, desperately needed by the world. But it must be applied sensibly and understood wisely. For, ill-placed or false, it will encourage crime, condoning it rather than deterring men from it.

39

The pursuit of nonviolence in the international field is like the pursuit of politico-economic utopia—a dream. It is laudably idealistic but, unfortunately, it is also ill-founded. The pacifism which preaches a total and absolute nonviolence, applicable all the time and in all situations, fails to recognize what is written all over the universe—the law of opposites. It is their balance which holds all things in the world, all creatures in Nature, together. In human life their conflict breeds violence, and their recession, peace. War can change its form, can lose its brutality, can be lifted to a higher level altogether where words displace weapons, and this will certainly happen. But war at worst, friction at best, will not disappear so long as the ego in man with its negative emotions is his ruler.

40

The common attitude which thoughtlessly proclaims that everything on one side of a case is good and everything on the other is bad, cannot be adopted by a philosopher. For it is dictated by the unconscious complexes of egoism. It brushes aside what is unpleasing or unselfish. It is not honestly concerned, as he is, with truth, the whole truth and nothing but the truth. A wise student, therefore, will not accept the demand to choose between two extremes. He will take something from each but tie himself to neither. The part of a fanatic who forces all questions into an "either-or" steel frame is not for him. These sharp divisions into two opposite camps are uncalled for. There is a third alternative which not only combines their own best features but also rises superior to them both. Philosophy seeks this higher view as the outcome of its refusal to take a partisan one, for partisan views contain truth but, because they are too prejudiced or too exaggerated or too one-sided, they also contain untruth.

Thus he will never make the common and harmful error of confusing sentimentality with spirituality. The propagation of the doctrine of pacifist nonviolence as a universal ethic arises out of such an error. Pacifism is a dream. The only practical rule is to meet force with force, to deal firmly when you are dealing with ruthless men, and to renounce the use of violence only when you are dealing with nonviolent men. So it is that while mystical ethics lend themselves to conscientious objections to war, such an attitude is defective from the philosophic standpoint. The philosophic student must be guided by the ideal of service and should not hesitate about the form of service whether it be soldiering or otherwise. Nevertheless, it is necessary to be tolerant and respect the inner voice of others.

There is nothing reprehensible about holding conscientious objections to the draft for military service at a certain stage of his growth for it grows out of his fine ideals. It is not a matter where anyone should attempt to dictate what he should do, for such a view is to be respected and the practice of tolerance is advisable in such an instance. Nevertheless, he should also realize that it is nothing more than a milestone from which he will one day move on. There is a higher possible view but if he cannot see its rightness or hasn't the inner strength to take it, he should not worry but do whatever he thinks is right. And this higher view is to sink his personal feelings, to realize that having been born among the people of his country and shared its life, he has incurred a karmic responsibility to share its protection too. If their ideals are different, that does not absolve him of responsibility. Only a deliberate renunciation of citizenship and transfer of residence to another country would absolve him—and once war has been declared, it is too late. As to taking up arms and killing an enemy, if need be, here again if it is done in defense of one's country against an aggressive nation, it is not a sin but a virtue. For he is not doing it merely to protect himself alone but others also. To that extent it is quite unselfish. Much depends on his motive. If a soldier fights selflessly as in a spirit of righteous service against a ruthless aggressor, he is acting egolessly. Again, the mere killing of a physical body is not a sin but the motive which brought about that killing can alone turn it into a sin or not.

41

He will not love men merely because they happen to have been born within a few miles of where he was born nor hate them solely because they happen to live a few hundred miles from it. His sympathies are too broad for that. Let the world not judge such a man by its own standards. Although he will externally comply with all that the State may legally demand and all that society may rightfully demand, he will internally be beyond all nationalistic or class favouritism, bias, and prepossessions. In its thought it may believe that he regards himself as, for instance, a Frenchman and a Catholic. But in his *own* thought he will really regard himself as a citizen of the world and a servant of God. There will be no room in his heart for narrowness and creedalism. Consequently, he will be completely tolerant and friendly towards all, including the members of different races and religions who approach him. But will they be so towards him?

42

India's much-vaunted contribution of nonviolence to the world's ethics was in fact, taken from the West, for Gandhi took it directly from Tolstoy.

43

The practice of nonviolence is prescribed in two different forms, one for laymen and the other for monks. No founder of any religion who has himself understood the Truth demands from laymen that extreme form which only the monks should give.

44

If it would be wrong for the monk, who has renounced worldly life, to resist evil, it would be foolish for the householder not to do so.

45

Pacifism is a natural and inevitable consequence of the monkish and mystic view of life. Monks may rightly submit to martyrdom, but philosophers must resist the evil forces and even fight them to the end.

46

The whole of the *Bhagavad Gita* is a warning against the folly of nonresistance to evil.

47

The problem of conscientious objection to war is an extremely difficult one. Arjuna was taught in the *Bhagavad Gita* to fight and to do his duty in the defense of his people, but he was warned to fight impersonally, without anger and without hatred. Yet how few can be caught up in the passions of war or the dangers of war without feeling some antagonism towards those on the other side? It is an almost impossible ideal for most persons.

48

Those who follow spiritual ideals will have to take their stand. Unless they recant those ideals, they must oppose the evil.

49

Nonviolence is a good. Violence is an evil. But in the compulsory choice between violent defense against violent aggression or passive submission to such aggression, it is often the lesser of two evils. For the first may bring the aggressor to suffer the consequences of his crime whereas the second may condone it. The first may re-educate him to abandon his evil ways whereas the second may encourage him in them.

50

There are savage creatures, moral monsters and insane animals who look like men but have only partially risen into the human species in their passage up from the lower ones. Having human faces and limbs, digestive and sense organs, is not enough to render them worthy of human classification.

51

With a wise mercy, which need not be stretched too far but must not be stretched too little, we must temper natural desire to punish the violent criminal adequately.

52

The pacifist who believes that his attitude will affect the war-makers and alter their attitude is as irrational as the sparrow who appeals to the hawk for his life to be spared. But pacifism has a far sounder basis than this weak one.

53

The adherence to nonviolence is not a sign of ignoble weakness but rather of noble wisdom. The folly of war cannot be reconciled with the dictates of reason.

54

To use violent means for the defense of nonviolent ideals can only lead to the loss of those ideals.

55

What is conquered by violence must be maintained by violence.

56

Nonviolence is not a doctrine of practical defeatism and emotional surrender. On the contrary, it is, in these atomic days, the only sure road to a real victory rather than to the illusory one which modern warfare brings. Nor is it a doctrine of escapism.

57

Whether it be right or wrong, this refusal to take human life under any circumstances is noble and magnificent. It must be admired even by those of us who cannot agree.

58

The decision to accept nonviolence will be made, not necessarily on an exalted plane of moral values but on a practical plane of superior effectiveness. It will be not because we have been spiritually transformed that we choose the pacifist way but because we have reached an impasse and have no other way out from world-wide suicide than this one. We are in no position any longer to make any choice at all.

Part 2:
THE INTELLECT

It is inborn in the human mind to wish to *know*. If this begins with the endless surface questions of a child's curiosity, if it continues into the deeper questions of a scientist's probing investigation, it cannot and does not stop there. For the higher part of the mind will eventually come into unfoldment, that union of abstract reflective thought with mystical intuition which is true intelligence, which needs and sees a view of the whole of things. And so the knowing faculty enters the realm of philosophy.

1

THE PLACE OF INTELLECT

Its value

Let us honour intelligence, and not insult it, for it is as much from God as piety.

2

The intellect cannot lead us to infallible truth, yes, but it can keep us from straying into roads that would lead us to utter falsehood.

3

What was called "Reason" in *The Hidden Teaching Beyond Yoga* and what was honoured as "Reason" by the Cambridge Platonists is a mystical plus intellectual faculty and not merely an intellectual one. It is not merely a coexistence but a fusion of the two capacities.

4

If we reverse the words of Descartes, whose thought helped usher in the age of science, and proclaim, "I am, therefore I think" we come nearer to the truth.

5

True intelligence is the working union of three active faculties: concrete thinking, abstract thinking, and mystical intuition.

6

The intellect can only speak for the Overself after the Glimpse has vanished and turned to a mere memory. That is to say, it is really speaking for itself, for what it thinks *about* the Overself. It has no really valid authority to speak.

7

The wisdom of God cannot be found by the intellect of man.

8

The fragment of knowledge which the finite mind can absorb and hold is so little that we must remain humble always.

9

He may recognize the truth with his intellect and yet be unable to realize it with his consciousness.

10

The intellect ought to work only as a servant, obeying intuition's orders in practical life or filling in details for intuition's discoveries in the truth-seeking quest.

11

These competing tendencies of intuition and reason may, however, be harmonized in a balanced personality. All mystics have not advocated the paralysis of intellect—even Jacob Boehme wrote: "Human reason, by being kept within its true bounds and regulated by a superior light, is only made useful. Both the divine and natural life may in the soul subsist together and be of mutual service each to the other."

12

We should not rightly expect such a deliberately evoked intuition to act always as a substitute for reason. Its help is to be sought only when reason is baffled. We must not on the plea of the superiority of intuition desert our parallel duty of evolving reasoning power. We are endowed with intelligence, with the faculty to reason things out, with the ability to box the compass of our own life, and it is our task to use this most common of all potential qualities a little more frequently than we appear to do at the present time.

13

The greatest intellect is as nothing when compared with the intelligence, the so-called subconscious mind, which directs the involuntary functions of the body.

14

Intellect, reason, and intelligence are not convertible terms in this teaching. The first is the lowest faculty of the trio, the third is the highest, the second is the medial one. Intellect is logical thinking based on a partial and prejudiced collection of facts. Reason is logical thinking based on all available and impartially collected facts. Intelligence is the fruit of a union between reason and intuition.(P)

15

The truth is not against intellect but above it, not opposed to thought but beyond it.

16

None of these ultimate problems can be solved by the intellect: those who imagine they do so, deceive themselves. And if they communicate their specific solutions to disciples or followers they, unintentionally perhaps, mislead them. Human thought can go so far but no farther.

17

The "truth" which intellect can attain is a perpetually moving one. Thinking can never arrive at a final conclusion that is completely final, or at an absolutely true "truth."

18

Cerebral thought is an activity which, if it dominates a person as it does with most people, prevents intuitions from deeper levels of consciousness gaining entry. It also prevents other minds from entering, thus barring hypnotic suggestion and telepathic transfer.

19

Ordinary thinking is wholly related to experience connected with the five senses. It entirely misses the higher dimension which is the content of such insight.

20

The same power which caused man to fashion a crude wooden plough eventually enabled him to fashion a motor-driven plough. That power was and is intelligence.

21

The power to discriminate between the false and the true, to decide between the right and the wrong, to judge all the varied factors which present themselves to the senses, is the power of intelligence.

22

Intuition is often the explosive climax of a long slow process of hard thinking but whether it comes swiftly or slowly it must always be ready to justify itself at the bar of reason, for the latter is our only reliable guide to truth. Man may lay reason aside only when its fullest use has led him to the point of transcending it. To ignore it before that moment is to fall prey to extravagant fancies which are likely to lead the mind completely astray.

23

He accepts all that mystical intuition can tell him about his own and the universal being. But he sees that it will not be weakened, it will only be supported checked and balanced if he listens also to what the rational intellect can tell him.

24

Unless every question is seen in relation to the Overself it is not seen rightly. Therefore, whatever answer is gained cannot be the final one.

25

If man's intellect is subject to error and illusion, how can it distinguish correctly the final Truth which is not subject to error, and the absolute Reality which is not subject to illusion?

26

Life is an enigma to those who think, who have felt the intellectual urge to probe its meaning and the emotional urge to find a conscious relationship with it. Yet, if they pursue the attempt to satisfy these yearnings, they do not get far. The theories and beliefs offered from different sources too often contradict one another. Life continues to evade the deeper questions.

27

The intellect, by its criticism and research, can serve and supplement the intuition's work, can round and balance it; the service need not nullify it. Such a collaboration ought to be encouraged, not excluded as the more religious devotee in the past often excluded it.

28

Thinking about the Overself is inferior to experiencing the Overself but in its own way and on its own level it is helpful.

29

Reason with a small "r" is the logical use of thoughts, which is a mediate process; but with a capital "R" it is the intelligent use of the understanding, which is a direct immediate thing: intuition. Kant used it somewhat in this sense—but went only part of the way into a semi-agnosticism, semi-knowledge of the truth. So the term got fixed into its lesser meaning alone: the Kantian use of it is somewhat obsolete and best not used by laymen.

30

The intelligence, as something more than intellect alone, can be used to carry his thinking to the verge of an intuition which will light up some of his understanding. But such a success requires certain preconditions: a measure of equilibrium in his personality, a measure of self-discipline in his character, intensive pondering on the truth.

31

There are no final conclusions in these matters. It is better to accept the truth and let life remain inconclusive than delude oneself. But this is not to support those who claim that the only truth is that there is no Truth, or those who assent that all is mere opinion.

32

Intuition speaks with its own authority but what does it lose if it has the support of argument?

33

When intellect comes to understand that its own existence implies a superior existence which is its origin, it has served its highest function. When it accepts the fact of intuition and serves it by laying itself down in stilled prostration, there is born Intelligence. Then alone does truth appear and peace bless us.

34

Intellect obstructs the light of the Overself.

35

The intellect, which so usefully serves the purpose of analysis or exposition, discussion or explanation, is useless for the purposes of acquaintance with, or comprehension of, the essence of things, creatures, life, or mind. It is not capable of "touching the Untouchable," to use an expression borrowed from the most ancient and, at one time, the most secret Asiatic philosophy.

36

Human thinking can only lead to, and produce, another thought, or series of thoughts. It cannot get beyond itself, cannot rise to any object that is not of the nature of a thought.

37

The intellect is incompetent to solve the mystery of man by itself. But in the absence of a properly developed intuition it can render certain useful services to protect and guide the seeker. If it is not to be relied on altogether, it is nevertheless not to be abandoned altogether.

38

Colin Wilson: "All thought chases its own tail" seems to be Lao Tzu's meaning in his line "going far means returning."

39

To evoke thoughts, make mental images, or gather words about the Overself is to remain just as much outside it and inside the ego as ever.

40

Commentaries upon truth and expositions of it are not identical with truth.

41

It must never be forgotten that such intellectual conceptions of Reality are mere photographs taken by the camera of imagination or diagrams drawn by the reason. They are not the object itself.

42

What the intellect is unable to grasp is truer than what it can. That part of man—the intuition—which operates in this sphere brings the truth-seeker to a satisfaction that is more intense. Why? Because it withdraws him from the illusions and errors to which the intellect, however sharply formed, is necessarily subject. However, the intellect can help by submitting, and serve by formulating into suitable words what the intuition reveals to it.

43

The dangers of developed intellect are pride and complacency, over-analysis and over-criticism.

44

The untrained and uneducated mind necessarily has shallow views. But the academically trained and educated mind may still have distorted prejudiced or narrow views, even though they are deeper and better informed. Only a free philosophy, based on insight, uninfluenced by social pressures, can produce truly reasonable minds.

45

He must develop and nurture all the powers of intellect, but without its pride, arrogance, or conceit.

46

The intellect can quite expertly give its support to any position the ego desires it to take up. It can become instrumental in the search for truth only as it becomes freed from egoism.

47

The danger that intellect will rule over mankind is as catastrophic in the end as has been the danger of emotion and passion ruling over mankind.

48

There is a dead intellectuality which, although quite unable to penetrate to the mystical heart of things, yet carries itself with an arrogant air of supercilious self-assurance!

49

He must know that so long as various complexes sway the mind it is not possible to take a detached impartial view of any situation to which those complexes have reference. Therefore, one aspect of such a situation will be seen, but not another, and any decision taken, any action called for, will be unbalanced and unwise.

50

The gluttony of the intellect is as hard to curb as the gluttony of the stomach, and often much harder because less recognized for what it is.

51

The ordinary intellect submits to the rule of passion, self-interest, desire, appetite, custom, and appearances; hence the knowledge it obtains may easily be illusory and is always undermined by doubt. The purified reflective intellect disregards the pull of these forces and tries to see things as they really are. Hence its knowledge is stamped with greater certainty.

52

Every man who is capable of thinking in a disinterested manner—and therefore capable of thinking truthfully—must come to this realization. It is a most unfortunate fact, however, that such disinterested thought is extremely rare, that men are prone to wishful thinking, to mental outlooks more or less strongly coloured by their personal desires, prejudices, and social positions.

53

The possession of half a dozen imposing university degrees may just as easily hinder a man's approach to philosophy as help it. It will do so if it generates emotional pride and intellectual self-conceit, if it makes him sceptical of intuitions and antithetic to prayer, if it prevents him from approaching the Overself with humility and love so that he cannot weep at his estrangement from it.

54

When the intellect has produced its sharp pointed criticisms and the voice or pen has formulated its logical emphatic sentences, in the end, in old age, or after many a lifetime, the man will have to drop his arrogance and submit humbly to the higher power within.

55

If there is a string of mistaken judgements running through a man's life, even though he believed them to be accurately reasoned when he passed them, be sure that one end of it is being pulled by his own faults and deficiencies.

56

We have seen in certain lands the results of intellectual activity when placed at the service of materialism greed and sensuality. Its worst phases are then made manifest, especially its craftiness and lack of conscience, its trickery and dishonesty.

57

Men who are unable to create, criticize. Thus the work they do hangs upon the work of other men.

58

The pompous public figure who mounts the highest stilts of oratorical eloquence is not necessarily one whit wiser than the humble adept who seldom brushes the air with words and who prefers depth of thought to dissipations in speech.

59

A smug and conceited mind may become spiritually inert.

60

The pontifical self-important formality of such statements is intended to create an impression. It does. But we must penetrate their surface. Then we find there is some hollowness beneath them.

61

When malice and egotism get into a mental picture, reliability goes out of it.

62

Cleverness may be admired but cunning is reprehensible.

63

When the mind is hazed and feeling glamoured, reason and judgement are at their feeblest.

64

But with stronger thinking power there comes also intellectual pride and egoistic conceit. He must offset them by humbling himself deliberately before the higher self. He must not hesitate to pray daily to it, on bended knees and with clasped hands, begging for its grace, offering the little ego as a willing sacrifice and asking for guidance in his darkness.(P)

Its limitations

65

It is true that no man can arrive at the truth about God through his own thinking, which is merely the ego thinking. But it is also true that through keen, close, and sustained reflection he can arrive at the truth which perceives the ego's limitations, the intellect's limitations, and thereby know the time has come to suspend such efforts to stop and to surrender in mystical meditation to the non-thought side of his being.

66

Idea is not the ultimate reality, it is only a manifestation of something which is its ultimate reality. The latter seems to be an abstraction. Intellectually it must be so because it is beyond the power of finite, human mentality to conceive it. But it may not be beyond the power of a higher faculty lying latent within us to have the experience of this reality—at least for a time. It is not known how to verify whether this is so or not unless the intellect humbly realizes its own limitations and voluntarily abnegates itself at a certain stage. In most cases this is done prematurely, hence the self-deceptions and hallucinations which are rife in mystical circles, but in the philosophical mystic's case it would come only after the fullest use of critical thought and analytic reasoning. This is the proper moment for such a suicidal act. For in the end he will be brought to such an abrupt turn. Perhaps Jesus' statement, "Except ye become as little children ye shall in no wise enter the kingdom of heaven," is appropriate here, if understood as an invitation not to foolishness but to surrender of all human pride.

67

If you are trying to grasp the great Mystery do not make the mistake of unwittingly holding on to the intellect while doing so.

68

When he has climbed to the peak of a series of abstract thoughts, they may end abruptly and the higher faculty of intuition may then become active.

69

The philosophic mystic seeks to stimulate thinking to its highest degree until finally it turns round on itself and examines the very nature of the ego—of the personal mind. Both practices lead in the end to the same result, the stoppage of thinking.

70

Is it not strange that the most intense, the most active pursuit of thought leads to human knowledge, whereas the complete cessation of thought leads to divine knowledge!

71

Thinking achieves its highest object when it leads to its own rest and the mind transcends all thoughts.

72

Where intellectual knowledge puffs up a man, insight humbles him, has indeed the very opposite effect.

73

For the intellectual type, the essence of his need is to see that he is *not* his thoughts, that they are but projections thrown up out of consciousness. He *is* that consciousness, the very knowing principle itself.

74

A time comes when the searching intellect humbly recognizes at last that it can never recognize pure Spirit, but only its ideas, opinions, fancies, and imaginations about Spirit. If it follows this up to the fullest consequence and ceases all its theological or metaphysical or occult studies, it lays itself open to be penetrated by the intuition.

75

The work done by original deeply penetrative thinking can go far, can uncover much not yet known; but it cannot solve the mystery of the thinker himself, unless it renounces its right to do so and lets the diviner Self take over in utter silence.(P)

76

The same intellectual quality which obstructs the inner path or blinds the inner eyes of so many sceptical people actually helps the path of less egocentric persons. The intellect is not to be condemned. But its presumptuousness in arrogating supreme, unchecked, and unbalanced control of a man, is to be condemned.

77

The mind will go on having doubts and asking questions, making problems for itself and creating illusions, as it has always done in the past. That is, it will do so until it attains Truth, or abides in the Stillness.

78

He need not abandon rigorously logical thinking because he is cultivating mystically intuitive feeling. But he should know its limitations.

79

He must not depend on lesser faculties alone—good though they are in their place—when a higher faculty exists, when the intuition shines out of its certitude. Not the impure, ego-warped, narrowed, emotion-swayed and intellect-dried thing which serves so many; not man dictating to God but more humbled before God. A seeker must become free from fanaticism before the eyes can see. Let no one impose suggestion's power nor authoritarian rule; rather should the mind empty itself until Pure Consciousness is there.

80

Weak minds which perceive the defects of logic, instead of rising above it into reason, fall below it into instinct or impulse.

81

The silent mind receives spiritual guidance and allows grace to approach; the thinking mind deals with the world and attends to its activities.

82

Only when the intellect, after admiring its own massive historical achievement, will turn upon itself and perceive how puny is that by contrast with the still-awaited answer to the question, What am I?—only then will the possibility of higher forces coming to its aid be realizable.

83

Krishnamurti: "Into crowded minds no revelation is possible. In the stillness of the mind, that admits, 'I do not know,' illumination is more apt to be achieved."

84

In telling us where knowledge must end and mystery must begin, in being forced to describe the Absolute by telling us what it is not and then confessing that it can go no farther, the intellect surrenders to its limitations and acquires that quality of humility which is an essential condition for receiving grace.

85

Correctly used, its limitations understood, its emotional and egotistic biases discounted, intellect may enable a man to think properly. It can then have a liberating effect; otherwise it is likely to have a corrupting one.

86

The limitations of intellect must be recognized, for then only will a man be ready to try the philosophic techniques whereby words are used to rise above words, thoughts directed so that he may extract himself from all thoughts.

87

To develop intellect and then to know when to drop it, is to become its master. It then fulfils its proper purpose and serves man instead of dominating—and therefore unbalancing—him.

88

The last act of human intellect, when it reaches its highest level, is to recognize its own limitations and surrender its own authority. But the surrender is not to be made to another human intellect! It is to be made to the intuition.

89

It is not that he is called upon to reject all his own knowledge and refuse the offerings of his intelligence. But since he is striving to enter a state where the stillness precludes all questions and all answers, all mental concepts and mental images, he must make a beginning where the way to it is possible.

90

If you try to make Mind a topic for analysis, worship, or discussion, it is no longer the unseen uncomprehended Mystery but a projection, whereupon it is at once objectified and becomes an idea-structure. Such an act falsifies it. You honour it more truly if you stay silent in voice, still in thought.

91

With so much education and information, so many particular pieces and fragments to keep together and carry in his mind, how is it possible for anybody to keep it really peaceful?

92

Paradox transcends ordinary familiar experience and baffles ordinary logical thinking. Its leap can be made only by intuition, if he lets it function, or by faith if he can trust the sages' teaching.

93

Even the intellectual theory is worth studying despite the intellect's limitations. It acts as a set of red signals pointing out both dangers and deceptions, wrong ways and pitfalls.

94

The intellect which changes hour by hour has no existence in the absolute sense. And it surely does not represent the ultimate possibility of experience. Thus, one can stop its movement for a time through profound meditation and be then aware of a deeper level of mind whence all these intellectual changes spring up but which is itself relatively unchanging. How to know whether this deeper level is worthy to be called enduring reality is a question that is beyond most mystics.

95

Humanity is discovering that it cannot solve its old problems in the old way—the logical thing to do is to try a new way. In an age of materialistic intellect and materialistic religion such as ours, that new way must consist of turning towards a spiritualized intellect and a spiritualized religion. The first step for the intellect to take is humility; the first step for the religious feeling to take is obedience. The intellect must sink down in the self-abasement of constant prayer to the Higher Power; the religious feeling must obey sincerely and honestly the admonitions given it by the great prophets. The intellect must no longer go on deceiving itself and the religious feeling must no longer go on deceiving God.

96

The intellect has to become baffled and exhausted by its own activity in search of the Overself, must despairingly know that it has no possible chance of ever knowing the truth by its own self-defeating procedures, must realize that it is running round and round in a circle, and must finally abandon the effort altogether. At this very point a great opportunity awaits the seeker, but it is also here that so many go off at a tangent and miss their chance. Either they label the quest futile and illusory, losing further interest, or they take shelter in a hierarchical religious organization which imposes dogmas and demands complete submission to its authoritarian rule.

97

The intellect can never stop asking questions. It has millions always in reserve. But in the end there is only one important question. So why not ask it in the beginning and save this long circular detour?

98

When logic fails, men often betake themselves to occult, mystic, and even primitive paths.

99

If the end is to sublimate thinking altogether, why go on collecting more and more thoughts from teachers and traditions—all outside one's self?

100

How haughty the intellect may become! It does not understand that there is an invisible circle around it labelled "Pass Not!"

101

Some intellectuals have too many questions, give up in the end and turn agnostic or join the Catholic Church or, like Hume, spend the rest of their years shallowly.

102

Unless intellectual thinking understands its own limitations and therefore knows when to stop its own activity, it will not lead man to truth but mislead him. But if and when it is willing to deny itself at the correct time, it will allow intuitive thinking to be born and that will lead him still nearer to the goal.

103

The same man at different times of his life may hold different views. It is unrealistic to demand that everyone should be consistent throughout the course of a lifetime.

104

The intellect is only the totality of transient thoughts; it is not a separate and self-existent thinker.

105

The telephone operator in a business who attempted to manage all the departments of that business independently of the chief executive would be a usurper. The intellect is the telephone operator of our psyche and undertakes more than it is really capable of when it undertakes to decry the Soul.

106

The intellect's desire for total explanations of the universe is impossible to satisfy, save with self-deception.

107

The intellect produces thoughts without weariness. It looks for change instead of looking inside itself for its originator.

108

To start with the data and come to the conclusions, joining the two by a series of logical steps, is the way of ratiocinating intellect. But we need to guard against inaccuracy of thought and speech as well as against narrowness of mind and feeling.

109

Kant saw how the mind forms its ideas under definitely limited conditions, and how it cannot help but do so, and that these ideas are merely the best it can produce under those conditions, not at all the truest ones.

110

We make the mistake of looking for a philosophical system that will confirm our preconceived beliefs and views.

111

How few are really and sincerely seeking to establish truth; how many seek rather to establish victory. They can point out the errors in other people's conclusions, opinions, and beliefs, but are blind to the errors in their own.

112

"Against stupidity the gods themselves strive unvictorious." —Schiller.

113

There is a simplicity which is too much like stupidity to be worth cultivating.

114

Neither tries to take in the other party's case but each presents only his own. Neither is willing to listen or believe the other side has any case at all. So reason never really gets a chance, only ego-centered self-interest. Each is far removed from any real wish to find the truth as it really is, objectively.

115
To limit one's ideas to those of the environment in which he happens to be born is a common fault.

116
Many aspirants fail to realize that they move mostly in the realm of their own personal ideas, and not necessarily in the realm of utter truth.

117
The intellect is endlessly curious, ever wanting to *know*; this is why its activity is hard to still.

118
Intellectual acumen is useful on this quest, but alone it is quite insufficient.

119
If thoughts and ideas are removed, what is left of the intellect? What is it if not the aggregate of all these mental activities?

120
A *doctrine* comes into being through theorizing by intellect or activity by feeling, that is, it is an opinion or a belief. An *item of knowledge*, for example scientific knowledge, is neither.

121
The intellect has to receive truth before it can be satisfied. And it requires that truth to be presented by giving reasons and using logic, if it is to be acceptable.

122
The work of the intellect in tracing causes to effects, in analysing situations and substances, in forming theories and making studies, and even in synthesizing the results of all these operations is still a limited one.

Its inward vision

123
Let no one mistake intellectual understanding for the wholeness of knowing, rather let it be to him a spur and a help to reach deeper within himself to the Overself in full surrender.

124
The situation may be summed up thus: If the activity of thinking is directed towards external objects and inspired by the desire to attain or

retain them, it binds a man to his spiritual ignorance. If however it is directed towards God or his divine soul and is inspired by the desire to attain it, then it leads him to spiritual intuitions.

125

To understand intellectually is good but to glimpse intuitively is better. Best of all is not merely to look at truth but to enter into it.

126

When you are going through the intellectual analysis you must think as sharply as possible. You have to hack your way through these woods by the sharpness of your thinking. This is where the clarity of thoughts and their formulation into exact phraseology is so necessary. You must not be vague and hazy about ideas; you must penetrate them with clear understanding. It is only later when you have reached the meditation stage that this activity is put into abeyance, because then the effort is to still thought.

127

Thus we see how reason, so far from being despised as "anti-spiritual," has actually led us, when allowed to complete its work and not stopped by materialist intolerance, to the profound spiritual truth of our being. What we have next to do is to *realize* this truth through ultramystic exercises.

128

Nevertheless, the endeavour to grasp what is beyond its reach is not a wasted one, for it carries the intellect to the very limits of its own being and then invokes its higher counterpart to come to the rescue.

129

First there must be intellectual understanding of the truth of his real being, then he can advance to the practices which lead to its realization.

130

He should always try to distinguish between knowledge which is acquired by the intellect and spiritual intuition which is bestowed by spirit.

131

Where ordinary thinking cannot penetrate, holy thinking can.

132

There are certain deep questions which a developed intellect will have to ask but which cannot be answered in the intellect's own language.

133

The intellect's finest function is to point the way to this actual living awareness of the Overself that is beyond itself. This it does on the upward path. But it has a further function to perform after that awareness has been successfully gained. That is to translate that experience into its own terms, and hence into ordinarily comprehensible ones, both for its own and other people's benefit.(P)

134

Reasoned thinking may contribute in two ways to the service of mystical intuition and mystical experience. First and commonest is a negative way. It can provide safeguards and checks against their errors, exaggerations, vagaries, and extravagances. Second and rarest is a positive and creative way. It can lead the aspirant to its highest pitch of abstract working and then invite its own displacement by a higher power.(P)

135

Like the two sides of the same coin, so it is that a thing thought of is thought of always by comparison with something not itself, that all our thinking is therefore always and necessarily dualistic, and that it cannot hope to grasp Oneness correctly. Hence the logical completion of these thoughts demands that it must give up the struggle, commit voluntary suicide, *and let Oneness itself speak to it out of the Silence.* But this must not be done prematurely or the voice which shall come will be the voice of our own personal feelings, not of That out of which feeling itself arises. Thinking must first fulfil, and fulfil to the utmost, its own special office of bringing man to reflective self-awareness, before it may rightly vacate its seat. And this means that it must first put itself on the widest possible stretch of abstract consideration about its own self. That is, it must attempt a metaphysical job and then be done with it. This is what the average mystic rarely comprehends. He is rightly eager to slay his refractory thoughts, but he is wrongly eager to slay them *before* they have served him effectively on his quest.(P)

136

These studies do indeed open up the loftier faculties of human intelligence, faculties which bring us to the very borderland of insight.

137

To learn that Reality is beyond the intellect's capacity to know it is to learn something about it. To learn what it is not may seem useless to some people but that does prepare the mind, as well as the way, for the positive knowledge of it through insight.

138

A reality which is not conceivable by human thought because it transcends thought itself, therefore it is also not describable. But what thought can do is to establish what IT is not, and even more important that IT *is*.

139

It is by its pondering over these very contradictions paradoxes and puzzles of an intellectually scientific view of the world that the intellect itself is unconsciously led first to engender and ultimately to accept a mystically intuitive view of the world.

140

Why must we always try to arrive at formal conclusions? Why not let ideas work of themselves in the subconscious?

141

This philosophy does not come within the range of any recognized system. This is because it refutes all standpoints, including those which it adopts itself temporarily as a means of leading the student higher. And when no other view is left for examination and attack it says, "Truth itself is beyond thought and speech, but the way to it embraces them." Reality itself is beyond touch and ideation but the way to it can be pointed out. You must eliminate from the definitions of both truth and reality everything which might mislead you to regard concepts as the final goal. Just as a man may use one thorn to pick another from his flesh and then throw both away, so you must use right concepts to remove erroneous ones. Finally you must discard them all.

142

Because critical, rational thinking has to be transcended during certain phases of this quest, we should not overvalue it. But let us not therefore fall into the opposite error and undervalue it. Even if it could no nothing more than keep us from stumbling, it would be worthwhile. But it can do much more than that.

143

When intuition quietly confirms what intellect argues, when it gives a deeper sanction to reasoned conclusions, we come closer to the truth of the matter.

144

The intellect has its own limitations but it can lead a man—if properly guided by correct thinking or by hearing and reflecting upon words of those who have already written them—to the very verge of the limitations where a single leap into passivity will dispel darkness and bring light.

145

Among those masters who taught the tenet of three levels of understanding was the brilliant intellectual and mystic thirteenth-century medieval Ibn al-Arabi, of Spain, who was honoured by the title "Teacher of the Age." He described them as (1) ordinary intellectual acquisition of information; (2) temporary emotional conditions, mental glimpses, and mystical experiences of unusual uplift; (3) permanent perception of the Real.

146

We must beware of falling into unreason at any point on this path. For it is reason that leads up to insight even though it is incapable of reaching beyond itself.

147

It is not that reason must be abandoned and all its values thrown aside, but that reason itself now points to the intuition which transcends it. "My work was good, and it was well done," says reason, "but to take you farther, into a sphere that is not properly mine, where an entirely different faculty must bear you, would be imposture."

148

The intellect cannot know its source but it can explain *why* it cannot know. More, it can go farther and tell us that there is a source and that it is transcendent, wrapped in eternal stillness.

149

Man's self is not his thoughts but the *consciousness* which makes those thoughts possible. He stands in somewhat the same relation to them that they stand to the body: he uses them and partially expresses himself through them.

150

No thought can assume a clear and distinct form in the mind of a man until he has pinned it to a picture if it be concrete, or to words if it be abstract.

151

During the time that anyone is engaged in the activity of thinking, he is not in himself but in the thoughts.

152

No idea can give us full and lasting support, for after all it is only a thought; but a true idea can give us much help over many years. But only being established in Being can support us in every way and all the time.

153

We cannot underestimate the importance of the leading ideas which direct and control a man's thinking. Man possesses creative power. He may pour his molten imagination into new molds, then solidify it, and through sheer intensity of will give birth to his own brain-child.

154

The mind can be put to a high or a base purpose. It can be a friend or a devil at your side.

155

If intellect were an undesirable faculty to use and thinking were part of the evil in us, then this assertion should not itself be supported by any argument for that would be illogical and inconsistent—since it involves the use of thinking!

156

Most of us move from one standpoint to another, whether it be a lower or a higher one, because our feelings have moved there. The intellect merely records and justifies such a movement and does not originate it.(P)

157

When you utter the words "I know" you inevitably imply a duality of a thinker and his thought, of subject and object.

158

Only those thoughts are true for such a man as can lodge comfortably with the other thoughts already reposing in his mind!

159

We ordinarily know any object while we are both separate and distant from it.

160

Dynamite reposes in moral neutrality. The use that is made of it determines its goodness or badness. In the same way, reason and thought are spiritually neutral. They hinder or help the inner life only according to the way they are used, the roads which they take, and the aims which they set for themselves.

Reason, intuition, and insight

161

My criticism in earlier books of intellect as an unsatisfactory guide to truth, and of intellectualism as yielding a lot of contradictory opinions, was misunderstood. It was directed against intellect, not reason: I differentiate between both. Intellect uses logical method, reason uses a higher one. Theological philosophy is based on logic. Scientific philosophy is based on reason. I uphold rationalism against intellectualism, the thinking power in man against the classifying power, the mind which evaluates thoughts against the mind which merely collects and describes them.

162

So long as these two faculties of human mind—reason and imagination—are surrenderd to its animal side, so long will they prevent the real human being from being born.

163

The victories of reason are the only enduring ones.

164

When we abdicate reason for unquestioning belief, when we sign away our birthright of private judgement to another man, we part with a precious possession.

165

Reason is active in the developed man. He cannot stop it from demanding a cause for an effect.

166

I took this use of the term "Reason" from Aristotle, who made it higher than ordinary intellect, as well as creative, spiritual, eternal, and undying.

167

The faculty of discrimination which we are to use in the pursuit of truth is not the intellect but the true Reason, which itself judges the intellect and rejects or confirms what it says. The Indian sages call it *Buddhi* and have even assigned to *Buddhiyoga* a status not a bit lower than that given to the other yoga paths.

168

The conclusions to which reason comes can only have obligatory force upon the reason itself, not necessarily upon the whole integral being of man. We are finally to decide the problems of life by the integration of all our human nature and not merely by the judgement of a particular part of it. To make life a matter only of rational concepts about it is to reduce it, is to make a cold abstraction from it, and thus to fall into the fallacy of taking the part for the whole. Metaphysical concepts may fully satisfy the demands of reason but this does not mean that they will therefore satisfy the demands of the totality of our being. They satisfy reason because they are the products of reason itself. But man is more than a reasoning being. His integral structure demands the feeling and the fact as well as the thought. Hence it demands the experience of nonduality as well as the concept of it, the feeling as well as the idea of it. So long as he knows it only with a limited part of his being, only as empty of emotional content and divorced from physical experience, so long will it remain incompletely known, half-seized as it were. It is at this crucial point that the seeker must realize the limitations of metaphysics and be ready to put aside as having fulfilled its particular purpose that which he has hitherto valued as a truth-path.(P)

169

It is impossible for the modern mind to encounter such experiences without seeking their explanation. And therefore it is of little practical use for a master to tell his followers not to trouble their heads about the reason why such things happen or not to ask questions about the meanings and purposes of the world.

170

My use of the term "reason," although with a capital "R" in *The Hidden Teaching Beyond Yoga*, seems to have been misunderstood by several persons. This forced me to add an appendix to the chapters in order to clear the matter in their mind. Reasoning, in its highest sense, transcends mere logic and welcomes the alliance of meditation; out of their union comes wisdom, peace, balance, and so, blessing. There is a translation from the Sanskrit of the *Katha Upanishad* made by Professor Mishra of the University of Barcelona, published with a preface by Suresh Radhakrishnan, President to India, who was then lecturing at Oxford University. In this translation there are two verses which use the term. Here is the first:

The man whose chariot is driven by reason holding well the reins of his mind, reaches the end of his journey, the Supreme Pervading Spirit.

And the other verse is:

Beyond the senses is the mind, and beyond mind is reason. . . . Beyond reason is the great Self.

171
We may reject reason's ideas about Divinity but in the end it is reason we have to rely on to support the ideas which authority, tradition, emotion, or faith put forward.

172
The agnostic, even the atheist, is a believer, too. Only he has more faith in the validity of reason than in the validity of intuition. Yet it is only the reason's own vanity that asserts that *its* validity is a higher one.

173
Just as we ought not misuse emotion, so we ought not misuse reason. We may use reason to justify an intuition, provided we use it faithfully and not to flatter our prejudices or prepossessions. We shall then be as ready to examine critically searchingly and impartially our own conclusions as those of an opponent.

174
Reason properly used will critically examine an emotion which is leading one astray, whereas improperly used it will uncritically defend such an emotion. It will not hesitate to puncture the ego's inflated complacency in the first case whereas it will support this complacency in the second one.

175
How often is reasoned judgement pushed aside by mere physical appeal which obscures what is below the surface.

176
Common sense assists the triumph of reason over sentimentality.

177
The faculty of reason also has two phases; the lower is practical and reaches perfection in the scientist; the higher is abstract and reaches perfection in the metaphysician.

178
If we bury our reason alive, so much the worse for us. Its wraith will rise up one day and sneer in revenge at our silly errors and self-made troubles.

179
The utmost use of the reasoning faculties cannot always provide for every factor in a situation. There are some which only intuition can

grasp—the karmic factor, for instance. This explains the miscalculations of men who possess the most highly developed rationality but who lack a counterbalancing development of intuition.

180

Expect no favourable opinion of spiritual truth from a man who looks at life through the medium of the senses alone, whose reason is enslaved by them, and whose intuition is effaced by them.

181

To depend on feeling as a guide to truth is to depend on a truncated method which is inadequate to the task. The only complete basis for our enquiry is feeling plus reason, the only results which possess unquestionable validity are those achieved by feeling plus reason. The power of intuition alone can enable us to discriminate between the real and the unreal and it alone can eliminate all doubts by eliminating contradictions.

182

There is no reason why reason itself should not be appeased.

183

This intellectual power is not to be allowed to crush the heaven-born intuitional sense by its sheer weight but is to be fused with it.

184

The intellect can present opinions—some very plausible and logical, others very weighty and fact-supported. But only the intuition can penetrate those layers after layer of spiritual experience which reveal the truth about man's link with God.

185

If the intellect's workings are not warmed by the heart's movements, it can only approach the reflected images of truth, not truth itself.

186

The disputations which follow the activity of intellect melt away in the harmonies which follow the upwelling of intuition.

187

The sin of the intellectual is when he allows intellect to block intuitive feeling, to serve only the animal body or to disregard the testimony of all those who, since early antiquity, have solved the problem of being and experienced the mind at its best level. Such men may have the finest brains, the greatest erudition, but themselves remain uncorrupted by these possessions.

188

The intellect is not competent to establish the existence of God, which only a higher faculty can know and consequently make any valid assertions about. But neither is it competent to disprove the existence of God since it can disprove only those finite matters which it can deal with: God, being infinite, is outside its reach in every way.

189

The intellect cannot be used to ascertain the ultimate truth without becoming involved at the end in inexplicable contradictions. Some of them are: There is an ego—there is no ego. The world is real—the world is unreal. Any idea or statement about fundamental being, whether of man or cosmos, can be countered by its opposite.

190

The simple education of the intellect, whether as a hoarding of information or a training in reasoning, becomes mere vanity if not accompanied by the balancing cultivation of the intuition.

191

What we need is a third point of view which shall fall into neither of these two extremes of emotional credulity or rational scepticism, whilst reconciling what is sound in both. This exists in the intuitive point of view.

192

There is always a risk that in taking a too intellectual view of the universe and in practising a too methodical system of yoga, the aspirant may get caught in the machinery of both intellect and method. If he is unable to extricate himself then whatever benefit he derives from both will always be on the lower plane. The transcendental insight which he seeks will then be as elusive as ever.

193

If he seeks guidance concerning the correct course to pursue, he can better get it from the still centre of his being than from the restless chopping of his intellect.

194

It is better to be intelligent when he is searching among ideas and doctrines than to be credulous—otherwise he may mistake human absurdity for divine mystery—but he can be so only if intuitive feeling is at work along with the reasoned thinking.

195

His own mind acts as a medium which interprets each experience, event, object. Hence it colours necessarily if unwittingly or even reshapes what is received by consciousness. And in the case of the Real, the end result for him is a paradox. He cannot know It without transcending himself. He cannot transcend himself without rising above the knower-and-known duality.

196

Where intuitive feeling will guide him aright to his best decisions, calculating intellect will not infrequently step in with doubts or fears and rob him of them.

197

The contribution of intellect is indispensable. But it is not enough. It leaves a most important part of the psyche—the intuition—still untouched.

198

The danger of slipping into this overstress on intellectual activity and not retaining the healthy balance between it and intuitional activity, is large and real.

199

The intellect has so dominated the modern man that his approach to these questions is first made through it. Yet the intellect cannot provide the answers to them. They come, and can only come, through the intuition.

200

When a difficult and important decision has to be made, the mind can impartially take in both the pros and cons, can circle all around the facts, yet in the end return baffled to where it started. Reason exerts itself in vain and only exhausts itself in such a process. The next step is to try outside advice, authority, or, if one can, intuition.

201

The intellect may be convinced and confess to the truth but the faculty which actually recognizes it is the intuition. It is the latter's light falling upon, and passing through, the intellect which really certifies an idea to be true.

202

Semantic analysis and reasoned reflection help to uncover the lesser errors, the little illusions. The intellect cannot go beyond its own limitations, however; a higher faculty, insight, is needed to uncover the larger errors, the major illusions.

203

The intellectual knowledge of the Truth is merely its shadow and not the Truth itself. The Truth is a higher state of awareness which leads you out of the little personal and physically materialistic everyday life into a new world of being—the world of your higher self which transcends these things. It is a real experience and not a mere speculation. It brings with it the peace which passeth understanding of which Saint Paul spoke, frees you from anxieties, fears, and all other negative ideas. It reveals to you that God, in the sense of a Universal Intelligence and Universal Power, is actually the basis of all existence.

204

Spiritual self-realization is the main thing. Study of the teachings concerning cosmical evolution and the psychical evolution of man are but intellectual accessories—things we may or may not take on our journey, as we like. That part of man which reasons and speculates—mortal mind—is not the part which can discover and verify the existence of God. We are not necessarily helped or hindered on the divine path by taking up the lore of science or by becoming versed in the ways of sophistry. Once we live out our spiritual life in the heart, the rest sinks to second place.

205

What the Overself really is defies adequate statement. For reason falters and fails before its mysterious Void. It dares not claim a capacity beyond what it actually possesses. Thus the mystery of the world is the mystery of a soluble riddle hidden within an insoluble enigma. Nevertheless, we need not despair. For even if metaphysics is unable to explore this mysterious territory, it is at least able to point out its location. That is a definite gain. But that is not all. What reason cannot do can yet be done by the faculty which towers transcendentally above it—insight.

206

Logical thinking about a proposed course can never be equal to intuitive guidance about it. For the first is limited by the ego's capacity and experience whereas the second transcends them.

207

The intellect cannot know itself; it must have an object; but that which is behind it does know it. That Overself is the only entity which can know itself, which fuses subject and object into one.

208

Although the intellect in us cannot grasp the Real, cannot do more than think about what it is *in relation to* itself, there is something else in us which can successfully do so. This is insight which, unfortunately, few have cultivated although all have it.

209

It can only be translated into thinkable language by a process which elaborates this instantaneous and simple experience into a lengthy and complicated metaphysic. It is only through such insight that a man may attain enduring wisdom, not through intellect.

210

Changes of view are inevitable so long as he has not attained insight, which is marked by its sureness of itself, thus contrasting with the intellects's doubts, hesitations, and waverings.

211

Only after reason matures to its fullest extent can we look to the dawning of a perfect intuition, or "insight" as I prefer to call it.

212

The belief that the unaided reason of man can solve all his problems is merely an expression of reason's own arrogance. Unless it co-operates with mystical insight, its best solutions of ultimate questions will either be fictitious ones or contradictory ones.

213

At the end of all this work what does he get? Does he touch reality? The answer is no. He simply gets one thought instead of another, replaces an old thought by a new one. There is here a danger that the replacement may be the exact opposite of the thought which it replaces—as if he were substituting a correct concept for an erroneous one. But this still does not bring him into reality, the knowledge of which is Truth. There is indeed only one way out of this impasse and that is to recognize that the plane of thoughts and concepts is not the plane which holds the real but must be transcended. This realization is a kind of crisis which enables him to admit that the way of the intellect is in the end a circular way leading from one thought to another and that it must be transcended. But the thinking has led to one useful result, though it is indeed a negative result: it has told him what reality is not, and the use of thought has enabled him to destroy the belief that thought is the way to the goal. This reminds one of Ramakrishna's illustrative metaphor about the use of one thorn to remove another which had got stuck in the finger. And so, this point reached, it is but one step further to perceive that the consciousness which holds all thoughts is what he's really seeking and not those projections from it which appear as concepts, ideas, and thoughts. There, in this consciousness, he can come to peace: the peace of the silent Mind, the transcendental Mind. Once he has become steeped deeply in this realization, he perceives with full clarity that it is not the movement from one set of beliefs or one set of ideas to a new one which is going to complete his search but the redirection of attention to THAT which is behind all thoughts—the reorientation of concentration to THAT which is in the gap between two thoughts.

If this is done with perseverence and sustained with patience, Truth dawns upon him either slowly or swiftly and then stays with him forever and cannot be broken by any form of materialism in thinking, of dualism in belief, or personality cult in practice. He looks henceforth only to the infinitude of Being which is within him, within the cosmos, and has always been so. If indeed in meditation the world disappears, he does not need to go so far as the Advaitans and assert that there is no world! If in wide activity it reappears, he knows it is still a phenomenon, an appearance made by mind, issuing forth from mind, and the Ultimate Mind was there and is there now. Whatever form thoughts and concepts may take, he knows them for what they are and does not let go of That which is their ultimate origin. This is real knowledge, for it is practice, it is life and not a concept.

214

No single human faculty is alone adequate to the search for truth. All must be used, including intuition, and finally crowned by a new one—insight.

215

Men who have daily experience of a divine presence will not waste their time arguing whether or not a divine power exists.

216

The absence of a universal consensus amongst philosophers certainly does indicate the inability of intellect to arrive at indisputable truth. But the only alternative which could be proposed—that of an integral develop-ment of all sides of our nature—is superior, yet still not enough. For the other sides—that is, feeling, mystical intuition, and mystical experience—will also suffer from the same deficiencies. There is the same possibility of endless contradiction here. One arrives, therefore, at the conclusion that a new faculty is really needed wherewith to ascertain ultimate Truth, one which, if it is attained, will function in precisely the same manner in all persons. Such a faculty was, it is believed, used by sages like Krishna and Buddha. It can be given the name of "insight." The purity of this insight must necessarily be a consequence of the purity of the entire character and mentality of the individual who has it. This applies not only in the moral realm, but also in the intellectual and emotional realms of his being. For the very tendencies of a virtuous nature which helped his progress in earlier stages must now be discarded as much as those of a vicious nature. The very tendencies of the intellect which brought him to his spiritual standpoint must also be discarded. Only by this ruthless self-pruning can he respond quite impersonally to reality and not falsify it. It is, presum-ably, the same as the divinization of the human mind.

217

The gulf between intellectual revelation and personal realization is greater than that between thought and action.

218

The depth of insight is not to be measured by the length of intellect.

219

Thought bedims consciousness instead of expressing it, coffins the universal Mind into the narrow ego. Man began to think when he began to forget his Overself. However, the forces of evolution will so work that one day he will learn to remember his divinity and yet use his intellect at will without losing this remembrance.

2

THE SERVICE OF INTELLECT

The cultivation of intelligence is one of the supreme duties of man. Fact-fed thinking—hard, deep, rational, and thorough—is what converts vague surmise into unbreakable certainty, blind belief or tormenting doubt into irrefutable knowledge, and native error into new truth.

2

By forming clearer ideas of the Overself's activity, he can better co-operate with it, and more effectually remove the obstacles which obstruct that activity within him.

3

Unless he exercises his reason—and that at its subtlest pitch—how is he going to wake up from this dream of spinning planets in which he sleeps by the mesmeric power of some unseen and unknown Sage?

4

All knowledge is beneficial to man in varying degrees. The knowledge of his own soul, being the highest degree of human knowledge, offers the greatest degree of benefit to man.

5

It is to those who follow traditional religion that this analytical approach (which could disturb faith) has little to say. Yet for others outside the traditions—atheists, materialists, and agnostics—it will certainly be of help.

6

Man did not first know through his eyes or hands that electricity exists but only through his powers of reasoning. We know in our best moments that we are merely *recipients* of power, goodness, and understanding.

7

What the higher self is trying to do in us may be obstructed through ignorance or assisted by knowledge.

8

Intellect is most useful as a servant but most tyrannical as a master. It may hinder progress or accelerate it. Hence, although the philosopher thinks as keenly as any other man, he does not allow his whole self to be submerged in the thinking process.

9

When man refuses to use his intelligence in settling his affairs it is only because he has not sufficiently developed his intelligence to be able to use it in this way. However, philosophically speaking, he is blinded by the ego and so seeks satisfaction rather than truth. Such a one does not know that truth brings satisfaction in its train.

10

The magnificent spectacle of the universe does have a meaning but it is only discoverable when we put such prejudices aside and accept the deliverances of analytic reason concentrated in its impeccable and searching quest.

Cultivation of intelligence

11

As his conception of the truth becomes clearer, his aspiration to realize it in his life becomes stronger. This is so and must be so.

12

It is wise to be intellectually familiar with the various ways of approach to the Overself, for this expands one's outlook and enlarges one's tolerance; but one should also know what is the correct way for oneself.

13

The intelligence which man possesses will not merely enable him to distinguish between truth and falsity in the consideration of external things, but will finally fulfil itself in enabling him to distinguish between the truth and falsity about his own internal being. That is to say, it will lead him to the knowledge of his own true self, his Overself.

14

Many of the opinions which have found lodgement in his head are not there through impartial investigation or intelligent enquiry but through the accidents of prejudice, bias, or heredity.

15

In all intellectual and scholastic studies, there is a secondary result which, whether recognized or not, is their most valuable one when judged from an evolutionary standpoint. It is the power of concentrated attention. Even if the student fails to master his subject or to solve his problem, nevertheless to the extent that he sincerely and diligently *tries*, this power is necessarily drawn upon, used, and developed. Both the mental effort needed to attend to the subject or problem and the desire to wrest the meaning of it, benefit the student even when his studies fail in their specific object. From the one he progresses a step forward toward greater ability to concentrate. From the other he gets a stimulus to his aspiration for truth. One day both will be applied to the spiritual quest.

16

He lifts himself above the herd, and becomes a student of philosophy, who sees how most people come to rest or even go to sleep in mere opinion. They have not enquired further whether it be truth—perhaps because they lack either the intellectual competence to do so or the preliminary knowledge of comparative opinion which shows up its contra-dictoriness, perhaps because they begin to find truth displeasing to their biased temperament and disagreeable to their prejudiced mind, perhaps because they are overawed by the massive impressiveness of tradition, authority, and established institutional teaching, or finally perhaps because the truth might prove disturbing to their personal position.

17

When clever able experienced and idealistic men tell you, for example, that a particular doctrine negates all that Christ stood for, and when other men, equally clever able experienced and idealistic, tell you that it fulfils Christ's ideals, then you have a clear illustration of the truth that some people are able to hold on to their present views only by shutting their eyes and stopping their ears to other ones.

18

The intellectual study of these truths is not without great value. It prepares him for their eventual realization, nourishes his soul, strengthens his higher will, and encourages his finer hopes. Moreover, holy reverence is born of itself as he meditates on the picture of universal intelligence which thus unfolds before his gaze.(P)

19

When it is said that all is opinion, it must further be said that all views of God exist in the minds of men as their opinions, too. The value of such opinions is only what these men give to it. For a view which is beyond the mental capacity of an unevolved person is of little value to him, whereas it may be life-saving to an evolved truth-seeker.

20

If the critical sense were lacking, how could a man perceive the insuffi-ciency of earthly aims, the transitoriness of earthly life, and the unsatisfac-toriness of earthly happiness? And without such perception why should he turn away to seek spiritual satisfactions?

21

Every man who has enough capacity to reflect upon his life-experience, has also to acknowledge that some power superior to himself—let him call it chance or God, fate or spirit—exists.

22

It is the philosopher's business to reject falsehood and therefore he refuses to swallow misleading statements merely because they have been well-baited on the surface with the sugar of true ones.

23

So much that we esteem as solid fact is quite often nothing more than merely imagination. Enquiry is necessary.

24

The same intellect whose activity deters most men from discovering God's presence within themselves can be used to discover this presence. Something like this was noticed by Francis Bacon in England, and he put his idea into one of his essays.

25

It is queer and comical how those who have studied a subject only casually and hurriedly, will often be quite dogmatic and most positive in their conclusions about it.

26

Time and thought, experience and experiment, study and practice, initiation and instruction are all needed to teach a man how to distinguish between the final truth and its countless counterfeits. With growing enlightenment and increasing confidence, he becomes more expert.

27

The intensity with which a view is held tells us something about its holder, nothing about the truth of that view.

28

When they must form an opinion, come to a decision, make a judgement, or choose between alternatives, men consult past experience, listen to authority, obey tradition, or yield to the strongest elements in their own personal character.

29

The imagination creates its own idols which it worships as the true God. Therefore reason must be called in to cast them down.

30

Disillusionment about pseudo- or half-truths often precedes discovery of the real or full truth.

31

Too many simple persons, whether Orientals or Occidentals, do not seem able to distinguish between mere mythology and authentic history. The development of a discriminating faculty is as necessary in religion as in the marketplace.

32

If the mind has been trained to reject falsehood, be it born from within self or received from others, it will be better able to let the Truth shine unhindered in itself.

33

The first value of correct teaching is that it purges the seeker of many errors in understanding. This purgation in its turn saves him from committing many errors in conduct. Here is its practical value. The second value is that its light instantly exposes imposture, charlatanry, exploitation, or evil in other teachings and in their exponents.

34

There are true as well as false opinions, adequate as well as groundless beliefs. We may freely hold opinions and beliefs, provided they are supported by sufficient evidence.

35

Before enlightenment can be received into consciousness, a measure of sharpness to discern the real from its appearance, as well as of detachment, must be acquired.

36

We learn to discriminate in practical affairs and among material things as to what they seem to be and what they really are. But the faculty can be applied on a much higher level of existence and a more abstract one, depending on the cultural or personal quality of a man. Its highest application is to separate the Truth about God, the Universe, and oneself from its appearances and their Realities.

37

With contradictions eliminated or reconciled, with errors corrected and new fertile concepts introduced, and with his ideas ranged in an orderly pattern, he can attain some intellectual clarity.

38

Not only was there some fact as well as some exaggeration in Anatole France's assertion—sceptic and cynic though he usually was—that "all is Opinion!" but it could be restated as "All is secondhand opinion!"

39

They wittingly or unwittingly impose their own opinions, theories, beliefs, and concepts upon the object perceived or the happening experienced. The result may come near to, or be far from, the truth, depending on their advancement, but it is unlikely to be the whole truth.

40

The value of metaphysical knowledge lies in the fact that it is a safeguard against error for it shows how to discriminate between reality and the appearance of it. Neither the deceptions of individuals nor the errors of mystical experience can then succeed.

41

Even if a man succeeded in getting others to accept his views, even if everyone accepted them, it is unlikely that they will accept them always.

42

Every opinion has been written down in the books, including the opinion that truth requires us to hold no opinion.

43

Suggestion from outside enters largely into the opinions and beliefs, the views and outlook, of masses of people. It is just as true, possibly truer, of the mystically minded, be they seekers or gurus, be they Orientals or Westerners. What is really known—rather than echoed back—dwindles down to a residue.

44

He may be poised in the tranquillity of these grand concepts or poisoned by the negative fogs of false ones.

45

Convert a man to your opinion and you have him for long; compel him to adopt it and you have never really got him.

46

We must work hard to elicit the truth from the medley of beliefs and opinions which rule us, and to extract the reality from the medley of illusions and glamours which hold us.

47

Any fool can say "I know," that is, can have an opinion.

48

Mass stupidity is not, and never can be, a satisfactory substitute for individual intelligence.

49

Far too often private opinions are passed off as God's oracles, man-made institutions as God's instruments, and group propaganda as factual history. The masses, lacking both discrimination and information, are led like sheep by the mass media.

50

How can a credulous fool attain supernormal wisdom? How can the man who is unable to discriminate intelligently in small matters suddenly become able to discriminate in transcendent ones? The jump is not possible.

51

Most people do not know the difference between an opinion and a truth, and do not make the effort to distinguish between them.

52

Is it not better to force illusions into accord with the realities than to go on being pleasantly deceived by them?

53

We must not be doctrinaires; we must not sit at the sanctified feet of the god of opinion.

54

The intellectual purificatory work begins by clearing his mind of errors, illusions, and superstitions. These things lead him astray, both during meditation and out of it, from his search for truth.

Balance of intellect and feeling

55

Sincerity is not enough. Every aspirant needs this, of course, but he also needs other things. An aspirant may be totally sincere, yet may take a wrong direction. His mind may be filled with erroneous beliefs despite his sincerity. So to his sincerity he should add right knowledge, for this will guide him, this will uphold him, and this will safeguard him.

56

The result of a solely intellectual outook devoid of religious faith or mystical intuition, is failure to offer mental peace or cherish moral goodness.

57

We are not casting stones at intellectual knowledge; it has its place. But let it be kept in its place. Let it not become a usurper. The higher mysticism first satisfies the intellect's demands, then transcends them. It does not, like the lower mysticism, reject or ignore them.

58

Gotama, the author of *Nyaya Sutras on Logic*, defends the value of intellect as follows: Although the intellect admittedly cannot grasp reality (Brahman), it is nevertheless necessary in order to set a standard, to show what reality is, as such, so that it shall be recognized. A pair of scales cannot weigh themselves but they are necessary in order to weigh other things. Similarly, the intellect cannot yield reality but can measure it so to speak or indicate what is and what is not reality. Hence it is most valuable as a corrective to mysticism and yoga.

59

The moral code which a man obeys is itself the result of his view of life, whether the latter be imposed on him from without or developed from within.

60

The futility and unwisdom of utter reliance upon feelings, unchecked by reason, was tragically evidenced by the sad case of Nijinsky, the famous Russian dancer, who after delighting audiences in the world's chief capitals became insane and for more than twenty years had to withdraw from his artistic career and pass most of his days in a sanatorium. Nijinsky kept a diary in the early days of his illness, in which we find sentences like the following: "I am God. I am God. I am God." Throughout those pages Nijinsky insists on feeling rather than thinking as a source of wisdom, and feeling he defines as "intuitions, proceeding from the unconscious." The man who claimed to be God was, however, unable to fulfil himself as a human being. Why? Because he was really unbalanced for he rejected utterly the claims of Reason, and he denounced "mental" people as being "dead."

61

(1) Yes, mystical experience *must* collaborate with rational thought. But there is a higher kind of mysticism, which prunes away the accidental and penetrates to the essential. (2) Intellectual knowledge is certainly relative. But what lies beyond it is *for us* ultimate truth. That there may be a truth beyond this in turn need not concern us at present, for nobody could either dispute it or demonstrate it. (3) The urge for higher knowledge is *not* an act of the ego but a prompting from the Overself. That it gets mixed, in its earlier phases, with egoistic desires is true but these slowly fall away.

62

The intellect is a faculty that man is endowed with, not by Satan to trap him, but in accordance with the divine World-Idea. Man is learning how to use it. If he is using it wrongly today, the consequences will tutor him in time and he will use it rightly tomorrow.

63

When the mystical bent of mind is not steadied by rational reflection, there is grave danger of mistaking satisfaction for truth, utility for knowledge.

64

Socrates taught that character was somehow dependent on intelligence: the better quality of the one was a consequence of the better quality of the other. Therefore cultivate clear intelligence, he said. Long after, Spinoza repeated this advice.

65

The need of coping with life forces us to develop intelligence or else to go on suffering the consequences of being stupid.

66

Even the world-picture of a higher condition available to those who will work and sacrifice for it is not without value. It shows a model to use and emulate, a standard to seek and form oneself by.

67

It is not enough to mean well, it is not enough to believe one is doing right, it is not enough to be earnest, sincere, innocent of evil motives. It is just as essential to possess a balanced mentality, sound reasoning capacity, and unbiased attitude. The Spanish Inquisitors were sometimes saints, Hitler was an ascetic. Many who have brought misery upon mankind were men of excellent private character: the defects of these people were mental rather than moral, and led them to bad thinking and worse judgement. The moral of this is plain: intelligence must be cultivated as fully if not more so than emotions.

68

The role of reason in the human psyche is to keep its balance.

69

The education of a man is worth no more than what he is worth inside himself. If he is evil within, he will be aided by a developed intellect to do more harm to others than he would have been able to do without it. If he is good within, he will have more capacity through education to do good to others.

70

A thorough mastery and understanding of the Hidden Teaching—even if it be intellectual only—will help to refine, educate, and to some extent, even dissolve the ego, if the knowledge thus obtained is applied. Truth is a dynamic, not a narcotic.

71

The mystic may sneer at reason, but when he wants to justify his mysticism, either to himself or to others, he has to fall back on reason to do so.

72

It has always seemed to me that the one great theme around which Shakespeare hung all his writing was, in his own words: "There is nothing good or bad but thinking makes it so." Certainly right thinking is even more important than right action. For if two men both perform the same deed rightly but one does so on false reasons and the other on true ones, the first is always liable to slip later into wrong action but not the second.

73

Our problems can never be solved by dealing with them as we do, in passion and prejudice, unless indeed we find a new passion for Rightness and a new prejudice for Truth.

74

The integrity of his intellectual conscience will one day demand from every man a search for spiritual knowledge to confirm, sustain, or even replace his present spiritual faith.

75

The studies should stimulate him to start, continue, or intensify the exercises, regimes, and practices, but they cannot act as a substitute for them.

76

It is easier to substitute feeling for thinking when it is hard to balance the claims of opposing doctrines.

77

Without deserting the use of sharp reasoning, yet without abandoning the piety of worshipful feeling, he follows obediently the light which has been shown him. Using the symbols of mysticism, it is a harmonious co-operation of head and heart.

78

We must fearlessly subpoena our faith to appear before the court of common sense; if it is afraid to do that it is not worthy of being held.

79

He wants the vigorous facts, not the vague sentimentalities. He wants mysticism but only after ridding it of its deficiencies and thrusting aside its limitations.

80

The mystical attack upon intellect has sufficient basis to justify it up to a certain point. But when it goes beyond that point and unreservedly praises the holy imbecile and listens with bated breath to his utterances, it renders a disservice to mysticism. If all this enormous human evolution is to end in men feeling like children and acting like fools, is there not a danger that they may go farther and turn into idiots? Life today is too challenging to be met successfully by the brainless or foolish. It is also nonsense for any mystic of the religious devotional school to say that intellect is useless and unnecessary on the spiritual path. It may be so on his particular path—although even there his assertion is arguable—but it is certainly not so on the other paths. How can it harm a seeker to acquire all possible knowledge about the quest, to know all that he can gather from the history of mysticism, the biography of mystics, the psychology of mystical states, and the philosophy of mystical thinkers? Thus equipped, he is surely better equipped to find his way in what is, after all, a dim and obscure territory. And how can he learn these things without studying books, listening to lectures, discussing ideas, and exchanging experiences with others?

81

If men of high intelligence are trained in theology, at some point the intelligence is forsaken or led to subserve faith.

82

The cleavage of the mental functions in the form of an irrational attitude towards religion combined with a rational attitude towards everything else, is quite common. It is not distant from the mental disease called schizophrenia.

83

Each mistake in action is the result of a preceding mistake in thought.

84

What is lost by bringing a higher intelligence to the study of spiritual topics? Nothing—if the person is sufficiently balanced to use it properly.

85

Too many mystics of the emotional-devotional type have, while rightly scorning intellect's limitation, wrongly decried reason's services.

86

Dynamite serves the mining engineer and the road builder very well. Fire serves the kitchen cook very well. But if she brings dynamite into contact with fire in her kitchen, both may destroy her. Knowledge is not only her power but also her protection.

87

When the aspirant has great devotion to the Overself but little understanding of it, Nature will halt him at a certain stage of his spiritual career and compel him to redress the balance.

88

The educated mind is repelled by superstition, the reasonable mind by fanaticism. Yet both need the fortifying support of a spiritual teaching.

89

Every error rejected and every truth accepted strengthens a man in character and mind.

90

Just as the religious devotee will be moved sooner or later to seek personal experience if he lacks it, so the mystical votary will be moved to seek intellectual enlightenment if he too lacks it. But such an inner movement will only develop where aspiration is strong and continuous, sincere and self-critical.

91

A man's consciousness of himself includes not only his thoughts and acts but also the understanding of them.

92

The intellectual, the scientist or politician, businessman or professional, who has become cold, dry, materialistic, and insensitive, is unbalanced. Yet he thinks he is so levelheaded.

93

A man can get intoxicated by his intellectual-logical thinking as he can with wine, or as the mystic with devotional rapture. The fine balance needed for the clear reception of truth is then absent.

94

All correct thinking must be, and is, accompanied by intense reverence; whilst all ardent devotion of the Divine must be rightly directed towards That which is genuinely divine—and not towards that which is often erroneously thought to be so. If this development is one-sided, there is then the danger that can be seen illustrated anywhere one goes—that is, of knowledge degenerating into dried-up intellectualism, no longer able to influence morals nor control conduct, and of devotion degenerating into superstitious hysteria.

95

To perceive the truth intellectually for the first time through someone else's eyes or book is very important. And to glimpse the truth intuitionally through one's own experience is still more important.

96

Many people lack the broad knowledge which is necessary to form proper judgements or humanitarian appeals; many lack the patience which is necessary to scrutinize these appeals at all adequately while most people lack the impartiality to analyse a situation with insight. This is where the philosopher's counsel may be useful.

97

Even from a rigorously practical standpoint the man who is incapable of reasoned thought is less likely to get on in the world.

98

He will not forget, in being reasonable, to be reverent also.

99

Care is to be taken that the deceptions into which both his logic and his sentimentality are liable to fall, are avoided by the use of sharp discrimination.

100

He has not only to guard against wishful thinking and comfortable believing whenever these collide with truth. He has also to guard against passion-distorted thinking and emotion-warped believing.

101

It is not enough to be emotional about his faith. He ought also to be able to give a coherent statement of the reasons for it.

102

When academic learning runs to excess to the point of becoming dry pedantry bereft of common sense it becomes a nuisance to those who seek truth.

103

If instruction and education leave a person in ignorance of the World-Idea and in illusion concerning the world and self, then they are incomplete, and inadequate to prepare him for life.

104

Those who are unable to think or afraid to think may leap eagerly at the gospel of avoiding thought altogether. For them a bland blankness may bring peace. But how long can it last in the face of life's stern insistent problems, tragedies, or responsibilities?

105

The spiritually paralysed modern mind often skims the surface of things with great brilliance but the poor thing is completely unable to penetrate them.

106

In a region where yogic aberrations and mystical excesses abound so freely, the value of a scientific attitude is immense.

107

His reverential feelings will not be reduced or weakened if supported by intelligence; rather they will be richer, deeper, and balanced.

108

It is not enough to purify the moral nature of evil and sin. It is also needful to purify the intellectual nature of error and delusion. Hence moral discipline must be complemented by an intellectual one.

Doubt and the modern mind

109

If there is one prime feature of the modern mentality it is that reason has replaced faith. We begin by calling into question what our forefathers believed. In the good old days we assumed everything and proved nothing; now we assume nothing and prove everything. The change is fundamental.

110

The weak point of both the ancient sophists and our modern "rationalists" is that they have made a dogma of our doubt. They have set it up as though it were an end in itself instead of a means to an end—truth.

111

Scepticism must in the end, after it has criticized and destroyed everything else, turn its criticism on itself and doubt itself.

112

We do not overcome our doubts by suppressing them, we do not meet our misgivings by denying them, and we do not refute falsehood by shirking questions which happen to be inconvenient.(P)

113

I am too much aware of the diversity of intellectual truths to regard them as other than merely relative. Therefore I prefer a light scepticism.

114

Is it not ironic that the only creature in the universe which doubts God's existence is also the only one—up to that grade—which contains the proof of that existence? The countless germs, worms, insects, reptiles, and mammals below man lack the rational capacity to question, while the higher types of individuated beings above him know too much to utter such a doubt.

115
Reason begins by being sceptical of everything else. It ends by becoming sceptical about itself.

116
It is unwise sceptically to let these truths vanish from our sight, as though we had not even heard of them, for then the groove of old sufferings will have to be cut anew.

117
These secret doubts, these inward vacillations, must be faced and overcome.

118
To doubt is not to deny. We must begin with doubt in order to clear the ground but we would be in a sorry state if we were to end in it. The assertion that all beliefs are relative and untenable, is itself a belief and therefore equally untenable.

119
No doctrine is so sacred that it is not to be questioned. Man cannot escape from his duty to doubt. Each generation must reflect in its own way on the conundrums of existence and be vigorously alive to its own problems, which are not wholly the problems of other epochs, and must face them in a fresh living manner.

120
But when uneasy doubt is pushed to the extreme of settled cynicism, when needful caution is elongated to paralysing cowardice, when scepticism is grown so big that it cannot let the divine get past it into his heart, then the man falls into a bog of materialism and becomes its pitiable victim.

121
Doubt has a legitimate use in the world of thought. Without it, we should be at the mercy of every charlatan, every fool, every exploiter, and every false doctrine. We need not be ashamed therefore to avail ourselves of it at times. Doubt tears the veil off deceit and exposes humbug hidden beneath benevolence.

122
We need not be afraid to question everything, to doubt everything, even the words we use and our own very selves. We have nothing but falsehood, illusion, and self-deception to lose if we take nothing for granted.

123

How shall we begin this study? The best way is the only way for us. We must begin by doubting everything; thus alone may we hope to end by knowing everything.

124

Although we have to begin our metaphysical life by doubting accepted values, we cannot end there; we cannot live forever in an atmosphere of suspended judgement. The process of active living demands that sooner or later we commit ourselves to a definite, if tentative, standpoint, even without reaching absolute certainty. Doubt, therefore, is a provisional and not a permanent attitude.

125

Because truth has been bound up with such absurdities, often for self-interested motives, it behooves us to accept no message without due investigation and deep caution.

126

Because people do not feel their inward divinity, they often deny it. In ancient and even medieval times they were satisfied that it did exist because their simplicity, their uncultivated intellects, created no barriers to this feeling or to faith in it on the authority of tradition and their prophets. We must understand the inevitability of their present scepticism and prove *the fact* of the Soul as logically, as evidentially as possible. Yet to offer intellectual proof alone is not enough, although a truly excellent step forward. We must also show them *how* to get the experience of verification for themselves.

127

Scepticism makes conditions which require that truth be presented in a rational form and argued out. Otherwise the intellectual reactions to it will not be fair and just to its value.

128

The value of metaphysical scepticism is to overcome mental inertia, to liberate us from dogma, and to teach us tolerance. It frees us to search for higher truths and nobler values.

129

They may try to escape from their doubts, perhaps by stifling them, perhaps by ignoring their very existence, perhaps by going to the guru and getting his reassurance again. This course may succeed for a time, even for a lifetime. But it is not conducive to their true welfare.

130

There are two ways open to a sceptic. One is to seek the actual experience of transcending intellect and becoming aware of the Overself; the other is to obtain intellectual proof of it. The first is a hard and long way; the second short and easy.

131

Just as the very presence of suffering starts a search for its relief, so does the very existence of doubt cause a search for truth to begin.

132

We must begin by suspecting the data furnished by our five senses. We must learn that appearances are dubious, that they are not to be accepted without searching enquiry.

133

Not only is he to question the dogmas which orthodoxy hands him but even the doubts which scepticism offers instead of them.

134

Those sceptics who reject the possibility of attaining truth are already stating something as truth and thereby refuting their own theory.

135

Because there is no room in philosophic study for naïveté or gullibility, those who suffer from these mental disabilities should first get cured.

136

Where belief comes too easily, error may follow too quickly.

137

To doubt everything and stop at that point, to assent to nothing but criticize every presentation, to meet all affirmative statements with the sceptic's questions—this is the product of sharp intellect, blunt speech, and negative feeling.

138

If a man is too suspicious of being deceived, he may err when truth is presented to him, and so miss the chance of acquiring it. Balance is needed here as elsewhere.

139

To bring one's natural scepticism into a fine balance with the intellectual sympathy these subjects demand is not an easy task, but he must try to do it.

140

We can accept nothing on trust as far as the quest of truth is concerned, although we can and needs must accept most things on trust, so far as the practical purposes of life are concerned.

141

No argument is capable of moving the absolute sceptic, for he does not look into its truth but only into its weaker places.

142

If you do not know whether God exists do not fall into the error of denying that he does exist. It is an error because it is something which we do not know and to make such a positive statement has no justification.

3

THE DEVELOPMENT
OF INTELLECT

When intelligence is applied so thoroughly as to yield a whole view and not merely a partial view of existence, when it is applied so persistently as to yield a steady insight into things rather than a sporadic one, when it is applied so detachedly as to be without regard to personal preconceptions, and when it is applied so calmly that feelings and passions cannot alter its direction, then and only then, does a man become truly reasonable and capable of intellectually ascertaining truth.(P)

2

We must think before we can understand the soul's existence; we must understand before we can realize it.

3

The earliest beginnings of thought, as apart from instinct, when it was itself still but a lurking tendency, belong far back in primeval time. The human intellect as we find it today, so rich and developed an instrument for the consciousness of the ego, did not arrive at this fullness without a series of graduated stages.

4

We have had plenty of scientific thinking, business thinking, and political thinking long enough, but we have had very little inspired thinking. That is the world's need.

5

The intellect is cradled in selfishness but runs the evolutionary track into reason where it will one day finish at the winning-post of selflessness.

6

The animal acts as its instinctive drives bid it act whereas in man this instinctive nature is made up with and consequently modified by, the awakening intellect's need to consider, compare, and judge.

7

He who wants to go back to the simple medieval life is welcome to it. He who wants his rooms cleaned with old-fashioned brooms that raise a cloud of dust and leave it hanging in the air until it can find safe lodgement in throats and lungs, is welcome to the dust. There are others, however, who react differently to such a situation; who are resolved to take advantage of the skill of human brains and the fact of human advance. They have thrown away the unhealthy broom and adopted the vacuum cleaner which removes and swallows the dust instead of filling the air with it. We are not writing a thesis on domestic hygiene. We are writing in this strain because it is highly symbolic. It shows quite vividly the difference between the backward looking mentality and the forward looking one. The student of philosophy belongs to the second category. He sees the futility of propagating a switch-back to medieval methods when we are in the midst of the greatest technical transformation mankind has ever known. He knows that modern conditions must be faced with modern attitudes. However, he takes "modern" to mean whatever has attained the most finished state as a consequence of progressive development. He knows it does not mean whatever is merely fashionable at the moment, as materialism was fashionable in intellectual circles and sensualism in youthful circles until very lately. His vision is larger than that of his contemporaries, because it encompasses more. They are modern only in a chronological sense, but backward in a spiritual one.

8

It is the faculty of reason which differentiates human beings from all Nature's other creatures. It is this which sets man beyond the animals. But reason untouched by the finer promptings of the heart, and unillumined by the sublimer intuitions of the mind, degenerates easily into selfish cunning, and degrades instead of dignifying man.

9

It may be they find it too hard to make the crossing from the older way of thinking to what is demanded of them by the new knowledge: a willingness to accept paradox. For otherwise they get only a half-truth.

10

Reason gradually becomes paramount as man develops through life after life.

11

How few are even aware of their intellectual dishonesty! Through his exclusive possession of the capacities for independent choice and self-control, as well as his privilege of individual responsibility, man is set apart from the animal.

12

What this age needs to seek is a new intellectualism, a new science, one informed by deeper spiritual feeling and protected by higher spiritual ideals.

13

A high quality of thinking is being done by men who are probing now for the better life of tomorrow. They are coming to the only possible conclusion about the validity of determinism on the basis of known facts when regarded by the *whole* mind of intellectually mature man—the mind which uses both its abstract and materialistic thinking capacities and, consequently, verges on the truly intuitive. I am reminded of Bacon's well-known remark about the slight use of reason leading to atheism and the adequate use of it leading back to religion.

14

Although men are born with latent mental power and potential intelligence few use these qualities to their utmost possibilities. Man arises out of the mysterious womb of the Infinite, yet he is to be found everywhere as a pitiful creeping creature, full of moral frailties, finite indeed. Yet the unseen mental being of man is the silent workman who really constructs the edifice of his happiness.

15

Spiritual teaching must be expounded today in a form suited to the modern need. The doctrines so revealed should be methodically progressive and the explanations should be systematically developed.

16

At last the living growing entity has reached a kingdom of Nature where it can develop the power to think not only about material topics but also about spiritual ones.

17

Early humanity possessed a mind that thought in terms of images and pictures rather than in terms of logical sequence. But it developed marvelous memory as a consequence and entire volumes of sacred books were handed down for centuries by oral tradition before they were committed to writing.

18

The man of the twentieth century must seek truth in his own fashion. The question of how many angels can stand on the point of a pin does not interest the modern mentality.

19

This longing to know more may, at the start, be motivated by the desire to earn more but, in the end it will be motivated by the search for Truth.

20

Where we do not know the different sides of a case, where we have not ascertained the various facts behind the answer to a question, it is wiser to suspend judgement, fairer, if possible, to refrain from taking action.

21

The course of evolution has made the intellectual stride of man a necessity but it has not made such utter imbalance as prevails today a necessity.

22

The intellectual wondering, seeking, and questioning which make a man study or aspire, follow or join, often attain a degree of some ardour. But this does not prevent the same man from changing his mood and mind in later years.

23

We humans dominate the earth planet, not by our physical strength but by our mental power.

24

Through the many changes of experience in the many lifetimes on earth—and later elsewhere—the mind grows. It wants to move upward from mere curiosity to actual knowledge. It inquires if there be any purpose in life to be fulfilled—if there be a purpose. It demands to know if there is a God yet doubts the possibility of finding a sure answer.

25

But if this increased knowledge and sharpened brains predominate over mystical experience and religious intuition, then disequilibrium is created. Truth appears only to the perfectly balanced mind, but to the disequilibrated one it appears materialized perverted or falsified.

26

The medieval period was impelled by theological sources, and the modern period by scientific ones.

27

The benefit of university education has reached a much higher percentage of people and in a much larger number than during any earlier century.

28

Has world-thinking progressed enough consciously, deliberately, and honestly to set up the search for truth? The answer is that individual world-thinkers have done so but taken as a group humanity has not done so.

29

The intellect is in process of being developed and its limitation must be accepted as such. The time spent in deploring that fact is time wasted. For the important thing is not that it is not the highest faculty in man, which is admitted, but that its development does not really oppose itself to the highest spiritual development, which is not often admitted.

Independence and individuality

30

It is not enough to be a collector of other men's ideas. He must also be an original generator of his own. He must go into the pure silence to think independently, to analyse problems and consider them for himself, and to pray for enlightenment.

31

Unless one is prepared to part with a wrong habit of thinking, unless one is willing to eradicate all limited conceptions which blur clear-sightedness, unless, in short, one is willing to reorient the mental outlook completely, it will never be possible to penetrate the world illusion.

32

The student of philosophy must enforce in his own mind the clear difference between views based on wishful thinking, and views based on adequate knowledge and comprehensive understanding.

33

Before it can search for truth the mind must be set free: otherwise it merely seeks either the confirmation or rejection of previously held ideas, systems, opinions, and creeds.

34

It is not enough to express your willingness to learn. You must also be willing to unlearn.

35

It is possible, and must become his object, to develop a completely impartial intellect.

36

It is one thing to have caught a vague notion in the mind, and another to think it out and make it intelligible.

37

The philosophical student, having thoroughly scrutinized the bases of his outlook and attitude, reveals his wisdom and humility by confessing ignorance where he cannot claim knowledge. It is then always possible for him to learn something here. But the undeveloped or undisciplined mind is not ashamed to make a pretense of knowledge where in fact there is none.

38

It is too much to expect that his mind can understand what is quite beyond it; but when repeated, the effort tends to "stretch" the mind's capacity.

39

It is not enough to acknowledge his misjudgements. He ought also to enquire into the defective qualities which led him into making them.

40

The farther he travels from egocentric existence the clearer and straighter will be his thinking.

41

Be willing to accept a truth even if the man who utters it is only half-literate, if his statement is ungrammatical, his words are mispronounced, and his voice stutters irritatingly. But the experience is more enjoyable, the effect deeper, if the truth is expressed impeccably and enriched by a fine culture.

42

The man who puts up a barrier of egoistic prejudices or superiority complexes cannot hope to penetrate into the secret circle of truth-knowing. Only he who is ready, tentatively, to shift his intellectual standpoint for that of another is at all likely to be admitted into the sacred treasure house of wisdom.

43

We must not shelve a single fundamental but awkward question. The sanctity of truth is inviolable.

44

Thinking must move at every step with rigid rationality if it is not to degenerate into mere mental effervescence.

45

We want precise understanding and exact description of every science and do not abandon our demand even when the more delicate matter of a method of spiritual illumination is in question.

46

The humility which can say "I do not know" is a first step to the confidence which can say "This is a fact."

47

If they begin to question, really and deeply question, then even the simplest statement brings them into difficulties whose existence, previously, they had never suspected.

48

Men learn best because they concentrate best in a quiet unruffled atmosphere. This requires a secluded site, tall buildings, and high enclosing walls, peaceful lawns, and tree-bordered walks.

49

Most Western people dislike abstract generalities: they prefer concrete facts. They believe in first appearances rather than in second views. Against such a tendency truth must struggle bravely for survival. If Westerners were more balanced they would realize they could keep their facts and their first views—nobody asks them to disregard the practical and the apparent—but they could also have the abstract and the long view, thus achieving balance, and with it, truth.

50

The depth and width of his research must equal the depth and width of his reflection.

51

Where are the answers to men's questions? He must elicit them for himself one by one.

52

There is little harm in putting into the mind ideas above its level. At the worst, they may bore it, but at the best they might stretch it.

53

Quite often, when a truth or a judgement is carried to extremes, it loses some, or much, or all of its validity.

54

If we have sought for truth in directions which have yielded negative results, it is time to take a new direction.

55

A man whose cultural rise has depended upon self-education alone deserves praise and admiration for his effort. Nevertheless he would have done better to seek also a formal education. This would complete and elevate what he has learnt by himself by providing him with higher standards, competent instruction, and well-tested knowledge or by affording personal help with questions, uncertainties, and problems.

56

He must be frank with himself and know what he does not understand and what he does and not accept mere opinion for solid fact.

57

It may be hard, a rough stony obstructed path, for the common man to find his way into philosophy, but the tension is well worthwhile. He has to stretch his mind, but there are moments of relief, of joyful discovery, of encouraging perception.

58

Before you can get clear expression of meaning, you must get a clear mind. You must nurture a tendency toward sharply defined thoughts and exactitude of understanding. You must give definite shape to the inchoate ideas which float through your mind like clouds, and thus arrive at complete possession of your subject.

59

He will not consciously refuse to readjust his views whenever they are shown to be out of harmony with the facts of life.

60

If such questions have never entered their minds, it is hardly likely that the answers themselves will.

61

Correct thinking may annihilate superstitions and uncover deceptions, but unbalanced thinking may create new ones.

62

The mind needs a long training in truthful thinking into which the ego does not obtrude itself before the hidden reality begins to respond.

63

This uprooting of old familiar but fallacious beliefs discourages some persons but encourages others.

64

The ordinary man makes a hasty judgement of the matter, or follows his personal wishes, but truth requires a deep well-considered examination.

65

If the capacity to comprehend philosophy is not inborn, then it can be slowly acquired by anyone who thinks it worth the effort.

66

If so many seekers do not find truth pure and unadulterated, but only its impure adulterated variety, it is because their way has been blocked by self-serving partisans interested only in triumph for their own group, position, or argument, their own prejudice, attraction, or bias. Discovery of truth requires not only a willingness to take in the facts which serve one side of a case, but also to refrain from ignoring or belittling those which serve the other side. It is not in an atmosphere of favouritism or hostility that truth appears but in a deep calm bereft of egoistic urges. This is why some sort of preparation for it is necessary, some kind of training.

67

Only he who is capable of sustained intellectual effort is capable of understanding this philosophy.

68

Some people can understand philosophy and some most monumental concepts in an unclouded flash, but most people can understand even its simplest ones only by slow degrees. Here first acquaintance is not enough. There must be many subsequent meetings before intimacy can be established.

69

Thinking must not only approach these studies as worshippers approach a temple shrine, with the reverence they deserve, but must also become alive and dynamic.

70

The intense intellectual joy of discovering a new truth—new, that is, to oneself, but as old perhaps as thoughtful humanity itself—equates with the intense aesthetic joy of creating or appreciating an art work.

71

In the human body the cerebral nervous system, with which man's mental faculties are associated, does not develop until long after all the other chief organs have developed. This is symbolic of its evolutionary importance. In the human life, the thinking power does not attain full maturity until long after all the chief decisions, such as the choice of occupation, marriage-partnership, and religious affiliation have already been made. How much human error and consequent misery must therefore arise from the lateness of this development.

72

Younger mentalities need to think in terms of definite sense impressions, of physical feels sights and sounds. More developed mentalities can think in terms of abstract ideas, of general metaphysical principles. The first group is the most numerous.

73

We must first give intellectual assent to philosophical teachings before we can hope to gain practical demonstration of their worth.

74

It is hard, perhaps impossible, to give absolute proof of any statement or any fact; but a reasonable proof may be given. Life is too short to wait for the one so we have often to accept the other.

75

The continual and untiring quest of truth is what distinguishes the philosophic attitude toward life. The intellectual discipline which this involves is irksome to the ordinary mind. For it demands the scrutiny of facts, the unveiling of assumptions, the examination of reasoning processes leading to conclusions, and the probing of standpoints to their ultimate ground.

76

Patience is needed, for the time factor is still there; the ripeness of mind of the prober is still essential, and it must not limit itself by preconceived ideas. It is at the threshold of an astounding realm, where so much that was correct on other levels collapses here and is no longer correct.

77

One sees their anxiety to understand a doctrine which is on too abstract a level for them and pities the bewilderment with which they end. Yet for such there is an easier way, bringing a more successful result. It is to take up the study of mentalism first, and only after that proceed to the study of Advaita.

78

The work of research proves endless. The task of collecting all the data has no finish to it, and if we are to arrive at any conclusion at all, there is some point at which we have to cut short our investigation and reflection. Thus, by the very act with which we serve the cause of practical truth, we render a disservice to the cause of theoretical truth. The very means whereby we make a decision, join a party, take a side, or evaluate a right and a wrong produces only a makeshift result.

79

We must think our thoughts out to their inevitable conclusions and not stop halfway when the process becomes decidedly unpleasant.

80

Memorized knowledge is inferior to thought-out understanding.

81

It is one thing to begin to suspect the fallacy of these views; it is another to be completely certain of it. A long road lies between the two states and it passes through uneasiness, anxiety, wretchedness, and anguish.

82

The hand of experience sows a good many doubts in the field of his early beliefs.

83

We learn truth partly by experience, partly by intuition, and partly by instruction.

84

Therefore, one of the first steps upon this path is to accept, tentatively at least, the reasonable propositions laid down here and to allow the mind to work upon them in a sympathetic manner.

85

Memory depends on interest, attention, and concentration. However the path does not depend on memorizing; we leave that to the academic philosophers of the universities. It depends on getting understanding, brain-changing not brain-packing.

86

It is inevitable that, as his search for truth becomes keener and deeper, his thought will become more precise.

87

So far as education consists of knowledge and information, it depends on memory, which is a function of an ego built up by the past and present experiences.

88

It is not only a matter of temperament as to which view he will accept, although that factor is obviously present, but much more of development. How far has he journeyed in the understanding of life and the mastery of self?

89

The first impulse to gather facts—that is, to know—was the first step taken by primitive men out of their backwardness towards science. The first impulse to explain those facts—that is, to know, understand, and complete—was the first step taken towards metaphysics.

90

Take what you can find that is congenial to your mind, appealing to your heart, and conformable with reason and evidence.

91

To isolate the genuine truths from all the possible fantasies is hardly a work for beginners.

92

When your mind can move from point to point, from idea to idea with alert nimbleness, it is ready for philosophy.

Comparison and synthesis

93

After a man has studied comparative religion, comparative metaphysics, and comparative mysticism, taking the East as well as the West in his stride, he is better fitted to come to right conclusions about truth, God, reality, the soul, and life's purpose.

94

We should talk about these matters, not in any spirit of animosity—of which the world is sadly too full—but in a spirit of mutual enlightenment, as of brothers calmly consulting to assist each other towards the elimination of mistakes. We must discuss these questions in the detached manner of the philosopher, and keep out those angry emotions and acrimonious words which often escape partisans in theological discussion.

95

It is not at all hard for anyone with enough brains to state a case for being good and then to state a case of equal strength for being bad. Logical argument alone cannot provide a final test of the truth of any case.

For this we must go also to impersonal feeling, mystical intuition, and, not least, practical life.

96

The recognition that the synthetic view is the only right viewpoint will initiate a new epoch in the world of thought.

97

For every argument that is set up and defended, there is always a possibility to set up another argument whereby it is contradicted or destroyed. The only qualification of this seemingly hopeless position is that we approach nearer truth as the contradictions lessen.

98

A *dialogue* where both seek to learn, is what ought to take place, not a *polemic* where each listens only to himself!

99

The region of logical intellect offers no durable abiding place for the questing human mind. Every argument can be met by another of equal force, every opinion cancelled by another of equal weight; nor is there any end to the process except escape from this region altogether. But the escape should be on to a higher region, to that of genuine intuition, and not to a lower one like that of superstitious belief.

100

The futility of a solely logical attempt to solve problems concerning the human being, and his nature, relations, and activities, is shown by the many cases where men of equal intellectual capacity and academic status offer conflicting interpretations of the same fact or arrive at opposite conclusions from the same premises.

101

Too often a study is made from a single angle only and neglects all the others. The result is a narrowed, limited understanding which leaves out factors that may be much more important. Each one omitted is, by implication, denied. A philosophical view takes as many aspects as possible into account to get nearer the full truth.

102

The Truth is found intellectually not at one end of a pair of opposite alternatives, not by making a choice between two concepts only, but by grinding and synthesizing the interplay of forces and experiences which must be taken into account.

103

His conclusions are not hastily and impulsively reached. They follow the gathering of sufficient evidence, which means sufficient to give both sides of a case. He gives careful thought to it before he gives an opinion about it.

104

He may go so far even as to put himself in the receptive mood which would make it possible for him to see a variant teaching in the light with which its followers see it. (One can, perhaps.) He may try to understand and sympathize with a viewpoint that may or may not have much to recommend it. But if he should permit himself to respond thus, he would have to return from this standpoint anyway, for his critical intellect would, upon resuming renewed activity, ask insistent questions.

105

The time comes when the seeker must sift out all the doctrines he has received and let those go which lack reasonableness, the sound of truth, the lofty tone of impersonality. And even after he has sieved away the ideas born of narrowness, pettiness, bigotry, prejudice, and false sentimentality, he has still to choose those which he can usefully work with.

106

He will collect his ideas not from books alone, but also from various other sources, orthodox and unorthodox, conventional and off-beat.

107

The student should train himself to note, study, and state accurately views which he could not join in himself. In order to do this he will have to keep his emotional feelings against them out of his examination of statements. He will have to suspend his intellectual judgement of them also. However firmly he may hold his own views upon any subject, it is a useful discipline to subdue the ego and put himself into the mentality of those who hold different views and to try to understand why it is that they hold such views. This will be a valuable exercise in keeping bias out of his thinking and the conceit of always being right out of his opinions.

108

Men who are specialists in a single profession are usually men whose minds run in a single groove. Each can contribute his own viewpoint quite creditably, but he cannot understand and sympathize so readily with the viewpoint of another man whose experience lies along totally different lines. Even if we go farther and attempt to step beyond such limitations into a synthetic viewpoint and gather up into one coordinate whole the contributions of all our modern mentors, we shall yet fail to arrive at the deepest understanding of the world's problem. This is because these men deal not with root causes but with effects, the effects of profounder causes which ultimately take their rise in subtler, less obvious sources.

109

The difficulty in getting at the truth about controversial questions, whether they be economic, political, religious, or metaphysical, is that the advocate of a particular side pushes forward the good points of his own views and the bad points of his opponent's views, whilst at the same time he suppresses both the bad points of his own and the good ones of his opponent's views. Consequently the only way to form a fair and just estimate of the question is to construct our own picture, frankly and impartially incorporating in it all the essential points from both sides and those which they may have missed, too.

110

Intellect is sharpened by frequent discussions and endless disputation.

111

We ought to put such a discussion, which deals with the sublimest topics that confront the human mind, upon a dignified basis. If we argue merely for the sake of scoring an intellectual victory over the opponent, or getting the upper hand over him, we argue wrongly. If, however, we argue with the sole desire that truth may appear out of the conflict of viewpoints, we argue rightly.

112

Philosophy points out that we have to study a subject not only from the outside but also from the inside—that is to say, not only critically but also sympathetically—if we would arrive at a just estimate of it. Those who paint it all black with defects or all white with virtues, and omit all intermediate or half-shades, make a serious mistake.

113

Our approach to every doctrine must be to take its truth and leave its error. But we must do this in appreciation rather then in disparagement.

114

There is a need to develop flexibility by practising the shift of attitudes, to see why others hold their beliefs, and to be able to stretch one's own thought so as to enter sufficiently into theirs. This produces sympathetic understanding, but the opposite—critical judgement—must not be forsaken.

115

There may however be one result of such comparative study which is as unpleasant as it is undesirable. If it is overdone and independent thinking underdone, it may breed confusion in the understanding and contradiction in the feelings. The more books written from different points of view he reads, the less certain of his knowledge he may become.

116

Concepts or ideas are clues, pointers, signposts to truth, perhaps helps towards the search, but ought not to be referred to a level beyond that of the intellect, which is limited. Fixation and dogmatism should be avoided. Words, definitions, even bibles are not absolute, but relative to our present mental state.

117

When a man begins to lay down in advance the conclusions to which his thinking is to lead him, he is not really seeking truth.

118

We must so care for facts that we welcome them even when they are personally and profoundly distasteful. Nothing can be gained by shutting our eyes to them or by concealing them from our mental horizon, or by examining them with partiality and prejudice.

119

If we are to view the problem of truth aright, we must view it in proper proportions. We waste much mental energy in whole-heartedly denying this or contending for that; truth is like a diamond; it has several facets: we could be better employed seeing *all* the facets than in splitting them up. Analyse all round a subject's head, but do not split its hairs.

120

He who cannot reject his personal preferences at the higher bidding of truth; he who has no aptitude for reflecting upon abstract philosophical ideas or is unwilling to overcome inertia and labour at its creation; he who impertinently matches his individual *opinions* against the proved facts of science or philosophy as though they were of equal or superior value— such a man is quite unfit for this knowledge and can never master it.

121

The very fact which may be put forth in support of one point of view may be triumphantly hailed by someone else as a proof of a different point of view!

122

Even full debate and discussion cannot lead to full truth about any issue, spiritual or secular, when all the necessary information is not there. But even if it is there, it will twist and pervert truth if the minds approaching it are seriously flawed.

123

Too many arguments have mere egoistic self-expression as their purpose, and not the pursuit of truth. Neither arguer is really interested in seeing the fallacies and weaknesses of his own case, but only those of his opponent's. Neither will be willing to abandon his own standpoint or theory no matter how much evidence or facts disprove it.

124

This battle of conflicting explanations is not necessary, since both refer to different aspects of the subject and as such are both correct.

125

Conventional people, fond only of commonplace ideas, may feel shocked at some philosophical statements. They do not see that their thinking is falsified because they have prejudiced their quest of truth from the start, because it is done within the context of conventional attitudes. How few can free themselves from the thick incrustations of prejudice; how many are unable to approach an idea with calm, impersonal, detached open-minded-ness! Most people naturally pick out from a teaching those views which please them and reject the others. Only the seeker who has disciplined himself morally and intellectually will be heroic enough to take unpleasing views along with the pleasing ones. Philosophy's teaching will appeal, and can only appeal, to those who have striven to escape from dogmatism, who have shaken off widespread prejudices and outgrown crudely materialistic ideas, and whose minds are sufficiently developed to realize the value of free views and flexible attitudes. Where that has been insufficiently achieved, a special discipline is prescribed to complete the preparation.

126

Any man can fool himself by the trick of finding out just those facts that fit his fancy. All such pickings are easy, but they are also worthless. Any fuddle-minded person can twist and turn a state of affairs into a painfully sorry caricature of itself. But in doing that he is simply twisting his own head, in order to ignore conveniently what he does not wish to see.

127

The appreciation of a doctrine ought to be balanced and reasoned, not exaggerated or hysterical. The wish ought not to be made the father to the evaluation of it, nor to the judgement of its results.

128

We must rid our minds of this cant. We must clear our eyes of this cataract of prejudice which covers them and dims the sight against our real remedy.

129

When a man's thinking unconsciously mixes up the central issue of a problem with diverse other issues, and does not keep that entirely to itself, his conclusions are likely to be self-deceptive ones.

130

When a man first starts to think, he has to pass through the disease of mental measles, and get not a few obnoxious prejudices out of his head.

131

People who live in the suburbs of thought have the sheeplike mentality which fears originality.

132

When I meet with certain persons or certain books, I am often reminded of a certain sentence in Roman Seneca's writings: "There are many who might have attained to wisdom, had they not fancied they had attained it already."

133

A small mentality can only mangle a large truth.

134

Such people are constitutionally incapable of perceiving any other truth besides the new one which they happen to have embraced at the moment, dazzled by its blaze as they are.

135

People can see every half-truth and every quarter-truth, but they can not see the obvious truth. This is because they are so sated with self-interest and prejudice. The aspirant, too, may be crammed full of prejudice and have enough self-interest to fill a bank but—he knows it; he is trying to disentangle it, whereas they go on in blissful ignorance and imagine they are envisaging facts when they are only pampering to prejudice.

136

It is a common habit to belittle ideas and practices simply because they are unknown or less familiar, but it is not a wise habit.

137

When he finds that the truth is not what he had always supposed it to be, he is either shamed and humiliated or surprised and exhilarated.

138

It is possible to know some things; only to believe other things: while the residue may be hoped for—nothing more.

139

It is not an uncommon experience to observe how some persons project their own fancies on outer happenings, meetings, and persons—in other words, bringing their own thoughts and imaginations into real events and confusing the two.

140

The latest knowledge is not the last nor the latest governmental form the final and best.

141

The conventional mentality thinks and therefore speaks in clichés. Its capacity for independent activity does not exist.

142

It is a common enough mistake among the thoughtless to confound the abstruse with the absurd.

143

This is surely something that should appeal to a reasonable and reflective person. That is why few will be found at first to listen to it, for few take the time to reflect; most are led by the nose since they are led by prejudice.

144

There are so many men who believe that they know very well where they stand, but who believe wrongly.

145

The mass mind, with its ignorance of higher laws, its confused state resulting from this ignorance and from the varied pressures, suggestions, traditions, or authorities imposed on it from outside and opposed by resistances or desires from inside, is *at first* thrown into greater confusion if challenged by a messenger of truth.

Authority and the past

146

His mind acknowledges no criterion of truth, no convention of goodness, no taste in beauty merely because convention tradition or society supports it. He has to examine it first; he has also to find out what other minds in olden and medieval as well as modern times, in widely differing Oriental lands as well as Occidental ones, thought of these matters; finally he has to consult his own reason and, above all, his own intuition and compare all these views quite impartially and without selfish interest.

147

We must apply human reason, not supernatural "revelation," to all our problems, if they are to yield proper solutions.

148

Modern man is being led to spiritual truth by a new path, by reason's discoveries rather than by revelation's dogmas.

149

Exaggerated respect for established views can soon lead into servitude to them.

150

Men dispute over truth and fail to agree and have done so for three thousand years at least, according to Chinese records, four thousand at least according to Egyptian traditions, and longer still according to Indian beliefs.

151

The educational institutions purvey information but only great souls can provide inspiration.

152

We should not defend sound truths on unsound grounds nor should we defend unsound truths on sound grounds. It happens often that erroneous religious doctrines or false mystical teachings are defended by declaring that they pertain to a higher dimension and transcend the intellectual capacity to understand when in fact they also transgress against its capacity to reason correctly.

153

It is his inalienable privilege to hold whatever opinion he pleases, as it is to hold whatever religious belief sustains him. But it must be said that there is a vast difference between what he has inherited and accepted unchanged from society or family, and what he has arrived at by his own diligent, determined, original, and independent research.

154

Authority, the two kinds of experience—ordinary and mystic—logic, reason, intuition: each of these is to be regarded as a valuable help in eliminating error or doubt and ascertaining truth or fact, but none is to be regarded as the only means of doing so.

155

There are very few right-thinking people for the simple reason that there are very few people who ever think at all. Oh yes, there are multitudes of people who shuffle ready-made thoughts in their brains, just as they would shuffle cards at a table—after they had been handed the cards!

156

This freedom which must be given to the intellectual approach to and communication of truth forbids a narrow rigid conformity to any one of the known systems, whose *comparative* study is itself a beneficial consequence. It must apply to all of them, even to the terms and images used by the mind.

157

In this kingdom of Truth I accept no authority save that of Reason.

158

Rationalism must replace superstition. Reason must reign supreme. All arbitrary assumptions must be discarded. The mind must preserve its honest integrity. Thought must be set free from authority. Inquiry must be fearless, full, and unbiased.

159

We may accept the judgement of authority but only after we have examined the history and tested the worth of such authority, be it book or man, tradition or institution.

160

He is wary of falling into superstition, whether sanctified by religion's faith in the intangible or by science's incapacity for it.

161

Since these mahatmas disagree on certain points, it is obviously safe to follow them only on those points where they do agree.

162

He will study several different teachings, approving here, disapproving there, suspending judgement often, but committing himself to none. He can afford to wait for the most satisfactory one or to remain permanently free.

163

Before we try to rid ourselves of traditions we ought to make sure that we have learnt their best lessons.

164

He who is discontented with conventional dogmas and who disagrees with orthodox authorities must be willing to think in isolation.

165

When he is unreceptive to new ideas unless they have first been authenticated by a certain particular teacher, cult, or book, he is trapped in a closed system.

166

Judge every source, and the teaching which emanates from it, independently. Make use of confirmatory or negatory comment to help you in the matter but do not follow any of them in utter blindness. For you cannot evade your personal responsibility. Whether you accept or reject a teaching, just because you accept or reject a particular institution or authority, your judgement will be there anyway hidden in your belief, only it will be there unwittingly.

167

There is no need to depart from reason but only to illumine or inspire its working by intuitive revelation. But where one is unable to provide this himself, then he ought to go to the great masters for it, or consult their writings if they are unavailable through distance or inaccessible through death.

168

Since all teachings are related to the stage of development, the time in history, and the area where they are given out, they must be regarded as relative. This means, in the end, that they are arguable and, even more, that they are personal opinions, speculations in someone's mind.

169

To study the imaginations and theories of limited minds upon this subject is to waste time and squander energy.

170

Are we to reject every machine, ship, carriage, and alphabet merely because Lao Tzu recommends us to do so, and he is an illuminated soul? This shows up the childishness of setting up a single absolute authority to cover and govern every facet of living and thinking.

171

Even if a belief were held throughout the world, it is not thereby proven true. It may still be a world-wide self-deception or, more likely, traditionally received suggestion.

172

He who has made this research a serious matter, who has travelled widely in its cause, listened, seen much and read more, who has become well educated in the subject and quite sophisticated in its application, is entitled to hold views even though they do not coincide at all points with the traditional ones.

173

No human authority can be final for all authorities are liable to make mistakes. He has to settle these questions in a scientific manner by appeal to facts and reason or, where it is not possible to get the facts, to make it quite clear to himself that he is holding a belief as an opinion and nothing more. Certainly, it cannot be held as a truth when it is held only as an opinion.

174

By refusing to be tied to a particular school, one remains free to study as many of the doctrines of the different schools as he wishes. The teachings of one organization should help him to see the limitations of another.

175

Instead of merely repeating certain sentences which you have read or been taught, think them over for yourself. If you were really the Real how could you become Illusion? If you were the True, how could you succeed in deceiving yourself so far as to become the False? If ignorance, error, and illusion can happen to the One Mind, then they are just as powerful as It.

176

It is not other men's knowledge and power that we have to live by in the end, but our own.

177

Those who are able to think deeply upon such matters and are also quite well-informed, will find that much of their thinking has been done for them already by sages who preceded us.

178

Such a man does not ask whether this idea is included in the body of ideas which he has hitherto accepted by inheritance or tradition, education, or choice. He asks rather whether it is true.

179

Ideas are imposed upon the mind from various sources, accepted consciously or subconsciously, swallowed, and later regurgitated as if they were one's own! Such is the power of suggestion!

180

Learn from the past without becoming a mere imitator of it.

181

If we allow authority in doctrine to step beyond its rightful place, then instead of fulfilling a useful function it paralyses our powers of thinking.

182

Whatever the reason does to dissolve superstition serves to open a way to discover another truth.

183

When a stronger mind imposes its ideas on a weaker one, it is called teaching. When the weaker mind receives them passively (because of its trust in the guru's authority, his presumed knowledge of what he talks about) it is called learning.

184

The independent thinker cannot conform to the opinions of his age merely because he happens to be living then; he will not cut the cloth of his thoughts to patterns by his contemporaries but always to his own.

185

When he begins to scrutinize the religious and intellectual authority behind what he is taught or receives, and especially their sources, questions come up, doubts filter in.

186

A man's high position in one field of activity does not necessarily add great weight to his pronouncements in a totally different field. His personal knowledge in the second one may be absolutely nil.

187

Acceptance of a teaching ought to come from a deeper level than surface attraction only. There ought to be understanding also.

188

The power of mind needed to find truth is not commonly possessed. Those who lack it can benefit by the discoveries made by the sages. But they ought to test them in their own life-experience to confirm whether they be true.

189

Other men also have striven for self-mastery, have sought for truth since centuries ago. He should take advantage of their discoveries and secure the benefit of what they have learned.

190

Whatever is learnt from this valuable heritage of the past must still be applied in the present to make it a living force in one's own existence. This brings it to full meaning instead of remaining half-lost.

191

Those earlier statements of truth have their value; but it is unwise to forget the time and place of their making, for we must remember our own, too.

192

It is not by wholesale swallowing of traditionally accepted doctrines that we are going to expand our intelligence.

193

Amid such diversity of schools, the bewildered student would do well to pause and study the history of thought before choosing among the many rivals competing for his favour. Amidst such a chaotic welter of ideas, he should look rather for a master key which will reconcile them all than for a single satisfying system, because undoubtedly each has its special contribution to make towards the cause of Truth. The key exists and search will find it out.

194

There may be no sense of recognition, no feeling of ancient familiarity with these teachings, and yet they may have a strong appeal and attraction for him.

195

It is not enough in these days to quote scripture. There are many who do not hold it in awe and who consequently remain unconvinced. It is now necessary to quote facts also.

196

He need not share the timid concern for consistency. He need not be imprisoned forever in views which he held long ago. He need not be intimidated by his own past record, if at different periods of his life he has slowly changed or abruptly altered his world-view. Had he not been a seeker, quite probably this would not have happened, and he would have remained sunk in the ignoble complacency of thoughtless orthodoxy.

197

The Buddha: "Do not believe merely because the written statement of some old sage is produced."

198

Why not accept the best of the past? It is at the least as valuable as the best of the present, while having the added advantage of having been tested by time.

199

These writings have roused some sleeping minds, and galvanized some sleeping souls. With that their work was done: teaching must be sought elsewhere.

200

It is not easy to struggle against ancient and strong-rooted errors. For some of the seeming escapes turn out to be merely another kind of error.

201

I open the Old Testament and encounter the sentence: "There is nothing new under the sun." This judgement, made thousands of years ago, is echoed in memory by the more recent one of Jean de la Bruyere: "Everything has been said." Yet books keep on pouring, like a flood, from the presses. So, old thoughts circulate in new minds.

202

Most people look to the East for living representatives of this knowledge and to ancient or medieval literature for written records of it. They fall into the faith that the distant is better, and the dead are wiser.

203

Is he to remain the prisoner of his own past thinking or is he to free himself from it? Is he to remain faithful to everything he once believed even after he has found it to be no longer true or only partly true? Has long habit so committed him to certain ideas that he can no longer escape into better and larger ones?

204

These people pulled down the blinds over their minds soon after reaching maturity, because they did not desire to see any horizon wider than the musty dogmas which they possessed.

205

The independent-minded seeker will welcome truth from any quarter, any era, will be avid for whatever fragments of it he can find, and wherever he may find it.

206

Why hide views which a wide experience and wider study have forced into supremacy? I respect what the past has bequeathed us but this must not be allowed to enchain us to them alone.

207

He should take these old texts and render their ideas more intelligible to his own generation.

208

The search for the spiritual truth and the spiritual self cannot be economically done, in terms of energy and time, if the work and discoveries of others are ignored. So the records left by past men and the experiences of present ones are worth our study. They give it a spiral pattern; it moves around through them, turns, and climbs higher.

Books

209

The understanding of such deeply metaphysical writings calls for an effort on the reader's part to use his own mental energy as actively as the author had to use his own during their creation. The reader's task is, of course, immeasurably easier than the author's for he has had the pioneer work of track-laying performed for him; but even so it is hard enough.

210

The reflective study of these high-grade writings forces the mental growth of the student. The absorption of their spirit elevates him for a while to the spiritual plane of the author.

211

Are books nothing more than pieces of paper—as a famous Hindu saint once said to me? Have they brought no positive help to suffering men, no guidance to bewildered ones, no light to groping minds, no peace to agitated hearts, no truth to deluded seekers, no warning to misguided masses? If they have, this alone would be their justification. They have their place even in the most unspiritual and in many spiritual lives. The confusions arise only when the limitations of this place are ignored, or not perceived. Mystics who condemn intellect, and therefore books which speak for, or from, the intellect, should keep their condemnation within its own proper limits, too. With this plainly said as a safeguard, we may move over to the restricted standpoint of the Hindu saint. The need of silencing the intellect is paramount. If it is ignored in favour of the reading of endless books, or the writing of numerous notes extracted from them, the man keeps his intellect constantly active and thus prevents his mind becoming still! What is the use of accumulating notes and books, which are *outside* him, when the mind which must be conquered is *inside* him? Each book that is read represents a stirring up of thoughts whereas what is required of him is a silencing of them. There is no limit to the number of books that can be read or notes made. Even working twenty-four hours a day, he could go on activating intellect until he died, thereby avoiding his duty in meditation. Reading is useful in the preliminary stages to convince him, to clear his doubts, and finally to tell him what to do, that is, to practise mind-stilling. But if he does not do it, his knowledge is wasted.

212

In this matter of reading books, we should be truly grateful for their plentitude, their helpfulness, and their variety. And for those interested in the Oriental modes of thought, they make readily available teachings, ideas, and traditions which not so long ago were available only to the few who were wealthy enough or brave enough to make the long journeys to strange remote lands.

213

There are mystics who show in their sayings a contempt for books about mysticism. They would be better advised to point out that it is only when a certain development is reached that the quester should turn aside from his books in order to practise what he learned from them, should stop reading and start meditating. Certainly reading is not enough and the work should not stop with it; there is need to go inwards by way of meditation and thus turn theory into practice. But this is far away from the total rejection of religious, mystical, and philosophic literature those anti-intellectual fanatics urge upon their followers. The very fact that texts were composed thousands of years ago and that they have been written continuously ever since shows that there is a real need for them. They can and do help seekers.

214

It is unfair of those who perceive the limitations of the intellect to decry books. Only if they find themselves suffering from the Dark Night of the Soul for a time are books likely to be of little service or make little appeal. At all other times inspired work can give some reassurance or restore some calm, just as perceptive work can give needed intellectual food. But if, during the press of personal preoccupations, they do nothing more than remind us of larger issues, they still render a service.

215

We are helped indeed every time that we discover in somebody else's writings an idea which has been trying to formulate itself in our own mind but which could not pierce the clouds of obscurity, vagueness, and uncertainty which surrounded it.

216

Even though it is indirect and not personal, the help which is given thousands of people through the printed sheet possesses a worth which only those who benefit by it can properly estimate.

217

When he finds his own inner experiences described in the pages of a book, he feels more assured about their reality.

218

Metaphysical books are best studied when alone. The concentration they need and the abstraction they lead to, are only hindered or even destroyed by the presence of others.

219

Those who complain that this philosophy is unintelligible, thereby expose their own insufficiency of intelligence and their own lack of mental capacity wherewith to grasp its position and conclusion. For there must be an affinity between the creativeness of the writer and the comprehension of the reader; without it both will be peering at each other through an opaque frosted-glass window.

220

Many persons have never even had the access to books on these subjects, nor the chance to get tuition personally. But now all that is changed. For all who can read can uncover today the once-hidden wisdom of the East. And today the proportion of those who can read is not only immensely larger but is rapidly enlarging.

221

It is true that reading sheets of printed paper cannot take the place of personal inner experience. But this does not stamp them as useless. They provide bridges to support the aspirant and thus help him find his way from his present familiar state to the farther one he seeks to reach.

222

No teacher and no book, however inspired, can transform a disciple into something new. What they can and usually do is to kindle the disciple's latent capacities, to bring out his innate views, and to clarify his vague tendencies.

223

Books can be used to stimulate thought or to escape from it: it depends on the reader whether they are used to help fulfil the duty of thinking for oneself or to evade it.

224

Through books we may borrow the experience of others and save ourselves costly experiments. Such living by proxy is painless.

225

Where a teaching is said to be based on an ancient tradition yet never quotes a traceable source, an original document, one may need to use some caution in quoting it.

226

He will learn to know some truth better through experience than through books but more truth through both together.

227

The mystics may decry intellect and disparage the worth of literature. But how many men have turned in hard periods to the classics among books and got power against depression, got wisdom, guidance, or consolations from them!

228

In the masterworks of the Eastern ancients, in the profounder classics of the European heritage, and even in the fewer outstanding American pieces, there is enough material for study.

229

We can usually find refuge from the world of action by taking to the world of books. Then, stress and turmoil left behind, and restfully ensconced in chair or bed, pictured scenes may be enjoyed, or ideas received, which act like a holiday.

230

Live in the atmosphere which great books bring, their truer and wider ideas, their finer exalted ideals.

231

Most men are not yet built to wait in the silence for the visitation of the spirit of truth. It needs must be described in words for them, by the intellect for their intellect.

232

So long as men have thinking minds, so long will they need teachings, instructions, explanations, and clarifications. It is in vain that Krishnamurti and Pak Sabuk claim to have no teaching: they give one through their talks and writings, whatever name be affixed to such communication.

233

Erasmus went so far as to call the books written by saints "wherein is so much of them, in which they live and breathe for us . . . the holiest and most efficacious of sacred relics."

234

Some of us cannot afford to wait until the hair turns grey around our temples before acquiring a modicum of wisdom. We need it before then. For us therefore there are books, the recorded wisdom of other men, the inscribed experience bought by *their* pain and *their* struggle.

235

Out of the silence of the dead past there are a thousand inspired voices to speak to the living present. If the aspirant will listen to them, these voices of noble and illumined men may instruct and guide him through different stages of the quest. They are to be heard in books both well-known and little-known.

236

Are scriptural revelations the only ones worth heeding? Have not high truths, even great teachings, appeared in the world's thought, poetry, and intuition—outside religion, outside officialdom, outside the academic halls, outside the institutions and organizations?

237

We must admire and praise the exact, accurate, and scrupulous methods of academic scholarship.

238

A tenet which fails to be interesting or helpful because it mystifies one's mind should be put forward a second time in plainer language.

239

When we put these abstruse ideas into popular language, we must be careful not to do so at the cost of sacrificing their significance.

240

A founder of a cult or a religion has to claim inspired prophetic authority, but an author can give his ideas on a merely intellectual basis.

241

If a man who purports to speak or write on behalf of any teaching lets his own personal ideas get mixed into those he received, the resulting product will be adulterated and could even be distorted.

242

Most of the texts of the hidden teaching, like the *Upanishads*, do not disclose the logical steps by which their conclusions are attained, but only affirm the conclusions themselves. This was done because it was left to the teacher to expound vocally and supply personally what had been left out. But this is unfortunate for modern students, for teachers who know the Overself are almost non-existent.

243

Condensed in thought, summarized in statement, the Hindu *Upanishads* and similar works needed a teacher to expound and explain them. But this is not to say that intuition and intelligence cannot, if sharpened properly, cut through alone into their meaning.

244

The academic writers and authorities must be honoured for their painstaking study, their diligent documentation of statements made and evidence offered, their search after, and later assembly of, records needed to understand a particular topic or subject.

245

It is a help first, to clear his thoughts and second, to communicate them to other men.

246

Even those who take philosophy as a merely academic pursuit are not wasting their time. Learning what the world's thinkers have put forward as their best wisdom or sharpest observation has its place and value in the intellectual life, just as comparative study of religions has its value in the religious life.

247

To read what others have written is to read what others have thought or fancied.

248

These great verities will always bear restating. They are too important to be said once and for all.

249

If every knower of the divine were to live as if he were struck dumb or as if his writing hand were paralysed, none of the great world revelations, truth-statements, or gospels would have come down to us. Only the enlightened sage is entitled to say that silence is the best teacher for he alone has the power to use it adequately. But such geniuses are extremely rare and for anyone else to utter the phrase is merely to babble words, to mislead and to confuse. In what way does it serve the hearer or the reader?

250

The highly compressed sentences of a Lao Tzu teach us more that matters than the prolix extended pages of a merely book-taught but dry mind.

251

Sometimes a man's words are wiser than he knows. Sometimes he speaks a truth above his ordinary knowledge. But these times are rare.

252

It is not easy to give a list of philosophical books to be studied. First of all, philosophy has a higher definition than the current one, for what usually passes under that name is only metaphysics. There cannot be any philosophy without the advanced forms of meditation practice which have been called ultramystic for want of a better term. Metaphysics is guided by the light of reason alone, and admirably, so far as it goes, but that is not far enough. This is because all the thinking in the world will in the end only yield a conclusion, which is another thought. The Overself is not a thought, but Being. However, there is such a thing as the "Metaphysics of Truth" which is reasoning—disciplined, chastened, and checked by the highest possible mystic experience. There are no books on this subject available in English yet, but there are a few, hundreds or thousands of years old, available in the East. Unfortunately, they are written either in Sanskrit, Pali, Tibetan, or Chinese. Of these, a few only, about half a dozen, have been translated into English. But these translations were made by philologists without the experience of advanced yoga to guide them, hence they are unintelligible. It would be an utter waste of time to try to understand them. Fortunately, some of these documents have been reviewed with the assistance of qualified guidance. Some day, probably in a philosophic magazine, hundreds of pages of notes and translated excerpts from these little-known texts will be published for the benefit of students. Meanwhile, one who is inclined to do so may study the works of some of our Western metaphysicians, but only in part. For they have gone astray and lost themselves either in gross errors, in half-errors, or in fanciful speculations. Keeping such reservations in mind, the student may read Berkeley, Schopenhauer, Kant, Russell, Bergson, Spencer, Fichte, Joad, Radhakrishnan, Hamilton, Malebranche, Locke, Hegel, and Monsieur Cousin. These may be said to come nearest, in particular points only, to the hidden teaching. However, it is not wise to plunge into such a course alone and unguided, for he will emerge with more bewilderment and confusion than before.

253

A beginner may certainly aid his search for knowledge through wide reading and, possibly, through attendance at suitable lectures. Some very fine works have been written by the philosophers and mystics of all ages. These writings may bring into his life a little emotional inspiration, intellectual guidance, and power of will to help his struggle through the years of long and unavoidable endeavour, and they can to that extent act the part of a teacher and guide.

254

Is then our writing nothing more than black ink on white paper? Have we nothing to communicate that is sublime enough to survive its reading?

255

The book can be one of his mentors at a time when he is too young to have a correct set of values, and it helps to supply the deficiency.

256

Erudition, education, even scholarship—if put under the proper restricting limits—offer useful contribution.

257

At last he can meet with an expression of truth that has a recognizable face.

258

Each time we read such truth it comes with liberating freshness and becomes a stimulant to aspirations. The degree of its power to help us is conditioned only by its writer's ability to catch its heart and convey his perception.

259

It is better to look twice at some assertions. Sometimes it is wiser to look beneath the words themselves and scrutinize the character of the writer himself.

260

The final realization of truth is not found in any documents however sacred and however worthy of men's highest regard they are held to be. But they may confirm the realization, may also give a reference-point when attempting to communicate it to other men.

261

Just as the man who stands on the summit of a Himalayan mountain does not need the testimony of an altitude meter to tell him that he really has ascended to a loftier level than that of the plains, so the man who enters into his spiritual being does not need reason's proof, someone else's say-so, or scripture's test to tell him so.

262

There are many who read through such writings only to fasten on those paragraphs which agree with their own beliefs.

263

Every kind of material appears nowadays upon the printed page, from utter nonsense to lofty wisdom. An editor may place impartially on the same page of his newspaper or magazine the inspired utterance of a new prophet alongside of the reported description of an ephemeral triviality. Indeed, the triviality may be given the greatest prominence, whereas the inspired truth may be tucked away at the bottom of a column!

264

You may write historically about a country or a man but not about THAT. It is out of time, beyond all events, happenings and changes. There is no difference, not even the hint of a hint, between what it was and what it is. There is in this sense, nothing at all to write concerning the Real.

265

The worst books are mere repetitions and the best are mere exercises in intellection.

266

Most such books are limited by the fact that the author's sources of knowledge are mainly intellectual and only somewhat intuitional. He has received his knowledge chiefly from large-scale reading.

267

No single book should be made into an infallible bible, even if it be worshipped by a million men.

268

The intellectuals, caught in a trap of ever-lengthening discursive knowledge and analytic thought, listening to endless discourses and reading the ever-appearing books, live behind a wall of non-understanding.

269

The experience of illumination is worth a library of books.

270

It is not very inspiring to read these spiritual commentaries, however rarefied their metaphysics may be. For they lack verve. The reader's feelings are not stirred, he never gets even a single fitful glimpse of the kingdom of heaven.

271

The words of the book can carry you to a certain point in consciousness. When this is reached you can go farther and higher only by closing the book! It has served you well but you must turn now to a new source. Let thoughts come into quietude; intuition will take their place: a holy presence will be felt: surrender to it.

272

Constant attention to God will awaken in one's own awareness some of the knowledge he is seeking in books and spiritual study.

273

A book which is unintelligible to the reader may be so wise as to be above his head, but on the other hand it may be so lost in turgid, enigmatic mystification that it is below his head. The annals of both religion and occultism bear witness to this fact.

274

The greatest lies and the greatest truths appear on paper.

275

The same printed page causes different reactions in different readers.

276

People do not give enough weight to the fact that even if claim or criticism is printed from inked linotype on white paper, its correctness is not a whit more guaranteed than if it were not.

277

He projects his own thought into what he reads, imposes his own conception on the author's and then believes he has understood him correctly!

278

The religious or even the mystical writer is not concerned with the accuracy of his statements, the meaning of his words, or the regard for facts as is the philosophic writer. On the contrary, he writes with abandon, revels in emotion and seeks to incite it.

279

We tell the student to study but we do not tell him to believe everything that he sees in print. He is to study in order to find a single true idea among several false ones, he is to read for the few true ideas among many half-true ones. That is, he is to read discriminatingly.

280

If you know the precise sources of a man's inspiration, you will be able to measure more correctly the truth of his proclamations. But you cannot discover them from his own statement, for he may be mistaken or unaware. To get at them, you must add critical analysis to sympathetic self-identification with him.

281

If you mentally correct a false statement which you hear or a false teaching which you read, you defend yourself against it.

282

A spiritually inspired book should be read slowly and followed reverently.

283

When you approach a volume containing the true LIGHT it were better that you put aside the old and established canons of criticism which elsewhere serve you so well, but here are about as useful as a candle on a stormy night.

284

In no matters short of ultramystic experience need he discard reason and reject scientific knowledge at the bidding of any book, however sound its other instruction may be. He may remain equally unenthusiastic over theological fancies which once provided serious occupation to bored individuals who, having deserted the world, had somehow to fill their time. He need waste no time over metaphysical sophistries and logical hair-splittings which agitated dreamers who, having lost their firm footing on a toiling and suffering earth, became aviators before airplanes were invented.

285

A continual round of reading may yield pseudo-progress, the feeling of making continual growth, but after all it will only add more thoughts to those he already possesses. Only by thinking out for himself what he is reading—and for this he will need abstention from it—will he be able to add understanding to it.

286

Take them easily, do not worry about any parts you do not understand just now. You will find that after a year or two, if you come back to read those parts again, they are becoming clearer.

287

It is better to go to the primary texts themselves, even though it takes longer to delve sufficiently into their meaning, than to wade through the secondhand commentaries of others. There is, however, an exception to this rule, and that is when a writer with penetrative insight and creative power takes hold of a text and puts its meanings and relations before us with all the skill that he possesses so that the words bring about an intense emotional and mental reaction in the reader. We need not look to dry academic pundits for such works. Only when the mystical level of study and understanding has become insufficient will he be ready for a new and higher level of philosophic study.

288

A statement which puts into portable form the wisdom learnt through many years, even many reincarnations, is worth a little analytic thought.

289

The great texts are worthy of deep repeated study.

290

If any chapter in any book has some nutriment for you, accept it, but if not then skip that chapter. No one is bound to accept *every* thought of any writer, nor is likely to, human mentalities being as widely variant as they are. No author is fit and qualified to meet and remove all the doubts of the same human being, let alone of all human beings.

291

Every reader is a guest of every author whose pages he opens. But whether he is an understanding guest or a bewildered one depends on two things at least: on how clearly the work is phrased and on the development which the reader's mind has reached.

292

If what he reads becomes his own thought, communication is complete. The writer triumphs.

293

Without denying his services or reducing his role, both of which are obviously large and important, it is still necessary justly to criticize and calmly to reject the flaws in his teaching. To accept them merely because they bear his name would be not only to support the myth of one man's infallibility but also to be disloyal to the search for truth.

294

If a man is unable to think for himself on such abstruse matters, he ought to refer to the works of those who are able to do so; but he should look for such works as are stamped with originality and individuality, so that he can get his thoughts at first hand and not at second or third hand.

295

Few have the time to go through every word in the ancient texts. So let us pick out those sentences which have a peculiar importance, and also those which are most often misinterpreted and misunderstood.

296

The reading of metaphysical books requires a continual exercise of reason, a constant effort to concentrate thought, and a keen probing into the precise meaning of its words.

297

What is the purpose of your reading? Is it merely to kill time? But if you are out to learn, if you want to feel that you have progressed as a result of your reading, then you must realize that there is a wrong way and a right way to read. Remember you have not mastered any study until you can restate it in your own words. The best way to master the essence of a book or lecture is to select only the meaning of it, state it in your own words, and apply the meaning to examples drawn from your own experience, and not from the lecturer's or author's.

The wrong way merely wastes time for the serious student. It scatters your thoughts and diffuses your mental powers. It weakens your mental energy. And when you try to remember what you have read the net result is—nothing! Moreover the wrong way has no effect upon your active life—the way you work and live. That remains unbenefited by your study.

Now there is a better way to read.

4

ABSTRACT THOUGHT

Facts and logic

The way to deal with facts is not to ignore them but to meet and master them. The happiness got from the first will always be illusory whereas that got from the second will always be genuine.

2

Philosophy is not interested in twilight-gropings for occult phantoms or deceptive speculatings to exercise fancy. It seeks and accepts only verifiable facts.

3

But observation must be unprejudiced, sharp, and intelligent to produce the facts, and facts are apt to be obstinate and intractable.

4

By skilfully selecting some facts but suppressing more facts, by emphasizing a few and ignoring many, by distortion and dishonesty, a case could be built up for evil as good and for good as evil.

5

The futility of logic lies in this, that where facts please a man's fancy he will trot them forward in his oh-so-logical argument, whereas where they are not to his taste, he will unblushingly suppress them.

6

Those who take the trouble to form a rational opinion upon any matter by investigating the facts at first-hand, have a stronger claim upon the attention of the thoughtful than those who receive ready-made opinions from books or hearsay.

7

It should never be necessary for anyone to encircle the fine philosophy of the Spirit with the unworthy defenses of a refusal to face facts.

8

We may measure the worth of a teaching by pressing it to its ultimate theoretical conclusion and by ascertaining clearly its ultimate practical destination.

9

How factual is their teaching? Do its tenets find confirmation in rigid observation in the factor of experience and the thoughts of reason? This is what he must ask himself if his training of the intellect is to bear spiritual fruit.

10

Even men of much experience find it hard at times to arrive at positive decisions on worldly matters when these offer as many arguments for one conclusion as for a different one. Even their matured minds may sway back and forth, unsettled and uncertain at such a time until they decide to wait for the turn of events to give them a positive directive what to do.

11

It bespeaks a well-matured well-balanced mentality if judgement is withheld on what appear to be fantastic claims until they have been investigated.

12

A statement which holds a half-truth because it is based on a selected half-fact removed from a contradictory context, can neither be accepted nor denied. It must be analysed and its parts carefully measured until its truth and its falsity are likewise properly revealed.

13

Time will either develop or deform this idea.

14

We must build a flexible system for the facts, not for the probable exceptions to the facts.

15

Facts are as hard to find as they are disconcerting to the demagogue.

16

We must closely distinguish between what we believe and what is fact. In this philosophy we deal only with facts. All else, whether theory, hypothesis, inference, axiom, or postulate, we discard because it is merely belief. We are unable to accept them because we deal only in proved facts.

17

What anyone is in no position to appraise or evaluate he ought not to reject or condemn.

18

Whoever presents such ideas must be ready to offer the evidence for them, to validate them with sufficient reasons, to defend them with sufficient facts.

19

The open-minded questioner who is not too hasty to come to a conclusion but first assembles sufficient data, and that in an ambient circular course which moves around all sides, will get rewarded.

20

So to magnify a fact as to render it out of proper proportion to other facts, is to make it a cause of imbalance in the mind and error in judgement.

21

Deliberate over-emphasis of a partial statement of truth is sometimes useful and necessary but always dangerous because liable to misunderstanding.

22

Subconsciously fearing to look at the facts as they are, he becomes an innocent at large.

23

If the facts are distasteful, his imagination will adulterate them to suit his palate. If this cannot be done, his devoted service to an imperfect theory will submerge them altogether.

24

Where there is gathered a sufficient number of facts on which to base a reasonably correct decision, it is still possible that one more fact, of an importance outweighing all the others, could induce a man's mind to alter the decision.

25

The order of his thoughts may be perfectly logical yet the truth of them may be largely absent. For the premises with which they start may be ready-made theories, the facts upon which they rest may be less important than those which they ignore, and personal factors may have unconsciously accepted the one and chosen the other.

26

Just as mysticism may give the dangerous illusion that it is dealing with reality when it is not, so logic may give the equally dangerous illusion that it is dealing with truth when it too is not doing so.

27

To call a man a "philosopher" when he is only a mere logician is to demean the word. Logic is a useful tool, for certain limited purposes, but it can as easily lead a man into great error as into great wisdom.

28

Let them not mistake exercises in logic for penetration into truth.

29

Logic is always beset by the serious charge that its so-called truths are fallacious ones. For instance, it insists on the law of contradiction, the law which says that a statement of facts cannot be true and false at the same time. But the careful study of illusions produces conclusions which falsify this law. We do not mean by this criticism to declare logic to be useless.

We mean only what we have elsewhere written, that it is a good servant but a bad master.(P)

30

If our original assumptions are wrong, then the irony is that the more logically we travel from them to our conclusions, the more distantly we travel from truth.

31

We have to learn a little logic because we ought to bring our judgements into proper connection with our premises, and because we ought to test the reality of their implications.

32

If we begin our quest of truth with any assumption, at the end we gain nothing new, nothing which was not already there in the beginning. And when we then remember that we started with a mere belief, we realize that there is and can be no certainty about our final conclusions, no matter how rigidly logical we have been during the journey. We begin with imagination and end with it. This is not philosophy, but poetry. There is no other road for genuine philosophy than to depend on facts, not on presuppositions.

33

Carlyle: "In the eyes of the Pure Reason man is a soul but in the eyes of logic only a biped."

34

When the hailstones of truth fall upon these fields of worthless assumptions and these growths of false logic, the result will be not a little entertaining.

35

It is not enough to offer evidence, however plausible it may be. Proof is better, and more convincing.

36

No simile or metaphor, used to help explain an idea, should be pressed too far for meaning, wrung-out too much for consequences or implications. Take what you can from it and then let it go. It is only a starting-point and not a finishing post.

37

Truth cannot be found by addition, that is, by piling one bit of information on top of another. Nor can it be found by calculation, that is, by arranging these bits in plausible logical forms.

38

Logicians pride themselves that they can offer with their "law of contradiction" a perfect test of truth. They call it the fundamental law on which reasoning rests. Put into a few words it declares, "A proposition cannot be both true and false." The extraordinary thing about this law is that its own truth cannot be proved by logicians themselves. They can offer an indirect or roundabout proof by assuming the contrary, and affirming that a proposition may be both true and false. The significance of such a statement, however, is as even the tentative denial of the law implies, that at the same time it may also be true. But this is a contradiction. Therefore, the law must be true. Unfortunately for the logicians, such a proof is hardly valid because it is applying the very law which is called into question. So they are forced to content themselves by regarding the law as a self-evident one.

39

He must be careful in his definition, progressive in his logic, and consistent in his attitude.

40

Thinking is a kind of guesswork. Logical thinking is intelligent guesswork. At its best it is limited by the thinker's nature, development, experience, and so on.

41

The conclusion to which a person will arrive after thinking upon the problem of the world will inevitably depend on the standpoint from which he starts.

42

It might seem that we devoted too much space in *The Hidden Teaching Beyond Yoga* to the chapters entitled "The Worship of Words" and "The Arbitrament of Thinking Power." There were, however, quite a few reasons why we did so and one of them was that mystically minded persons—who naturally composed the larger portion of our readers—had to be led to a higher octave of mysticism, the philosophic. But this could only be done by encouraging them to think for themselves, to cease taking certain dogmas blindly and certain men at traditional valuations, and to learn discrimination between the merely emotional and the authentically spiritual. One of the finest roads to such independent thought is the analytic striving to find out truth by words, phrases, and statements.

43

We must also clearly state a situation before we can profitably reason about it. We must define a problem before we can understand it.

44

The principle of non-contradiction is important. Without it, no rational philosophy can be constructed, no true knowledge obtained. This principle declares that the same thing cannot be in the same sense both affirmed and denied, it cannot be and not be. For instance, it is impossible to involve any object in the contradiction of being both hot and cold at one and the same moment. Any so-called reasoning which offends this primary principle can lead only to insanity and not to truth.

45

We must reason from relevant facts until we reach more remote truths.

46

He who examines and enquires will necessarily become the foe of hollow, meaningless formulae.

47

It is better to submit these statements to rational weighing in the scales on one's independent judgement rather than to accept credulously or dismiss wildly.

48

Without the slightest training in the science of evidence, people airily deliver themselves of judgements that will not stand expert dissection for five minutes.

49

Metaphors do not make arguments: they merely illustrate them.

50

Fling up the coin of their rhetoric and when it comes down on the ground of test, you will know it to be base.

51

Assertion is not demonstration. They mistake their personal prejudices for sound reasons. The fact that it is their pleasure to hold certain opinions, constitutes for them sufficient argument. As a result their folly is sent into the world as philosophy. Any doctrine which demands a hearing today, must render sound reasons for its appearance.

52

It is an elementary axiom in logical science that we can understand the relation between two given facts from their relation to a third fact.

53

Take karma, for instance: they may mouth this doctrine a hundred times yet, never having thought it out for themselves, they do not understand its far-reaching implications.

54

It is open to anyone to disregard the facts of a situation, if he wants to, but he is likely to bump into them if he moves about long enough.

55

Thinking can lead us nearer to the kingdom of heaven if it is of the right kind. But it can also lead us nearer to the gate of hell, if it is not.

56

A theory may be solidly based on observed facts or it may be mere conjecture to support a bias.

57

Such a faulty conclusion is a fitting reward for those who judge hastily on insufficient evidence.

58

The facts are there, but such thick mists of different speculations have fallen upon them that we stagger among them as though we were blind.

The need for precision

59

The need is not for further mumbled, vague, or utopian and unrealistic proposals that are more words than practicable suggestions, but for specific and serious ideas.

60

When the facts are incomplete and the reasoning is incorrect, the conclusions are hardly likely to be unbreakable.

61

By the aid of logic a man may as easily deceive himself as he may delude others.

62

Fanatical partisans full of pet theories naturally become intoxicated over them; thus they are unable to see straight and perceive truth until they recover their intellectual sobriety again.

63

The soundness of a theory does not depend upon the number of its adherents.

64

Such half-articulate nonsense atones for the poverty of its philosophical authenticity by the pose of its linguistic authority.

65

We can discuss, accept, or deny a statement when it possesses some meaning. But when it is quite unintelligible, then we are entitled to ignore it.

66

It is quite natural for those whose thinking flounders incoherently, to hold views which stop inconclusively.

67

The flimsy materials out of which some "philosophies" have been constructed are fit only for the attention of the fabulist, certainly not for the serious scientist. The entire structure rests on a base of fiction unmixed with the concrete of a single fact. One may well exclaim with Macaulay, "When the consequences of a doctrine are so startling, we may well require that its foundations shall be very solid."

68

To oversimplify such a problem is to falsify it.

69

If the assumptions with which they start are inaccurate, then the conclusions with which they finish must be regarded as unacceptable.

70

We may accept such doctrines only by strengthening faith and weakening reason.

71

He is one of those foolish persons who believe all thinking which passes through their brains must necessarily be correct and logical thinking.

72

The quality of metaphysical thinking must inevitably deteriorate and its independence of movement be discouraged if it is to be conditioned by personal authoritarianism.

73

Those who live under idealistic delusions are not less foolish than those who live under realistic ones.

74

To the precise kind of mind, the use of generalizations is a perilous venture.

75

Between the melancholy blacks and dazzling whites of these two positions, no allowance is made for intermediate shades.

76

We may admit their devout emotions while we rebut their doubtful reasonings.

77

It is amusing to hear these bigots set down their theories and call them facts, or revere them as propositions about which there could be no more doubt than about the theories of Euclid.

78

The question itself is direct enough but his reply is a dissertation on some other subject. This reminds me of a Tamil proverb about the bazaar shopkeeper who is asked for salt, but fails to admit he has not got it in stock, and instead replies that he has got lentils!

79

It will catch the careless and thoughtless, and all those who accept extreme claims without receiving definite proof.

80

It is time that they refrained from making wild generalizations out of isolated particulars.

81

We must bring such a teaching to the test by running the rule of common sense over it. It is then that we discover its claims to be weak and extravagant. The sonorous prose in which its gospel is gathered together plays a trick upon its readers, if not upon its author also. The path from its facts and promises to its conclusions and perorations is covered with a haze of obscurity and vagueness. It is in this eye-covering haze that the logical trick is performed.

82

If the variety of doctrines, the contradiction of tenets, and the fierceness of arguments are fully noted, what else can be said than that personal opinion is the real basis of most teachings, seldom factual knowledge or firsthand authority?

83

We must be on our guard against the impressive obscurities of immature philosophers.

84

Those who will read this statement with an ironical smile have my full sympathy and assent. For once I read similar statements with the same ironical smiles—nowadays I am too weary to argue; I prefer to agree with my adversary quickly, for I have realized that experience is not merely the best teacher; it is the only teacher.

85

If he is too easily vexed by other people's criticism, this is because the ego is still upholding his pride and vanity.

86

Philosophy disdains to lower itself into the use of a criticism which is merely destructive. But it does not hesitate to accord a proper place for a criticism which is courteous, dignified, honest, constructive, and useful.

87

Those so-called intelligentsia who regard life on a purely intellectual level, separated from its spiritual aspects on the left and its ethical aspects on the right, still have the self-illusion that they are dealing with reality.

88

The solemn, staid exponents talk as though the advocate were also the arbiter. They put forward their own silly theories with such thick veneers of impartiality that one wonders how anyone can have the tremendous temerity to turn round and say they are wrong!

89

We could criticize a foolish philosophy from its first postulate to its last conclusion; we could rend its illogical arguments and self-contradictory claims into a thousand pieces; but it is not worth the trouble doing so, while our time is worth more than being wasted upon such profitless work.

90

Some people are unable to walk unaided in the world of thought, and directly they step into it, they call out for a pair of crutches in the form of a dogma.

91

These literary authorities deem it undignified to be lively and hence sink into a stagnant pool.

92

There are literary wasps, who fight and try to sting though never provoked, since it is in their miserable nature.

93

As a rule the wise man will not spare strength to engage in polemical thrusts. But when the inner monitor bids him enter the fray, he has no other recourse than to submit.

94

The worthless reputation of such criticism is exemplified by the fact that the opposition of these narrow-minded critics forms the best service they can render our doctrine.

95

Argument is a language they cannot understand, because logic is a science they have never learned; but invective and ridicule are something that they can understand, something that will arouse their passions and cut their feelings and corrode their credulity.

96

I have been studying this question only about thirty years but my critic has been studying it only about thirty minutes.

97

It is not their published statements that are so significant as the omissions from their statements.

98

When such critics cannot meet your impersonal arguments, they will assault your personal character.

99

To tell most people the simple, if subtle, truth is to provoke them to partisan wrath.

100

To such unintelligent objections, we may well answer with old Dr. Johnson, "I have found you a reason, sir—I am not bound to find you an understanding."

101

These people possess a remarkable talent for finding out difficulty in what is perfectly plain. They complain at our arguments because, in brief, the latter have been directed to a higher intellectual level than that of a boy of ten.

102

Argument can be refined, dignified, and courteous and still remain argument. But the crude and immature think it necessary to express themselves by abuse and vilification in order to prove their points!

103

The pompous pedantry of some academic circles is not less unbalanced than the illiterate inarticulateness of those who scorn them.

104

These lopsided characters who make intellect their sole judge, guide, and support have imprisoned themselves in it and refuse to leave their jail. Are they not foolish?

105

They use their minds only to deal with matters and to answer questions arising from their personal desires and social situations, only for the private satisfaction of their earthly interests. A higher use of it makes no appeal.

106

We must not only renounce such an unsatisfactory doctrine, but also denounce it.

107

In the new loyalty to a narrower view of truth, they abandon the High, the Holy, the Beautiful, and the Refined. The practical benefits of their education are plain; but why become a dwarf to get them?

108

They are imprisoned by their own illusory concepts and unless something or someone from outside comes to release them they will continue to be captive, limited, and unnecessarily lost in illusions.

109

The meaning of a word or phrase may be multiple, which is why translations vary, why interpretations are disputed, and why statements in bureaucratic jargon leave some persons uncertain and others unclear. Hence lawyers are hired, teachers of semantics arise, and sects flourish. But turn to numbers and one knows precisely what one is dealing with. They fulfil their function without debate. No mist arises. So Pythagoras can boldly assert: "The universe is founded upon numbers."

110

The power of abstract thought has characterized the best class of minds since time immemorial.

111

Abstract thinking shifts the mind's attention to quite a different level. Such thoughts do not have an outer appearance. They take no shape. They are to be comprehended—known by being understood.

112

Few venture to do more than peep beyond the portals, for they are unable to bear the hard strain of prolonged philosophical thinking.

113

However noble they may be morally or however abstract they may be metaphysically, it is not by living in the ideas in his mind that a man can ever live in his true self. Somewhere in his field of consciousness all thinking must be transcended if he is ever to do this.

114

The logic of your thinking must be as universally valid as mathematics. Nobody can cheat mathematics.

115

Men understand more easily what they can see, touch, and hear—that is, images, forms, and pictures—in short, symbols. These are the idols honoured by simpler minds. But when they develop their minds sufficiently they become able to think in terms of simple arithmetic progressing to the laws of geometry, and from algebra on to higher mathematics.

116

The fact is it is utterly impossible to form an abstract idea in the mind. We can only think of particular ideas.

117

When the sage does indulge in the luxury of a conversation with an inquirer or spiritual aspirant he usually adopts the Socratic method. There is probably no more powerful or effective method of compelling a man to *think*, to exercise his *own* reason, instead of repeating parrot-like phrases, than this of thrusting question after question at him.

118

The first use of general principles, the first worth of general theories is to economize thought and thus to avoid going over the same ground again and again.

119

This is a remarkable and little-known power of abstract reflection—
that, just as one thorn may be used to pick out a second from the skin, so a
line of thinking can be so used as to bring all thinking to an end.

120

Why did Pythagoras put mathematics among the necessary preliminary
disciplines for the study of philosophy? Here was part of the way to
counteract man's natural materialism. It trained him to think abstractly, to
hold pure ideas whose exactitude and truthfulness were indisputable. And
he supported the teaching by pointing to the fact that the universe was
founded on number. Finally, the higher use of mathematics was as an aid
in symbolizing metaphysical principles.

121

When we begin to operate with abstract concepts in the practical world,
we begin to know their true worth.

122

Except as an intellectual exercise, I would discourage abstract speculation upon which so many intellectuals have frittered away their time, as
our medieval theologians frittered theirs.

123

We seek truth for various reasons. One is because it possesses a certitude
that gives us anchorage and rest.

124

Mathematics is fortunate in having been able to invent a language of
symbols and signs which is adequate to the most exacting demands of
precision. The connotation of each sign is definite. It derives a fixed
meaning from the common universe of discourse which is implicit as the
background of both speaker and hearer. The mathematician must give
every symbol he uses a clear meaning in his own mind as well as to those
who are to read his symbols. Therefore, he is compelled to provide a
common medium of understanding about which there can be no two
opinions. Mathematics is thus placed in a position of superiority in reference to language and rigorous reasoning when compared to other subjects. It provides perfect instruments for the expression of an idea. The
meaning of the arithmetical minus sign is forever invariable and forever
precise.

125

The man who has thought well about thinking itself may put forward
more clever ideas in a single hour than others do in a single week.

126

The brain of the intellectual man multiplies thoughts but the brain of
the yogi subtracts and reduces them.

127

Thinking in terms of mental images is a valuable faculty, but thinking in words alone is not less valuable. Both are needed to the balanced person.

128

The value assigned to the symbol X must be strictly adhered to throughout the series of equations and, being predetermined, no confusion concerning what it stands for can ever arise. But when we turn to words we find them to be imperfect, elastic, and indeterminate. When we deal with mathematical symbols we expect and find a determinate meaning has been assigned to them, but when we deal with words we cannot always expect and often fail to find any fixed meaning at all.

129

The ordinary man who is used to dealing only with concrete things his eyes can see and his hands can touch, quite pardonably feels, when he is asked to deal with abstract conceptions, that he is at once out of his depth.

130

When one does not know his Real Self, that is, his own deepest being, it is of little avail to ponder on difficult questions of an intellectual nature.

131

The symmetry of the universe's patterns appears best in the figure of a circle.

132

The ability to think abstractly and metaphysically is not a waste of time as so many scientists, activists, and practical men of the world think. On the contrary it is needed as a counterbalance to the ability to think concretely.

133

So long as a man gets all his ideas from experiences gained through the *body* alone, so long may he pardonably accept the belief in materialism. But as soon as he begins to get them from *thinking* alone—and the difference can not be properly grasped until he has practised meditation sufficiently and successfully—so soon will he see the falsity of this belief.

5

SEMANTICS

Semantics requires us to train ourself in clear communication so that we shall be able to weigh the effect of our words upon people.

2

We begin by making a scientific analysis of the meaning of each major term used in a linguistic expression. We proceed by exposing with the utmost clarity and exactitude the implications hidden beneath the superficial meaning of each concept. We conclude by examining the general purport of the entire linguistic form, whether it be a phrase, a sentence, a paragraph, or a page.

3

The need of semantic discipline was recognized thousands of years ago by Patanjali, the Yoga authority whose approach to the subject was so thoroughly scientific. He wrote: "There is confusion of word, object, and mental image because one is superimposed on the other."

4

I esteem Socrates because he was the first European to bestow attention upon the search for real definitions.

5

The analytic logicians do a needed work, just as garbage collectors do, but it does not give us anything. The semantic probers do the same with the same results. Both have their place, but it is a limited one. Error starts when they cross their limits.

6

We study *meaning* from two angles: (a) ruthless analysis of words used without any corresponding meaning at all, mere blab words like "intuition," "god," etc., and (b) words which have a meaning, but are used by different persons in different senses.

7

Semantics deals with those subtleties of language which escape the notice of uneducated people and are ignored by those who shirk a little labour.

8

If ever the importance of semantics was demonstrated to the whole world, it was during the twelve months after the war ended. For then Russia on the one side and Britain and America on the other quarrelled openly about the meanings of rules for postwar policy made by three heads of state at Potsdam. Issues of grave moment to the lives of millions of people were involved in those rules.

9

If such a sentence is not to be a mere juxtaposition of words, if it is to be something more than verbal confusion, we must test its meaning by reference to the facts of verified and criticized experience, and we must discover if it corresponds to something discernible in the actual world.

10

Semantics is really a part of logic.

11

When it comes to expressing metaphysical thought, the student should choose his language carefully.

12

Questions which are wrongly put need not be answered. Silence is their only fitting response.

13

The evaluation of linguistic factors forms an important determinant of the validity of philosophic ideas.

14

We get out of the marsh of dubious data on to the firm ground of fact only when we observe a strict semantic discipline.

15

We can define only by contrast and discrimination. Light defines itself by contrast to darkness. All definition is therefore relative and forms a duality. Meaning arises only by separation of one thing from another. Hence the meaning of one word is entirely relative to that of another. We can think of what the word "hot" means, for instance, only by thinking of its opposite "cold"—similarly for "tall" and "short."

16

Why make difficult topics still more difficult for students by unclear obscure writing? This is one reason why from the beginning of my career I aimed at a direct, to-the-point style.

17

Do not ask an analogy to correspond to a situation in every way. It is enough if it usefully illustrates a single point, if it makes that point easier to understand.

18

We must ask people "What do you mean by this word, 'real', 'unreal', etc.?" This semantics is the very beginning of Vedanta.

19

Words may cloud understanding or help it. If they are semantically clear they may help to explain themselves but still leave the fact behind them untouched. This happens when firsthand knowledge is lacking, when only hearsay or speculation or tradition prompts them.

Clarity is essential

20

Mind and its expression in language are thoroughly interwoven and to improve one is to improve the other.

21

We must begin by looking into our thoughts and examining what sort of ideas we form when dealing with such words and especially when dealing with abstract words. We must attend carefully to what passes in our own mental comprehension the moment an abstract term is used.

22

We have begun our studies not by learning new matter but by unlearning the old. So much that we take for granted is not knowledge at all but fantasy. For instance, we assume unconsciously that "B" must exist. The only way to cure ourselves of false assumptions is first to discover that they are assumptions. The only way to clear our minds of false learning is to inquire into all our learning and examine its warrant. And since all thoughts are embodied in words, we can carry out this essential preliminary task only by examining the words habitually used, the terms we have inherited from our mental environment, and to see how far they are justified.

23

It will not harm our spiritual affairs to bring more clarity into them. It will not help them to keep our thinking about them muddled.

24

He who can conquer language, conquers men.

25

Such semantic self-vigilance will have a chastening effect on his private thoughts, quite apart from his public talk or writing.

26

We start by elucidating the information contained in single words or in sentence constructions, and our procedure is to question not the word or sentence itself but the *meaning* assigned to it.

27

We have to get the meaning of certain words by going within, to find by internal experience the correct definition of Spirit, Thought, and Love.

28

If this new scrupulousness requires him to reform his speech, he should do so. If a spiritualized semantics is needed for his thinking about truth, he should take it up.

29

The philosopher must ask each word to yield thoroughly a definition which possesses an exactitude that may well terrify the ordinary man. He must become a hunter and wander through the forests of verbal meaning to track down real meaning. He will not rush prematurely into utterance. Words are cheap for the ordinary man but dear for him. His studied hesitation leads, however, closer to truth. This interpretational discipline must be vigorously applied until it leads to a thorough understanding of all concepts which are the essential counters in philosophical research. For when men go astray in their definitions of these highly important terms, they will surely go astray in their thinking, and thence be led astray altogether from truth.(P)

30

There are no words in human language in which Truth can find adequate expression.

31

Mind cannot grasp the Brahman because the *drik* is different from *drysam*: hence words, as the expression of thought, cannot express it. This is the reason, not as mystics say, that Brahman is too wonderful for words.

32

What do we mean when we use this "A"? We must mean something or we would not use it. Now we must either understand what we mean by it or else we do not understand it. Few persons will venture to assert that they understand "A." Consequently we do not understand what we mean when we use the term. But is there any difference between such a situation and one where we use a term like *gkmouch*? That is to say, is not "A" a meaningless sound?

33

We perceive things because we distinguish the form, colour, etc., of a particular one from others. After having done this, we affix a name to the thing so distinguished. The fact that we have perceived, distinguished, and named the thing makes us sit complacently back with the feeling that we have understood it. We deceive ourselves when we utter this word that is a name. For we have perceived only an appearance, namely, only as much as the five senses can comprehend. The reality behind this appearance has escaped us.

34

In work of a non-philosophic or non-scientific character, the duty of preliminary definition is not laid on the student because both author and reader may imagine what they please without doing much harm. Hence the philosopher need not become austerely insensitive to the charms of poetry and the fascination of fiction and the solace of humour. And he may himself rise above taking words in their literal meaning and move amid their attractions as simile and metaphor.

35

There are numerous "Gods" existing in the minds of different people, although all are denominated by this single term. Now if the primal instrument in this question of truth is thinking and if every thought must find words in which to express itself, it is essential for us to begin by defining every important term which we use, as and when we first use it. Definition must precede explanation; otherwise confusion will reign in the mental relationship between reader and writer. No instruction can be given, no discussion can take place effectively unless both first combine to define their terms and to state their positions. I cannot incur the danger of using a word with one significance given to it by my own mind and another given to it by a reader. We must both beware of the habit of inexact expression.

36

Clear concepts and lucid statements are not less needed by the metaphysical and mystical than by the scientifical.

37

The average man has not the patience to, and does not want to, inquire into meanings of words. He says, "My meaning is the right one and good enough for me." This implies that he knows, but in fact he does not because he has not examined it.

38

The intellect cannot work accurately with blurred concepts. Pitfalls wait to receive it under such conditions. This is one reason why the process of discovering and clarifying meanings leads its advance into truth.

39

Many think it useless to discuss the meaning of a term. This is often correct in the case of a logician who seeks merely to score a cheap intellectual triumph over an opponent, however dishonestly, but in the case of a true metaphysician who seeks truth in its genuine sense, such a procedure may be most helpful to him. At the least, it may point out pitfalls.

40

However approximate all meanings may be in view of the incessant development of language, we have to pin down the words used in philosophy to workable definitions. This sort of self-training is highly valuable and constitutes the beginning of philosophical wisdom. But where this quest is concerned we ought to avoid such simplicity of mind and not fall into fallacies as readily as the unthinking masses.

41

Words came to possess a power to influence man which, in primitive times, was widely recognized and raised by priestly society to the pedestal of magic. Sacred words or secret ones were embodied in all the primitive systems of magic and religion. Contrariwise, men even made scapegoats of mere words, so that evil spirits and gibbering devils had their evocatory names.

42

The mere use of a phrase—and especially its printed use—carries the suggestion that the thing for which the phrase stands is really what it is described to be.

43

Naturally, we would not know what the teaching of the Buddha was if we had had no communication in words—words were very much needed—but when there is no correspondence between words and meaning the teaching itself will lose its sense. The *Lankavatara* thus reiterates throughout the text that the Tathagata never teaches the Dharma fallen into mere talk.

44

Put this word on the torture rack and make it confess its meaning.

45

This is not a plea for the abolition of all abstract terms and all universal ones; they are immensely useful and necessary in the everyday affairs of practical life. It is a plea for the realization that the moment we drop the practical affairs from consideration and take up the philosophical quest of truth, we have to shift to a higher and stricter standpoint; we have to reject for the time being all such terms as are temporary counters that have no value in exchange and no corresponding significance.

46

Propaganda knows only two shades—black and white. Truth knows all the range of colours in between.

47

He will exhibit a caution of language suggested by experience and enforced by knowledge.

48

The nominalists of medieval times were realists whereas the conceptualists were idealists. The former abhorred abstract words as unnecessary mystifications and declared there was no such entity as India, but only individual Indians, for instance, that society is only the men who compose it. In a list of abstract universals which would be non-existent and which may be unveiled by semantic analysis, their definition would include: God, Time, Space, Matter, Eternal and Absolute Existence, Happiness, Motion, Justice, Evil, Spirit, Truth, Reality, First Cause, and even "I."

49

We must keep things in their proper places to characterize them correctly and to use names with more precision. Theology should not be dressed in philosophic pretensions as magic should not be dressed in mystical pretensions.

50

The philosopher must demand as perfect an integrity in speech as possible. For him a word must be used rightly or not at all.

51

If we attribute meaning where there is none, we are telling lies to ourselves.

52

There is a profound difference between using words because they have been understood and merely repeating them because somebody else has used them.

53

If a man had arrived at some vital and powerful thought, the addition of a group of words can only stifle the newborn life; it can never render a faithful copy of the throbbing image which palpitated within the man's self.

54

I learnt from Locke to get my meanings clear in thought, then the expression could well take care of itself.

55

Those who are discerning enough can taste the elixir in true words.

56

To state a metaphysical truth in such a way that it will be more helpful to the recipient's understanding, it needs to be more precise and come directly to the point. It should not lose itself in high-sounding but vague terms. It should be, and be felt or visioned as, something quite clear.

57

The poverty of vocabulary is shown in the use of words like "marvellous" or "wonderful" or "nice" when precise ones are available. Accuracy in the use of words shows also a tidy mind.

58

Metaphysicians lost in the winding convolutions of their speculation, mystics whose works are pointless and incomprehensible as hieroglyphics—these belong to the old school. Tell us quickly what you mean, or keep silent, says the modern.

59
The repeated phrase sticks longer to the mind and memory. But if repetition is overdone it becomes an irritant or a bore: the author is then simply nagging the reader.

60
Semantics has its part in the self-training of a quester. Its study makes him cautious of what he says and critical of what he reads and clear about what he understands.

61
The forms taken by language reflect character and evolutionary status. If refined elegant and grammatically correct then the speaker is a superior person. But if replete with slang, vulgarity, crudeness, his language is spoilt and he shames what he could be.

62
What is needed today is not a continuation of that enigmatic, puzzling, metaphorical, or overcautious language of the Middle Ages—a style taken up perhaps to avoid religious persecution or civil prosecution—but straightforward, direct, and honest expression, not to hide Truth, but to deliver it openly.

63
Wherever possible let us not use a language remote from common understanding. Where this is not possible, then the student must make the effort which is necessary to arrive at comprehension.

64
Truth in the higher sense can not be communicated by words, but in an indirect symbolic sense the knower of Truth may seek for and find words that will accurately give out what his consciousness knows as being Truth.

65
Words are valuable in telling us about something, but they can never take the place of that something itself.

66
By working on his own consciousness in the proper way he may hope to come to an impersonal state where the words he speaks, the products of his pen, are less coloured by the falsities of his ego, less distant from the egoless truth.

67
Articulate speech is not an absolute necessity for human intercourse. Mere gazing is said to be sufficient in the world of Samantabhadra to make one realize the highest state of enlightenment known as *Anutpattikadhar-makshanti*. Even in this world, says the sutra, the ordinary business of life is carried on most successfully among bees or ants that never use words. If so, we never need wonder at those Zen masters who merely raise a finger.

68

Why is it that there are speakers whose words are forgotten as soon as they are uttered? Why is it that there are lecturers whose addresses are lost to remembrance as soon as the audience leaves the lecture hall? Why is it that there are writers whose works are left unread to perish slowly on untouched shelves? In the last analysis it is because of the lack of truth. For those whose every sentence compels thought, whose every lecture is a notable event in the audience's life, and the appearance of whose every book is hailed with holy joy, are those who think truth and can therefore speak and write it.

69

We seek a truth which is unvarying and universal. Define your terms and then examine them to discover whether they are related to facts or not.

70

Only those who seek facts rather than phrases, who respect the meaning of words, are not likely to be overwhelmed by them.

71

The right use of spiritual, religious, mystical, and metaphysical terms, with the attempt to get full consciousness of their meaning, may help the development of spiritual understanding.

72

When a word becomes so vague that it carries different meanings in different mouths, the way in which it is being used should be specifically clarified.

73

Serious students are willing to struggle for the meaning, but busy workers and professionals may feel that their energies are not up to the demand.

74

We lose our way in all this meaningless verbiage, but we may begin to find it by learning to use words that we really do understand.

75

A statement which purports to give the whole truth, whether about a man's character, a legal situation, or a cosmic scheme, is usually less incomplete than other statements, but it is still incomplete.

76

Once a word has transmitted the meaning in its speaker's mind without failing at any point, it may be said to be effective.

77

He says foolish things because he holds foolish thoughts. When wisdom enlightens his mind, he will utter fewer words, but they will be more prudently uttered.

78

The symbol is a substitute for reality.

79

Communication can only come into actual being where the collective verbal symbolism is understood in a similar manner by all who use it. If such common understanding is absent or only partial, then the representational value of the symbolism breaks down.

80

Many people know the meaning of a word without really understanding the meaning. This ignorance was shown up by Socrates in the simple but celebrated case of an onion.

81

They manage to pack the smallest quantity of thought into the largest quantity of words.

82

The instinctive faculty of animals and primitive men gives way in time to the thinking faculty of developed men who form concepts, invent words, and formulate phrases to accommodate what they try to express. In time the habit of thinking conditions them as it gets more strongly seated. When the need arises with further development for abstract thoughts, the words used tend to spread out their meaning, become more generalized and vague, and thus in a different way tend to limit consciousness still further. If the consciousness is to free itself from these limitations it must probe words more semantically and cut into concepts with more precision. This becomes important if the higher Truth becomes the object of a quest.

The problem with words

83

Whoever has read the blood-stained pages of history knows what terrors and what agonies have afflicted mankind when words were only half-understood or quarter-understood or quite misunderstood. When these dangerous interpretations of words have been let loose like beasts of prey in the name of religion or war, men, women, and children have in consequence been butchered. For religious scripture and monarchical proclamations are nothing but collections of words. When they are deified, words thereby become deified. Sect wars with sect over the interpretations of a few words in a single scripture and governments war with their own people over the interpretation of a constitutional phrase or a legal clause. Who then dares assert that the worship of words is of no consequence?

84

The failure to cultivate a scrupulous regard for truth in speech is one of the reasons why these seekers accept so easily teachings which are remote from or distortions of the truth.

85

The problems of metaphysics are often mere pseudo-problems. The dogmas of religion are mere dogmas of language, playthings of terminology, utterly divorced from universal fact and human experience.

86

We get the meaning of a statement from several factors, such as the text which contains it, the obvious intention of its writer or speaker, the mood which seems to dominate him at the time, and the ideas which it arouses in our own minds. The same sentence in a different text, written by a writer with a different intention and under a different mood, may arouse different ideas in us and thus yield a different meaning.

87

If the mystery of the Spirit is only to be written about in unintelligible language which makes readers only more puzzled than before, why try to communicate it?

88

For one who does not inquire, the writings of mystics and yogis will be full of meaning, because the reader may imagine as he likes. For a thinker, much in these writings is meaningless where their works are carefully examined. In Vedanta we do not want things which we cannot understand.

89

How many words, how many phrases, are but thick disguises which deceive their users and delude their hearers into the naïve belief that they contain real meaning. How many utterances are but hollow sounds, containing no sense and conveying no facts.

90

We can adequately solve a problem only after we have adequately stated it. We can thoroughly think our way to a solution only after we have thoroughly thought out its verbal meaning. When this is done it may even be found that the problem simply does not exist.

91

They have become inebriated by words and think they present convincing statements and arguments when they have merely lost themselves in the maze of their feelings. What is the sense of being so fervid if they are fuddled?

92

Much discussion is only much ado about nothing, because based on terms that express self-contradictory concepts or meaningless sounds.

93
We must not mistake lyrical outbursts in passionate prose for sensible maxims in careful phraseology.

94
We must beware of becoming obsessed by mere jargon, by long words which convey the conceit of knowledge but not its reality.

95
Talk to a Tibetan yak-herder about the internal combustion engine, tell him how the noisy explosion of gases starts a series of processes into operation, and although you may be using good Tibetan words they will not make sense to him. His consciousness can take in your sounded words but not your mental pictures.

96
The words which the clergyman pours into your ear every Sunday may be as empty of content as an unfilled box. The sentences which lie before you in black print on the white ground of a newspaper may be as meaningless as the gabbing of a verbose lunatic.

97
We must not mistake the glamorous rhetoric of the orator for the divine knowledge of the illuminati.

98
All unprovable statements of this character, all assertions based on the usage of ambiguous words, are outside the realm of true thinking and therefore need no refutation; they are ineligible for discussion, and incapable of yielding the slightest fruit upon examination.

99
Water which has any temperature at all, however low, necessarily has some heat. Therefore when we speak of cold water we are speaking of apparent and not scientific truth.

100
It is unfortunate that a sentence which has no factual content, no logical meaning, and no corresponding object in Nature, is shaped into the same grammatical form as a statement of fact which can be scientifically verified or as an account of experience which can be personally verified. The consequence is that careless readers are misled into illusory belief that they are reading about real things or reasonable events when they are doing nothing of the sort.

101
Before we go any farther it is desirable to define our terms. We have to deal with facts, truth, reality, God, and religion—all of which are among the most ambiguous words in human language. Everybody usually produces the first definition that pleases him, without caring to enquire and consider whether there are other definitions of a conflicting kind.

102

The cultural assumptions of earlier periods are embodied in such words and, without our awareness, are apt to mislead us when they are false to present knowledge of facts.

103

We are word-drugged!

104

We misunderstand each other often because we do not communicate our thoughts adequately or accurately enough to each other. And out of such misunderstanding there is born strife, conflict, and hatred.

105

When a word has become quite lifeless, when it is habitually used without any consciousness of a meaning attached to it, there is real danger of deceiving oneself every time it is so used.

106

Such a diet of empty phrases ("flapdoodle," as H.P. Blavatsky used to call it) would sicken any other stomachs than those of these foolish followers.

107

It is the role of words to give meanings or hide them, to explain truths or expound falsehoods.

108

Words may be cunningly or thoughtlessly used to cloud facts as well as reveal them.

109

The same words which express knowledge in one mouth, merely hide ignorance in another mouth.

110

Whether it be a professor entangled in a web of words or a labourer imprisoned in a cell of materialism, both misconceive the meaning of "real."

111

How can we get at truth when long but meaningless words or short but ambiguous ones are built like a barricade between it and us?

112

Abstract words like "justice" may easily mislead the thoughtless and call for care in use or reading, but that does not mean they are quite unnecessary. They have their place but they ought not to be permitted to transgress beyond their proper limit.

113

Too many bad doctrines exist today because their pleaders' eloquence has saved them. But man cannot live by talk alone.

114

Both the religious devotee and the philosopher may use the word "soul," for instance. But whereas the one is only dimly aware of its significance, the other is fully aware.

115

The word "soul" is so vague a word that the *Oxford English Dictionary* offers no less than twenty-five meanings for it!

116

The logic of thinking may be affected and influenced by wrong use of words, even by the wrong use of grammar.

117

We habitually speak of "sunrise" and "sunset" yet we know that those phenomena have nothing to do with the sun's movements, but only with the earth's daily rotation. Our very language is obsolete, unscientific, and misleading in this instance, and in many others.

118

Men who become so attached to words, phrases, and other symbols as to attribute a reality—either of meaning or fact—to them which they do not possess, become idolatrous worshippers of "the letter which killeth."

119

The use of slang is vulgar. The use of careless slipshod phrases is unworthy of an educated man. But the use of the word "God" in common swearing as "God damn it!" is quite unpardonable.

120

Glib slogans are too easily used by the young, the uneducated, or the emotional as a substitute for reason.

121

Some speak or write naturally in an enigmatic or obscure manner in order to lend more importance to the subject and thus by implication to their own depth of knowledge.

122

The semantic dangers of using abstract terms which are translated by different groups of people into different or contradictory concrete images, are plain enough in politics but, more subtly, they exist also in matters of religion and metaphysics.

123

It is unphilosophic to use the word "spirit" when what is unconsciously meant is "mind."

124

The profound philosopher tries to put his truth into terse terms. The shallow philosopher wades out into the deep waters of many words, loses himself, and half drowns his reader in the waves of time-wasting.

125

If we approach different theological authorities, we shall find that one attributes to such important words as "salvation" and "sin" meanings which are at variance with those attributed by the others.

126

Science has been helped in its advance because it has always sought to create a new term for every new conception, whereas philosophy has been hindered because its store of distinguishing terms lags far in arrear of its store of conceptions. With such an inadequate number of tools in its possession we need not be surprised why philosophy has been hard put to till its fields satisfactorily. It has had to pack two or more meanings in a single word; it has had to bear the burden of ancient words which caricature the newly discovered facts of today. It has found itself at times unable to say what ought to be said, at other times actually saying what should not be said, and at still other times trying to say what cannot be said. The poverty of the philosophical vocabulary can only be got rid of by inventing new words or borrowing from alien tongues, but philosophers are a conservative race.

127

Few people ever recognize that the language they use, and hence the thoughts they think, are filled with unexamined assumptions, with un-criticized suggestions from outside, with untested inheritances from other peoples' past.

128

If a seer or teacher, a prophet or mystic does not clearly know his own meaning when he makes a statement, there is little hope that others will be able to do so.

129

Language, which was invented to help primitive man, sometimes hinders his advanced brother. When it appears in the form of a profuse plethora of abstract words or of a loose phraseology which needs mending, he is likely to be led astray.

130

It is sometimes pleasant to deceive ourselves with specious sophistries.

131

Do they realize what they are talking about? Or are they merely repeating with no more understanding than a phonograph record what they have been told by someone else?

132

What remains when we purify the significance of this term of all hallucinatory and imaginatory elements? We must frankly confess that nothing at all is left.

133
Such muddy writing means only that there is uncertainty, obscurity, illogicality, or even error behind it.

134
Through the lips and the pens of those who know no better, language has deteriorated and coarsened.

135
When language is used so variously, it signifies anything or nothing; it becomes an instrument of thought which is sometimes intelligible and sometimes hopelessly unintelligible.

The meaning of language

136
Language evolved in response to the needs of the thinking process. Its own limitations prevent it from serving with the same adequacy what the thinking process itself serves to conceal—the silent depths of the Mind behind the mind.

137
When we analyse a spoken word we find it to be nothing more than a vibration in the air, which strikes the tympanum of the ear, a sound produced by throat, palate, lips, and teeth uniting to operate together. Speech therefore is thought made flesh. Every time we hear a word uttered we stand in the presence of this miracle. Familiarity has rendered it commonplace, but miracle it remains.

138
Just as the path of return from body-ruled intellect to divine intuition is necessarily a slow one, so the descent into matter of man's originally pure mind was also a slow process. The "Fall" was no sudden event; it was a gradual entanglement that increased through the ages. Pure consciousness—the Overself—is required even for the intellect's materialistic operations. We may say, therefore, that the Overself has never been really lost, for it is feeding the intellect with necessary life. All this has been going on for untold ages. At first man possessed only a subtle body for a long period; but later, *as his intellect continued more outward bent than before*, the material body accreted to him. This curious position has arisen where intellect cannot indeed function in the absence of the Overself, yet deceptively arrogates to itself the supremacy of man's being. Pretending to guide and protect man, it is itself rebelliously and egotistically blind to the guidance of the Overself, yet enjoys the protection of the latter. The intellectual ego-self is thus propped up by the Overself and would collapse without it, but pretends to be self-sufficing.(P)

139

THE WORD. I am the world's greatest tyrant. Yet paradoxically I am the world's greatest liberator. I decimate peoples, raise armies, ruin families, and destroy marriages. I make the lives of countless people happy, I also mar the lives of countless others. I bring wealth to some and poverty to many. I am the Word.

140

The right use of words has brought into being that immense store of recorded knowledge which is one of the most precious heritages man possesses. Today, through the understanding of words, we are able to shake hands with the world's most renowned sages, to have the privilege of a discussion with the distant wise, and to sit at table for an intellectual feast with the dead.

141

Only present-day Western language is strained when it deals with other than physical matters. We find it difficult to talk about mental matters with the subtle precision they demand. We tend to make things out of words in the same way that we tend to make facts out of traditions.

142

Let us first enquire into the nature and function of this code of communication called language. What was its origin? Primitive men soon found the need of making known their thoughts or perceptions to each other when they began to live together. Ideas, not being visible, could hardly be communicated by gestures whilst a suitable vehicle had to be found by men even to present them clearly to their own minds. Thus the word was born and made to stand for a thought. Herein they secured a tremendous advantage over the animals. The number of words which human beings could form and accumulate immensely outranged the few hoarse cries in which animals had perforce to express themselves. This development was rendered possible by the possession of a larynx.

143

Such is the extraordinary situation that language, which delivers most men from superficial ignorance, binds them the more closely to profounder ignorance.

144

Men like Maeterlinck, Fabre, Thoreau, and Burroughs have given the most painstaking and careful attention to the life and psychology of ants, spiders, beavers, horses, dogs, and even birds. What is the sum of their discoveries? They have found that these creatures of the animal kingdom, although unable to think and reason as creatures of the human kingdom do, nevertheless exercise an unerring intelligence, seemingly automatic and hereditary though it be, an intelligence which we call instinct.

Ants and termites closely organize themselves into a wonderful society where each has his appointed task and where all work individually with soldierly discipline and indefatigable industry for the common benefit, as is demonstrated by the way they store food for future communal use and the expert way in which they practise the art of warfare. Beavers build their dams across streams with the accuracy and ingenuity of skilled engineers. Large flocks of birds migrate with unfailing regularity to the same spot in some distant country every year, never losing their correct direction. A wild creature roaming the jungles will not touch poisonous plants, however hungry it be. A spider spins a web for its prey with the calculated accuracy of a mathematician and the refined grace of an artist. Nobody dare deny that some kind of intelligence, some activity of mind guides and directs multitudes of creatures all over the world and shows them how to feed and support themselves and their young, how and when to store food for the winter months, how to cure themselves when ill, what are the nourishing foods for them to take, and so on.

When however we ask in what way this animal mind compares with that of human beings, we soon observe one important difference. Science has ascertained that Nature invariably evolves a new bodily organ to perform a needed physical function: thus there was a time in the misty past when all creatures had no ears but grew them as the necessity of hearing sounds became more and more urgent. It was Nature's adaptation to inner need. There is one function which animals do not share in common with human beings and that is speech. They do not possess that delicate and intricate organ, the larynx. This is quite clearly because they do not feel the need of it. Even our primitive ancestors were once at the stage when they too were larynxless. Now language is the product of speech and came into belated being after men wished to communicate with other men. What is speech but uttered thoughts? And what are thoughts but the product of the working of intellect? And what is intellect but, to take the definition given in our first volumes, "the activity of logical thinking"? But logical thinking cannot be performed without using words. And words cannot be spoken without the possession of a larynx. If therefore Nature has failed to make the physical gesture of growing a larynx, it is because the mental needs of logical thinking have not compelled it, that is, such thinking is absent.

Many animals can see smell hear and taste with much greater acuteness than humans, but none of them can utter those magical words which will make a logically constructed thought known to another animal; none can frame words into phrases and then formulate the latter into sentences. The absence of spoken language among animals is itself a proof that they are not the ratiocinative creatures which human beings are. The splendid but limited intelligence they show and the remarkable perception of how and when to act which they possess are sufficiently remarkable to impress observers, but they are not the results of the same logical faculty which man uses; they are the results of a subconscious instinctive mental working. We admit this when we refer to it as "instinct." An animal submits to the guidance of this subconscious mind and does not balance up the pros and cons of a matter requiring decision, as the human's logical mind does. Some higher animals, like the elephant, the lemur, and the ape, may not conform to this description. But this is merely because they mark a transitional stage in evolution and are close enough to the human kingdom to exhibit exceptional traits. They have begun to manifest special characteristics of their own, to break away from the herd imprint, and thus to show that individuality which is a mark of man. This individual self-consciousness which man alone possesses in its fullness is the fruit of his possession of self-conscious intellectual processes.

145

It is not the words of any scripture—be they Latin, Greek, or Sanskrit—which have special power over men: it is what they themselves put into the words. That is to say, it is their faith, imagination, desire, and expectancy which invest the text with such power. But these states of mind *are their own*.

146

Language shapes thinking. Its forms and structures may permit or prohibit the entertaining of certain specific ideas by those who speak it. The languages of Europe and America, for example, promote materialism, whereas Sanskrit retards it.

147

Words are much like coins for we find those whose value is nil, and yet these counterfeits are freely passed into general circulation. We also find others that have become debased by misuse and still others which are worn thin by time and mean but half of what they once meant. Yet whether genuine, defective, or worthless, all are still tokens of negotiable utility with us.

148

Beware of words. To the ignorant they are expressions of human knowledge; to the wise they are expressions of human ignorance.

149

Whilst we have to use a materialistic vocabulary with which to demolish materialism, we are hampered greatly.

150

The first difficulty the mind has in formulating thought about the truth is that the very words it must use in such formulations are bound up with, and taken from, the illusion which the senses engender in it. The vocabulary which it must use in understanding or in explaining its experience of the world is itself based on the idea that the illusive is the real. With such a false idea to start with, it can give false meanings only to end with.

151

Although he may not know it at the time, each man who offers a statement about anything which exists in this world, any situation or condition even, offers an interpretation of it, suggests a meaning. This is done by the very words he uses, the very form he gives to the sentences. It is not a willed action, for he has no choice in the matter.

152

The use to which it is ordinarily put makes up a word's meaning; on this basis no word is entirely meaningless.

153

A tremendous advantage came when words were inscribed on clay tablets, styled on dried palm leaves, written on tough parchments or printed as marks on paper. Then, a man's thought was able to traverse the immensity of space as his voice never could until lately. Such was the birth of this complicated apparatus of language which represents things and thoughts by articulate sounds or written signs.

6

SCIENCE

Influence of science

The modern attitude, which has proved so significant in science, is safer. The era of mystery-mongering is past. Knowledge which is not verifiable cannot be received with certitude. Overmuch profession of the possession of secret powers opens the doors to imposture. He who is unable to offer adequate evidence had better not seek the public ear. It is only the supersession of human reason that has made it possible to support error for so many centuries.

2

The West has been training itself for two centuries or more along the lines of physical inquiry, and the fruitfulness of achievement has ordained that physical results, tangible and visible results, are the things which interest us most.

3

The scientific outlook is its own satisfaction. The practical rewards which attach themselves to it possess their value, but the consciousness of being able to appraise life correctly, wherever and whatever be one's environment, is immeasurably worthwhile.

4

Philosophy must build her structure with unimpeachable facts which means that she must build it with scientifically verified facts.

5

How often has mankind been offered concepts and conclusions, ideas and imaginations along with the vehement assertion that they are directly observed facts!

6

There is a certain measure of safety in the deliberate cultivation of rational thought based on observed fact as a guide to action. This is the way that science has travelled with the discoveries of, and profits by, natural law. This is the way that industry and commerce have travelled, with solid results for all to see. Its value, when applied to methods of achievement, is a proved one.

7

The sciences are useful to man and need not be cursed for the evil results of their abuse by man. He needs rather to learn how to make a better, more prudent, and wiser use of them.

8

The spirit of science—which happens to be the spirit of this age—has rationalized us, and we are naturally impatient of all misguided persons who appear irrational.

9

The scientific method has been sufficiently used and sufficiently popularized to bring about a radical change in the outlook of educated men. Revelations are no longer blindly accepted. The spirit of enquiry is awake, and these revelations can no longer be saved by placing them in watertight compartments, by setting up barricades beyond which the questing spirit of science is not allowed to proceed. Critical methods of examination must be everywhere applied. That which seeks to escape by hoisting a sacrosanct flag, is dishonest to itself and to others.

10

The area of European knowledge has extended far beyond that of old Rome. Science has penetrated every corner of our lives. It has come to stay. We must welcome the wisdom of the ancients but its formulation should be remolded in the light of present-day knowledge.

11

As the intellectual change of attitude is promoted by the discoveries of science and the reflections of scientists, religious, moral, educational, metaphysical, and social changes will follow as a logical consequence.

12

The mystics may scorn science, but it is science which has forced the different peoples of this earth to recognize their interdependence and to admit the need of brotherhood.

13

Electricity not only lights up the village street; it also lights up the village mind. For the intrusion of science stimulates thinking and scarifies superstition.

14

Both reason and science, which stand in the path of the mystic, assist the further progress of the philosopher.

15

Our chemical magicians wave their wands over a heap of tar and lo! it is transformed into fragrant perfumes, brilliant dyes, and valuable drugs.

16

The scientific knowledge accumulated in a single year nowadays exceeds the entire stock of knowledge of ancient Greece.

17

Modern man must be presented with a modern technique of spiritual unfoldment. He demands a scientific approach towards truth and there is no real reason why his demand should not be satisfied. He demands a simplified yet inclusive technique, and one that will be at the same time precise practical and immediately applicable.

18

Not loose but exact, not dilettante but methodical, not credulous but critical, not in haste to jump at conclusions but patient to get all the facts first—such is the scientific attitude which must be embraced by the man who would be a philosopher.

19

In an age of science, this stubborn refusal to relate causal facts to consequential ones, this blind determination to ascribe all happenings to God's will and none to man's doing, becomes childish.

20

Science is based upon the examination of Nature; so-called systems of philosophy are too often systems of discussion only or of abstract thought without any reference to, or test by, the facts of Nature.

21

Both for good and ill, science has imposed a dictatorship over the other ways of knowing and the other ways and results of experience. It has admittedly earned its position by the immense value and utility of its practical application, so visible all around us, as well as respect for the quality of its thinking—usually exact, factual, and accurate.

22

When we place science as an essential preliminary and integral part of this course, we must make clear that what is primarily meant by the term here is scientific education of the understanding and not the communication of scientific knowledge. Both are necessary in every curriculum, but whereas the former implies a development of intelligence, the latter is an accumulation of facts. We value the cultural aspects of science, its power to train the mind in correct thinking and proper enquiry, as being more important for the purposes of this quest than its practical aspects, which deal with physical techniques and material behaviours. We esteem the cautious, sceptical, and keenly enquiring method of approach which the scientist uses; the utilitarian results of such a method are not our special concern. The meaning of this difference becomes clearer when it is stated that the colleges have produced many science graduates who possess much scientific knowledge, but little scientific training. They have assimilated a fair amount of scientific knowledge through the use of memory and other faculties, but they have not organized their reason and sharpened their intelligence by the assimilation of scientific principles. The study of philosophy demands a certain mental equipment, a preliminary expansion of the intellectual faculties, before it can become really fruitful and actually effective. The knowledge of a number of facts contained in a number of books is not sufficient to make a scientist; such a knowledge is sterile from the viewpoint of this quest, however valuable it be from the viewpoint of commercial and industrial development.

23

We are not likely to give up voluntarily the civilized comforts which science has given us, nor the machines with which it serves us. A return to tribalism, medievalism, and primitivity is unlikely.

24

Science brings material comforts in its hands as its offering to us. These things are not to be despised, but they are also not to be worshipped. Take them, O man, for you need them; but learn to become less absorbed in them.

25

There is nothing wrong in seeking to make Nature's energies and materials serve the needs of mankind. Technology is not *all* evil, as beginning escapees from a materialistic society so often believe. Even Oriental peasants have a simple technology.

26

Thanks to science I can look at my watch and thus determine with a precision that Copernicus never knew at what point of its rotation the earth is.

27

This century has seen revolutions in conventional thought like non-Aristotelian systems, non-Newtonian mechanics, multi-valued logics, which have destroyed ancient sacrosanct errors.

28

The value of truth as an intellectual ideal has greatly increased. We have used our brains during the last two or three centuries as never before. Science has made giant strides, and the pronouncements of the scientist are highly valued merely because we believe that he speaks impartially and impersonally as a truth-seeker.

29

Only a little over three hundred years ago did scientists begin to understand the language of the story. Since that time, the age of Galileo and Newton, reading has proceeded rapidly. Techniques of investigation, systematic methods of finding and following clues, have been developed. The discovery and use of scientific reasoning by Galileo was one of the most important achievements in the history of human thought and marks the real beginning of physics. This discovery taught us that intuitive conclusions based on immediate observation are not always to be trusted, for they sometimes lead to the wrong clues.

30

The upshot of this statement is that although it is a fact from the practical standpoint that your typewriter still rests on the table, it is equally a fact from contemporary knowledge—that is, the ultra-scientific stand-point of deeper enquiry—that the series of energy-waves which con-stituted your typewriter, the series of events which were originally present in the space-time continuum, are perpetually vanishing. What then is the meaning of this "fact"?

31

Science, keeping close to facts, restricts the mental activities whereas fancy, willing to disregard them, lends them wings.

32

It is a great merit of science that its method produces results that are definite, reliable, and predictable. We know that if the needed conditions are properly fulfilled, the result will not vary from previous results.

33

There is still a mystery at the core of the atom. Humility is as befitting before it today as it was a hundred years ago.

34

The scientific mode of thought is no longer limited to a few scientists. It has begun to permeate the educated world generally.

35

The religious way was to suppress awkward questions but the scientific way is to seek out the answers.

36

Modern physics, mathematics, and metaphysics are bridges towards each other.

37

It may properly be called a scientific method only if its results can be checked by observers anywhere in the world.

38

It ought to be remembered that a number of those who have espoused materialism have been led into it by their loyalty to truth, by their intellectual honesty, rather than by an evil nature.

39

Science is really or entirely an affair of the intellect because it deals with manifest forces and visible and discoverable facts.

40

(a) "The vulgar belief that Science has 'explained everything' is a hopeless misunderstanding. As we shall afterwards find, it would be nearer the truth to say that Science has explained nothing. (b) Science does not even try to refer facts of experience to any ultimate reality. That is not its business. (c) In a limited sense Science explains things, namely, by reducing them to simpler terms, by discovering the conditions of their occurrence, and by disclosing their history. What do we mean when we say that Physics has accounted for the tides or that Physiology has made some function of the body much more intelligible than it used to be? What is meant is that we have gained a general conception of the nature of the facts in question, and that we are able to relate them to some general formula. In this sense only does Science explain things, and it does not really get beyond a description."—Thomson, *Introduction to Science*.

41

Earlier scientists had to struggle too much to free their knowledge and discovery from the dogmas or persecutions of religion not to be antagonistic toward it. And they had also to struggle against the imaginative speculations imposed on them by metaphysics not to be friendly with it.

When science stands alone

42

The right use of science is the physical release of man. The worship of science leads to its wrong use and from there to the downfall of man.

43

The scientific mind, cautious to accept nothing more than the evidence justifies, scrupulous to achieve accuracy in observation, possesses the defects of its virtues. For it shuts out the complete view of a thing, since that requires the use of other faculties as well as the intellect it uses, faculties such as imagination and emotion.

44

Metaphysics must teach us to think and science must provide us with the necessary facts upon which to exercise our thinking. But if it omits mystical facts it is incomplete science.

45

The intellectuals, including the scientists, have substituted faith in intellectual processes for faith in religious ones. In the last case it is open belief; in the first one, it is masked, hidden, covered up, but still faith.

46

All of those who use the data of science to support their belief in intellectual materialism and to justify their scorn for religion and mysticism, deny the very source from which they ultimately draw their intellectual capacity to make their criticism. And to the extent that it lets them use it so, science itself becomes superstition.

47

The philosopher fully appreciates the high worth of the point of view of science and applauds its method, but he refuses to limit himself to them. For he knows that one cannot take all truth as one's territory unless one applies all sides of his being to the enterprise.

48

In striving to master their earthly surroundings, they do nothing wrong. Nor is this statement changed if they call on the scientific intellect to help them do so. Materialism begins and grows when the moral, the metaphysical-intuitive, and the religious points of view are submerged and lost in the process.

49

After the intellect has finished analysing this experience, judging it by science's light and with science's critical rigour, the subtle essence is lost.

50

With all our scientific knowledge and technical skills, we know little of our subconscious self, less of our spiritual self, and we are unable to control thoughts and even less able to concentrate attention.

51

There is no teaching—however scientific—which will not be found, on simple or severe analysis, to make some call on faith.

52

The thousands of scientists who throng the halls of culture today can tell us so much about the thousands of details existent in Nature or fabricated by man yet still cannot tell us why the entire cosmos is present here in space-time at all. They have a rich wealth of knowledge and can describe well what is happening but what it is all for completely eludes them.

53

Although the educational trend has stimulated interest in science above any other subject, a time will come when the educated person will find that he cannot live by science alone. The arts will demand and receive their due. The spirit will put in its gentle call. In other words, culture will have to complete itself.

54

If scientific progress has freed man from many drudgeries, it has enslaved him with many illusions. One of these is the belief that it is itself sufficient to guide and guard him.

55

Stupendous are the possibilities when the atomic forces will be toiling for us, slaving for us; but still they are only material possibilities.

56

Those who believe that science will remove all the troubles of man and all the flaws in man, have badly taken their measure of Nature.

57

The scientist can give us facts of which he has made certain, but why they should happen to be as they are, he cannot say.

58

The wheel revolved. Time circled around the globe. And men cast their faith from them. A new star had arisen, Science!

59

Science treats man as a higher animal, and has no better view of him. This is incomplete to the point of falsity, dangerous to the point of self-destruction.

60

The scientist boasts of his triumphs. But how great after all is his triumph over Nature if he is still unable to make even a tiny insect?

61

If knowledge fails to reconcile science with religion and philosophy, then civilization will become the victim of a politically directed materialistic scientific knowledge, and end by destroying itself.

62

Are the physicians and surgeons not already worthy to be called dead who know so little of their own selves, and so much of the bodies in which they are lodged?

63

Science has seduced us completely, so completely that we are able to live unaffected by the wisdom of the ancients and of the past as though it had never been. Science has become its graveyard. We do not understand that the realm of truth into which these ancients penetrated still exists.

64

When science leads man to deny his sacred source and to decry all personal testimonies to experience of its existence, science is no longer serving man but seriously crippling him.

65

Science is not the same thing as scientism. The latter involves a cult, the former a valid attitude. The victims of the modern higher education too often and too unwittingly are initiated and pressed into this cult, while all the time believing that they are being trained in the former.

66

The cold analysis by a scientist may find no thing present in man that will fit the term "Overself," nothing sacred, mystic, and egoless. But in making this analysis his principal instrument was the intellect, and this at once limited his result.

67

These tough-minded people cannot see that a state of consciousness can be real if they cannot bring it within their limited imagination.

68

What clergymen preached to them, scientists taught them to doubt.

69

They proclaim the relativity of all intellectual standpoints, all spiritual doctrines, but fail to see that their own standpoint and doctrine are also stamped with such relativity.

70

Scientific truth acquired from without is utterly different from Spiritual truth revealed from within.

71

They derive their own minds and all other minds, along with their bodies, from the primeval mud. Thus consciousness, the pitifully slender and fragmentary echo of an echo which is all we ordinarily possess, is degraded and falsified, so that its ultimately divine origin is utterly lost.

72

Einstein has demonstrated once and for all how experimental science can only reach relative truth and how absoluteness is unapproachable. And even in mathematics, too, where we imagine that exactness replaces approximation we shall find that absolute quantities are unattainable. It is impossible to mark with precision the fraction of a fraction of a fraction of a second which actually elapses before or after any given time-dimension which is read off the dial of a watch and thus falsifies our reading. It is equally impossible to measure with rigid certitude any dimension on the scale which shall not be a fraction of a fraction of a fraction of an inch shorter or longer than our supposed measurement. Nor has any scientific experiment yet arrived at an absolute zero in actuality but has merely approximated it.

73

The mystic, who knows more about the internal world than the scientist, is entitled to a hearing not less respectful than that to which the scientist is entitled because he knows more about the external world.

74

Are the computer, the auto, and the television enough to support a man when higher supports are lost or lacking?

75

There is no need to deny the beauty of a flower, a picture, or a landscape in order scientifically to affirm its chemical composition. There is room for both views.

76

It is the tragedy of one who knows too much to believe that the universe is an accidental conjunction of atoms but too little to believe that man himself is divine in essence, in origin, and in destiny.

77

There is in man a knowing principle. During his existence he applies it to particular and separate objects, creatures, the world outside, Nature. And now—to space! This spirit of inquiry has enabled him to bring the moon into his path of travel. But the Knower itself remains neglected, unknown.

78

The scientific approach is insistent in demanding proof and requiring evidence.

79

Science has its bigotries no less than religion.

80

In cautiously trying to shut out from its examinations and understanding of facts the human factors which falsify them, the modern scientist shut out also those which are all-important in the examination and understanding of himself.

81

They are still trying to know by touch of the hand or sight of the eye what only stilled concentration of mind can reveal.

82

The same education which frees a man from superstition may cause him to miss the subtler knowledge of his real inner being, so that his mind wrongly believes itself to be a product of the body.

83

Science examines the universe and reads from it the laws of existence. The scientist cannot go beyond the unseen energy from which the atom is derived. But the metaphysician, using pure intelligence alone, can pursue the question: What is fundamentally real in all this?

84

The scientific attitude should have been used to keep superstition and imposture, fanaticism and fancy, confusion and untruth out of religion. Instead it was used to destroy religion in many minds.

85

Scientific knowledge can be extended indefinitely but it will not be able to do more than help body and, to a lesser extent, mind: salvation it cannot give us.

86

Those intellectuals who limited themselves only to the knowledge of present-day science and to the methods of present-day research have only themselves to blame for the world-wide menace of self-destruction at which they now shudder.

87

The disintegration of the atom which science has so amazingly achieved is an immense symbol of the disintegration of man which the scientist has brought about. The results of both are not only equally disastrous but also intimately related.

88

The consciousness which has gone into these remarkable inventions of the nineteenth and twentieth centuries can be traced back to the primary consciousness of man, and that is the divine part of his being, the Overself. But all these inventions serve a material purpose, and man's use of them could have been foreseen, for they have been used only to draw him deeper down into materialism and farther away from the higher goal which has been set for him by the World-Idea. Science is neutral. What he has done to apply its discoveries shows the kind of thought which is uppermost in his mind, and that the use of these inventions is for selfish, exaggeratedly selfish, purposes by individuals and by nations. The negative purposes have predominated over the positive use made of them.

It is clear enough that with the terrible weapons now in the hands of the human race, and with the low moral ideals which it holds, sooner or later they will be used to destroy the greater part of the population of the planet.

89

The atomic bomb could not have fallen on Hiroshima if the science of mathematics had not been formulated by developed human intellect. That human ethics failed to develop so far—and was even rejected by science— was a failure which turned white magic into black magic.

90

Yes, science has progressed, and carried us all along with it. But where has it progressed, led us? We are faced not only with the nuclear war as a future possibility but also with the dangers and devastations of experimental atom fission as a present actuality. The grave changes in climate with their serious results for agriculture, animals, and life of man himself as well as the increasing permeation of water reservoirs, rivers and lakes and seas with destructive radiation, are definitely harming us today. I am not suggesting a revolt against science but offering a warning.

91

We must pity the millions who have become the shut-eyed, mesmerized creatures of their period, who are carried away too far from the shores of safety by the triumphs of science to understand what the terrible end of it all may be.

92

Science, which was to have served man faithfully, has become a trap. The more he uses it, the more dangerously is he trapped. But alas! he does not want to see how precarious is his situation, so the prophet must remain mute and obscure: waiting and watching the higher forces which are themselves watching for the inevitable result that will arrest this evil.

93

Great inventions have not given more aspirations but they have enlarged his power to communicate with others about them and have made it easier to serve some of them. But unfortunately for him, they have also enlarged his power to communicate evil ideas and made it easier to serve evil desires.

94

Where science is balanced by the intuitive heart-forces it brings well-being to man but where it is controlled by the cold selfish head-forces alone it brings him to black magic and destroys him.

95

Science which, with its early promise of utopian progress, was to bring cheer to the heart, has actually brought fear to the mind.

96

Philosophy respects science, but not the abuses of science. When they occur, they create materialism in metaphysical thought, pollution in industrial application, and unbalance in religious criticism.

97

Scientific progress has given us useful gadgets, but terrible poisons. Instead of the paradise to which the enthusiasts of the last century asserted it was going to lead us, we now look forward with much anxiety, for it is beginning to look more like a hell upon earth.

98

When man extended the simple tools which he used into the early simpler machines, the development was an inevitable consequence of his developing mind. The change was a useful one and brought him conveniences or comforts unavailable to the monarchs and millionaires of previous centuries. But when this was pushed farther and farther, faster and faster, its inherent dangers appeared, human safety was imperilled, human health ignored, and human sensitivity crushed. Technology grew into a monster.

99

It is proper for man to use the world, to exploit science, only as long as he does not permit them to enslave him.

100

The knowledge got through the eyes and ears may, when united to reason, lead only to selfish cunning and cause destructive suffering to others. But when it is united to both reason and intuition, it can lead only to wisdom and bring good to others. The world today is undergoing this danger and ignoring this remedy. Consequently, the more science dis-covers about the atom, the worse will be humanity's suffering.

Science and metaphysics

101

If and when the scientist who observes phenomena and tabulates facts tries to sink a shaft deep down through them, he will strike the stratum of metaphysics. He may despise it, he may withdraw in disgust, but if he continues to push his shaft he will not be able to escape having to investigate his phenomena and facts in the way that the metaphysician investigates them. Nor will he be able to stop even there. If first thought makes a common man into a scientist, and second thought into a meta-physician, third thought will make him into a philosopher.

102

Few people outside the Royal Society know that Sir Isaac Newton, whose book, the *Principia*, changed science to its foundations, was not only one of England's greatest men of science but also one of her most ardent students of mysticism. There is a large mass, estimated at one million words, of unprinted papers which he left behind in a box at Cambridge—papers which must surely have been well known to his bewildered biographers but which have never been published out of fear of harming Newton's reputation by the mere revelation of this interest in a subject which was for so long taboo in scientific circles. After Newton's death Bishop Horsley inspected the box with a view to publication, but on seeing some of the contents he slammed the lid with horror. The existence of these papers is well known to, and has been testified by, Sir Robert Robinson, President of the Royal Society, who, asking how Newton could be both a mathematician and a mystic, himself answered that it was because he "perceived a mystery beyond and did his best to penetrate it." Also it is well known to the late Lord Keynes, the famous economist, who was moved by them to exclaim that Newton's "deepest instincts were occult," and that "the clue to his mind is to be found in his unusual powers of continuous concentrated introspection."

In a lecture given to a small private audience at the Royal Society Club in 1942, Lord Keynes said this about Newton: "Why do I call him a magician? Because he looked on the whole universe and all that is in it as a riddle, as a secret which could be read by applying pure thought to certain evidence, certain mystic clues which God had laid about the world to allow a sort of philosopher's treasure hunt to the esoteric brother-hood. . . . He believed that these clues were to be found partly in certain papers and traditions handed down by the brethren in an unbroken chain back to the original cryptic revelation in Babylonia. . . . All would be revealed to him if only he could persevere to the end, uninterrupted, by himself. . . . All his unpublished works on esoteric and theological matters are marked by careful learning and extreme sobriety of statement. They are just as sane as the *Principia*."

A large section of these papers seeks to deduce secret truths of the universe from apocalyptic writings; another examines the truth of Church traditions; a third deals with alchemy, the philosopher's stone, the elixir of life, and the transmutation of metals; a fourth consists of copies of ancient mystic manuscripts or translations of them.

There, in the University Library at Cambridge, about half of these silent memorials of Sir Isaac Newton's secret studies still rest today, while the other half were sold by auction and dispersed in private hands in 1936.

Newton's library had such titles in it as Agrippa's *De Occulta Philosophia, Fame and Confession of the Rosie Cross*, Geber's *The Philosopher's Stone*, several of Raymond Lully's works, and four of Paracelsus'. His own personal annotations appear in most of the volumes. He studied Jacob Boehme very closely and copied long pieces from his works.

Even such a hard-headed scientist as Professor E.N. da C. Andrade was forced to confess, at the Tercentenary Celebrations in 1946, "I feel that Newton derived his knowledge by something more like direct contact with the unknown sources that surround us, with the world of mystery, than has been vouchsafed to any other man of science. A mixture of mysticism and natural science is not unexampled—Swedenborg has important achievements in geology, physiology and engineering to his credit."

Archbishop Tenison said to Newton: "You know more divinity than all of us put together."

103

The moment it comes to consider the life-force in Nature and the mind in entities, science can get at the final truth about them only by handing over the task to metaphysics and mysticism—only by calling in concepts that are no longer scientific in the orthodox sense.

104

Science has passed through its short-lived materialistic phase and is plunged in the midst of a revision of all its nineteenth-century categories.

105

It is no use denouncing science for the horrors of war, the miseries of industrialism, and the unbelief of materialism. The way to conquer the evils arising from the unethical abuse of science is to go right inside its camp and win it over to philosophy.

106

There is this vital difference, that whereas the scientist can only *observe* the object into which he is investigating, the mystic can *participate* in the one upon which he is meditating. In the first case, there is a knowing in separation from it; in the second, a knowing in union with it.

107

Nuclear research has shown that the atom consists of energy alone. It is but an aggregation of energies. It has shown that there is nothing, no "thing" at the world's root. But only free minds and discerning eyes among scientists see clearly that this establishes the existence of Spirit, which is no formed thing, and overthrows the doctrine of materialism.

108

We are moving toward the day when science, instead of negating religious faith, will actually nourish it.

109

Man's body is formed of chemical compounds yet man himself—with his flights of sacred aspiration and intellectual speculation, his adventures in artistic creation and appreciation—has little resemblance to a chemical compound.

110

We may develop the scientific intellect until its visible achievements and results astound us even more, but they will always be relative to time and place, always subject to human limitations. But there is another line we could take for development, one that works with the metaphysical intellect. This need not set up an opposition to science, for it is not concerned with empirical work. It is a faculty of abstract thinking, seeking the large generalized archetypal ideas. When it succeeds in finding them, their verification is to be got by letting the intellect lapse and letting the pure knowing element reveal itself. In this way consciousness moves to a higher level.

111

The proper method of overcoming the evils of a materialistic intellectualism is not to escape back into a pre-intellectual attitude but to let it grow side by side and in proper balance with the spiritual attitude, not to refuse to look at the problems it raises but to try to solve them through such an integral endeavour.

112

Metaphysics, starting from one end of the path, must eventually meet science when it has advanced sufficiently far to test all its hypotheses by physical experience. Science, starting from the other end of the same path with physical research, must eventually meet and hand its problems over to metaphysics when it seeks to arrive at a large general view of all its accumulated data. The metaphysical Idea, must verify itelf by the scientific Thing. The scientific Thing must understand itself to be the metaphysical Idea.

113

If God is not the inner reality of this universe, then Matter is both its inner and outer reality. There will then be no room in the thinking mind for any belief other than materialism, no plea for religion, no admittance to a spiritual metaphysics.

114

So long as they choose to look at the phenomena of the universe only within the perspective of their own limited assumptions and refuse to look at any evidence outside them, so long will those scientists who still reject everything non-material remain the victims of their own prejudiced and biased judgement. But the others—and they are increasing—who genuinely practise the scientific method of investigation and therefore come with an open, patient, and experimental mind, are moving forward to the formulation and verification of reliable truths, laws, and principles.

115

Philosophy does not attempt to explain what it is the business of science to explain. Hence it does not oppose the aims of science nor does it fear the further progress of science. On the contrary, its regard for fact makes its teachings consistent with those of science. It simply leaves to science the filling-in of the details of the world's picture, itself supplying the outline.

116

It is impossible for the scientist to conclude his thinking about the observations which he has made of Nature and the facts which he has amassed in the laboratory without venturing into metaphysics. If he is afraid to make such a venture then he must leave his thinking inconclusively suspended in mid-air.

117

We thus see that philosophy is the integral development of science, a continuity of the same austere point of view. But whereas science deals with particular groups of concrete perceptions, philosophy deals with abstract generic concepts.

118

Science which first made materialism seem the most plausible explanation of life, through the careful observation of facts and close reasoning upon those facts, has since refuted itself. It is enabling philosophy to put the hidden teaching upon firm and rational foundations.

119

The scientists as such cannot set foot in a region like that of pure Mind. They must rise above their scientific limitations and convert themselves into mystical philosophers first.

120

The scientists have reached a region of investigation where each turn of the page of the world-problem reveals another page which is even harder to read. The newer problems are metaphysical ones. Therefore, when science ceases to be such and becomes metaphysics, it fulfils its highest purpose.

121

To move from physics to metaphysics is to move farther from touchable things to more abstract conceptions, from pictured images to compre-hended ideas, from concrete forms to mind-held abstractions. The first leads to materialism, if the research stops there and goes no further. If, however, he pursues the enterprise and looks for origins, sources, and primary causes, he must end up as a mentalist.

122

Science, using the method of analysis to find the truth about things, must afterwards add the method of synthesis or it will get only a half-truth. This need not mean surrendering the mind to speculation, imagina-tion, theorizing, fantasy, or so-called metaphysics, but rather using its creative faculty and its power of understanding—in short, using intel-ligence which is derived from intuitive feeling and correct thinking.

123

So long as science does not pause to reflect adequately upon its own self, its own character and its own foundations, so long is it necessarily mate-rialistic. But after it has taken the trouble to do so, which means after it has fulfilled its higher purpose by turning metaphysical, it cannot help re-nouncing its materialism.

124

The scientist remains loyal to his self-set goal. He will sooner or later be compelled by the logic of his discoveries as much as by the logic of his reflections to turn himself into a philosopher and continue his quest in the still higher sphere of philosophy.

125

In the last one hundred years even the sciences, particularly the fields of nuclear physics and biology, have moved so far ahead that they have opened the way for principles and teachings, the knowledge and practices of true philosophy.

126

Life will be better guided when scientific knowledge lets itself be joined to spiritual consciousness.

127

The speculative metaphysician *starts* by postulating the existence of some self-sustaining eternal principle, whereas the scientific metaphysician *ends* with such a principle.

128

Those who question the soundness of these ideas are nearly always those who are still mesmerized by materialistic superstitions. It is impossible for them to cope with life's higher requirements because they persist in thinking sensately.

129

Because the spirit of man is neither scientifically measurable nor immediately experienceable, the educated modern mind too often rejected its reality and denied its utility.

130

He should feel not less reverent and not less worshipful even though he is expunging superstition and working with science. Does this surprise anyone? Can he still become a philosopher without any intellectual embarrassments, self-betrayals? Yes he can and assuredly a more effective one.

131

The same science which formerly separated him in belief and understanding from the divine Mind, later, by its confirmation of the universal laws and powers, draws him nearer to it.

132

In view of the spirit of the times, the attitude and findings of modern science must be respected and harmonized with the mystic's. Both Blavatsky and Steiner saw this and tried to accommodate science in their presentations. However, since their day there has been a revolution in scientific theory which has made this work easier, much easier.

133

Science has carried itself to the broadest possible dimensions. Now it must carry itself to the deepest.

134

The fear of yielding to personal feeling in his thought about the world became so exaggerated in the scientist that it shut out the pleading and rejected the services of impersonal feeling, which manifests itself through intuition. This is why he came to the denial of mystical doctrine and scorn of mystical experience. But such undue one-sidedness could not last indefinitely. Its end is within sight.

135

The hope of educated men who understand and appreciate the services of science but who deplore its dangers and recognize its limitations, lies in the investigation and development of consciousness.

136

When men awaken to a more emotional realization of what science has done to them—as opposed to what it has done for them—there will be an urgent demand for a reinterpretation of science itself. The old interpretation will be discarded as dangerous.

137

When the scientist recovers his lost quality of reverence—not necessarily expressed through some established religion—for some mysterious Greatness present in the cosmos he investigates, something which escapes analysis or description but arouses feeling and wonder, his work will not suffer but become fuller and his understanding become more satisfying.

138

It is a meaningful historic fact that Francis Bacon wrote the first notable book in the English language of a philosophical—by which I do not mean theological—kind and the first notable book of a scientific kind in the same language. He was a Creator, a Pioneer, a Pathfinder.

139

Faith in science is no longer the alternative to faith in religion—except for one-sided, narrowed minds in either camp. Rather are there now complementary faiths.

140

The scientist who seeks to learn the origin, history, nature, and laws of the physical universe and the psychologist who probes into the working of the human mind—both must at some point of their investigation consider the questions "Who Am I?" side by side with "What Is the World?" Next they cannot afford to ignore the mystery of the Deity. Finally it will be found at some point on their way that they need to impose a self-discipline and an ethical code upon themselves.

141

Having emptied human life of its spiritual meaning, turning it into a "fortuitous conjunction of atoms," science is now nearing the point where it will have no other course than to restore the meaning, but in a rational intelligent way.

142

Whoever adores the Highest Beauty, whether through Nature's scenery or art's fabrication, through prayer or meditation, song or poem, feelingly and sincerely, is not wasting his time, whatever materialists may say. Even the intellectual mathematician or astronomer contemplating on infinity or space, can use this approach as worship.

143

Science seeks an explanation of the universe based on the facts. Its attitude is correct, of course, but from another standpoint, incomplete.

For its approach starts from outside and tries to stay there. Metaphysics starts from inside and supplies what is lacking. But unless it penetrates to the deepest fact at the start, it gets mixed with speculation, theology, or guesswork. What is this fact? Consciousness! One day the two—science and metaphysics—must meet.

144

It is one of the greater yet sadder ironies of the modern world that Bacon, who is considered one of the founders of its science, is used only to point the way to materialism. He himself says in one of his "Essays" that "a little philosophy bringeth men's minds to atheism, but depth in philosophy bringeth men's minds about to religion."

145

There is no need to be dismayed at the negative attitude of scientists towards this philosophy. He has only to compare their present-day outlook with that of three-quarters of a century ago to realize that great progress has been made.

146

The recent findings of physical scientists are strikingly revolutionary when compared with the conclusions of those who worked in Darwin's day. But what is most astonishing is that they support the discoveries made by Asiatic thinkers who lived long before modern science appeared.

147

Every thoughtful scientist now knows that just as matter has turned out to be a manifestation of force, so force will eventually turn out to be a manifestation of something higher; he perceives that matter is really an appearance behind which stands the reality force; so an ultimate reality must be reckoned as standing behind force. In other words, there is but ONE Reality and various forms under which it appears.

148

Atomic science needed mathematical formulae and equations to carry on its work. They are, after all, symbols and abstractions, that is, pure concepts. So too physical science now needs metaphysical concepts to carry its work further. The refusal to do so on the objection that metaphysics is not physics leaves the scientist powerless to answer his own ultimate questions.

149

The last great discovery awaiting science is the scientist himself. By this I do not mean the acquisition of more and more information about him, nor the exploration of the various kinds of thoughts and emotions belonging to him. I refer to a sustained stubborn concentration penetrating his consciousness *in depth*.

150

It is pathetic to hear men reason in so shallow a way that they find nothing more than mere chance in the coming together of nuclear forces to make a world. It is saddening to observe them slip into so great a mistake with so little resistance and so large an insensitivity, for it shows that in this matter they think and feel in a one-sided and ill-balanced way. But just as materialism came as an opposition to superstition masquerading as religion, as a corrective gone too far, so there are little signs of beginnings of new dawns.

151

The materialist who sees only the animal side of man is usually brutal or sensual, whereas the materialist who sees also the intellectual side is immeasurably more evolved. But both miss the intuitive side.

152

A science devoid of the life-giving power of intuitive feeling leads to its own self-destruction in the end.

153

Science must pass from concrete observation to abstract thought if it would pass from mere fact to the ultimate meaning of its fact.

154

When science begins to stammer it is time for it to turn for help to philosophy.

155

The science-suffused Western mind can follow this thread of thought into the subjective sphere without undue difficulty.

156

Jeans sees in the universal orderliness an evidence of God's design. Eddington sees in it an evidence of what the human mind can contribute to its own experience.

157

Some of the Japanese nuclear physicists have picked up the clue afforded by their laboratory work and found in Buddhism's highest metaphysics a satisfactory world-view.

158

The facts of philosophic mysticism cannot be proved beyond doubt so easily as those of physics. They cannot be classified and organized and utilized in the same way. Yet this is not to say that the scientific method is inapplicable here.

159

The nineteenth-century science, which depressed thinkers with the view that matter was the only reality and man the product of blind chemical and mechanical forces, began to go out forcibly with the nineteenth-century ideas of warfare when the atomic bomb exploded over Hiroshima.

160

Those who seek escape from our present troubles by turning back to a revival of medievalism have somewhat muddled their thinking. Science admittedly took the wrong turning when it entirely separated itself from the *truths* of religion, mysticism, and metaphysics, but it took the right turning when it separated itself from their fantasies. So what we have to do today is to go back to the pre-Renaissance and pre-Reformation times and re-learn abstract thinking, mystical practices, and religious notions, but at the same time recast them in modern form and refuse the superstitions which were then entangled in them. But this will be equivalent to a spiritual re-creation; it can hardly be called a mere return. There is moreover one prime objection to following the way of the medievals which effectually bars it for our liberated era. Their minds were fettered to the walls of vested interests and dared not go outside them. No genuine progress is possible under such conditions.

7

METAPHYSICS OF TRUTH

It is not my work to enter into academic debates. That is necessary, yes, but others will have to undertake it, and this of course they can do only after mastering the teaching for themselves. The problems involved have been discussed by the cleverest intellects of mankind for thousands of years and still they remain to be discussed, still they remain unsettled. It is obvious that they can not be settled on the level of merely rational argument. The truth about them can be arrived at only by a higher faculty—insight. Each person must rediscover it for himself by developing this faculty. There is no other way; for anyone's say-so, least of all mine, has no validity for others. If this result seems unsatisfactory, the blame is neither mine nor anyone else's. But from my point of view, it is not unsatisfactory for it forces those who want to test the truth of this teaching to work hard at their own ultramystic development. Even if I am proved wrong in the sequence, their gain in character alone will surely be worthwhile. I have earlier written that the way up for and from science will lead to metaphysics. But obviously the conflict of doctrine in the metaphysical world makes this a dubious region. So I must qualify my statement; it is a metaphysics supported by science and inspired by mysticism, that is, the metaphysics of truth.

2

Constant reflection on metaphysical and ethical themes reaches a point where one day its accumulated weight pushes him around the corner into a mystical realization of those themes no less surely than meditation might have done.

3

Although every tenet of the metaphysics of truth is worked out with strict rationality and scientific respect for facts, there is a hidden support in transcendental knowledge running right through them all.

4

If philosophy harmonizes the two opposite elements of metaphysics and mysticism, it also transcends them through the ultramystic contemplations. The present volume carries the quest to a height where all reasoning reaches its ultimate limit and must then be dropped. At such a point it becomes necessary to separate the purely rational and ratiocinative portion of this teaching from the advanced-yoga—that is, ultramystic—portion. Accordingly the phrase "metaphysics of truth" will be used henceforth to indicate only the former portion.

5

The whole intellectual structure is supported by a solid core of super-intellectual insight.

6

The metaphysics of truth is set out in such a way that the student believes he is proceeding step by step purely by logical deduction from ascertainable facts, that his reasoned thinking upholds the findings of transcendental experience, whereas not only is he doing this but at the same time is proceeding upon a path which conforms to his own latent insight. It kindles a higher intelligence in its students. Consequently the sense either of sudden or of growing revelation may often accompany his studies, if he be sufficiently intuitive. The *authentic* metaphysics of truth can bring him close to the mystical experience of reality. Then the trigger-pull which will start the experience moving need only be something slight, perhaps a printed inspired sentence, perhaps just a single meeting with one who has learnt to live in the Overself, or perhaps a climb in the mountains. For then the mind becomes like a heap of dry wood, needing only a spark to flare up into a blazing pile. The close attention to its course of thought then becomes a yoga-path in itself.(P)

7

If the metaphysical mysteries are profound for him, then he need not see their disclosure. It is enough to live rightly and worship daily.

8

One day, if this kind of metaphysical thinking is carried on sufficiently, rightly, and concentratedly, his intellect may overreach itself, even lose itself in that wonderful faculty, intuition, or even slip farther into inspiration. This is a mysterious event where something grander takes over by a process which is certainly not mechanical.

9

Human knowledge may be relative, but the truth that there is an imperishable reality back of the cosmos, is an absolute one.

10

The final triumph of metaphysical thinking carries in itself the end of such thinking. Logic vanishes when its own work is done, when the intuition which it unwittingly invoked and successfully called into existence is born.

11

It would be as great an error to suppose that, because of its transcendental character, truth is inconsistent with reason as it would be to suppose that it is attainable by unaided reason alone.

12

The intellectual construction of the metaphysics of truth occurred subsequently to the living realization of truth. The latter finds a logical support in the former, although for the one who has finished treading the path of enlightenment such support is not necessary.

13

If these words will convey some illumination to his mind, it can be only because they are alive with truth.

14

Human intelligence has penetrated to the fact that behind the world-show there is a Reality but cannot penetrate the latter itself. Both science and metaphysics concur in this discovery, but no human writing has ever described it or can ever do so.

15

Whether it is ever possible to put into words that will not be idle ones truths of our real being has been a question whose answers are well argued for and against. But whatever the judgement may be, who can doubt that similes, metaphors—that is, symbols—may be offered, suggestive hints given forth, and clues left behind by those whose knowledge and experience carries authority. And these, too, are only words. Those who say that, in this matter, human language is suspect, completely untrustworthy, and utterly helpless, that its use here can only set up false images and fresh illusions, are going too far. It is to condemn us to hopelessness. And it does not explain why Lao-tzu, Buddha, Krishna, Jesus, John of the Cross, and Ramana Maharshi spoke or wrote despite their avowals. Of course their communication is all a matter of reference to levels. On the ordinary practical level—the immediate one—expression through any art, be it music, painting, drama, or literature, is not futile and does give something, does affect its audience. If it be given by an enlightened man to those still groping in darkness or dusk, it has its place and is justified. But on the ultimate level, with the mind absorbed in the Void, what is there to say? And to whom could it be said? Silence then becomes the correct attitude. When humanity attains this level, the descent of divine teachers and their words will not be needed.

16

If the enigma must be put into worded statements to satisfy demands, then they must be paradoxical ones. Those who require smooth, eloquent, and uplifting utterances may get comfort. But the truthful way is in the end the better way.

17

These teachings carry human thought as far as it will go; beyond them there can be only what superhuman beings could comprehend. This illumination is the final one, the terminal result and reward of all the arduous search of man's questing mind.

18

Truth clears away the remaining illusions which effort and instruction failed to clear away.

19

Metaphysics is ordinarily concerned with the criticism of superficial views about the experienced world and the correction of erroneous ones, whilst it seeks to construct an accurate systematic and rational interpretation of existence as a whole. This is good in its own place because we shall be all the better and not worse for finding a metaphysical base for our beliefs. It is quite clear however that metaphysical systems cannot alone suffice for our higher purpose, for being based on personal assumptions, reasoning, or imaginations, if they partially enlighten mankind they also partially bewilder by their mutual contradictions. Hence philosophy steps in here and offers what it calls "the metaphysics of truth." This is an interpretation in intellectual terms of the results obtained from a direct mystical insight concerned with what is itself incapable of intellectual seizure. Through this superior insight it provides in orderly shape the reasons, laws, and conditions of the supersensuous experience of the Overself, unifies and explains the experiences which lead up to this consummation, and finally brings the whole into relation with the practical everyday life of mankind. It is the sole system that the antique sages intellectually built up *after* they had actually realized the Overself within their own experience. *Such a point needs the utmost emphasis for it separates the system from all others which carry the name of metaphysics or philosophy.* Whereas these others are but intelligent guesses or fragmentary anticipations of what ultimate truth or ultimate reality may be and hence hesitant between numerous "ifs" and "buts," this alone is a presentation from firsthand knowledge of what they really are. It bars out all speculation.

Just as science is a rational intellectualization of ordinary physical experience, so the metaphysics of truth is a rational intellectualization of the far sublimer transcendental experience. It is indeed an effort to translate into conventional thought what is essentially beyond such thought. As expressed in intellectual language, it is scientific in spirit, rational in attitude, cautious in statement, and factual throughout. It is devoted to the relentless exposure of error, the fearless removal of illusion, and the persevering pursuit of truth to the very end—irrespective of personal considerations. It seeks to understand the whole of life and not merely some particular aspects of it.(P)

Speculation vs. knowledge

20

When metaphysical thought abstracts itself from the rest of human nature and works in solitude, unmoved by feeling and unmoved to action, the result is useless for living although interesting for theory.

21

We need free minds to deal adequately with religious and physical problems. The doctrines erect obstacles to this accomplishment in their own way. The merely intellectualist doctrinaires, who have worked things out quite neatly and logically on paper, for instance, erect for themselves and their followers their own stumbling blocks to the attainment of truth. For without authentic mystical experience, of which they are so ignorant, life and man cannot adequately be understood.

22

Metaphysics instead of being, as it could and should be, a fertile field, has become instead a stagnant pool.

23

Metaphysics is an interminable maze. Well might Dante's line be written over its portal: "Abandon hope all ye who enter here." For men lose themselves within its tortuous labyrinths and end in bewilderment, agnosticism, or pseudo-knowledge.

24

The failure of metaphysics begins when it becomes speculation based on imagination, when its ideas are derived from other ideas instead of from observed facts.

25

The study of speculative metaphysics may chill off religious belief but the study of the metaphysics of truth brings with it deep religious feelings.

26

The prosaic man in the street fears to enter the domain of metaphysical study because it seems like a vast and void obscurity. And he is right. It is. But it need not be.

27

The unsatisfactoriness of most Vedantic metaphysics is that it limits itself to ontology. The unsatisfactoriness of most Western metaphysics is that it limits itself to epistemology. Both are one-legged creatures. A satisfying full-limbed system must first begin with epistemology and then end with ontology.(P)

28

Our advice is: study metaphysics to its bottom and then make good your escape from it before you become a mere metaphysician! Once you start using metaphysical jargon you are lost.(P)

29

After the French revolutionary armies successfully entered Italy and reached Padua, Napoleon visited the ancient university there. He went into a classroom and heard the professor of metaphysics expounding a theme. "Bah!" exclaimed the man of action and walked away. His disgust may have arisen from the lack of any practical foundation to the professor's statements, or from the theological bias which he detected in them. In any case it showed his opinion of metaphysics in general.

30

Through every epoch of history the best minds of Orient and Occident have devoted arduous efforts to solve this problem of truth. They succeeded in establishing a few important principles, but these were generally lost amid the fog of ungrounded speculations and the mist of meaningless words.

31

Unfortunately, although there are hundreds of books on metaphysics to instruct the novice, they are also there to confuse him. For where, as in most cases, they are not certified by the sublime experience of insight, they tell him what is, after all, but reasoned guesswork. And the guesses are naturally numerous, different, contradictory.

32

It is the business of science to deal with the course of things but the business of metaphysics to deal with the reason of their being.

33

The student who becomes fatigued by metaphysical quibbling and victory-seeking pedantry may be reassured. He does not *have* to endure all that.

34

This type of metaphysician, who deals only in verbal quibbles, first stands on his head each time he wishes to take a look at the world. We need not be surprised therefore at the atmosphere of farcical unreality which pervades his writings.

35

Through the portal of a merely metaphysical world-view one enters a dry barren realm which, although it is actually remote from experience, yields the deceptive illusion that it is the very essence of experience. Here the student may perform successful logical somersaults and verbal contortions but he cannot successfully realize truth.

36

When plagued with metaphysical points as he often was, Gautama unfailingly adopted this point of view: In his own words, "And why have I not elucidated these questions? Because they profit not, they have not to do with the fundamentals of true doctrine, therefore have I not elucidated them."

37

The failure of unspiritual and unmystical metaphysics is the failure of a mental attitude which is forever trying to look at so many sides of a problem that it never arrives at any conclusion at all.

38

When he has thoroughly grasped the philosophy of truth, he will find that none of the criticisms which mystical votaries and religionist followers will freely pour down upon him can shake his adherence to it. Indeed they will actually confirm it! For almost all such criticisms will reveal to his trained eye the unpurified egoisms, the hidden complexes, the emotional overweighting, and the distorted or incomplete thinking which keep down the progress of their own utterers at its present level.

39

But if it is only ordinary metaphysics, then it cannot bring the student to such an experience, although it can give him good intellectual exercise and logical discipline if he wants these things. Ordinary metaphysical thinking is a kind of mental groping about in the dark, whereas that used in metaphysics of truth is like walking along a well-made road direct to a goal. This is so because the system itself is built up after and upon the mystic experience. Metaphysical self-debate for merely logical purposes is not meant here.

40

There are two kinds of knowledge: the ordinary kind which supplies information about a particular thing object or person and the higher kind which leads to wisdom. A man may correctly understand the handling of an electrical appliance and yet be a fool in the handling of his own life.

41

Buddha found the metaphysics of his time had run riot in worthless speculations and puerile logic-quibblings. He realized that only by making a clean sweep of the subject altogether could such speculations and quibblings be got rid of. Consequently, he enjoined upon his disciples to enter into no metaphysical controversies, but to apply themselves to the practical task which they have to achieve—liberation.

42

When metaphysics departs from the search for truth and roams about in mere speculation, it engages in such verbal trifling as whether movement is possible!

43

The trick of evading a direct question by giving a vague, abstract answer was known to metaphysicians called "eel-wrigglers" by Buddha.

44

If it is to be measured by values, then the first inheritance from philosophy is intellectual: it tells us what we need to know about self and how to find it out; and it teaches us about the world on a level that is left out by science—the metaphysical.

45

The metaphysics of truth has no recognized place in the academic world, as academic teaching is really based more or less on materialism.

46

Theological instruction is materialistic. Although this is a strange thought, a little reflection will show that, like the scientific knowledge of today, it is based on materialism—that is, as matter in itself being different from mind. The metaphysics of truth is based on *insight*, a faculty latent in all people but developed only in a few.

47

Some metaphysicians mostly write for each other, which is why the outside public finds them hard reading.

48

The philosopher does not denounce materialism so much as the one-sidedness which claims it to be the only aspect of existence. On the theoretical side it has its truth, and on the practical side it is worth attention. The name is used here not only in its narrow scientific sense, but also in its broad coverage of blind attachment exclusively to physical objects. Such ideas lead to mechanism without humanism, technological progress without care for negative consequences, atheism and anti-religion, and denial of psychological, mystical, and metaphysical experience.

49

The Pali texts of the Southern Buddhist school contain great wisdom but they also greatly contain unimaginative pedantic hair-splitting of the true scholasticism. It is strange how such sterility develops when men desert normal living for monastic retreat. This one-sidedness leads to the queer metaphysical illusion that the fine-spun intellectual analysis of life will suffice to yield the secret of life. On the contrary, it can no more do this than the scientific analysis of the materials out of which an organ is made, can yield the secret of its ethereal musical charm.

50

Reason is always proudly self-conscious of its worth. Just as the emotional devotee glories in abasing himself so the metaphysical student glories in exalting himself. Here he must be warned on one danger. Hence he should make a point of cultivating a sense of his personal unworthiness in other directions. He should hold to a wise humility as being one of his best safeguards.

51

Thinking can resolve all our doubts but it can do so only after it has been pushed to its farthest possible end, which means to its most metaphysical end.

52

Those who disparage this philosophy as intellectualism talk nonsense. Right *understanding* is essential, said Buddha. Said the Blessed One: "It is through not understanding this doctrine, Ananda, through not penetrating it, that thus mankind fails to extricate itself from suffering, rebirth."

53

The metaphysician who has lost himself in a jungle of intellectual subtleties which end nowhere must retrace his steps and achieve balance through yoga practice.

54

There is no unvarying answer to the question, What is Truth? The standpoint of one who asks it must inevitably delimit the nature and form of the answer he will receive, whether it come from life itself or from the sage who knows.

55

When we shall have worked out a criterion of truth we shall thereby be in possession of a clue to truth.

56

His metaphysical work must be thought out with heartfelt reverence.

57

Whoever presents a final statement of truth, deceives himself.

58

Metaphysics enables the mystic to make clear and conclusive to himself the principles on which his inward experience is based. This helps him, not only by satisfying the need for intellectual understanding, not only by supplying weapons to fight both his own doubts and the criticisms of sceptics, but also, by giving directional guidance, enabling him to avoid errors in mystical practice.

59

Because philosophy aims to develop a fully rounded psyche, it does not share the fanatic and extreme points of view of some medieval Western mystics and modern Indian yogis who banish every intellectual pursuit from the aspirant's path and who regard study as not merely being useless but as even being harmful. It is true that if a student is forever reading and never digesting what he reads, or never acting on it, he will make little progress. Nevertheless he cannot be said to be entirely wasting his time, for he will be gaining information. And if his reading includes works by the great masters, he will also be gaining inspiration. If, moreover, he has learned to read properly, he will be gaining yet a third thing and that is stimulation in thinking and reflecting for himself. Yes! An inspired book and a good reader if brought together are not necessarily an unspiritual combination, but the qualifications which we earlier made should be remembered. What he reads should be digested. He should learn to think, to create his own ideas under the stimulus of what he reads. Otherwise the more he reads, the more bewildered he may become with contradictory ideas and doctrines. And again reading and thought must lead to action and not leave him uselessly suspended in the world of dreams and theories.

Philosophy does not adopt the anti-intellectual attitude of so many medieval ascetics and their modern inheritors. For it declares that metaphysical thinking can lead the thinker to the very threshold of mystical intuition. It asserts that by persevering in abstract reflection he may earn the grace of the higher self and be led nearer and nearer to the highest truth. But there is one qualifying condition for such a triumphant achievement. The thinker must first undergo a self-purificatory discipline. His thoughts, his feelings, and his actions must submit themselves to a prolonged training and a constant regulation which will eliminate or at least reduce those factors which falsify his thinking or prevent the arisal of true intuition. Therefore his character has to be improved, his egoistic instinct has to be struggled against, his passions have to be ruled, his prejudices have to be destroyed, his biases have to be corrected. It is because they have not undergone this discipline that so many people have been led astray by the thinking activity into a miserable materialism. For philosophy asserts that the ordinary man's thinking is corrupted by his lower nature, with which it is completely entangled. Therefore he must free that thinking to a large extent from the thraldom of the lower nature if it is to lead to true conclusions, if it is to lead to the recognition of its own limitations, and if it is to invite intuition to arise and replace it at the proper moment. Just as education of intellect and practice of courtesy lift a man from a lower class of society to a higher one, so purification of thought, feeling, and will lifts his mind into a realm of higher perception than before. So philosophy welcomes and includes metaphysical activity into its scheme of things.(P)

60

Metaphysics is best assimilated through the printed word because it calls for close and continued thinking. Mysticism, on the other hand, is better assimilated through the spoken word, because it touches the emotions.

61

The religious devotee loses nothing worth keeping when he passes his faith through the sieve of scientific inquiry and metaphysical sanction. If the result is the dropping out of useless superstition and unfactual dogma, his religion will be all the stronger, all the more triumphant.

62

The mystic disdains to seek or receive a metaphysical explanation of his method and its results, disdains the contribution of intellect. He is like a man who refuses to have a bandage removed from his eyes and persists in walking blindfolded.

63

Metaphysics says that it is impossible to arrive at truth if we take a limited standpoint of the whole, or if we take our facts from a single state like that of waking instead of all the three states of existence—of waking, dream, and sleep.

64

The metaphysical scientist and the scientific metaphysician scorn the masses for making God in their own image. It never occurs to them that they but duplicate the process when they set up an arid dry unemotional and frigid concept as Deity. For it is a dull and dreary God precisely like their own colourless character. For the metaphysician and scientist over-rate a particular phase of human make-up—intellect—and underrate another phase—emotion—when each should be valued in its own place. To make intellect primary is to upset the proper balance of life. It has a most important place but that place is subordinate to the higher values of life.

65

The theories of metaphysics need to be proved by the facts of life, by the discoveries of man, and by observation of the world.

66

The final test of the worth of the doctrines to which a man subscribes is what he himself is. By this test there are numerous men who are not metaphysicians like himself but who tower far above him in character. You may call yourself a philosopher but you have proved yourself to be but a metaphysician.

67

The words we use belong to the limited range of conditioned existence. How then can they be of actual service in describing the Unconditioned? The only service they can render is a symbolic or suggestive one. Reality cannot be expressed in any of the positive terms we know, for there is nothing like it in the familiar world. It may be hinted at negatively.

68

Truth can only be upheld by truthful arguments.

69

It is useless to discuss or study this subject before you have made clear to yourself what conception of truth you entertain in your mind.

70

Unless we can find a criterion of truth which shall be fully competent to adjudicate between this host of contending theories we shall merely wander without end and without a goal. For this alone can provide us with an adequate assurance of finality.

71

Is there any criterion whereby we can distinguish error from truth? The only answer to this question which will be universally valid is that the sole criterion must be reason based on experience.

72

Neither the quibblings of logic nor the quarrels of experience can constitute ultimate tests of truth. For logic may ignore, distort, suppress, or forget facts, while human experience is too limited.

73

The metaphysical system may be only a reflected image of the Truth, but still it is as faithful an image as present-day human intellect can show. Therefore, it is most helpful to the seeker who is groping his difficult way and needs all the guidance he can get.

74

As a metaphysical system, it may not be acceptable because considered to be a mere abstraction, remote from life and unfit for modern use. It is not. It is the law of all being, the science of all life, the truth of all existence. As such it is not for theoretical study only; it is just as much for practical application to every problem of life.

75

Any fool can be happy with any falsehood, but the prudent man will want his truth to bear up to any examination, however severe, and any test in experience, however varied.

76

Some individuals have undergone tremendous physical ordeals. It is the realization of such horrible experiences which underlies the Buddha's declaration that life in the flesh is a form of suffering, a declaration which the Western mentality usually rejects. Again with the terrible war that gripped mankind like an octopus, the doubt that may have been felt as to whether or not there is any use in metaphysical strivings brings home the same point. If life on earth were really satisfactory, few of us would ever engage in such striving, but it is because of its dissatisfactions that so many of us are sooner or later driven to seek inner solace. It would be an error, however, to set up metaphysical striving as being in opposition to ordinary human activity. On the contrary, it is complementary, and is an effort to carry on that activity more wisely and more satisfactorily. Where metaphysical effort leads to desertion of activity, then it loses its way. Certainly at such a time as the present, metaphysics should help us and inspire us to do our utmost in this great struggle against the forces of evil.

77

These are truths not only when they are known by the intellect, but also when they are felt by the emotions. The two must come together and be two sides of the same coin.

78

All theories must be brought to the test of experience and not only of reason, authority, and intuition before their value can be finally stated.

79

The modern school of existentialist metaphysics gives too much weight to passing experiences and too little to permanent principles, too much to appearances and too little to the realities, too much to the political economic and social, too little to the moral ethical and spiritual phases of human life. This brings about an unbalance and a half-truthness in its conclusions.

80

The doctrine of Advaita is after all a conception existing in a human head, for it had to take shape in that head, even if it had been revealed by the god Shiva or Vishnu or Brahma as Indian myth and legend would have us believe. Even if the doctrine were revealed in the deepest mystic experience by the discoverer digging within himself, it still remains a mental concept interpreted and formulated by the discoverer himself.

81

Those who need more intellectual sustenance than mysticism gives, may turn to metaphysics.

82

The intellectual who aims only at classifying and analysing kills the finer subtler part of that which he is dissecting; the artist who yields his feelings in love of it receives its soul.

83

If we remain true to the logical course of our thinking, we shall be forced in the end to accept the truth of philosophy.

84

The intellectual point of view is necessarily a developing one and its search for truth an unending one. It can never secure or offer any final formulation since reality is beyond the intellect's touch, even if it comes within the intellect's understanding.

Issues and adherents

85

What is self? What is thought? What is reality? These are accepted by metaphysics as three of its chief problems.

86

The immense growth of human knowledge in modern times has rendered it completely impossible for any single man to acquire even half the sum total in his lifetime. It is therefore of immense value to consider the relation of different branches to one another and to find those leading principles which shall coordinate all this mass of knowledge into a consistent whole and thus bring them within a single comprehensive purview. Metaphysics occupies itself with such an important task of unification, such universality of scope, and such an effort after unity in which all facts fall into place. This is possible to metaphysics alone.

87

Kant's mistake was to imprison human possibility within the intellect, to make the Spirit quite inaccessible. Hegel's error was in the opposite direction. He brought intellect into a false closeness to the Spirit and wrongly made history the chief preoccupation of the Absolute!

88

In the end, a man's actions are based on his metaphysical assumptions.

89

Plato, "the wisest of the Greeks," regarded the intuition of the poet and artist as being inferior to the insight of the metaphysician, because it could give no reflective explanation of itself.

90

Logical Positivism is a school which has excellent critiques to offer concerning matters of purely physical reference but which is completely misleading and mischievous when it wanders farther into matters of purely metaphysical mystical and non-physical reference. According to Logical Positivism, words are formed to deal with what is visible and tangible to us, to what the senses can grasp. The presupposition here is that this is all that exists. But this presupposition is wrong, as metaphysics demonstrates and mysticism reveals, for an immaterial and infinite mind is the source and sustenance of the senses themselves. The high priest of this school writes: "Let us find out how we teach the meaning of expressions, words and sentences to children and to primitive people; then we shall know what is meant by meaning!" The fallacy here is that we are neither children nor primitives. Both these classes are naturally materialistic, naturally take appearances for reality. We as adults are capable of abstract reflection and profound enquiry which free us from such naïve materialism. We may now comprehend why Logical Positivism, taking its cue from children and primitives, is such a materialistic school.

91

Hegel's use of terms in his dialectic system may perhaps be looked upon as follows: (1) The use of a set of intellectual concepts constitute his Thesis; (2) The use of an opposed set of such concepts is his Antithesis; (3) The use of noetic ideas or intuitions becomes his Synthesis.

92

Berkeley's acceptance of the distinction between primary and secondary qualities is antiquated and unnecessary. *All* the qualities are basically present together.

93

Hume's critique of causation and Berkeley's critique of matter still remain themes which scientists ought to ponder over.

94

For those who have devoted several years to its detailed study, this teaching is not a matter of pious belief or fanciful thinking but a tested fact and demonstrated truth. Nor, for them, does it depend upon the say-so of some bygone man or the tradition of some bygone century. It depends upon procurable evidence and appeals to scientific attitude.

95

When specialism is overdone, as in the case of such schools of mental and logical analysis as those of Logical Positivism and Semantics, it topples over into errors.

96

The tendency for rationalism to enter all the departments of life— although it is still weak in most of them and vigorous only in the department of science—is a necessary inevitable and evolutionary one. It is to be accepted, not to be deplored as the mystical sentimentalists and religious traditionalists deplore it. In the end it will lead man out of the materialism it creates for him, and into loftiest comprehension of the truth about himself and the world—philosophy.

97

To the extent that every man assumes certain elemental propositions about his surroundings—whether his assumptions are derived from instinct, convention, or education—to that extent he is unconsciously a metaphysician. It will not do therefore for him to say that he has no use for metaphysics or to disparage those who seek to arrive at such propositions more consciously and more rationally.

98

René Guénon's books take a standpoint which attracts an increasing number of Europeans. It needs to be understood thoroughly. It represents the latest of several of his own personal phases—including Catholic, Sceptical, Hindu, and lastly Muhammedan-Sufi. Guénon makes two important contributions to thought. First, he rightly perceives that science can add metaphysics not to displace itself but to complete itself. But what sort of metaphysics shall it be? If merely a speculation or a dogmatism, then that may lead only to further error. It must be a metaphysics based primarily on the mystical intuition and secondarily on the metaphysics of Truth, whose principle tenet, mentalism, is raised both out of observed facts, out of man's sense relations of the external world and his experience of it, and out of mystical seership. Is Guénon's system of this kind? Unfortunately, it is only partially so. Therefore, its grand truths suffer from certain insufficiencies and some errors. Second, Guénon rightly sees the existence of a universal crisis, but he misses one chief purpose and result of this crisis and that is its tremendous destructiveness. It is breaking adherence to past tendencies and shattering old forms. He fails to see that any return to vanished tradition could never be an internal but only an external one. It would lack reality, naturalness, and vitality. Yet his work possesses special importance not only, as he believes, for Western seekers who have thrown off conventional religious fetters but especially for the more intellectual.

99

On Spinoza's Doctrine (by PB): (a) Spinoza taught that God was the whole of things in the universe. This brought him into the category of pantheism. Philosophy says this is true but only part of the truth. For God is not only immanent in the universe but also transcends it. God still would be God even if there were no universe. (b) He declared that the unknown reality was Substance. Philosophy says this is only an attribute of Reality and as such still not the ultimate itself, any more than the quality of fragrance is the flower itself. (c) He believed in Causality, as science did in the nineteenth century, and as all must do who do not comprehend the final truth that Reality is nondual, hence leaves no room for the duality of cause and an effect. Spinoza's pantheism made him declare that everything is God. This is the theological outlook. The philosophical one declares that everything is a manifestation of One Infinite Reality. For if the ego also is God, then who is God? (d) Spinoza's teaching that God has two attributes, Mind and Matter, that reality has two aspects—mind and body, made him a dualist. Philosophy knows only one reality—Mind. It admits causality only for the immediate and practical purposes of the illusory world. (e) His teaching on how to live so as to fulfil the proper purpose of life is identical with philosophy's teaching. He saw that man so far must become wholly free inwardly, and as free as possible outwardly. This is to be achieved by self-mastery, by overcoming desires, subjugating passions, and simplifying existence. This brings true happiness.

100

The philosophy of Martin Heidegger is heavily based on Heraclitus and Parmenides. In his opinion their thinking is still the basis of Western culture.

How far is he mystical? The simplest answer to this question is that according to Heidegger Being is finite and time-bound, which is not the way in which mystics usually express themselves. He is also a nationalist and thinks that one can only philosophize in Greek and German . . . Several years later I heard that Heidegger had changed or developed his views: he now took a mystical stand, especially regarding Time.

101

The semantic philosophers, like Chase, who say that 'me', the senses, and the world are fundamental have gone so far, but no farther, into truth. They have not stopped to ask what is 'me'? The 'me' is only the body. What are the senses? What is the world? All these questions they have not gone into deeply, but we must give them every credit for their work on language. They have gone on the right track but they are afraid of going farther. That is why Vedanta says one must be determined to go to the *end* in quest of ultimate truth.

102

He will not be able to avoid the influence of metaphysics, anyway, for he will be subject to it at third hand, but in greatly diluted homeopathic doses, through the ministration of religion.

103

Every man has his own abstract view of his relation to the universe. In most cases it is either an unconscious or a half-conscious one. But still it is there. To the extent that he seeks to make it a fully conscious and adequately truthful one, he becomes a metaphysician.

104

When we consider the purpose why anything came into existence, we call that purpose its reason. When we consider the means or medium through which it came to exist, we call the latter its cause.

105

A shy little man shocked the Western world of metaphysicians with his critical analysis of the very foundations of their knowledge. Such was Immanuel Kant and such was the startling effect of his magnum opus, *Critique of Pure Reason*, which appeared in 1781 to amaze the learned. It was the logical, if late, result of the purpose fixed thirty-five years earlier, when Kant wrote to someone: "I will enter on my course and nothing will prevent me from pursuing it. I have already fixed upon the line which I am resolved to keep." He gave European thinkers a nut on which many have broken their teeth, though none has yet succeeded in breaking the nut. He indicated the limits of the human mind and proved, as conclusively as it can be proved, that human reason was utterly unable to penetrate into the reality of things, which necessarily transcends it.

He courageously accepted the conclusions of his own rigorous reasoning. He admitted that metaphysics as a science transcending all sciences, as an intellectual quest of God, was doomed to failure. The rational could never discover the Suprarational.

Kant, after all, was a rationalist. He worked primarily with purely intellectual concepts not with mystical ones. Consequently he shared the limitations of such a narrow standpoint. He recognized that his ideas pointed beyond themselves, but he did not venture to make the journey himself. Besides, professors have to consider their posts first and truth afterwards and truth often comes off second best. But Kant, being a thoroughly honest man who had already found that the full and free expression of his views brought threats of dismissal from the State authorities, probably refrained from entering religious mysticism and fell into silence about it because the intellectual revolution he advocated was itself a tremendous enough advance. He used logical reasoning to show that what lay beneath all our reasoning was beyond our knowing, that the essence of existence was beyond finite perception, but he did not say that there was no essence. It *is* there, whether we know it or not.

106

Causality is the foundation stone of the world creation problem. When it is displaced the entire structure of every cosmogony—religious and scientific—collapses.

107

Against this Correspondence Theory of Truth it suffices to point out that it is impossible to lay one's idea upon the fact to see if it is an exact copy; it is impossible to take the impression in one's mind and ascertain whether it is perfectly like the original throughout. Moreover, if the fact itself is directly known for what it is, the question of its truth ought not to arise, whilst if it is unknown how can it be discovered whether the idea corresponds with it?

108

What is the difference between the concepts of existence and Being? Hegel has tried in his ponderous way to express it metaphysically and only intellectually.

109

Bergson's study of memory convinced his mathematical mind that the fleshly brain was far less, and quite other than, the invisible mind. They were in two different categories. This is how he came to reject the materialism with which he started.

110

Even metaphysicans may misunderstand each other, as when Kant wrongly thought that Berkeley had tried to establish that things experienced in space are mere imaginations. Kant then proceeded to waste his own and his readers' time disproving what Berkeley never claimed.

111

G. Lowes Dickinson, the Cambridge don, read Plato and Plotinus in the original Greek. They led him to believe that there might be a way toward ultimate truth and ultimate experience. But time made him more cautious and in the end he lost this belief. The human mind was quite inadequate to find answers to ultimate questions, he decided, and kept this scepticism until the end of his long life. As for yoga, he was willing to grant its mind-over-body power but was unwilling to test it, as he feared its dangers and suspected its delusions.

112

Hegel would rationalize the Overself just as the Hindu mystics would irrationalize it. Hegel's metaphysically rational Absolute satisfies the head but leaves the heart untouched.

113

Because Spinoza was a mathematician as well as a metaphysician the few who admire and honour him as such are surprised when Richard Church, himself a poet, called him "every poet's friend." Or he is denounced by others as "a pantheist," for this led him into alleged heresy. "He shows us Mother Earth as he showed it to Wordsworth."

114

What a pity that Kant did not put his meanings more directly, clearly, and compactly, for then his greatness as a transition thinker would have emerged with less difficulty for most readers.

115

Even though Kant proved that the human mind is so limited by its nature that the Real eludes it, he did not stop there. For he went on to prove also that it could still get clues, hints, or slender notions which confirm the basic spirituality of the Real.

116

We must gladly welcome the recent interest in writings like the Dane Kierkegaard's, for even if they are not wholly emancipated from religious bias, they are excellent transitions from orthodox religion to mystical religion. They prepare the reader who accepts them to accept mysticism itself as his next forward step.

117

This habit of persistent daily reflection on the great verities, of thinking about the nature or attributes of the Overself, is a very rewarding one. From mere intellectual ideas, they begin to take on warmth, life, and power.

118

If we want to trace out what is real in either human or universal existence it is essential that we separate appearance from reality, effect from cause, and object from subject.

119

Can the infinite impersonal Mind really play at being the little personal ego as one school of metaphysicians assert?

120

Hegel limited the Absolute when he limited access to it only through the faculty of Reason.

121

Metaphysics must act as a custodian of the truth and as a guardian of the road to it. To refuse to submit to its discipline is equivalent to choosing a different goal, and another road than truth.

Its spiritual significance

122

Metaphysical knowledge is the rain, devotional fervour is the sunshine. Both are needed to bring the plant to flowering and fruition. But rain attracts people less than sunshine. And so we find that most aspirants avoid the labours of metaphysical study for the pleasures of mystical practice.

123

The day when the seeker must wrestle with the problems of metaphysics is usually postponed until he is thought to be ready for them, which means until much of his life has passed away. However, this suited the convenience of ancient times, when the general mental level of mankind was much lower than it is today. There is more disadvantage than advantage in such postponement, and the sooner this study is undertaken the better for the seeker himself.

124

The philosophic student knows that the same thoughts which rear their heads and obstruct the mystic from attaining Thought can be turned round and used to help him attain it. But to achieve this successfully there must be metaphysical knowledge.

125

Those who make philosophical writings their constant study are using life profitably.

126

He must study the great teachings of philosophy with something like passion.

127

When thought hits into one's passions and prejudices, few people care to draw a line of hard thinking unto its bitter end. The consequences of philosophical brain activity can be too dreadful for weak mortals. Only he who has made thought his lord and king can accept its commands.

128

Philosophy provides its mystical students with a scientific basis and a metaphysical background. Thus and thus alone can they get a secure position in the intellectual world of today. Let him turn these ideas over and over in his reflections until they are quite comprehensible.

129

Philosophy provides for the intellectual and emotional needs of evolving spirituality, not merely, as does mysticism, for the emotional needs alone.

130

Metaphysics has no pictorial images and emotional appeals to offer its votaries. Hence it is at a disadvantage compared to religion or art. The abstract ideas which it gives instead can satisfy only an uncommon kind of intellect.

131

Metaphysics gives itself the work of uncovering intellectually life's deepest secret.

132

But let it not be thought that the metaphysical effort is a wasted one. On the contrary, it is essential for training the mind to think correctly about the Overself, for supplying it with the firm conviction that such an ultimate reality does exist, and for encouraging it to take up the practical quest of ultramysticism; whilst after the latter quest has been successfully realized the metaphysical effort again becomes useful when the sage seeks to communicate to others a precise report and accurate explanation of his own grand experience.

133

But if we say that every attempt of the intellect to judge the nature of reality involves it in a maze of contradictions, that in short the Overself is impenetrable to thinking, this is not to say that thinking is useless and metaphysics is sterile. For the negative knowledge which they provide enables us to confirm the validity of ultramystic insight as well as to reject the validity of lower-mystic intuition. Moreover, there is a certain chaotic vagueness about the lower-mystic experience, into which philosophic enquiry introduces the cleansing breeze of system and understanding and thus brings into the clear light of self-consciousness what is genuinely real in that experience.

134

Once he begins to bestow his thought upon thought itself, he begins a path of enquiry which, if pushed to its farthest end, will bring him into astonishing discoveries and, if he follows them into practical application, beneficial changes.

135

A metaphysical faculty is required to understand the truth. However sharp a businessman's intelligence may be, or a scientist's intellect, truth will be beyond their grasp if this faculty is lacking. But the lack may be repaired. Steadfast determined and resolute study will develop the needed equipment.

136

Metaphysical study may exercise the reason, but if it is the metaphysics of truth it will also unfold the intuition. Therefore, it is also a holy path.

137

If a man will constantly think about these metaphysical truths, he will develop in time the capacity to perceive them by direct intuition instead of by second-remove reflection. But to do this kind of thinking properly the mind must be made steady, poised, concentrated, and easily detached from the world.(P)

138

His conduct will be better, his mind wiser, and his heart happier if he seeks and gains a knowledge of the divine laws governing the universe than if he refuses to do so.

139

The task of philosphy is to see through every situation from its beginning to its end, from its core to its surface, but this it can only do if it approaches the situation with an entirely impartial mind, with a perfectly trained power of concentration, and with a thirst for facts rather than opinion.

140

This is the training which frees his mind from the influences of origin, the compulsions of environment, the suggestions of education.

141

Mystical teachings were too often in the past presented in a form which demands blind faith or which is hard to understand. Philosophical teachings are presented in a comprehensible form and so logically that they arouse mental trust.

142

He alone is fit to study metaphysics who can use logic rigidly yet not get so intoxicated by its use as to forget that its syllogisms are only of limited applicability.

143

From all these metaphysical studies he will derive even without seeking it a lofty tranquillity and a noble impersonality.

144

We must climb this pyramid of reflection to the grand apex of truth.

145

The worth of metaphysics to us is relative to the work which we put into it, to the degree of hard thinking which we achieve under its direction. For it demands sustained enquiry into facts, careful assessment of the value of statements, and careful judgement of conclusions.

146

People turn from metaphysics as from a dry and forbidding subject. Yet for those to whom it is a pathway to Truth, its statements carry the attractiveness of a good novel; its books possess the readability of a good biography.

147

An important value of a metaphysical outlook lies in the conscious understanding it bestows of what we ordinarily experience unwittingly and unreflectively.

148

Such thinking is admittedly difficult. The average man habitually regards the flat toneless tenets of ordinary metaphysics as something to make his head ache. He possesses a veritable fear of entering their cloudy domain of unprofitable remoteness and useless logical hair-splitting. Nevertheless, their subject is too important to be ignored without involving him in definite intellectual loss. And more men have a capacity for comprehending it than are usually aware of being able to do so. In some, the metaphysical tendencies have been lying dormant waiting for a suitable opportunity or a fit environment to rise and manifest themselves, but neither opportunity nor environment being propitious they have wrongly thought the subject to be beyond their range. Only when the passing years bring the needed change do they discover that the intellectual significance of experience discloses itself to them with increasing clearness and interest just as the inner content of a novel increasingly discloses itself.

149

Those who pride themselves on being practical and who consequently (such is their reasoning) dispense with metaphysical theory as a useless encumbrance, may learn with surprise that there are students of meta-physics who are not less practical than they are and who find in their studies the best foundations for their management of day-to-day living.

150

The mystic who has not this clear metaphysical knowledge may attain a limited goal, but even then, because his effort is not a guided one, much of it is lost in blind striving.

151

The concepts formed by common sense will not avail us here.

152

Without the knowledge of this metaphysical system, he is like a traveller in a strange land, who is ignorant of his whereabouts, unprovided with a map, and unguided by a native.

153

Readers must again be reminded and must ever keep in memory that the term metaphysics is used here to indicate the particular system called "Metaphysics of Truth" alone. This warning is a needed one. For perhaps in no other study have men so lost themselves in mere verbiage, so strayed afar from actuality and reality.

154

The study of the metaphysics of truth prepares the mind for mystical revelation, helps it to become mystically intuitive.

155

A high grade and inventive engineer's mentality is better suited to grasp the metaphysics of truth than most others.

156

It trains the mind to move guardedly along the path from reasoned thinking to conclusive judgement, to proceed cautiously and not pre-cipitately when opinions are formed, and to form them not at random but only after sifting factual evidence from idle hearsay.

157

There is this to be said for such study, that it brings to us ready for assimilation what others have had to purchase by long experience and arduous research.

158

He must have the courage not to be frightened away from these doctrines merely because at first sight they seem absurd. If he will take the time and trouble to make a comparative research, he will find that great minds in ancient Greece and Rome and Egypt, in medieval Europe and Asia, as well as a growing minority in the modern world found these ideas reasonable.

159

The grades and levels of spirituality as well as the schools and systems of metaphysics may be studied from the outside.

160

Unsound theoretical principles can never lead to sound practical deeds. Therefore, metaphysical study is required.

161

Most men fall into easy acceptance of the belief that abstract thinking and mystical experience are too vague and too intangible to spur emotion and influence action. This is one reason why most men do not even trouble to investigate mysticism or study metaphysics.

162

The value of a systematic course in philosophy is that it gives a solid foundation. A casual self-education lacks this, has no teacher to question or to organize its reading; it picks up knowledge in bits and pieces—too fragmentary and scattered to be complete.

163

Too many people are too fatigued, whether by their work or by the stress of modern conditions, to be willing to read books demanding an effort of close intellectual attention. They feel that they need writings which give them something instead of requiring the reader to give anything, which inspire, counsel, and console.

164

The partisan, the sectarian, and the fanatic should keep away from philosophy for they might then get cured of their ailment.

165

So subtle is the metaphysics of truth that the mind unpractised in concentration will soon waver in following it; the heart, unpurified of desires, will soon weary in applying it. The Long Path work is absolutely necessary as a preliminary.

166

Hitherto we have used the thinking faculty to extend our hands and lengthen our legs, that is to say, to create ingenious tools, instruments, and devices and to invent amazing land, sea, and air vehicles. This has brought us powers surpassing those of most animals but they do not make us more than clever animals. The evolutionary hour is now at hand when we must also use thinking for higher purposes, when we must let it guide us not merely to mass production or quicker locomotion but to the dignity of our own divinity.

167

A slow measured delivery of these unfamiliar metaphysical and mystical explanations helps the hearer understand better and accords with the dignity of the subject.

168

Metaphysical study lifts a man into the clear keen air above personal considerations.

169

Those who left divine forces outside their world view have become baffled, confused, and hesitant.

170

There is nothing wrong in asking that the search for, no less than the statement of, truth should be reasonable.

171

Although he cannot be relieved of the great strain of studying its metaphysical side, for it clarifies the meaning of human existence, he can be helped to bear it more easily.

172

Metaphysics makes us exercise intellectual muscles which have got flabby because they are little used.

173

The basic ideas of this teaching have been transmitted down through the ages but only to a selected few.

174

Because the metaphysics of truth deals with root ideas, and because in a mentalist universe such ideas are naturally more potentially powerful and more important than materialist ones, the metaphysics of truth becomes the most worthwhile study in which man's intellect can engage. For these ideas provide him with the right patterns for shaping physical existence.(P)

175

The contemplation of universal laws and metaphysical truth chastens the feelings and elevates the thoughts. This study causes man to forget himself, to turn aside from his little ego, and thus helps to clear a path to discovery of his Overself.

8

INTELLECT, REALITY,
AND THE OVERSELF

The Insufficiency of Intellect and Reason (Essay)

Intellect can perceive what belongs to reality, not reality itself. The metaphysician deludes himself into thinking that he has seen the world in all its varied aspects, but what he has really seen is the world in all its *intellectual* aspects only. Moreover when he thinks that he has put together the results of one science with another, uniting them all into a harmonious whole, he omits to reckon that such are the limitations of human capacity and such the rapidly growing vastness of scientific knowledge, that no man could ever combine all the multitudinous results. He could never acquire an intimate knowledge of them during a single lifetime. Therefore he could never develop a complete philosophy of the universe as a whole.

The intellect fulfils itself practically when it discovers that each idea it produces is incomplete and imperfect and therefore passes on to replace it by a further one, but it fulfils itself metaphysically when it discovers that every idea which it can possibly produce will always and necessarily be incomplete and imperfect.

Now so far as they are almost entirely metaphysical works, these two volumes [most likely, *The Hidden Teaching Beyond Yoga* and *The Wisdom of the Overself* are meant—Ed.] have no option but to make their appeal chiefly to reason alone. And expounding the special and unique system called the *metaphysics of truth* as they do, they have to start where possible from verifiable facts rather than mere speculations. But whatever other importance they ascribe to reasoning as an instrument of truth-attainment applies only to the particular stage for which it is prescribed, which is the stage of metaphysical discipline and certainly not beyond it. Although the status bestowed on reason in every metaphysical system beginning with science must necessarily be a primary one, its status within the larger framework of the integral hidden teaching can only be a secondary one. This teaching possesses a larger view and does not end with science or limit itself to the rational standpoint alone. How can it do so when metaphysics is merely its intermediate phase? We must rightly honour reason to its fullest extent, but we need not therefore accept the unreasonable doctrine that the limits of reason constitute the limits of truth.

Our senses can perceive only what they have been formed to perceive. Our reason similarly cannot grasp what it was never formed to grasp. Within their legitimate spheres of operation, the deliverances of both sense and reason should be acceptable to us, but outside those spheres we must seek for something that transcends both.

But the basic cause why reason is insufficient exists in the fact that intellect—the instrument with which it works—is itself insufficient. Reason is the right arrangement of thinking. Each thought thus arranged depends for its existence on another thought and is unable to exist without such a relation, that is, it suffers from relativity. Hence a thought cannot be considered as an ultimate in itself and therefore reason cannot know the absolute. The intellect can take the forms of existence apart bit by bit and tell us what they consist of. But such surgical dissection cannot tell us what existence itself is. This is something which must be experienced, not merely thought. It can explain what has entered into the composition of a painting but, as may be realized if we reflect a little, it cannot explain why we feel the charm of the painting. The analytic intellect describes reality sufficiently to give some satisfaction to our emotions or our intelligence, but it does not touch this baffling elusive reality at all. What it has dissected is not the living throbbing body but the cold dead image of it.

When reason tells us that God *is*, it does not actually know God. The antennae of intellectual research cannot penetrate into the Overself because thinking can only establish relations between ideas and thus must forever remain in the realms of dualities, finitudes, and individualities. It cannot grasp the whole but only parts. Therefore reason which depends on thinking is incompetent to comprehend the mysterious Overself. Realization is to be experienced and felt; thought can only indicate what it is likely to be and what it is not likely to be. Hence Al Ghazzali, the Sufi, has said: "To define drunkenness, to know that it is caused by vapours that rise from the stomach and cloud the seat of intelligence, is a different thing from being drunk. So I found ultimate knowledge consists in experiences rather than definitions." The fact that metaphysics tries to explain all existence in intellectual terms alone and tries to force human nature into conceptual molds, causes it to suppress or distort the non-intellectual elements in both. The consequence is that metaphysics alone cannot achieve an adequate understanding. If it insists upon exalting its own results, then it achieves misunderstanding.

Metaphysics proves the existence of reality but is unable to enter into it. Indeed, metaphysics must in the end criticize the desert-sand dryness of its own medium of thinking and not make the mistake of regarding thought-activity as the ultimately real, when it is itself only a section cut from the whole of human experience and existence. The intellect offers a reality which can never be a felt reality but only a described one and then only in negative terms. Intellectual work can only paint the picture of reality; we have to verify this picture by realizing it within our own experience. The final office of reasoned thought is to reveal why reason is not competent to judge reality and why thinking is not competent to know reality.

The moment we attempt to understand what reality is, we get out of our depth because our own thinking must move in a serial sequence which itself prevents us from escaping the particular space-time form which confines us to a particular world of appearance. Just as, because it has entered our space-time experience, we can take hold of an artist's production but not the mind behind it, so and for the same reason we can take hold of the screen which cuts us off. This is because we can think of existence only in a particular shape or relative to a particular thing, not of existence that is formless, bodiless, and infinite. We have to localize it somewhere in space. Because space and time are forms taken by rational knowledge, because they are only conditions existing within personal consciousness, they do not enter into the knowledge of consciousness of that which is beyond both rational thinking and personal selfhood.(P)

2

No idea is ever really outside another, nor is any idea ever outside the mind, and all ideas, all that which is seen, can only *theoretically* be separated from the thinking seeing mind. As psychologists we have had in thought to separate seer from seen, so that we might learn at length what the nature of pure mind really is; but as philosophers we must now merge them together. It is because thinking must always have an object with which to occupy itself that it can never penetrate the Overself, for here there is only the One. We must renounce thoughts and things if we would enter into the Absolute. Because in this ultimate state there is no more awareness of an individual observer and an observed world, the distinction between individual mind and individual body also ceases. Everything, including our *separate* selfhood, is voided out, as it were. The resultant nothingness however is really the essence of everything. It is not the nothingness of death but of latent life. Human thought can proceed no farther. For when "not-two-ness" is established as the Real, the logical movement from one thought to a second can only prolong the sway of "two-ness" over the mind. In this pure being there can be no "other," no two, hence it is called non-dual. The integrity of its being cannot really be split. If the Overself is to be actually experienced, then it must be as a realization of the Infinite One. To divide itself into knower and known is to dwell in duality. The antithesis of known and knower cannot enter into it just as the opposition of reality and illusion is meaningless for it. The oneness of its being is absolute. The return to this awareness, which regards the world only under its monistic aspect, is the realization of truth possessed by a sage. When rational thinking can perceive that it cannot transcend itself, cannot yield more than another thought, it has travelled as far as it can go and performed its proper function. Metaphysical truth is the intellectual *appearance* of reality, the rational knowledge of it; but it is not reality itself, not realization. For knowing needs a second thing to be known; hence metaphysical knowledge, being dual, can never yield realization which is non-dual.

Reality must stand grandly alone, without dependence on anything and without relation to anyone; it ever was, is, and ever will be. It is this inability of human reason to grasp the super-rational, the divine ineffable, that Omar Khayyam tried to express in his beautiful quatrains which have been so widely misunderstood by Western readers. If the *Rubaiyat* of Omar is only a drunken refrain from a wine-shop, then the New Testament is a mere scribble from an out-of-the-way corner of the Roman Empire. The cup of language is too small to hold the wine of the Absolute. A thought of Mind as the Void is still a "something" no less than a thought of great mountains and therefore prevents us from realizing the Void.

Now when we grasp the basic nature of human thinking, that it is possible only by forming two opposing ideas at the same time as the concept of black is formed by the contrast against white, we can then grasp the fundamental reason why such thinking can never rise to awareness of the Absolute unity. We cannot think of eternity without thinking of time too. For our conception of it either prolongs time until imagination falters and ceases or negates time altogether into timelessness. In neither case do we really comprehend eternity. Why? Because intellect cannot lay hold of what lies beyond itself. We humans know a thing by distinguishing it from other things, by limiting its nature and by relating it to its opposite. But the infinite has nothing else from which it can be distinguished or to which it can be related, whilst it certainly cannot be limited in any way.

Our earlier division into a dualism of observer and observed must now come to an end. But let us not make the error of mistaking it for the final stage. There still lies a path beyond, a path which leads to the ultimate where both observer and the observed become one.

The Real can never be stated because it can never be thought. Therefore it is quite clear that ordinary means of knowledge are unable to grasp it.

But such knowledge is not useless. For if religion can give us a symbolic idea and mysticism an intuitive idea of the Infinite, metaphysical knowledge can give us a rational idea of it. And to possess such an idea keeps us at least from falling into errors about the reality behind it. If metaphysics can never perform the task it sets itself—to know reality—it can perform the task of knowing what is *not* reality. And such a service is inestimable. The function of reason is ultimately a negative one; it cannot provide a positive apprehension of the Overself, but it can provide a clear declaration of what It is not. Reason can demonstrate that the Overself can possess no shape and can in no way be imagined.

Nevertheless we may have both the assurance and the satisfaction that our thinking is correct but we have neither the assurance nor the satisfaction of consciously embracing that with which this thinking deals. We may have formed a right mental image of God but we are still not in God's sacred presence. We must not mistake the image for the reality which it represents. Whatever discoveries we have hitherto made have been made only within the limited frontiers of reasoned thinking. Exalted and expanded though our outlook may now be, we can still do no more than think the existence of this reality without actually experiencing it. The mere intellectual recognition of this Oneness of Mind is no more sufficient to make it real to us than the mere intellectual recognition of Australia's existence will suffice to make Australia real to us. In the end all our words about the Overself remain but words. For just as no amount of telling a man who has never touched or drunk any liquid will ever make properly clear to him what wetness is unless and until he puts his finger in a liquid or drinks some of it, so every verbal explanation really fails to explain the Overself unless and until we know it for ourself within ourself and as ourself.(P)

Index for Part 1

Entries are listed by chapter number followed by "para" number. For example, 7.6 means chapter 7, para 6, and 7.24, 26, 49 means chapter 7, paras 24, 26, and 49. Chapter listings are separated by a semicolon. Please note also that, for the reader's convenience, the first number in the right-hand running heads throughout the text indicates chapter number.

Index for Part 2

Entries are listed by chapter number followed by "para" number. For example, 3.246 means chapter 3, para 246, and 3.237, 244, 256 means chapter 3, paras 237, 244, and 256. Chapter listings are separated by a semicolon. Please note also that, for the reader's convenience, the first number in the right-hand running heads throughout the text indicates chapter number.

The 28 Categories from the Notebooks

This outline of categories in *The Notebooks* is the most recent one Paul Brunton developed for sorting, ordering, and filing his written work. The listings he put after each title were not meant to be all-inclusive. They merely suggest something of the range of topics included in each category.

1 THE QUEST

> *Its choice —Independent path —Organized groups —*
> *Self-development —Student/teacher*

2 PRACTICES FOR THE QUEST

> *Ant's long path —Work on oneself*

3 RELAX AND RETREAT

> *Intermittent pauses —Tension and pressures —Relax body,*
> *breath, and mind —Retreat centres —Solitude —*
> *Nature appreciation —Sunset contemplation*

4 ELEMENTARY MEDITATION

> *Place and conditions —Wandering thoughts —Practise*
> *concentrated attention —Meditative thinking —*
> *Visualized images —Mantrams —Symbols*
> *—Affirmations and suggestions*

5 THE BODY

> *Hygiene and cleansings —Food —Exercises and postures*
> *—Breathings —Sex: importance, influence, effects*

6 EMOTIONS AND ETHICS

> *Uplift character —Re-educate feelings —Discipline emotions —*
> *Purify passions —Refinement and courtesy —Avoid fanaticism*

7 THE INTELLECT

> *Nature —Services —Development —Semantic training —*
> *Science —Metaphysics —Abstract thinking*

8 THE EGO

> *What am I? —The I-thought —The psyche*